How to Govern AI Responsibly

A Guide for Ordinary Institutions

2026

Publisher: BoD · Books on Demand GmbH, Überseering 33, 22297 Hamburg,
bod@bod.de
Print: Libri Plureos GmbH, Friedensallee 273, 22763 Hamburg
ISBN: 978-3-6963-9530-8

How to Govern AI Responsibly A Guide for Ordinary Institutions

How to Govern AI Responsibly A Guide for Ordinary Institutions

Table of Contents

Part I: Foundations

Chapter 1: Why Ordinary Institutions Need AI Governance

The moment has already passed

There is a temptation, when confronted with the subject of AI governance, to treat it as a future problem. Something to address once the technology matures, once regulators issue clear guidance, once someone more senior makes a decision. This temptation is understandable. Governance feels like overhead. It slows things down. And the tools themselves seem to be working fine — the chatbot is answering questions, the software is screening applications, the system is flagging anomalies — so why create bureaucracy around something that isn't broken?

The temptation should be resisted, because the moment it describes has already passed.

AI systems are not arriving in institutions — they have arrived. They are embedded in the software organizations already use, often without a deliberate choice to adopt them. They are being offered by vendors as standard features. They are being installed by well-meaning staff who found a useful tool and started using it. And in many cases, no one in the organization has a complete picture of where they are, what they are doing, or what happens when they go wrong.

That is the governance gap. Not a future condition to prepare for. A present condition that already needs managing.

This chapter explains what is driving that gap, why it matters for institutions that are not technology companies, and why governance — understood plainly as having a system for making responsible decisions — is no longer optional for any organization that uses, plans to use, or may be pressured to use AI.

What has actually changed

Artificial intelligence has existed as a field for decades. What changed in the early 2020s was not the invention of intelligence in machines but the accessibility of capable AI systems to organizations of every kind. For most of its history, AI was the province of large technology companies, well-funded research labs, and institutions with specialized engineering teams. Building with AI required expertise, infrastructure, and capital that most schools, hospitals, nonprofits, and government agencies simply did not have.

That barrier collapsed with remarkable speed. Large language models became accessible through simple application programming interfaces. AI features were bundled into productivity software that tens of millions of organizations already paid for. Consumer-grade tools became powerful enough to do work that previously required professional assistance. What had been an exotic capability became a commodity.

This changed the governance situation in three important ways.

First, it changed who was making decisions about AI adoption. In earlier eras, AI decisions were made by technologists — people who understood both the power and the limitations of the systems they were deploying. When AI became a feature of standard software, adoption decisions moved to procurement departments, department heads, and individual staff members who often had no technical background. The person approving a contract with an HR software vendor is not typically in a position to evaluate whether that vendor's AI screening tool is statistically fair. The teacher downloading a grading assistant is not necessarily equipped to consider what data it retains or how its outputs were validated.

Second, it changed the pace of adoption. Deliberate technology projects have cycles — planning, evaluation, piloting, rollout. AI features embedded in existing software appear with a product update. Standalone tools spread through organizations informally, one user at a time. By the time leadership is aware that a tool is in use, it may already have become embedded in workflows, with staff depending on it and data flowing into systems outside the organization's control.

Third, it changed accountability. When an institution built its own technology systems, responsibility for those systems was relatively clear.

When institutions use AI through third-party vendors — which is now the dominant mode of adoption — accountability becomes distributed across contracts, service agreements, vendor commitments, and institutional policies in ways that require explicit governance to manage.

None of this is a reason to reject AI. Many of these tools offer genuine value. It is a reason to govern AI — to have a system for making decisions about it, monitoring its use, and responding when things go wrong.

The word that intimidates and why it shouldn't

"Governance" is a word that lands differently depending on the audience. For some, it suggests board-level strategy and formal policy frameworks. For others, it sounds like compliance bureaucracy — forms to fill out, committees to sit through, approval chains that slow everything down without adding value. Neither association is quite right for what this book is about.

For the purposes of this book, governance simply means having a system for making responsible decisions.

That system does not need to be elaborate. For a small nonprofit, it might be a single policy document, a designated staff member who reviews new AI tools before they are adopted, and a clear way for staff to report concerns. For a large hospital, it might involve a cross-functional committee, a vendor review process, an audit schedule, and an incident response protocol. The scale differs; the essential logic is the same.

The essential logic is this: consequential tools deserve deliberate management. AI systems make decisions that affect real people — which job applications get screened in, which patients get flagged for follow-up, which content gets shown to students, which claims get denied. The people affected by those decisions deserve to have someone accountable for them. That accountability is what governance creates.

Governance is not about slowing things down. It is about being able to say, when something goes wrong, that your organization knew what it was using, had a process for evaluating whether it was appropriate, had someone responsible for monitoring it, and had a plan for responding. In the absence of governance, none of those things is true — and the cost of that absence, when something does go wrong, is almost always higher than the cost of having put governance in place.

Why every institution type is affected

It is tempting to think of AI governance as a problem for large corporations or government agencies with sophisticated technology operations. Institutions on that scale certainly need governance, and some of the highest-profile AI failures have occurred there. But the governance challenge is not proportional to institutional size. It is proportional to the impact of the decisions being made.

Consider the range of institutions already navigating these questions.

Schools and universities use AI in grading assistance tools, plagiarism detection, admissions screening, student support chatbots, and behavioral monitoring systems. Each of these touches the educational experience and life prospects of students. A plagiarism detection tool that produces false positives at higher rates for non-native English speakers is not a software inconvenience — it is a fairness problem with serious consequences for individual students. A behavioral prediction tool that flags certain students as at-risk based on demographic patterns may channel resources in ways that help some students and stigmatize others. The educator who adopts these tools without evaluating them carefully, and without any process for monitoring their effects, has taken on a responsibility they may not realize they hold.

Hospitals and healthcare providers use AI in clinical decision support, diagnostic imaging, patient triage, appointment scheduling, prior authorization processing, and billing. The stakes here are self-evidently high. Clinical AI tools have been found to perform differently across racial and ethnic groups, to reflect historical biases in the data they were trained on, and to produce recommendations that clinicians may follow without adequately understanding their basis. An AI system that influences which patients receive what care is not just a technology system — it is a component of medical practice, with all the ethical and legal weight that carries.

Nonprofits may seem less obviously implicated, but many use AI in ways that affect the people they serve: screening clients for program eligibility, assessing housing or food insecurity, allocating scarce services, and communicating with vulnerable populations. A tool that automates eligibility decisions for a housing program may embed criteria that disproportionately exclude certain applicants. A chatbot deployed to answer questions from crisis line callers may fail in ways that have severe consequences. The mission of a nonprofit — to serve people in need — is directly implicated by the fairness and reliability of the AI tools it uses.

Government agencies at every level use AI in law enforcement, benefits administration, child welfare, permitting, tax compliance, and public service delivery. The coercive and consequential nature of many government decisions — denying a benefit, flagging a fraud, issuing a license, placing a child — makes the accuracy, fairness, and explainability of AI systems especially important. Government institutions also face distinctive accountability obligations to the public they serve. Citizens affected by automated government decisions generally have a right to explanation and appeal that may be difficult or impossible to provide without adequate governance of the underlying systems.

Businesses of all sizes use AI in hiring, performance management, customer service, fraud detection, pricing, credit assessment, and content moderation. Employment decisions shaped by AI screening tools have attracted substantial legal scrutiny in multiple jurisdictions. Customer service AI that fails certain users disproportionately — for example, voice recognition systems that perform worse for certain accents — creates both ethical and reputational problems. Pricing algorithms that systematically charge certain customers more raise consumer protection concerns. The business case for governance is partly ethical but also plainly commercial: reputational damage, regulatory liability, and litigation are costly, and they are disproportionately likely to arise from AI failures that adequate governance would have caught.

The institutions in this list have very different cultures, missions, resource levels, and regulatory environments. What they have in common is this: they are using tools that make or influence consequential decisions, and those tools require management.

The specific risks that make governance necessary

Governance exists because there are real things that can go wrong. Responsible leadership requires understanding what those things are. A complete taxonomy of AI risks appears in Chapter 3, but the most important can be introduced here.

Bias and discrimination. AI systems are trained on historical data. When that data reflects historical patterns of discrimination — in hiring, lending, criminal justice, healthcare — the systems trained on it tend to reproduce those patterns. This is not a technical glitch but a structural feature of how most AI systems learn. Without deliberate attention to how systems perform across different demographic groups, institutions using AI may find that their tools produce outcomes that would be unlawful or deeply unfair if produced by human decision-makers — and in many jurisdictions, the source of the discrimination does not exempt the institution from liability.

Hallucination and unreliability. Generative AI systems — systems that produce text, images, summaries, or recommendations — can produce outputs that are fluent, confident, and wrong. This phenomenon, sometimes called hallucination, is not a flaw that better versions will necessarily eliminate; it is a characteristic of how these systems generate outputs. When staff use AI-generated summaries, citations, or analyses without verification, errors propagate into institutional processes and decisions. The confidence with which AI systems present incorrect information makes this risk particularly difficult to manage without explicit policies about when and how AI outputs must be checked.

Overreliance and automation bias. Research consistently shows that humans defer to automated systems at rates that exceed what the accuracy of those systems would warrant. When AI recommendations are presented with apparent authority, clinicians prescribe differently, hiring managers screen differently, and case workers assess differently than they would with the same information presented differently. This is not a failure of individual judgment but a predictable human response to apparently authoritative automated systems. Managing it requires governance: policies about when humans must independently review AI-assisted decisions, and training that helps staff understand the limits of the tools they are using.

Privacy and data protection. AI systems require data to operate. Many AI tools are trained on institutional data, process institutional data in real time, or retain outputs that contain sensitive information. When institutions deploy AI tools without understanding what data those tools collect, where it goes, and who can access it, they take on privacy risks they may not have chosen. Many jurisdictions have laws governing the use of personal data in automated decision-making; compliance with those laws requires understanding what the tools do.

Vendor dependency and accountability gaps. Most institutions use AI through third-party vendors rather than building their own systems. This creates a distinctive governance challenge: the institution is accountable for the outcomes of the tool, but the institution does not control how the tool works. Vendor contracts often provide limited insight into AI system performance, limited rights to audit, and limited recourse when things go wrong. Without deliberate governance, institutions may find themselves bound to tools they cannot evaluate, cannot fix, and cannot easily replace.

Reputational and legal exposure. AI failures attract attention. When a healthcare system's AI tool is found to have discriminated against patients, when a school's automated monitoring system is found to have surveilled students beyond its disclosed scope, when an employment platform's screening tool is found to be systematically biased, the reputational consequences are serious and lasting. Legal exposure follows in many cases. These outcomes are not hypothetical: they have already occurred at institutions across sectors. The organizations that avoided them, or managed them well, typically had governance systems that allowed them to detect problems earlier, respond faster, and demonstrate that they had acted responsibly.

The argument that this is too much trouble

Organizations that have not yet invested in AI governance sometimes make an implicit argument that amounts to this: the cost and friction of governance exceeds the benefits, especially given uncertainty about what governance should look like.

This argument deserves a direct response.

The friction argument — that governance slows things down — rests on a comparison between the current informal state and a hypothetical governed state. But this comparison misses what the current informal state actually costs. In the absence of governance, decisions about AI tools are made ad hoc, by whoever encounters them first, using whatever criteria happen to be salient. Some of those decisions will be good; many will not be. The costs of the bad ones — remediation, liability, reputational damage, harm to the people the institution serves — are typically much higher than the cost of a systematic review process that might have prevented them.

The uncertainty argument — that it is hard to know what governance should look like — is more legitimate, but it is also exactly what this book is designed to address. Institutions do not need perfect governance. They need adequate governance: a system that is proportionate to their risk exposure, practical enough to actually be used, and clear enough about roles and processes to function reliably. The chapters that follow provide exactly that.

There is also a strategic dimension to this question. AI governance is increasingly not optional in a regulatory sense. The European Union's AI Act imposes obligations on institutions that use certain categories of AI systems. Several US states have passed or are developing laws governing AI in employment, healthcare, and other domains. Regulatory scrutiny of AI is increasing across most jurisdictions. Institutions that have built governance systems proactively are substantially better positioned to comply with emerging requirements than those that have not.

What governance does not mean

It is worth being explicit about what this book is not asking institutions to do.

Governance does not mean refusing to use AI. The goal is responsible use, not abstention. Many AI tools offer genuine value — they save time, improve consistency, extend reach, and help institutions serve more people more effectively. Governance is what allows institutions to capture that value while managing the risks that come with it.

Governance does not mean having AI expertise on staff. This book is written for leaders, managers, and staff who are not technical specialists. The frameworks, checklists, and templates it provides are designed to be used by people without backgrounds in machine learning, statistics, or software engineering. Understanding what questions to ask and what processes to have is not the same as understanding how transformers work.

Governance does not mean creating a dedicated AI team or bureaucracy. For most institutions, responsible AI governance is a function that can be embedded in existing roles and processes — procurement review, risk management, training, incident reporting — rather than a separate organizational unit. The scale of governance should match the scale of the institution.

Governance does not mean treating AI as uniquely dangerous. AI tools carry risks, but so do many other tools institutions use — financial systems, medical devices, personnel management software. The governance approach this book describes is the application of general principles of responsible institutional management to a specific category of tools.

What governance does mean is this: when your institution uses an AI tool, someone knows it is being used, someone is responsible for it, there is a process for evaluating whether it is appropriate, and there is a plan for what to do when something goes wrong. That is not a high bar. It is the bar below which no institution using AI should fall.

The institutions that have already learned this lesson

The case for AI governance is not merely theoretical. A substantial and growing body of real-world experience demonstrates what happens when institutions use AI without adequate governance — and what adequate governance looks like in practice.

Healthcare institutions have encountered AI diagnostic tools that performed significantly worse for patients of certain backgrounds, leading to misdiagnoses and delayed treatment. Those institutions have had to confront the question of whether they had done adequate pre-deployment testing, whether they had monitoring systems that would have caught the problem earlier, and whether their vendor contracts gave them the access and recourse they needed. Some did; many did not.

Educational institutions have encountered AI proctoring and plagiarism detection systems that produced false positives at higher rates for students with certain disabilities, from certain linguistic backgrounds, or with certain physical characteristics. The resulting disputes — with students, with families, with accreditation bodies — have been costly in time, resources, and reputation.

Government agencies have encountered automated benefits determination systems that contained errors affecting thousands of claimants, and social services tools that made recommendations with systematic biases reflecting the historical patterns in their training data. Courts in several countries have grappled with the use of algorithmic risk assessment tools in sentencing and parole decisions, finding that the opacity of those systems made due process guarantees difficult to honor.

Businesses have encountered hiring algorithms that screened out qualified candidates based on characteristics correlated with protected classes, customer service AI that failed users with certain accents or disabilities, and fraud detection systems that flagged legitimate transactions at disproportionate rates for certain demographic groups.

These are not the failures of reckless organizations. Many of them occurred in institutions that had good intentions, competent staff, and genuine commitments to serving their users well. They occurred because those institutions adopted AI tools without adequate processes for evaluating what those tools did, monitoring what they were doing, and responding when things went wrong.

The institutions that avoided these failures — or detected and addressed them early — had something those institutions lacked: governance.

What the rest of this book provides

This chapter has made the case that AI governance is necessary. The rest of this book explains how to do it.

Part I continues the foundational work: clarifying what governance is and is not, identifying the specific risks that matter most for ordinary institutions, explaining how AI systems work in plain language, and mapping who in an institution is responsible for what.

Part II turns to building the governance system itself: forming the team, establishing principles, writing policy, inventorying AI use, screening new use cases, reviewing vendors, and managing data.

Part III addresses the ongoing work of responsible AI use: ensuring human oversight, testing before deployment, rolling out safely, monitoring continuously, building AI literacy among staff, and communicating with stakeholders.

Part IV addresses failure: incident response, special governance considerations for generative and autonomous AI, legal and regulatory context, auditing and accountability, and knowing when and how to stop using a system.

Part V provides practical tools: a starter policy, intake form, vendor questionnaire, testing checklist, incident report template, monitoring dashboard template, and glossary.

None of this requires technical expertise. It requires the same thing that responsible management of any consequential institutional function requires: clarity about what you are doing, who is responsible, what could go wrong, and how you will know if it does.

That is what this book provides. The moment to put it to use is now.

Chapter 2: What AI Governance Is — and Is Not

Starting with clarity

Few words in organizational life accumulate as much baggage as "governance." It arrives in conversations already carrying associations — board meetings, compliance frameworks, audit committees, legal exposure — that can make it sound either more imposing than it needs to be or more procedural than it actually is. Before an institution can build a system for governing AI responsibly, it needs a clear understanding of what that system is, what it is trying to accomplish, and what it is not.

This chapter provides that understanding. It defines the core concepts — governance, oversight, policy, and accountability — in plain language, explains how they relate to one another, and addresses the most common misconceptions that cause institutions to get governance wrong: doing too little because they think it means doing too much, or going through the motions of governance while missing its substance.

The definitions here are not academic. They are working definitions — the kind that help people in real institutions make real decisions about how to manage AI responsibly.

Governance: the system, not the document

Governance is a system for making and overseeing consequential decisions.

That sentence is worth unpacking. Governance is a system — a set of connected processes, roles, and structures that function together, not a single act, document, or committee. It is about making decisions — not just observing or commenting on them, but having clear processes for who decides what, on what basis, and with what authority. And it is concerned specifically with consequential decisions — those that affect people, resources, legal obligations, or institutional reputation in significant ways.

Applied to AI, governance is the system by which an institution decides what AI tools to use, on what terms, for what purposes, subject to what constraints, with what monitoring, and with what recourse when something goes wrong. It encompasses the full lifecycle of AI use — from the first question of whether to adopt a tool, through deployment and ongoing operation, to the decision to stop using it.

Three features of this definition deserve emphasis.

First, governance is prospective as well as reactive. It is not only about responding to problems after they arise. A well-governed institution has processes for evaluating AI tools before they are adopted, requirements for testing before deployment, and monitoring systems that detect problems while they are still manageable. This prospective dimension is what distinguishes governance from incident response — which, while necessary, is governance arriving too late.

Second, governance is distributed. It is not the property of a single person, team, or document. A chief executive who has approved an AI policy, a department head who has completed a vendor review, a frontline supervisor who knows how to escalate an AI-related concern — all of these are governance in action. The system works when all these roles function together. It fails when any of them is absent.

Third, governance is proportionate. The appropriate governance system for a large hospital deploying AI in clinical decision support is not the same as the appropriate system for a small nonprofit using an AI tool to draft communications. Both institutions need governance, but the scale, formality, and complexity of what they need are different. A common governance failure is over-engineering the system for small institutions — or under-engineering it for large ones. Proportionality is a design principle, not a compromise.

What governance is not

Understanding what governance is requires being equally clear about what it is not. Several common misconceptions distort how institutions approach the task.

Governance is not a policy document.

Many institutions believe they have addressed AI governance because they have written — or are planning to write — an AI policy. Policy is a necessary component of governance, but it is not sufficient on its own. A policy that sits unread in an employee handbook, that was written without staff input, that has no mechanism for enforcement, and that specifies no processes for decision-making or monitoring is not governance. It is the appearance of governance.

A policy creates governance only when it is paired with the institutional structures that give it effect: roles with clear authority, processes that staff actually follow, training that builds understanding, monitoring that reveals whether behavior matches policy, and enforcement that makes the policy meaningful. The chapters in Part II address each of these elements. For now, the point is simply that a document, however well-written, is not a system.

Governance is not solely an IT function.

In many institutions, questions about technology systems are routed to the IT department by default. This is appropriate for many technology decisions. It is not appropriate as the organizing principle for AI governance.

AI systems affect hiring, patient care, student outcomes, service delivery, legal compliance, and organizational reputation. These are not technical matters. They require judgment from people who understand the institutional mission, the regulatory environment, the needs of the people the institution serves, and the ethical values it is committed to upholding. An IT team may have essential technical expertise, but AI governance requires perspectives that IT alone cannot supply — from legal and compliance, from operations and program delivery, from human resources, from senior leadership, and in many cases from the people most directly affected by AI-driven decisions.

This is not a criticism of IT departments. It is a recognition that AI governance is an institutional management function, not a technical function. IT is a partner in governance; it is not the owner of governance.

Governance is not a one-time event.

Institutions sometimes treat AI governance as a project with a completion date: build the policy, stand up the committee, create the intake form, declare victory. This is a misunderstanding of what governance requires.

AI systems change. Models are updated by vendors. New use cases emerge. Regulatory requirements evolve. Staff practices drift. Problems that did not exist at deployment appear over time. Governance is only meaningful if it is ongoing — if there are regular reviews, active monitoring, periodic audits, and processes for updating policies and practices as circumstances change. A governance system built once and never revisited is a governance system that is decaying in real time.

Governance is not about prohibition.

Perhaps the most damaging misconception is that AI governance is essentially about saying no — restricting what staff can do, blocking adoption, applying precautionary brakes to tools that would otherwise be useful. This misconception leads organizations to resist governance, treating it as an obstacle to innovation rather than an enabler of responsible use.

Genuine governance creates conditions for saying yes confidently. When an institution has a clear process for evaluating new AI tools, it can approve them with justified confidence rather than accepting them without scrutiny or rejecting them out of excessive caution. When it has monitoring systems in place, it can allow experimentation knowing it will detect problems. When it has clear policies, staff can use AI tools without uncertainty about what is permitted and what is not. Governance is what allows an institution to use AI more — not less — because it has managed the risks that would otherwise make use irresponsible.

Oversight: governance in operation

If governance is the system, oversight is the system in operation. Oversight refers to the active, ongoing exercise of responsibility for AI systems — watching what they are doing, checking whether they are performing as intended, detecting problems, and intervening when necessary.

Oversight is what makes governance real rather than nominal. An institution may have an impeccable governance architecture — policies, committees, review processes, monitoring frameworks — and still have no meaningful oversight if the people responsible for those systems are not actually watching them, if monitoring data is collected but never reviewed, if concerns raised by staff are not acted on, or if reviews are scheduled but never conducted.

The concept of human oversight deserves particular attention in the context of AI, because one of the characteristic risks of AI systems is the erosion of meaningful oversight by humans. This erosion takes several forms.

The first is the automation of decisions that were previously made by humans. When a system automatically screens job applications, routes service requests, or flags suspicious transactions, the human decision-maker is no longer deciding at the same point in the process. The human may review or approve AI outputs, but the practical reality is that AI-generated recommendations strongly constrain the range of outcomes that human reviewers consider. If a human reviewer sees only the candidates that an AI system selected, they cannot correct the selection errors that the AI made upstream. Effective oversight in this context requires understanding where in the decision process human judgment is actually operative — and ensuring that it is operative at points where it can make a meaningful difference.

The second is the delegation of monitoring to automated systems. Many AI governance frameworks include monitoring components — dashboards, alerts, automated performance reports — that purport to track system performance. These tools are valuable, but they are also subject to a recursive governance problem: the monitoring of AI systems is itself partly automated, and the outputs of that monitoring require human interpretation and action. Dashboards that no one reviews, alerts that no one acts on, and performance metrics that no one understands are not oversight. They are the infrastructure of oversight operating without the human attention that gives it meaning.

The third is volume and pace. AI systems can process millions of transactions, decisions, or interactions in the time a human reviewer could examine hundreds. The sheer scale of AI-assisted operations can make meaningful human oversight feel practically impossible. This is a real challenge. The governance response is not to insist on human review of every AI output — that would eliminate the efficiency benefits of AI — but to design oversight systems that sample intelligently, focus human attention on high-stakes or high-uncertainty cases, and ensure that the categories of decision most likely to cause harm receive the most human scrutiny.

Effective oversight, in summary, is not passive. It requires active human engagement with the systems that governance structures are designed to manage.

Policy: governance in writing

Policy is the written expression of governance decisions. An AI policy states what an institution has decided about AI use — what is permitted and what is not, who is responsible for what, what processes must be followed, what values and principles govern decisions, and what happens when things go wrong.

A good AI policy serves several functions simultaneously. It creates clarity for staff — people who want to use AI tools appropriately should be able to consult the policy and understand what is expected of them. It creates accountability — when the policy specifies who is responsible for AI-related decisions, those people cannot later claim the responsibility was unclear. It creates a record of institutional values and commitments — a policy that articulates the institution's principles around fairness, privacy, and human oversight establishes a standard against which practice can be measured. And it creates a basis for enforcement — a policy that is never enforced communicates that institutional commitments are not serious; a policy that is consistently applied communicates that they are.

Several elements distinguish a functioning AI policy from a document that exists primarily for appearance. Chapter 8 addresses AI policy in detail; the relevant points for this chapter are definitional.

A policy must be specific enough to guide decisions. A policy that says "we are committed to responsible AI use" or "AI must be used ethically" provides no actionable guidance. Staff facing a real decision — whether to use a particular tool, how to handle a concerning AI output, who to contact when a system fails — cannot derive answers from these statements. Effective policy translates principles into specific requirements: this category of tool requires review by these roles before adoption; outputs of this type must be reviewed by a human before being acted on; concerns about AI performance must be reported to this person by this mechanism.

A policy must be proportionate to the institution's actual AI use. A highly detailed policy covering scenarios the institution will never encounter creates confusion and compliance fatigue. A policy that fails to address the AI systems the institution currently uses is a policy that cannot govern those systems. Effective policy starts with an honest inventory of what the institution is actually doing and builds requirements around that reality. The fact that policy should be updated as AI use evolves follows directly.

A policy must have visible leadership commitment. Staff take institutional policies seriously when they can see that leadership takes them seriously — when leaders refer to the policy in decisions, when policy violations have consistent consequences, when leadership itself complies visibly. A policy announced by email and never mentioned again is not a governance document; it is a liability shield that may not even serve that function well.

Accountability: governance with consequences

Accountability is the dimension of governance that ensures someone is answerable for what AI systems do. It connects outcomes — including bad outcomes — to the people and processes responsible for them.

Accountability in AI governance operates at multiple levels.

At the individual level, accountability means that specific people within an institution are responsible for specific aspects of AI governance. Someone is responsible for ensuring that new AI tools go through a review process. Someone is responsible for monitoring the performance of deployed systems. Someone is responsible for receiving and acting on reports of AI-related concerns. Someone is responsible for updating the AI policy when circumstances change. When these responsibilities are clearly assigned and understood, the institution has individual accountability. When they are diffuse, unclear, or unassigned, individual accountability is absent — and problems tend to fall into the gaps.

At the institutional level, accountability means that the organization as a whole can answer for the AI systems it uses. This is the kind of accountability that matters in a regulatory inquiry, a legal dispute, or a public controversy. An institution with strong institutional accountability can demonstrate that it had a process for evaluating the tool in question, that it had policies governing its use, that it had monitoring in place, and that it responded appropriately when problems were identified. An institution without this accountability can demonstrate none of those things, which typically results in worse regulatory and reputational outcomes regardless of what actually happened.

At the vendor level, accountability means that the institution has contractual and practical mechanisms for holding AI vendors responsible for the systems they provide. This is a frequently overlooked dimension of governance. Vendors often seek to disclaim responsibility for AI system performance, offering tools "as is" and placing the burden of evaluation and monitoring entirely on the customer. Institutions with effective governance negotiate vendor contracts that include performance commitments, audit rights, breach notification obligations, and clear processes for remediation. They are not simply accepting vendor tools; they are entering relationships in which accountability is explicitly allocated.

Accountability is the part of governance that gives it teeth. Without accountability, a governance system is a set of aspirations with no mechanism for enforcement. With accountability, it is a functioning management system.

The relationship between the four concepts

Governance, oversight, policy, and accountability are not the same thing. But they are not independent of each other either. They are related dimensions of a single coherent system.

Policy is the written foundation — what the institution has decided and committed to. Governance is the system that implements that policy — the processes, roles, and structures that put it into effect. Oversight is the active exercise of that system — the ongoing human attention to whether things are working as they should. And accountability is what ensures that the system is not merely nominal — the mechanism by which people and institutions are answerable for what happens.

An institution can have policy without governance — a document that is not backed by functioning processes. It can have governance structures without oversight — committees that meet but do not effectively monitor. It can have oversight without accountability — people watching what is happening but not empowered or required to act. And it can have accountability without policy — clear responsibility for decisions that are made without documented principles or constraints.

The goal is to have all four, functioning together. Not perfectly — no institution achieves perfect governance — but adequately for the risks it faces and the responsibilities it holds.

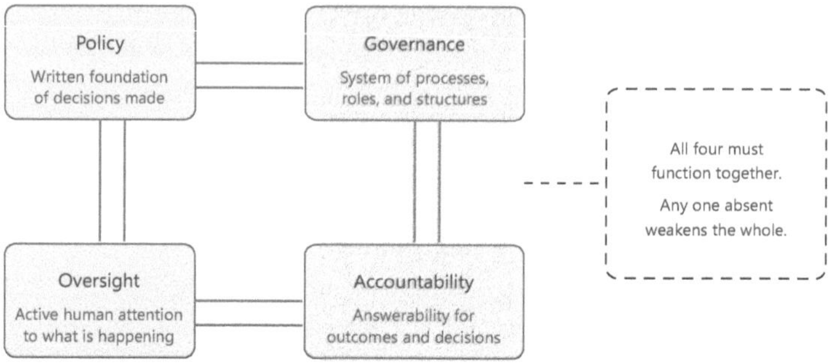

Six common misconceptions in practice

The conceptual framework above takes shape in real institutions through a set of common governance failures. Each represents a recognizable pattern — not a failure of bad intentions but a misunderstanding of what governance requires.

Misconception 1: Having a policy is the same as doing governance.

This is the most widespread governance failure, and it is almost always well-intentioned. An institution perceives the need for AI governance, forms a working group, drafts a policy, gets it approved, and communicates it to staff. Then the working group disbands, the policy document is filed, and the institution returns to normal operations with the sense that the governance question has been addressed.

What has been created is a policy artifact, not a governance system. Six months later, new AI tools have been adopted without the review the policy specifies, because no one has standing authority to conduct that review. Staff are using AI in ways the policy does not address, because no one has updated it in response to new developments. A problem has occurred that the policy would have prevented, because no one was monitoring for it. The policy document still exists, but governance does not.

The corrective is to treat policy as the beginning of governance work, not the completion of it.

Misconception 2: Governance is about controlling what AI does.

Institutions sometimes frame AI governance as primarily a technical challenge: if the AI system's behavior can be specified and constrained precisely enough, governance is achieved. This leads to investments in technical controls — content filters, output constraints, access restrictions — while neglecting the institutional processes that give those controls meaning.

Technical controls are a component of responsible AI use, but they are not governance. An AI system whose outputs are technically constrained can still be used in ways that are unfair, unaccountable, or harmful — if there are no processes for evaluating whether it is appropriate for a given use case, no training that helps staff use it well, no monitoring of outcomes, and no accountability for problems that arise. Governance is about how institutions manage AI, not about what the AI system itself does.

Misconception 3: Governance only matters for high-risk AI.

Some institutions reason that governance is appropriate for AI used in high-stakes contexts — clinical decisions, criminal justice, major financial determinations — but that low-stakes AI use does not require systematic management. A chatbot answering routine administrative questions, a tool that drafts internal communications, a system that schedules meetings — do these really need governance?

The answer depends on what "low-stakes" actually means. Many AI applications that seem innocuous have non-obvious risk dimensions. A communication drafting tool trained on certain data may produce language with systematic biases. A scheduling system may reflect historical patterns that disadvantage certain groups. A meeting summarization tool may retain sensitive information in ways the institution has not considered. The governance question is not whether a tool is superficially high-stakes but whether it could produce outcomes that affect people in significant ways — including ways that are not immediately obvious.

More practically: institutions that adopt selective governance — applying scrutiny to some AI uses and not others — create inconsistency that is difficult to manage. When governance applies only to a designated high-risk category and everything else proceeds without process, the category boundary becomes the governance frontier, and there are strong incentives to classify tools as outside the high-risk category to avoid process friction. Consistent governance is more effective than categorical governance, and it is simpler to manage.

Misconception 4: Vendors are responsible for their tools' performance.

When an AI tool fails — producing biased outputs, incorrect recommendations, or harmful results — institutions sometimes assume that the vendor bears primary responsibility. After all, the vendor built the tool, trained the model, and maintains the system. Why should the institution bear governance responsibility for something it did not create?

This reasoning is legally and practically mistaken in most jurisdictions. When an institution uses an AI tool to make decisions that affect people — employees, patients, students, clients — it is the institution that is accountable for those decisions under most applicable legal frameworks. Vendor contracts typically disclaim liability for AI system performance. Courts and regulators have consistently held that organizations cannot delegate their compliance obligations to technology vendors.

This does not mean vendors bear no responsibility — they do, and holding them accountable through contracts and procurement processes is an important part of governance. But it does mean that an institution cannot outsource its governance responsibility. The institution is responsible for evaluating whether a tool is appropriate before adopting it, for monitoring its performance once deployed, and for the outcomes that result from its use. The vendor's responsibility exists alongside, not instead of, the institution's own responsibility.

Misconception 5: Governance is for organizations that have made AI decisions. We haven't decided yet.

Institutions that are still deliberating about AI adoption sometimes defer governance on the grounds that they have not committed to using AI.

This is a mistake for a straightforward reason: decisions about whether, how, and under what conditions to use AI are themselves governance decisions. The deliberation process is governance. An institution that is deciding whether to adopt an AI tool is already doing AI governance, whether it calls it that or not — and the quality of that decision is better if it is made within a structured process than if it is made informally.

More practically, the assumption that governance begins after adoption misses the point that many institutions are already using AI without having made a deliberate adoption decision. Staff may be using publicly available AI tools in their work. Vendors may have added AI features to software the institution already uses. Governance that begins "after we decide to use AI" may already be starting too late.

Misconception 6: Governance is about protecting the institution from liability.

Defensive framing of governance — AI governance as risk management, as liability mitigation, as regulatory compliance — is not wrong, but it is incomplete. Governance framed purely defensively produces documentation-oriented compliance cultures that are technically in compliance but substantively empty. The goal of having a policy, conducting a vendor review, and filing an incident report is to demonstrate due diligence, not to ensure anything actually functions well.

The more accurate framing, and the one that produces better governance, is that AI governance exists to ensure that AI systems actually work as intended, actually serve the people they are supposed to serve, and actually reflect the values of the institution. The documentation and compliance dimensions follow from this substantive commitment; they are not substitutes for it. An institution that governs AI because it genuinely cares about doing right by its staff, patients, students, or clients will produce better outcomes than one that governs AI because it is worried about lawsuits.

What governance looks like at different scales

One of the most important practical implications of understanding governance correctly is recognizing that it is not a fixed architecture. The right governance system for a given institution depends on the institution's size, resources, risk exposure, regulatory environment, and the nature of its AI use.

For a small nonprofit with limited staff and modest AI use — perhaps a tool that helps draft grant applications and another that manages donor communications — governance might look like this: a designated staff member who reviews any new AI tool before it is adopted and checks a short list of questions; a one-page policy that staff read during onboarding; a standing item on monthly staff meetings for anyone to raise AI-related concerns; and an annual review of what AI tools the organization uses and how they are performing. This is genuine governance, not bureaucratic theater. It is proportionate to the institution's scale and risk profile.

For a regional hospital using AI in clinical decision support, radiology, discharge planning, and patient intake, governance appropriately looks much more substantial: a cross-functional governance committee with clear terms of reference; a formal intake process for AI proposals with defined review criteria; vendor contracts that specify performance requirements and audit rights; pre-deployment testing protocols with defined acceptance thresholds; ongoing monitoring dashboards reviewed on a regular cadence; incident response procedures with defined escalation pathways; and regular reports to the board on AI governance performance. The same principles apply, but the institutional architecture implementing those principles is much more elaborate.

The chapters that follow provide frameworks that can be scaled in either direction. The goal is not to make every institution's AI governance look the same, but to ensure that every institution's governance is adequate for its actual situation.

A working vocabulary

The terms introduced in this chapter will be used throughout the book. It is worth summarizing them briefly before proceeding.

Governance is the system an institution uses to make and oversee consequential decisions about AI — including what tools to use, how to use them, under what conditions, and what to do when things go wrong.

Oversight is the active, ongoing exercise of governance — the human attention, review, and intervention that keeps governance from being merely nominal.

Policy is the written expression of governance decisions — the document that records what the institution has decided about AI use, who is responsible for what, and what processes must be followed.

Accountability is the mechanism by which people and institutions are answerable for AI-related decisions and outcomes — the dimension of governance that gives it consequences.

AI lifecycle refers to the full arc of an AI system's use within an institution — from initial evaluation and adoption, through deployment and operation, to modification and eventual retirement. Governance applies across the entire lifecycle.

Use case refers to a specific application of AI within an institution — using AI to screen job applications, generate patient summaries, draft communications, flag suspicious transactions, and so forth. Governance operates at the level of use cases, not just at the level of AI in the abstract.

These terms, and others introduced throughout the book, are collected in the Glossary in Chapter 30.

The frame for everything that follows

The substance of this book — the frameworks, processes, policies, and tools in the chapters ahead — is grounded in the understanding established here. Governance is a system, not a document. It requires oversight that is active, not passive. It requires policy that is specific, not generic. It requires accountability that is real, not nominal.

The chapters in Part II describe how to build that system. Part III describes how to operate it. Part IV describes how to apply it when things go wrong. And Part V provides the practical tools that make it usable.

All of it rests on what this chapter has established: knowing what governance is — and what it is not — well enough to build it for real.

Chapter 3: The Risks That Matter Most

Risk as the reason governance exists

Governance does not exist for its own sake. It exists because AI systems can cause harm — to the people institutions serve, to the institutions themselves, and to the broader fabric of fairness and accountability that responsible organizations are expected to uphold. Understanding what can go wrong, and why, is the foundation on which every governance decision rests.

This chapter addresses the risks that matter most for ordinary institutions. It is not a comprehensive catalog of every possible AI failure mode — that would fill a separate volume and serve primarily to overwhelm rather than inform. Instead, it focuses on the eight categories of risk that recur most frequently, cause the most significant harm, and are most directly addressable through institutional governance: bias and discrimination, privacy violations, safety failures, hallucination and unreliability, overreliance and automation bias, vendor lock-in, reputational harm, and legal exposure.

Each of these risks is real. Each has already materialized in institutions of the kinds this book addresses — schools, hospitals, nonprofits, government agencies, and businesses of all sizes. And each is substantially more manageable when an institution understands it clearly before something goes wrong.

One prefatory note: these risk categories are not independent. They interact, compound, and cause one another. A hallucination that goes undetected because of overreliance creates reputational harm when it surfaces publicly, which creates legal exposure, which reveals that the institution had inadequate vendor contracts. The chapter addresses each category on its own terms and then considers how they relate.

Bias and discrimination

What it is

Bias in AI systems refers to systematic patterns in outputs that disadvantage or unfairly affect identifiable groups of people — typically, though not exclusively, groups defined by characteristics such as race, ethnicity, gender, age, disability, religion, national origin, or sexual orientation.

The word "systematic" is important. All systems produce errors; not all errors constitute bias. Bias occurs when errors are not randomly distributed but are concentrated in ways that consistently disadvantage particular groups. An AI hiring tool that rejects qualified candidates is making errors; an AI hiring tool that rejects qualified candidates at significantly higher rates when they attended historically Black colleges and universities is exhibiting bias.

Bias enters AI systems primarily through three pathways.

The first is training data. AI systems learn from historical data, and historical data reflects historical patterns of human behavior — including historical patterns of discrimination. A loan approval model trained on decades of lending decisions inherits the patterns of that era, including discriminatory patterns that were legal at the time, patterns that reflect systemic disadvantage rather than individual creditworthiness, and patterns that encode structural inequalities as if they were natural facts. A medical diagnostic model trained predominantly on data from one demographic group may perform worse for groups underrepresented in the training data. The system does not need to have been designed with discriminatory intent to produce discriminatory outcomes; it needs only to have been trained on data that reflects a world in which discrimination occurred.

The second is feature selection. The variables an AI model uses to make predictions — its "features" — can introduce bias even when the features themselves seem neutral. Zip code is a geographic variable; it is also a proxy for race in many contexts, because residential segregation has produced zip codes that are highly correlated with racial composition. Educational credentials are measures of qualification; they are also correlated with family wealth, which is correlated with race and ethnicity. Models that use these features as proxies for qualities they do not actually measure may produce systematically biased results.

The third is feedback loops. AI systems that learn from their own outputs — or from human responses to their outputs — can entrench and amplify initial biases over time. A content recommendation system that starts with slight biases in what it shows to different user groups will collect more data about the biased state than about any alternative, which reinforces the bias in subsequent learning, which produces a more biased system, which collects more biased data.

Why it matters for institutions

Bias is not only an ethical problem, though it is certainly that. It is a problem that arises specifically from how these systems work, makes them fail at their stated purpose, and creates consequences that institutions are responsible for managing.

In healthcare, biased AI tools can produce diagnostic recommendations, treatment suggestions, and risk assessments that perform differently across patient populations. Studies have found clinical AI systems that recommended less care for Black patients than for comparably ill white patients, not because of any deliberate design choice but because the historical utilization data used to train the system reflected historical disparities in care. A hospital that deploys such a system without adequate evaluation and monitoring is not delivering equitable care, regardless of its intentions.

In education, biased AI tools can affect which students receive enrichment opportunities, which are flagged for intervention, which are admitted to programs, and whose work is flagged for integrity review. AI proctoring systems have been found to produce higher false-positive rates for students with darker skin tones, non-standard backgrounds, and certain physical conditions. Plagiarism detection systems have been found to flag non-native English writing at higher rates than comparable native-speaker writing. Each of these failures affects real students in ways that can alter their academic trajectories.

In employment, biased screening tools have been among the most visible AI failures of the past decade. Algorithmic hiring tools trained on resumes of past successful employees systematically reproduce the demographic characteristics of those employees, excluding qualified candidates who do not match historical patterns. Performance evaluation systems trained on manager ratings inherit whatever biases were present in those ratings. The people most likely to be systematically excluded — those from groups that have faced historical discrimination — are also those the institution may have explicit commitments to include.

In social services and benefits administration, biased AI tools can determine which people receive housing assistance, food support, healthcare, or child welfare services. Errors in these contexts fall on people who are already in difficult situations, and the consequences of unfair exclusion can be severe.

What governance does about it

Governing bias risk requires action at multiple points in the AI lifecycle. Before adoption, institutions should require that vendors document how their systems were tested for differential performance across demographic groups, and what the results of that testing were. During review, institutions should evaluate whether the use case creates conditions for bias — whether the system is making or influencing decisions that affect people differently based on characteristics that should be irrelevant. During deployment, institutions should monitor outcomes across identifiable groups, looking for patterns that would indicate differential impact. And when patterns are found, institutions need clear processes for escalating, investigating, and remedying them.

The specific processes for each of these steps are addressed in the chapters on intake and risk screening (Chapter 10), vendor review (Chapter 11), testing before deployment (Chapter 14), and monitoring (Chapter 16). The point here is foundational: bias is not a risk that can be assumed away, and it is not a risk that vendors can be trusted to manage unilaterally. It requires active institutional attention.

Privacy violations

What it is

Privacy risk in AI refers to the potential for AI systems to collect, retain, use, share, or expose personal information in ways that violate the reasonable expectations of the people that information concerns, exceed the institution's legal authority to handle it, or create risks of harm through unauthorized access or unintended disclosure.

AI systems create privacy risks that differ in important ways from those associated with traditional software. Traditional databases store data that has been explicitly entered; AI systems can infer sensitive information from data that was not explicitly sensitive. A model trained on browsing behavior can infer health conditions, political beliefs, and sexual orientation with reasonable accuracy, even when none of that information was provided. A language model that has processed personal communications can retain and reproduce personal details in ways that users do not anticipate and that designers did not intend. These inferential and emergent privacy risks are qualitatively different from the risk of a database being breached, and they require different governance responses.

AI systems also create privacy risks through the way they are trained and operated. Many AI tools send user inputs to vendor systems for processing, storage, and in some cases model training. When staff use an AI tool to draft a letter about a patient, summarize a performance review, or generate options for a child welfare plan, the content they enter — which may include sensitive personal information — may be retained by the vendor, used to improve the model, or accessible to vendor staff. Whether this is disclosed, and whether it is consistent with the institution's legal obligations, depends on the vendor's practices and the terms of the institution's contract.

The categories of information most frequently implicated in AI privacy risk include health and medical information, financial information, information about minors, information about criminal history, and information about characteristics that are legally protected in many jurisdictions. Institutions that handle these categories of information as a matter of course — healthcare providers, schools, financial services firms, government agencies, social services organizations — face heightened privacy risk from AI systems and heightened legal consequences when those risks materialize.

Why it matters for institutions

Privacy violations caused by or through AI systems can harm individuals in direct and serious ways: exposure of health conditions to employers, disclosure of financial circumstances to unauthorized parties, revelation of protected characteristics in contexts where they invite discrimination, or exposure of information about minors in ways that create safety risks. These harms are not abstractions.

They also harm institutions. Data protection laws in most jurisdictions impose obligations that do not relax because the data was processed by an AI system. In Europe, the General Data Protection Regulation governs AI processing of personal data with strict requirements around lawful basis, purpose limitation, data minimization, and individual rights. In the United States, sector-specific laws like HIPAA, FERPA, COPPA, and the CCPA impose requirements that apply regardless of the technology used to process the relevant data. Institutions that use AI tools without understanding how those tools handle personal data may find themselves in violation of obligations they did not know they were assuming.

Beyond legal compliance, privacy violations damage trust. The relationship between an institution and the people it serves — patients and their healthcare providers, students and their schools, clients and their social service organizations — depends on the reasonable expectation that personal information will be handled responsibly. When AI tools undermine that expectation, the damage to the relationship may be more lasting than any legal consequence.

What governance does about it

Privacy governance for AI requires understanding, before adoption, exactly what data a proposed AI tool collects, processes, stores, and transmits; where that data goes; who can access it; how long it is retained; and what the vendor's practices are with respect to using it for model training or other purposes. It requires reviewing vendor contracts to ensure that data handling practices are consistent with the institution's legal obligations and stated commitments. It requires policies that specify what categories of information staff may and may not enter into AI tools, and training that helps staff understand why those limits exist. And it requires monitoring for unexpected data practices as vendor systems evolve.

Data governance for AI is addressed in detail in Chapter 12.

Safety failures

What it is

Safety risk in AI refers to the potential for AI systems to cause physical, psychological, or material harm — either directly, through outputs that endanger people, or indirectly, by contributing to decisions that do. Safety risk is not limited to dramatic scenarios of autonomous systems taking harmful actions; it encompasses the everyday risk that AI tools deployed in consequential settings will fail in ways that injure people.

The categories of AI safety risk most relevant to ordinary institutions fall along a spectrum of directness. At one end are AI systems that directly affect physical wellbeing — clinical decision support tools that recommend inappropriate treatments, medical imaging analysis systems that miss diagnoses, autonomous systems that control physical equipment or navigation. At the other end are systems whose outputs influence consequential human decisions — a risk assessment tool that incorrectly classifies a person as low-risk, a benefits eligibility system that incorrectly denies support, an AI assistant that gives incorrect guidance about medication interactions. Between these poles are systems that affect psychological wellbeing — AI tools used in mental health contexts, content moderation systems that expose people to harmful material, or chatbots deployed in crisis settings that respond inappropriately to expressions of distress.

Safety risk is heightened in domains where mistakes are difficult to reverse, where the consequences of errors are severe, and where users may not have independent means of detecting errors. Healthcare is the paradigmatic case, but the pattern appears across many institutional contexts: a school that uses AI to identify students in crisis, a social services agency that uses AI to assess child welfare risks, a nonprofit that deploys a chatbot to assist vulnerable populations.

Why it matters for institutions

The governance dimension of safety risk turns on a crucial distinction: the difference between a system that performs imperfectly and a system whose imperfections cause harm. All AI systems make errors. The question is whether the deployment context, the uses to which the system is put, and the oversight structures around it mean that those errors translate into harm.

A clinical AI tool that misses a finding in ten percent of cases is a different safety risk when radiologists review every output and exercise independent clinical judgment than when radiologists are expected to review hundreds of cases per day and in practice accept AI outputs without detailed review. The tool's error rate is the same in both scenarios; the safety risk is different because the human oversight is different.

This is the safety governance insight: safety risk is a product of both the system's technical performance and the deployment context that determines whether errors cause harm. Institutions that treat safety as purely a technical question — evaluable through testing alone — will miss the contextual factors that determine whether a technically acceptable system is deployed safely.

What governance does about it

Safety governance requires understanding, before deployment, what category of harm a system could cause and under what conditions — not only whether it can cause harm in the abstract, but what the realistic failure modes are given the specific institutional context, user population, and oversight arrangements. It requires establishing minimum performance requirements that reflect the safety implications of the use case, not generic acceptability thresholds. It requires designing deployment contexts that ensure meaningful human oversight at the points where safety errors are most likely. And it requires incident reporting systems that capture near-misses as well as actual harms, so that safety risks can be identified and addressed before they fully materialize.

Testing before deployment (Chapter 14) and monitoring and ongoing review (Chapter 16) address the operational dimensions of safety governance. The intake and risk screening process (Chapter 10) addresses the upstream question of how to assess safety risk before it reaches the deployment stage.

Hallucination and unreliability

What it is

Hallucination is the term used to describe a distinctive failure mode of generative AI systems: the production of outputs that are fluent, confident, and factually incorrect. The term reflects the phenomenology of the failure — the system generates text that reads as if it were accurate, cites sources that do not exist, describes events that did not occur, and attributes statements to people who never made them, all with the same apparent authority as outputs that are genuinely reliable.

Hallucination is not a bug that better AI systems will eliminate. It is a characteristic of how large language models work. These systems generate outputs by predicting likely continuations of their inputs, based on patterns learned from training data. They are not retrieving verified facts from a database; they are generating text that resembles factual text. When the pattern-matching process produces something plausible but false, the system has no reliable internal mechanism for detecting the error. It produces the hallucination with the same fluency as a correct output.

The practical significance of this varies considerably by use case. AI systems that draft text for human review, suggest options for human consideration, or help organize information create hallucination risk that is manageable through appropriate human review. AI systems whose outputs are acted on directly, incorporated into records without verification, or presented to others as authoritative create much more serious hallucination risk. The same underlying failure mode has very different governance implications depending on the deployment context.

Beyond hallucination in the strict sense, AI systems exhibit a broader range of reliability limitations that governance must account for. Performance can degrade when inputs differ from the distribution of training data — a medical AI trained primarily on records from one healthcare system may perform less reliably on records from a different system with different documentation practices. Performance can change when models are updated by vendors, sometimes in ways that are not disclosed to customers. Outputs can be sensitive to superficially minor variations in how questions are framed, producing different answers to what are effectively the same questions. And AI systems can perform well on average while failing systematically in specific subpopulations or contexts.

Why it matters for institutions

Hallucination and unreliability create direct operational risks. An AI system used to draft communications that contains fabricated information and is sent without review damages institutional credibility and potentially harms the people it concerns. An AI system used to summarize research or policy guidance that produces inaccurate summaries, and whose outputs are used without verification, causes decisions to be made on false premises. An AI system used in a legal or regulatory context that fabricates case citations — a failure that has occurred in actual legal proceedings — can produce serious professional and institutional consequences.

Beyond individual errors, unreliability creates systemic risks when it is not acknowledged. When staff are trained to use AI as a productivity tool but are not adequately educated about hallucination risk, the natural tendency is to treat AI outputs as more reliable than they are. This tendency is reinforced by the fluency and apparent confidence of the outputs, which do not signal their own unreliability. The result is a gradual erosion of verification practices, an increase in the rate at which errors propagate into institutional processes, and an increase in the difficulty of tracing errors back to their source.

What governance does about it

Hallucination risk is primarily governed through use case design and oversight requirements rather than technical controls. The relevant governance questions are: In this use case, what is the consequence of an AI error? Is there a human review step between the AI output and any action or communication? Are the people reviewing AI outputs adequately trained to evaluate them critically? Are there categories of output — factual claims, citations, numerical data, descriptions of specific individuals — that should always be independently verified regardless of the use case?

Policy for AI use should specify verification requirements that are calibrated to the consequences of errors. AI outputs used as first drafts for human revision require a different level of verification than AI outputs that are incorporated into official records or communications. Building AI literacy (Chapter 17) is essential to making these requirements effective: staff who understand how hallucination occurs are better positioned to evaluate AI outputs critically than staff who treat AI as a more convenient version of an internet search engine.

Overreliance and automation bias

What it is

Automation bias is the tendency of humans to favor automated recommendations over their own independent judgment, at rates that exceed what the accuracy of those recommendations would warrant. It is a well-documented cognitive phenomenon, observed across a wide range of professional domains, that has significant implications for how AI systems should be deployed and overseen.

The research on automation bias is unambiguous: when automated systems present recommendations, human decision-makers defer to those recommendations more than they would if the same information were presented in a non-automated format. Clinicians modify treatment decisions based on clinical AI recommendations even when their independent assessment differs. Hiring managers weight AI screening scores heavily even when their direct assessment of a candidate diverges. Pilots follow autopilot systems into unsafe conditions. The common thread is not that humans are irrational or negligent; it is that automated systems carry an aura of objectivity and technical authority that influences human judgment in predictable ways.

Several features of AI systems compound this tendency. The apparent precision of AI outputs — scores, percentages, confidence ratings — suggests a level of empirical grounding that may not reflect the actual reliability of the underlying system. The volume and speed of AI processing suggests a thoroughness that human review cannot match. And the presentation of AI recommendations in the flow of professional work makes them cognitively prominent in ways that increase their influence on decisions.

Overreliance refers to the behavioral pattern that automation bias produces: systematically deferring to AI recommendations without adequate independent evaluation. This manifests in various ways — declining to seek information that would allow independent verification, failing to probe AI outputs that seem unusual, accepting AI-generated summaries without reviewing the underlying sources, and reducing the depth of independent analysis because AI assistance makes the task feel already complete.

Why it matters for institutions

Automation bias and overreliance are particularly serious because they operate beneath the surface of institutional processes. An institution may have a policy requiring human review of AI outputs; that policy may be formally complied with; and the human review may still be substantially ineffective because reviewers are deferring to the AI rather than exercising genuinely independent judgment.

This creates what might be called governance theater — the appearance of human oversight without its substance. A committee that reviews AI recommendations but almost always accepts them is not exercising meaningful oversight. A clinician who reviews AI diagnostic suggestions but modifies them only in extreme cases may be providing less independent clinical judgment than the review requirement implies. An admissions officer who reviews AI-scored applications but weights the AI score heavily in their final assessment may be exercising less independent judgment than an informal assessment would suggest.

The practical consequences of overreliance are compounded by the fact that AI errors are not randomly distributed. AI systems fail in systematic ways — particular types of inputs, particular subpopulations, particular contexts — and automation bias means that those systematic errors are more likely to pass through human review undetected. The humans who are supposed to catch the system's failures are precisely the humans whose judgment is most influenced by the system's outputs.

What governance does about it

Governing overreliance requires attention to the design of human oversight processes, not just their existence. The governance questions are: Is the human review process designed in a way that supports genuine independent judgment, or does it present AI outputs in ways that anchor reviewers to the AI recommendation? Are reviewers trained to understand automation bias and to actively seek reasons to question AI outputs, rather than reasons to accept them? Is the rate of AI recommendation modification being monitored, and would an unusually low modification rate trigger review?

In high-stakes contexts, institutional governance should consider requiring that human reviewers form and document an independent assessment before reviewing the AI recommendation — not as a bureaucratic formality but as a structural intervention against automation bias. This is one area where the design of the process, rather than just the presence of the process, determines whether governance is effective.

Chapter 13, on human oversight and decision rights, addresses these design questions in detail.

Vendor lock-in

What it is

Vendor lock-in refers to the condition in which an institution becomes dependent on a specific AI vendor's systems in ways that make switching vendors costly, disruptive, or practically impossible. It is a governance risk because lock-in reduces institutional autonomy, constrains bargaining power, and can leave institutions without adequate recourse when vendor systems fail to perform, when vendor practices change, or when the vendor relationship needs to end.

Lock-in in AI contexts arises through several mechanisms. Data dependency occurs when an institution's data — training data, historical inputs and outputs, user interaction logs — has been stored in vendor systems in formats that are not easily exportable or that do not transfer cleanly to alternative systems. Workflow integration occurs when AI tools become embedded in operational processes in ways that make removal practically difficult without redesigning those processes. Contractual dependency occurs when long-term contracts without adequate exit provisions commit institutions to vendors for periods that may outlast the vendor's performance or the institution's needs. Capability dependency occurs when the AI capabilities an institution relies on are not available from alternative vendors at comparable quality, making switching theoretically possible but practically prohibitive.

Vendor lock-in is related to, but distinct from, the general problem of technology vendor dependency. AI-specific factors intensify the risk: the pace of AI development means that vendor capabilities and practices change rapidly; the opacity of AI systems means that institutions may not fully understand their dependency until they try to leave; and the competitive structure of the AI market means that capabilities are often concentrated in a small number of vendors with limited alternatives.

Why it matters for institutions

Lock-in matters because it affects an institution's ability to exercise governance at all critical points. When an institution is significantly locked in to a vendor, its ability to impose requirements, renegotiate terms, demand audits, require performance improvements, or exit a problematic relationship is severely constrained. A vendor that knows a customer has no practical alternative has less incentive to respond to performance concerns, privacy complaints, or governance requests.

The practical consequences have played out in institutions that have signed long-term contracts with AI vendors for core operational systems, only to find that the systems perform worse than represented, that the vendor is unresponsive to performance concerns, and that the contractual terms do not provide adequate exit rights or performance remedies. Healthcare institutions, in particular, have found themselves in situations where replacing an AI system embedded in clinical workflows would require months of operational disruption at a time when such disruption is not feasible.

Lock-in also affects regulatory compliance. If new regulatory requirements mandate changes to AI systems, and the institution's vendor either cannot or will not make those changes, the institution has a compliance problem that it cannot resolve unilaterally. This risk is heightened in rapidly evolving regulatory environments.

What governance does about it

Vendor lock-in is primarily a procurement governance problem — most effectively addressed before a contract is signed rather than after dependency has developed. Governance requirements for vendor contracts include provisions for data portability in standard formats, performance benchmarks with contractual consequences for failure, audit rights, breach notification obligations, and clear exit provisions including transition support. Chapter 11 addresses vendor due diligence and contract governance in detail.

Beyond procurement, governance should include periodic assessments of vendor dependency — mapping which AI systems are most deeply integrated into institutional operations, how difficult they would be to replace, and whether the terms of vendor relationships are adequate given the degree of dependency. Institutions that identify high-dependency situations should develop mitigation plans before those situations become crises.

Reputational harm

What it is

Reputational harm from AI refers to the damage to an institution's standing — with the public, with regulators, with funders or investors, with the communities it serves, and with its own staff — that results from AI failures or from the revelation that an institution has used AI in ways that are perceived as irresponsible, unfair, or deceptive.

Reputational harm can arise from actual AI failures — a biased system, a privacy breach, a safety incident — or from perceptions about how an institution has used or governed AI that may be only partially grounded in facts. The two are related: institutions with strong governance are better positioned to limit actual failures and to demonstrate responsibility when failures occur; institutions without strong governance are more likely to experience both actual failures and the additional reputational damage that comes from being unable to demonstrate that they acted responsibly.

Several features of the current environment amplify AI-related reputational risk. Public attention to AI failures is high and increasing. Media coverage of AI problems is substantial and often not technically nuanced — a system that performs marginally worse for one demographic group can be accurately characterized as "biased AI," which in public perception may carry more weight than the specific magnitude of the performance difference. Social media dynamics mean that AI failures can spread rapidly and be difficult to contain, particularly when they involve identifiable individuals or clearly sympathetic circumstances.

The nature of AI also creates distinctive reputational dynamics around transparency and disclosure. Institutions that use AI without disclosing it to affected parties — patients who do not know that AI influenced their treatment recommendations, job applicants who do not know that AI screened their application — face reputational risk not only from the AI system's performance but from the perception of concealment. Even if the AI performed well, the failure to disclose can be experienced as a violation of trust that is reputationally damaging in its own right.

Why it matters for institutions

Reputational harm from AI failures is not hypothetical. Healthcare systems have faced significant public criticism for deploying clinical AI tools that were found to perform differently across racial groups. Employment platforms have faced regulatory action and media scrutiny for algorithmic screening tools found to systematically disadvantage protected groups. Educational institutions have faced student and faculty backlash for AI surveillance and proctoring tools perceived as invasive and biased. Government agencies have faced court challenges and public criticism for automated benefits and sentencing tools whose opacity was incompatible with due process expectations.

The common thread in cases where reputational harm was most severe is not simply that something went wrong, but that the institution appeared to lack genuine awareness of what its AI systems were doing, to have prioritized efficiency or cost savings over the interests of affected people, or to have been more focused on defending its practices than on addressing legitimate concerns. Institutions that could demonstrate active governance — that they had evaluated the system carefully, had monitoring in place, responded promptly when problems were identified, and were genuinely committed to protecting affected people — consistently experienced less severe and less sustained reputational damage.

What governance does about it

Reputational governance for AI has two dimensions. The first is substantive: governing AI well — ensuring fairness, protecting privacy, maintaining safety, building in meaningful human oversight — reduces the frequency and severity of the failures that cause reputational harm. The second is communicative: being able to demonstrate, when something goes wrong, that the institution has acted responsibly. Documentation of governance decisions, evidence of pre-deployment testing, records of monitoring and response — these are not only accountability mechanisms but the evidentiary basis for reputational defense.

Chapter 18 addresses how to communicate with stakeholders about AI use in ways that build and maintain trust. Chapter 19 addresses incident response, including the reputational dimensions of responding to AI failures.

Legal exposure

What it is

Legal exposure from AI refers to the range of potential legal liabilities, regulatory sanctions, and compliance obligations that arise from an institution's use of AI systems. It is the category of risk that most reliably commands leadership attention, because it translates AI governance failures into financial and operational consequences that are quantifiable and difficult to ignore.

Legal exposure in AI takes several forms. Anti-discrimination law applies when AI systems produce outcomes that have a disparate impact on protected classes, regardless of intent. In employment, housing, credit, and many areas of public accommodation, laws in most jurisdictions prohibit practices with unjustified discriminatory effects — and those prohibitions apply to algorithmic practices as well as human ones. Data protection law applies when AI systems collect, process, or retain personal information in ways that exceed the institution's legal authority, fail to honor individual rights, or violate requirements for data minimization, purpose limitation, or security. Consumer protection law applies when AI systems make misleading representations, fail to perform as represented, or create unfair conditions for consumers. Professional licensing and liability frameworks apply when AI is used in regulated professional contexts — healthcare, law, financial services — in ways that fall below applicable professional standards.

Beyond these general frameworks, AI-specific regulation is rapidly developing. The European Union's AI Act establishes requirements — including conformity assessments, transparency obligations, and prohibitions on certain high-risk practices — for AI systems used in regulated contexts. Several US states have enacted or are developing AI-specific legislation governing employment screening, healthcare decision-making, and public sector use. Regulatory guidance from agencies in healthcare, financial services, education, and other sectors is increasingly addressing AI-specific issues.

Why it matters for institutions

The legal consequences of AI governance failures range from regulatory investigations and fines, to civil litigation by affected individuals and classes, to loss of licenses or accreditation, to contractual liability to counterparties. In high-profile cases, they also generate the reputational consequences described in the previous section, which may outlast the legal proceedings themselves.

Several features of AI-related legal exposure deserve particular attention.

Legal liability does not require intent. An institution does not need to have deliberately designed a biased AI system to be liable for its discriminatory effects. The relevant legal question in most jurisdictions is not whether the institution intended harm but whether harm occurred and whether the institution's practices were adequate. This means that the defense "we did not know the system was biased" is not a defense — adequate governance would have revealed the bias.

Vendor contracts are not indemnification. Many AI vendors include liability disclaimers in their standard contracts that attempt to shift responsibility for AI system performance entirely to the customer. Whether these disclaimers are enforceable varies by jurisdiction and context, but their existence means that institutions cannot assume that vendor relationships provide adequate legal protection. Institutions need to negotiate contracts that allocate risk appropriately and that provide contractual recourse when systems fail to perform as represented.

Regulatory requirements are moving targets. What was legally compliant AI practice two years ago may not be compliant today, and what is compliant today may not be compliant when new regulations take effect. Governance systems need to include monitoring of the regulatory environment and processes for updating institutional practices in response to new requirements. Chapter 21 addresses the legal and regulatory landscape in more detail.

What governance does about it

Legal exposure is reduced primarily by getting substantive governance right — ensuring fairness, protecting privacy, maintaining human oversight, documenting decisions — rather than by treating legal compliance as a separate exercise. An institution with genuine governance is, in most regulatory frameworks, an institution that is substantially compliant or well-positioned to become compliant. An institution that has governance in form but not substance is one that may have documentation without the practices that documentation represents, which can be worse than having no documentation — because it suggests awareness of obligations that were not met.

Beyond substantive governance, legal risk management requires adequate vendor contracts, monitoring of the regulatory environment, and processes for legal review of AI governance decisions in high-risk contexts. These are addressed in Chapters 11 and 21.

How these risks interact

The eight risk categories described in this chapter are analytically distinct but practically entangled. Understanding their interactions is essential for governance that addresses the full risk picture rather than treating each category in isolation.

Bias and privacy risks frequently co-occur. AI systems that use sensitive personal characteristics — even as inferred proxies — to produce differential outcomes create both discrimination risk and privacy risk. A healthcare AI that effectively uses racial data (derived from zip code or name patterns) to produce differential treatment recommendations is exhibiting both bias and unauthorized use of sensitive personal information.

Hallucination and overreliance compound each other in predictable ways. A system that produces confident but incorrect outputs is more dangerous when deployed in a context where automation bias causes reviewers to accept outputs without critical scrutiny. The interaction means that the risks cannot be managed independently: reducing hallucination risk without addressing overreliance leaves the pathway from AI error to harm open; reducing overreliance without addressing hallucination leaves the error source intact.

Vendor lock-in amplifies every other risk. An institution locked in to a vendor whose AI system exhibits bias, privacy problems, or safety failures has limited ability to compel remediation and limited ability to exit. Lock-in is not itself a harm-producing risk in the way bias or hallucination is; it is a meta-risk that limits the institution's capacity to respond to other risks.

Legal exposure is often the downstream consequence of multiple compounding risks. A bias risk that generates discriminatory outcomes creates legal exposure. A privacy risk that produces unauthorized data disclosure creates legal exposure. A safety failure that injures a patient creates legal exposure. Reputational harm may follow each of these, creating further legal exposure through loss of revenue, breach of contractual commitments, or regulatory scrutiny invited by public attention. The causal chains are rarely simple.

This interconnection has an important governance implication: risk management that treats each category separately, without attending to interactions, will systematically underestimate overall institutional risk. A bias review that gives a system a clean bill of health may nonetheless miss a privacy risk that is creating conditions for legal exposure. A privacy review that finds adequate data practices may nonetheless miss an overreliance risk that is eliminating the human oversight that was supposed to catch safety failures.

Effective governance addresses risk categories individually — because each requires specific technical and institutional responses — but maintains an integrated view of the full risk picture rather than treating each category as independent of the others.

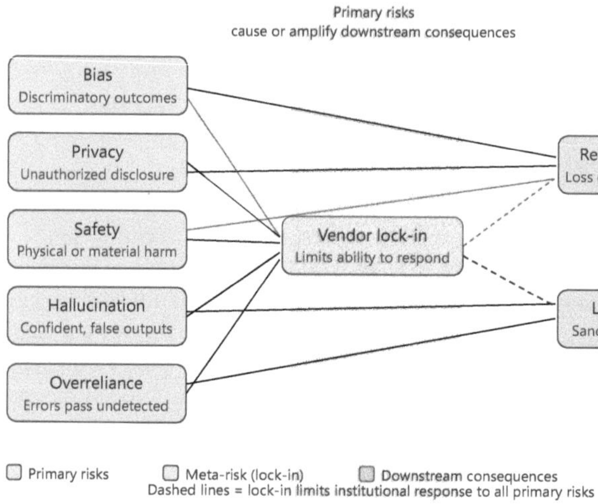

Risk calibration: not all risks are equal in all contexts

The governance implication of this risk landscape is not that every institution must address every risk category with equal intensity. Different institutions face different risk profiles, and effective governance allocates attention and resources in proportion to actual risk exposure.

A small nonprofit that uses AI primarily for internal drafting faces relatively limited bias and safety risk but meaningful hallucination and overreliance risk, because the realistic failure modes involve incorrect information entering communications or decisions without adequate review. A hospital that uses AI in clinical decision support faces meaningful bias, safety, and overreliance risk, because errors in those systems affect patient welfare in direct and potentially serious ways. A government agency that uses AI in benefits determination faces bias, privacy, and legal risk at the forefront, because the decisions affect legally protected rights and because the regulatory scrutiny of government AI use is intense.

This calibration is not about finding reasons to take some risks less seriously. It is about focusing governance resources where they matter most. An institution that spends its governance capacity on vendor lock-in analysis while its clinical AI tools are exhibiting differential performance across patient groups has misallocated its attention. An institution that conducts exhaustive bias audits of an AI tool used only for internal scheduling has also misallocated its attention, in the other direction.

The intake and risk screening process described in Chapter 10 provides a structured approach to this calibration — a way to assess, for any proposed AI use case, which risk categories are most salient and what level of governance scrutiny is proportionate.

Risk as an ongoing condition

A final point deserves emphasis. The risks described in this chapter are not conditions that can be permanently resolved. They are ongoing features of AI system deployment that require continuous governance attention.

A bias audit conducted before deployment does not guarantee absence of bias after deployment. Model updates, changes in the population using the system, shifts in the data it processes, and feedback loops built into the system can all produce bias in systems that previously showed clean results. A vendor that has adequate data practices today may change those practices. A system that performs within acceptable safety parameters under normal operating conditions may fail in edge cases that emerge only with scale or over time.

This is why governance must be ongoing rather than episodic, and why monitoring and regular review are central to any adequate governance system. The risks documented in this chapter are the reason monitoring is not optional. They are the reason that governance, once established, cannot simply be declared complete.

The system an institution builds in Part II of this book, the practices it adopts in Part III, and the responses it prepares in Part IV are all built on the risk foundation established here. Understanding what can go wrong, and why, is what makes governance meaningful rather than merely formal.

Chapter 4: How AI Systems Work in Practice

Why non-technical leaders need technical understanding

There is a reasonable instinct among institutional leaders to delegate technical questions to technical people. Governance of financial systems does not require a chief executive to understand double-entry bookkeeping at a detailed level. Governance of facilities does not require understanding structural engineering. Why should governance of AI require understanding how AI systems work?

The answer is that AI systems fail in ways that are specific to how they work, and governing those failures requires understanding their origins. A leader who understands that AI systems learn from historical data will immediately grasp why bias risk is structural rather than incidental. A manager who understands how language models generate outputs will understand why hallucination is not a bug to be patched but a characteristic to be managed. A procurement officer who understands the difference between a model and a system will know which questions to ask vendors and why the answers matter.

This chapter provides that understanding. It does not require technical background to read, and it will not transform readers into AI engineers. It will give institutional leaders and staff a working mental model of how AI systems operate — one that is accurate enough to support sound governance decisions and to ask the right questions of vendors, technologists, and subject matter experts.

The chapter proceeds through six components: models, data, prompts, outputs, workflows, and human oversight. Each is a distinct element of how AI systems function in practice, and each has specific governance implications.

Models: what they are and what they do

The basic idea

A model, in the AI sense, is a mathematical structure that has been trained to recognize patterns and produce outputs in response to inputs. It is not a database of facts, not a set of rules written by a programmer, and not a system that reasons the way humans reason. It is a very large collection of numerical parameters — weights — that have been adjusted through a training process to produce useful outputs for a defined type of task.

The training process works as follows. The model is shown a very large number of examples — text documents, images, records, data points — and adjusts its internal parameters to get better at producing correct or appropriate outputs for those examples. For a language model, the training task might be predicting the next word in a sentence given all the preceding words; for an image classification model, it might be identifying the content of photographs given labeled examples; for a fraud detection model, it might be distinguishing fraudulent from legitimate transactions given historical records.

After training, the model has learned patterns that it can apply to new examples it has never seen. A language model trained on vast quantities of text can generate fluent, contextually appropriate responses to questions it was never explicitly trained to answer. An image model trained on medical scans can identify potential abnormalities in new scans. A hiring model trained on historical applications and outcomes can score new applications.

What the model has learned is not knowledge in the human sense. It is pattern recognition — the ability to produce outputs that resemble the patterns present in its training data. This distinction is crucial for understanding both the capabilities and the limitations of AI systems.

Types of models in institutional use

Several model types appear with enough regularity in institutional AI deployment that governance leaders should understand their basic characteristics.

Large language models are models trained on vast quantities of text — often drawn from the internet, books, code repositories, and other sources — to generate, summarize, translate, classify, and respond to text. They are the technology behind AI chatbots, writing assistants, document summarization tools, and many customer service applications. Their defining characteristics for governance purposes are their generality (they can be applied to a wide range of text-based tasks), their fluency (their outputs are grammatically and stylistically competent), and their unreliability about specific facts (they generate plausible-sounding text rather than retrieving verified information).

Classification models are models trained to assign inputs to categories — spam or not spam, fraudulent or legitimate, high-risk or low-risk, qualified or unqualified. They are among the most widely deployed AI systems in institutional settings: hiring screening tools, fraud detection systems, clinical risk stratification tools, and content moderation systems are often classification models. Their governance implications center on the categories themselves (what does "high-risk" actually mean, and who decided?), the quality of the training data that defined those categories, and differential performance across demographic groups.

Recommendation models are models trained to predict which outputs — content, products, people, options — a user or system is likely to prefer or benefit from, given patterns in historical behavior and characteristics. They appear in content platforms, product suggestions, job matching, and clinical decision support. Their governance implications include the feedback loops they create (recommending what was popular in the past makes those things more popular, crowding out alternatives) and the ways in which "likely to prefer" can encode historical biases.

Predictive models estimate the likelihood of future events — a patient's probability of readmission, a student's probability of dropping out, a borrower's probability of default, an applicant's probability of success. Their governance implications are closely related to those of classification models: the definition of the outcome being predicted, the quality of the historical data, and the differential accuracy of predictions across demographic groups.

Generative models produce new content — text, images, audio, code — that did not exist before. Large language models are a type of generative model; image generation models are another. Their distinctive governance implications involve the authenticity and accuracy of generated content, intellectual property questions about training data and outputs, and the potential for generated content to be mistaken for authentic human-produced material.

What models cannot do

Understanding model limitations is as important for governance as understanding capabilities.

Models do not have access to information beyond their training data unless they are specifically connected to external information sources. A language model's knowledge is frozen at the point when its training data was collected; it does not know about events that occurred after that point, and it cannot check whether its outputs are consistent with current facts unless it is designed to retrieve and verify information from external sources.

Models do not know when they are wrong. A classification model that produces an incorrect classification does not flag the output as uncertain; it produces the output with whatever confidence score it was designed to attach. A language model that generates a fabricated fact does not signal its own unreliability; it produces the fabrication with the same fluency as a correct statement. This is one of the most important governance implications of how models work: the model's apparent confidence is not a reliable guide to the accuracy of its outputs.

Models do not generalize equally across all inputs. They perform best on inputs that resemble their training data and less well on inputs that differ from it. A model trained predominantly on data from one demographic group may perform less accurately for others. A model trained on data from one healthcare system may perform less accurately on data from a different system with different documentation practices. Performance on a test set drawn from the same population as the training data does not guarantee performance on a different population.

Models do not update their knowledge from deployment experience unless they are specifically designed and operated to do so. Most AI systems deployed in institutional settings do not continuously learn from new inputs in the way the public sometimes imagines. The model that processes an input today is functionally the same model that will process an input next month, unless the institution or vendor actively updates it.

This stability is actually a governance advantage — it means that tested systems do not change without deliberate action — but it also means that performance on current inputs may diverge over time from the performance that was validated at deployment.

Data: the raw material of AI

Training data and what it determines

Data is the raw material from which AI models are built. The training data — the collection of examples on which a model is trained — is among the most consequential determinants of model behavior. What the model learns to do, how accurately it does it, for whom it works well and for whom it works poorly, and what biases it encodes are all substantially determined by the training data.

This makes training data a governance matter of the first order. Several dimensions of training data quality are directly relevant to institutional AI governance.

Representativeness refers to whether the training data adequately covers the populations and situations the model will encounter in deployment. A medical imaging model trained primarily on images from adult patients may perform poorly on pediatric cases. A natural language processing model trained primarily on formal written English may perform poorly on text that reflects different dialects, writing styles, or linguistic backgrounds. A fraud detection model trained on historical fraud patterns may perform poorly on novel fraud approaches that differ from the historical pattern. When evaluating AI tools, institutions should understand how training data was collected and whether it represents the populations and situations the institution will deploy the model against.

Historical bias refers to the ways in which training data reflects historical patterns of human behavior, including historical patterns of discrimination and inequality. When models learn from data that reflects discriminatory practices — lending decisions that were racially biased, hiring decisions that reflected gender stereotypes, criminal justice outcomes that reflected systemic inequities — they learn to reproduce those patterns. This is not a failure of model design; it is a consequence of learning from history. It means that even technically well-designed models can produce discriminatory outcomes when trained on biased historical data.

Data quality refers to the accuracy, completeness, and consistency of training data. Models trained on inaccurate data learn inaccurate patterns. Models trained on incomplete data develop blind spots. Models trained on inconsistently collected data may behave inconsistently in deployment. Data quality is often invisible to end users — a model's outputs do not visibly signal that they were shaped by poor-quality training data — which makes it a governance risk that requires explicit attention in vendor evaluation.

Data recency refers to whether training data reflects current conditions. Models trained on data from several years ago may have learned patterns that no longer hold — occupational patterns that have changed, medical practices that have evolved, fraud techniques that have been superseded. When deploying AI tools, institutions should understand when training data was collected and whether the patterns it encodes are likely to still be valid.

Operational data: what flows through the system

Beyond training data, AI systems in operation process operational data — the inputs that users provide, the records the system accesses, and the outputs it generates. Governance of operational data is distinct from governance of training data, and both are necessary.

Operational data creates privacy risk when it includes personal information about the people an institution serves. When a healthcare worker uses an AI tool to draft a clinical note, the patient information they enter is operational data. When a social worker uses an AI tool to generate a case summary, the client information in that summary is operational data. When a hiring manager uses an AI tool to evaluate a candidate, the candidate's information is operational data.

The governance questions for operational data are: Where does it go? Who can access it? How long is it retained? Is it used to train or improve the model? Many AI vendors, particularly those offering large language model services, retain inputs and outputs for purposes including model improvement. Whether this is disclosed, and whether it is consistent with the institution's legal obligations and ethical commitments, depends on vendor practices and contractual terms.

Operational data also creates accuracy and contamination risks. When AI systems are used to process information that subsequently influences other systems or decisions, errors in AI processing can propagate through institutional data infrastructure in ways that are difficult to trace and correct. An AI system that incorrectly extracts information from documents, if that extraction flows into records that are treated as authoritative, creates data quality problems downstream from its own failures.

Data that institutions provide to vendors

A specific operational data risk deserves particular attention: the data that institutions provide to AI vendors as part of deploying or customizing AI systems. When an institution provides training data to a vendor — historical records, documents, case files — to customize a model for institutional use, it is giving the vendor access to institutional information under terms that the contract governs. The governance questions here are: What does the vendor do with this data? Does it remain within the scope of the customization project, or does it become part of the vendor's broader training ecosystem? What rights does the institution retain over the data it provides? What happens to it when the contract ends?

These questions have become more salient as AI vendors have developed practices around using customer data to improve their models. Whether customer data is used for model training, and under what conditions, varies by vendor and by contractual arrangement. Institutions that do not address these questions explicitly in procurement are accepting whatever terms the vendor's standard contract provides, which may not be consistent with institutional data governance obligations.

Prompts: how humans direct AI systems

What a prompt is

A prompt is the input that a human provides to an AI system to direct its behavior. For language models, a prompt is typically a text instruction, question, or request. For image models, it might be a text description of an image. For more specialized systems, it might be a structured input in a defined format.

The concept of prompting matters for institutional governance because the quality and design of prompts substantially affects the quality and appropriateness of AI outputs. A well-designed prompt that includes relevant context, specifies the desired output format, establishes appropriate constraints, and is tested across a range of inputs will produce more reliable and appropriate outputs than a poorly designed prompt. The same underlying model can produce outputs of dramatically different quality depending on how it is prompted.

In institutional AI deployment, prompting occurs at two levels. System-level prompting involves the instructions and context that the institution or vendor builds into the AI system to shape its behavior for the intended use case — the instructions that tell a customer service chatbot to stay focused on relevant topics, to respond in a particular tone, and to escalate certain types of requests to human agents. User-level prompting involves the inputs that individual staff members provide when they use an AI tool — the specific questions they ask, the context they provide, the formatting they request.

Both levels have governance implications. System-level prompts are a primary mechanism through which institutions can shape AI behavior to reflect their values and requirements. User-level prompts are a primary mechanism through which individuals can use AI tools in ways that were not intended, that exceed appropriate scope, or that produce harmful outputs.

Prompt governance

Institutions that use AI tools with significant user-level prompting — tools where staff provide instructions or questions directly to a language model — need prompt governance: policies and training that help staff use prompts effectively and appropriately.

Effective prompt use involves providing sufficient context for the AI to produce useful outputs, specifying the desired format and scope of response, and reviewing outputs critically before using them. It also involves understanding the limits of what prompting can achieve — a prompt cannot make a model reliably accurate on topics where its training data was poor, cannot eliminate hallucination risk for specific factual claims, and cannot substitute for the professional judgment that staff bring to their work.

Appropriate prompt use involves not providing information in prompts that should not enter the AI system — personal information about patients, clients, or employees when the vendor's data practices do not support such use, confidential institutional information when the confidentiality obligations are unclear, or information that is legally protected and whose transmission to a third-party system would violate applicable law.

Training that addresses both effective and appropriate prompt use is part of AI literacy development, addressed in Chapter 17.

Outputs: what AI systems produce and what they mean

The nature of AI outputs

AI outputs are the results that AI systems produce in response to inputs. For language models, outputs are text — responses, summaries, drafts, classifications, answers. For image models, outputs are images. For classification models, outputs are labels, scores, or rankings. For predictive models, outputs are probability estimates or risk scores.

The most important governance insight about AI outputs is this: an AI output is a prediction, not a determination. When a hiring AI produces a score for a job candidate, that score is the model's prediction of how likely the candidate is to succeed — based on patterns in historical training data — not an objective assessment of the candidate's qualities. When a clinical AI flags a patient as high-risk, that flag is the model's prediction of the likelihood of an adverse event, not a clinical judgment about the patient's condition. When a language model produces a summary of a document, that summary is the model's prediction of what a plausible summary would look like, not a verified extraction of accurate information.

This distinction matters because outputs that look authoritative — scores, rankings, summaries, recommendations — can create the impression that a determination has been made, when in fact what has been produced is a probabilistic pattern-match. An institutional culture that treats AI outputs as determinations rather than predictions is one in which automation bias is likely to be severe, human oversight is likely to be nominal rather than genuine, and errors are likely to compound before they are detected.

Output quality and its limits

AI output quality varies in ways that are not always visible in the output itself. Several dimensions of output quality matter for governance.

Accuracy refers to whether outputs correctly reflect factual reality. For classification models, accuracy is typically measured in terms of correct classification rates across a test set. For language models, accuracy is considerably harder to assess, because the fluency of outputs is independent of their factual correctness. An AI that produces a grammatically impeccable summary containing factual errors is producing low-accuracy output in a high-quality format — the kind of output most likely to be accepted without adequate scrutiny.

Consistency refers to whether the system produces similar outputs for similar inputs. Many AI systems exhibit sensitivity to superficially minor variations in how questions are framed, producing meaningfully different outputs in response to equivalent questions posed in slightly different ways. This inconsistency is a governance concern because it makes outputs harder to evaluate, harder to audit, and harder to defend when challenged. If an AI system that scores job applications would produce different scores for the same application depending on minor formatting variations, the scores cannot be treated as objective assessments.

Calibration refers to whether the confidence scores that AI systems attach to their outputs accurately reflect the actual reliability of those outputs. A well-calibrated model that says it is 90% confident in an output is correct about 90% of the time; a poorly calibrated model that expresses 90% confidence may be correct only 70% of the time. Many AI systems are overconfident — they express high confidence in outputs that are less reliable than the confidence score suggests. When confidence scores are used to make decisions about when to route outputs to human review, poor calibration can systematically direct the wrong outputs to and away from human scrutiny.

Explainability refers to whether the basis for an AI output can be understood and communicated. Some AI systems can provide some account of why they produced a given output — which features of the input most influenced the result, which historical examples most closely resembled the current case. Others function as effective black boxes, producing outputs whose reasoning is entirely opaque. Explainability matters for governance because it affects the institution's ability to audit outputs for bias, to explain decisions to affected parties, to fulfill due process obligations, and to identify and correct systematic errors.

What outputs are not

Several common misunderstandings about AI outputs deserve direct correction.

AI outputs are not neutral. The outputs of AI systems reflect choices — choices about training data, features, objectives, and performance criteria — that embed values and priorities. A hiring AI that optimizes for "fit with existing team" reflects a value judgment about what matters in hiring, one that may reproduce existing demographic homogeneity. A content recommendation AI that optimizes for engagement reflects a value judgment that engagement is what should be maximized, one that may promote emotionally provocative content at the expense of accurate or nuanced content. These are not neutral technical choices; they are choices with significant implications that governance must account for.

AI outputs are not authoritative. An AI output is only as reliable as the model that produced it, the data it was trained on, and the quality of the match between the current input and the distribution of training data. None of these factors is visible in the output format. An AI recommendation presented in a dashboard with a confidence score and supporting statistics looks authoritative regardless of whether the underlying model is reliable, the training data was representative, or the current input falls within the range of cases the model can handle well.

AI outputs are not final. They are inputs to human processes — first drafts to be revised, recommendations to be evaluated, scores to be considered. Treating AI outputs as final — acting on them without review, incorporating them into records without verification, communicating them to affected parties without independent assessment — eliminates the human oversight that is the primary mechanism for catching AI errors before they cause harm.

Workflows: how AI fits into institutional processes

AI as a component, not a system

In most institutional deployments, AI is not a standalone system; it is a component embedded in larger workflows. A clinical AI tool does not exist in isolation; it exists within a care delivery process that includes patient intake, clinical assessment, treatment planning, and follow-up. A hiring AI tool does not exist in isolation; it exists within a recruitment process that includes job posting, application collection, screening, interviewing, and selection. An AI drafting tool does not exist in isolation; it exists within a communication or documentation process that includes information gathering, drafting, review, and distribution.

Understanding AI as a workflow component, rather than as a standalone system, has important governance implications. It means that the governance of AI cannot be addressed only at the level of the AI component itself; it must address the workflow into which the AI is embedded. The same AI component — the same model, the same accuracy characteristics, the same risk profile — can have very different governance implications depending on where it sits in the workflow and what human processes surround it.

Consider two ways of deploying a document summarization AI in a legal services organization. In the first, the AI generates summaries that are then reviewed by a paralegal before being used in case preparation. In the second, the AI generates summaries that are stored directly in the case management system and used by attorneys as reference documents without a systematic review step. The AI component is identical in both scenarios. The governance implications are very different, because the presence or absence of human review in the workflow determines whether AI errors are caught before they affect case outcomes.

Workflow analysis — mapping where AI sits in institutional processes and identifying what human oversight is present at each stage — is a fundamental governance tool. It reveals risk concentrations that component-level analysis misses and identifies the points at which governance interventions can most effectively reduce harm.

Workflow integration types

AI systems integrate into institutional workflows in several distinct patterns, each with different governance characteristics.

Screening workflows use AI to filter, triage, or prioritize large volumes of cases, applications, or items — passing some forward for human attention and setting others aside. Hiring screening, fraud triage, content moderation, and patient risk stratification all use this pattern. The governance implications center on what is filtered out: cases or people that the AI routes away from human attention may receive no human review at all, which means that AI errors in the filtering stage can have complete and irreversible effects on outcomes. The base rate of false negatives — items that should have passed forward but were filtered out — is a critical governance metric for screening workflows that may never be visible unless specifically monitored.

Decision support workflows use AI to assist human decision-makers by providing recommendations, risk scores, relevant information, or draft outputs, which the human then incorporates into their decision. Clinical decision support, investment recommendation, case management tools, and many AI writing assistants use this pattern. The governance implications center on automation bias: whether the AI recommendation is genuinely augmenting human judgment or effectively substituting for it, and whether the presentation of AI outputs is designed in ways that support or undermine independent human evaluation.

Automation workflows use AI to handle processes end-to-end without human involvement in individual cases — routing service requests, scheduling appointments, sending communications, processing standard applications. The governance implications center on exception handling: what happens when the automated process encounters a case it cannot handle well, how the system recognizes and escalates those cases, and whether the escalation process is designed to deliver meaningful human review or merely to create a record that a human was nominally involved.

Augmentation workflows use AI to expand the capacity of human workers — enabling a clinician to review more patients, a teacher to provide more personalized feedback, a researcher to process more documents. The governance implications center on the dilution of human attention: when AI enables a human to do work at greater volume, the depth of human engagement per case typically decreases, which may or may not be appropriate depending on the nature of the work. A human reviewing ten AI-assisted summaries per hour is doing different work than a human writing ten summaries per hour.

Workflow risk mapping

Effective workflow governance requires mapping AI-augmented workflows to identify where risks are concentrated. This mapping exercise asks, for each stage of the workflow: What is the AI doing at this stage? What inputs does it receive and what outputs does it produce? What human oversight is present? What is the consequence of an AI error at this stage? Is there an opportunity to detect and correct AI errors before they affect outcomes downstream?

The answers to these questions identify the risk-critical governance points in any AI-augmented workflow — the stages where errors are most consequential, where human oversight is weakest, and where governance interventions can most effectively reduce harm. This mapping is a core component of the pre-deployment review process described in Chapter 14 and the ongoing monitoring process described in Chapter 16.

Human oversight: the essential component

What makes oversight meaningful

Human oversight — the active involvement of human judgment in reviewing, evaluating, and intervening in AI-assisted processes — is the primary mechanism by which governance converts institutional commitments into operational reality. It is what makes governance more than a set of documents, more than a policy that lives in an employee handbook. When human oversight is meaningful, errors get caught, biases get detected, and the gap between AI outputs and human values gets managed. When human oversight is nominal — present in form but absent in substance — governance fails regardless of the quality of the documents supporting it.

The distinction between meaningful and nominal oversight is critical and not always easy to observe from outside an institution's operations. Nominal oversight occurs when a human is present in the workflow but is not actually exercising independent judgment — when an approver signs off on AI recommendations without reviewing them critically, when a reviewer accepts AI outputs without independently verifying their accuracy, when an escalation process exists but is never used because the norm is to accept AI outputs without escalation. Meaningful oversight occurs when humans are positioned to actually catch errors, are motivated and able to do so, and have processes that make correction possible when errors are found.

The three conditions of meaningful oversight

Meaningful human oversight requires three conditions to be met simultaneously. When any one of these conditions is absent, oversight becomes nominal regardless of the formal governance structures that surround it.

Capability: The person exercising oversight must have the knowledge and access to evaluate the AI output critically. This means understanding enough about how the AI system works to know what kinds of errors it might make, having access to the underlying information the AI processed (not just its output), and having the professional expertise to form an independent assessment. A reviewer who does not understand the basis for an AI recommendation, who can only see the recommendation and not the inputs that generated it, or who lacks the domain knowledge to evaluate whether the recommendation is appropriate cannot exercise meaningful oversight.

Authority: The person exercising oversight must be empowered to deviate from the AI recommendation when their independent judgment calls for it. This sounds obvious but is frequently absent in practice. When institutional culture treats AI recommendations as authoritative defaults that can be overridden only with strong justification, when performance metrics reward speed of processing rather than quality of review, or when there are no formal mechanisms for documenting and acting on override decisions, the practical authority to deviate from AI outputs is limited regardless of formal policy. Meaningful oversight requires that overriding AI recommendations is a normal, supported, unstigmatized part of the workflow.

Timing: The oversight must occur at a point in the workflow where a human can actually affect the outcome. Review that occurs after a decision has been communicated, after a record has been finalized, or after an action has been taken is not oversight — it is after-action review. Meaningful oversight occurs before the point of irreversibility, at a stage where the human reviewer's judgment can actually shape what happens.

Designing for meaningful oversight

Because meaningful oversight depends on workflow design, not just policy commitments, governance must address how human oversight points in AI-augmented workflows are designed. Several design principles support meaningful oversight.

Separate AI output generation from AI output presentation. When an AI recommendation is presented to a reviewer at the same time they are collecting the underlying information, the recommendation anchors their information-gathering — they selectively attend to information consistent with the recommendation and discount information inconsistent with it. Presenting AI outputs after reviewers have formed an independent preliminary assessment, even informally, produces more genuinely independent review.

Design feedback mechanisms that capture override decisions. When a reviewer deviates from an AI recommendation, that decision should be recorded — what the AI recommended, what the reviewer decided, and if possible why. This creates two governance benefits: it provides data for monitoring override rates (an unusually low override rate may signal automation bias), and it creates a learning record that can improve both the AI system and the oversight process.

Calibrate oversight intensity to risk. Not every AI output in a workflow requires the same depth of human review. An AI that suggests meeting times requires less intensive oversight than an AI that produces a clinical risk score that will influence treatment decisions. Governance should establish oversight requirements that are calibrated to the risk profile of the specific output and use case — intensive review where consequences of error are serious, lighter-touch review where consequences are minimal — rather than applying uniform oversight requirements across all AI use.

Make escalation easy and normal. Reviewers who are uncertain about an AI output, who suspect an error, or who encounter an edge case the system appears to be handling poorly need a clear and easy way to escalate. Escalation processes that require extensive documentation, that pass through many approval layers, or that carry implicit signals of criticism about the reviewer's judgment will be underused. The governance standard should be that escalation is the routine response to uncertainty, not an exceptional event.

Putting the components together

These six components — models, data, prompts, outputs, workflows, and human oversight — do not operate independently. They form an integrated system, and the governance of AI systems must address the integration, not just the components individually.

A model's limitations create risks that are amplified or mitigated by data quality. Data quality determines what patterns the model learns, which in turn determines what kinds of outputs it produces. The outputs feed into workflows that either do or do not include meaningful human oversight.

Prompts, designed well or poorly, shape what outputs the model produces. Human oversight, designed for the workflow or bolted on as an afterthought, determines whether the risks inherent in the model, data, and workflow actually translate into harm.

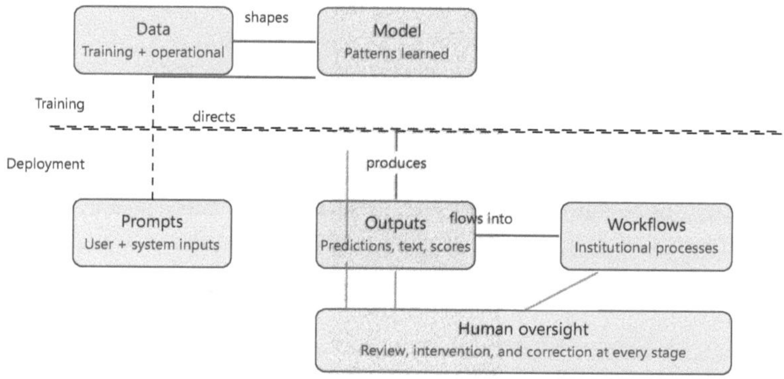

This integration means that governance failures can originate at any component and propagate through the system. A bias that originates in training data produces biased model outputs, which flow into workflows that may not have oversight designed to catch that specific kind of bias, which produce harmful outcomes that persist until monitoring detects them or an affected party raises a complaint. A hallucination that the model generates becomes a governance failure when the workflow lacks a verification step and the oversight process is too thin to catch it.

It also means that governance strengths at one component can compensate for weaknesses at another — within limits. Strong human oversight can catch many of the errors that result from imperfect training data. Strong prompt design can reduce the frequency with which language models produce unreliable outputs. Strong workflow design can ensure that consequential decisions receive adequate scrutiny even when model performance is imperfect.

The limits of compensation are important to acknowledge. Human oversight cannot compensate for systematically biased training data if the oversight process itself is subject to automation bias. Workflow design cannot compensate for fundamentally unreliable AI components if the volume of outputs makes genuine review impossible. The goal of governance is not to find enough compensating strengths to make weak components acceptable; it is to ensure that each component meets a minimum standard of quality, and that the integration of components is designed to add oversight rather than create gaps.

What this means for governance practice

The understanding established in this chapter has direct practical implications for how institutions govern AI. Several of the most important can be stated concisely.

When evaluating AI tools, ask about training data. Vendors will typically be willing to describe, in general terms, what data their models were trained on. The questions that matter are: Is the training data representative of the populations and situations this institution will deploy the model against? When was it collected? How were biases assessed and addressed? What is the documented performance across demographic groups?

When reviewing vendor contracts, address operational data. What data does the system collect from users? Where is it stored? Who can access it? Is it used to train or improve the model? What are the retention and deletion policies? These are not technical questions; they are data governance questions that procurement and legal teams are equipped to handle if they know to ask them.

When designing deployment, map the workflow. Where does the AI sit in the institutional process? What human oversight is present at each stage? What happens when the AI produces an output that is uncertain, unusual, or wrong? Where is the point of irreversibility, and is human review occurring before that point?

When training staff, address the nature of outputs. Staff who understand that AI outputs are predictions rather than determinations, that AI can be fluently wrong, and that their independent professional judgment remains essential are better equipped to exercise meaningful oversight than staff who have been trained only in how to use the tool efficiently.

When monitoring deployed systems, attend to the workflow, not just the model. Performance metrics for the AI component are necessary but not sufficient. Governance monitoring should also track whether human oversight is being exercised — override rates, escalation rates, error detection rates — and whether the integration of AI into workflows is producing the outcomes the institution intended.

These practical implications are elaborated in the chapters that follow. The technical understanding established here is the foundation on which all of them rest.

Chapter 5: Who Is Responsible

The accountability gap

When AI systems cause harm in institutions, a revealing pattern frequently emerges in the aftermath. Leadership assumed that IT was monitoring the system's performance. IT assumed that the business unit deploying the system had evaluated its appropriateness. The business unit assumed that procurement had reviewed the vendor's quality and compliance claims. Procurement assumed that legal had assessed the contract terms. Legal assumed that someone had conducted a risk assessment. No one had conducted a risk assessment, because no one had been explicitly assigned to do so, and each party had reasonably — but incorrectly — assumed that someone else had the matter in hand.

This is the accountability gap. It is not caused by negligence or bad intentions. It is caused by the absence of explicit, documented role definitions that assign specific AI governance responsibilities to specific people and functions. In its absence, AI governance work falls into the spaces between organizational roles, performed by no one, until something goes wrong.

Closing the accountability gap is one of the primary purposes of governance architecture. It requires mapping the full scope of AI governance responsibilities, assigning each responsibility to an appropriate role, ensuring that the people in those roles understand and accept the assignment, and creating the connections between roles that allow the overall system to function as a coherent whole rather than a collection of independent functions.

This chapter provides that mapping. It describes the AI governance responsibilities of seven key actors — leadership, legal and compliance, IT and information security, operations and program delivery, procurement, frontline staff, and vendors — and explains how those responsibilities relate to each other. It is not an organizational design guide; institutions vary too much in structure for a single design to be appropriate across them. It is a responsibility guide: a description of who owns what, in terms specific enough to close the accountability gap.

Leadership: setting the conditions for everything else

What leadership owns

Senior leadership — the chief executive, president, executive director, board, or equivalent — owns AI governance in the most fundamental sense: they are responsible for creating the institutional conditions that make governance possible. This is not a ceremonial or delegable responsibility. The evidence from institutions where AI governance has worked and where it has failed is consistent: when leadership treats AI governance as a real institutional priority, the rest of the organization follows. When leadership treats it as a compliance exercise to be delegated and forgotten, the rest of the organization responds accordingly.

Leadership's specific AI governance responsibilities fall into four areas.

The first is policy authority. Senior leadership approves the institution's AI governance policy — not as a rubber stamp on work done by others, but with genuine engagement in the values, principles, and commitments the policy expresses. When the policy addresses questions like "what level of human oversight is required for AI-assisted decisions that affect people's access to services," those are not technical questions. They are value questions that belong to leadership. The policy that leadership approves is the institution's public commitment to how it will govern AI; leadership needs to understand and genuinely endorse what that commitment says.

The second is resource allocation. Governance requires people, time, and in many cases technology and training investment. Leadership controls resource allocation. An institution whose leadership approves an AI governance policy but does not fund the staff time, training, and infrastructure that policy requires has created governance theater. Real governance requires real resources, and only leadership can authorize them.

The third is culture and tone. The institutional culture around AI — whether staff feel empowered to raise concerns about AI systems, whether compliance with governance processes is expected and enforced, whether AI failures are treated as learning opportunities or concealed, whether the commitment to responsible AI is genuine or performative — is primarily set by leadership behavior. When leaders ask about AI governance performance in the same terms they ask about financial performance, when they respond to AI failures with accountability rather than defensiveness, and when they visibly comply with governance requirements themselves, the culture follows.

The fourth is escalation and final decision authority. Some AI governance decisions exceed the authority of any single operational role. A decision to deploy AI in a context that carries significant regulatory risk. A decision to continue using an AI system after a significant failure has been identified. A decision to reject a vendor whose capabilities are attractive but whose governance practices are inadequate. These decisions need to reach leadership and be made at the appropriate level of institutional authority.

What leadership does not own

Leadership should not be the primary day-to-day operator of AI governance. The Chief Executive is not the appropriate person to conduct intake reviews of proposed AI use cases, negotiate AI vendor contracts, or monitor deployed AI system performance. Those responsibilities belong elsewhere. Leadership's governance role is to create the conditions for effective governance — policy authority, resources, culture, escalation — not to conduct the governance work directly.

The most common leadership failure in AI governance is not neglect of the high-level responsibilities described above but inappropriate delegation: treating AI governance as fully owned by a subordinate function and removing leadership attention until something goes wrong. The institution that has assigned AI governance to the IT department with no ongoing leadership involvement is not governing AI; it is hoping that IT will handle whatever arises, without the organizational authority, resources, or cross-functional access that genuine governance requires.

The board's role

Where institutions have boards of directors, trustees, or equivalent oversight bodies, those bodies have AI governance responsibilities that are distinct from operational leadership. Boards are responsible for overseeing institutional strategy and risk management; AI governance falls within both domains.

Specifically, boards should receive regular reporting on AI governance performance — not at the level of operational detail appropriate for staff, but at the level of material risk and strategic alignment. What AI systems is the institution using? What are the most significant risks associated with those systems? Are governance processes in place and functioning? Have there been significant failures, and how were they handled? Is the institution's AI governance posture consistent with its obligations and values?

Boards that receive no reporting on AI governance are not exercising their oversight responsibility. Boards that receive reporting but do not ask questions, do not request follow-up on concerns, and do not hold leadership accountable for governance quality are exercising the form of oversight without its substance. In an environment of rapidly developing AI capability and regulatory scrutiny, board-level AI governance engagement is not optional for institutions of any significant scale.

Legal and compliance: the regulatory and ethical framework

What legal and compliance owns

The legal and compliance function — whether it is a standalone department, a shared service, or a contracted relationship with outside counsel — owns the regulatory and legal dimensions of AI governance. This is a substantial and growing domain of responsibility.

Legal's primary AI governance responsibilities begin with regulatory monitoring: tracking the evolving landscape of AI-relevant laws, regulations, and guidance at the applicable jurisdictional levels. This is not a one-time assessment; it is an ongoing function. AI regulation is developing rapidly across jurisdictions, and institutions that were compliant under last year's framework may face new obligations under this year's. Legal needs to maintain current awareness of these developments and translate them into requirements that operational functions can act on.

Legal's responsibilities extend to contract review and negotiation. AI vendor contracts are among the most consequential documents an institution signs with respect to AI governance. They determine what the vendor is obligated to deliver, what liability protections the institution has, what rights to audit and data portability the institution retains, and what recourse is available when things go wrong. Legal review of AI vendor contracts should be thorough and specifically attentive to AI-relevant provisions: disclaimers of liability for AI system performance, data handling terms, audit rights, breach notification obligations, and exit provisions. Chapter 11 provides a detailed vendor due diligence framework; legal should be an active participant in that process, not a signatory at its end.

Legal also owns the assessment of AI use cases against applicable law. When a proposed AI use case raises questions under anti-discrimination law, data protection law, healthcare privacy law, financial services regulation, or any other applicable framework, legal is the function that evaluates those questions and advises on whether and how the use case can proceed. This advisory role needs to be built into the intake and review process, not called in after deployment when a compliance problem has already materialized.

Finally, legal owns the institution's response when AI-related legal or regulatory issues arise — investigations, complaints, enforcement actions, litigation. This reactive role is where legal's AI governance involvement is most visible, but its value is greatest when it reduces the frequency and severity of situations requiring that response.

Compliance as distinct from legal

In many institutions, compliance is a distinct function from legal — responsible not for providing legal advice but for ensuring that the institution's practices meet applicable regulatory and policy requirements. In AI governance, compliance's role is to operationalize the requirements that legal has identified: building them into review processes, audit programs, training, and monitoring systems.

Compliance typically owns the audit function — periodic assessments of whether AI governance practices meet established standards — and the reporting function — producing the documentation that demonstrates compliance to regulators, accreditors, funders, and other external parties. In regulated industries like healthcare and financial services, compliance may also own specific AI-related regulatory reporting obligations.

The relationship between legal and compliance in AI governance should be collaborative but distinct: legal identifies what the requirements are; compliance ensures the institution meets them in practice.

IT and information security: technical enablement and protection

What IT owns

The information technology function has a dual role in AI governance: it is both an enabler — making AI systems work technically — and a control function — ensuring that AI systems operate securely and consistent with institutional technology standards.

As an enabler, IT's AI governance responsibilities include infrastructure assessment (evaluating whether the institution's technical environment can support a proposed AI system), integration management (ensuring that AI systems connect properly with existing institutional systems), access control (managing who can use AI systems and under what conditions), and technical monitoring (collecting and maintaining the data about system performance that governance oversight requires).

As a control function, IT's responsibilities include information security assessment of AI vendors and systems (evaluating whether the security practices of AI vendors and the technical security of AI systems meet institutional requirements), data classification and protection (ensuring that AI systems handle data in ways consistent with the institution's data governance framework), and incident management for technical AI failures (diagnosing and responding to technical problems with AI systems when they arise).

IT also typically owns the institution's relationship with technology vendors at a technical level, including the technical dimensions of AI vendor evaluation — whether vendor systems meet technical performance requirements, how they integrate with existing infrastructure, and what the vendor's technical support and maintenance practices are.

What IT does not own

A critical governance principle is that IT's technical responsibilities do not extend to the substantive governance questions that determine whether an AI system is appropriate for a given use case. Whether an AI hiring tool is likely to produce discriminatory outcomes is not a technical question that IT is equipped to answer independently. Whether the data practices of an AI vendor are consistent with the institution's patient privacy obligations is a legal and compliance question, not a technical one. Whether an AI clinical decision support tool should be deployed in a specific care setting is a clinical and operational question, not an IT question.

IT should be a required participant in AI governance review processes — its input on technical feasibility, security, and integration is essential. But IT's participation should be additive, contributing technical perspective to a multi-functional process, not substitutive, replacing the substantive judgment of legal, operations, and clinical or program functions.

Information security's specific role

Information security — whether within IT or as a separate function — has specific AI governance responsibilities that deserve explicit identification. AI systems create security risks that differ from those of traditional software, and information security needs to be specifically attentive to them.

AI systems are potential vectors for data exfiltration: inputs provided to AI systems, including sensitive institutional data, may be accessible to vendors or transmitted to systems outside the institution's control. AI systems can be adversarially manipulated through carefully designed inputs that cause them to behave unexpectedly or to reveal information they should not. AI-generated content can be used in social engineering attacks. And AI vendor systems, like any external system the institution connects to, represent attack surfaces that need to be assessed and managed.

Information security's AI governance responsibilities include assessing these risks in the context of specific AI deployments, establishing security requirements for AI vendor relationships, monitoring for security incidents involving AI systems, and contributing security requirements to the AI governance policy.

Operations and program delivery: the front line of governance

What operations owns

Operations and program delivery — the functions that actually do the work the institution exists to do, whether that is providing healthcare, delivering education, administering benefits, serving clients, or running business processes — are where AI governance ultimately succeeds or fails. An institution can have excellent governance architecture at the policy, legal, and IT levels and still fail at governance if the operational functions that deploy and use AI systems do not own their governance responsibilities.

Operations' primary AI governance responsibilities center on use case ownership. When an operational function proposes to use an AI tool — for intake, assessment, case management, communication, quality assurance, or any other purpose — it owns that use case. This ownership includes initiating the intake and review process, providing the use case description and risk information that governance review requires, committing to the operating conditions — oversight arrangements, review protocols, escalation processes — that governance approval specifies, and being accountable for governance compliance in the day-to-day operation of the AI system.

Ownership means not delegating these responsibilities entirely to IT or legal. The operational leader who proposes to deploy an AI assessment tool in a child welfare program needs to understand what the tool does and how it will affect the program's practices. They need to ensure that frontline staff are trained appropriately. They need to establish the oversight processes that governance requirements specify. And they need to monitor whether the AI system is performing as expected and whether staff are using it appropriately.

Operations also owns the feedback loop between operational experience and governance oversight. Frontline staff in operational functions are the first to observe AI system problems — unusual outputs, apparent errors, staff misuse, unintended effects on service delivery. Operational leaders need to be the conduit through which that observation reaches the governance function: creating an environment where staff feel safe raising concerns, taking those concerns seriously, and escalating them appropriately.

The operations-governance relationship

The relationship between operational functions and the central governance function is one of the most important governance design questions for any institution. It needs to be collaborative and service-oriented rather than adversarial and bureaucratic.

Operational functions will resist AI governance requirements that seem disconnected from operational realities, that create friction without visible benefit, or that position governance as an external constraint on their work rather than a support for doing their work responsibly. Governance functions that understand operational contexts, that design review processes with operational feasibility in mind, and that are responsive to operational questions and concerns will find operational partners who engage seriously with governance requirements. Governance functions that are perceived as bureaucratic obstacles will find operational partners who look for ways around them.

This relationship dynamic is primarily a leadership and culture question, not an organizational design question. The governance function's authority and operational functions' accountability for governance compliance need to be clear. Within that clarity, the working relationship needs to be built on mutual respect for each other's expertise and genuine commitment to responsible AI use as a shared goal.

Procurement: governance at the point of commitment

What procurement owns

Procurement is the function responsible for managing the institution's relationships with external vendors — a role that gives it disproportionate leverage in AI governance. Many of the most consequential AI governance decisions are made, or foreclosed, at the moment a vendor contract is signed. Procurement owns the process through which those decisions are made.

Procurement's AI governance responsibilities begin before a vendor relationship is initiated. Procurement should be involved in any AI tool evaluation process where the institution is considering entering a vendor relationship, ensuring that AI-specific due diligence — beyond the standard vendor assessment — is conducted as part of the evaluation. The vendor due diligence framework in Chapter 11 describes what that due diligence should cover; procurement's role is to ensure the process occurs and that its results are adequately considered in vendor selection decisions.

During contract negotiation, procurement owns the process of translating governance requirements into contractual commitments. This includes provisions related to performance standards, audit rights, data handling obligations, breach notification, liability, and exit. Procurement may not have the expertise to evaluate the legal sufficiency of specific provisions — that is legal's role — but procurement owns the process of ensuring that the contract reflects the institution's governance requirements rather than defaulting entirely to vendor standard terms.

After contracts are signed, procurement owns the vendor relationship management process — the ongoing engagement with vendors that monitors compliance with contractual commitments, addresses performance issues, manages renewals and renegotiations, and maintains the institution's records of its vendor relationships. In AI contexts, this includes tracking whether vendors are fulfilling their commitments around system performance, data practices, and notification of material changes to AI systems.

Procurement as governance gatekeeper

Procurement's position in the AI vendor relationship gives it a unique governance function: it is the point at which the institution can most effectively shape the terms on which AI vendors operate within the institution. A procurement function that exercises this role seriously — requiring vendors to meet governance standards as a condition of institutional business, negotiating contracts that protect institutional interests, and refusing to sign contracts whose terms are inadequate — creates governance leverage that no other function can replicate.

This requires procurement to understand AI governance requirements well enough to translate them into procurement actions. Procurement staff who cannot articulate why audit rights matter, what data portability means, or what performance benchmarks should address will be unable to negotiate for those things effectively. Building AI governance literacy within procurement is therefore a governance investment, not a training expense.

The practical implication is that AI governance training and briefing should reach procurement staff as directly as it reaches operational and IT staff. Procurement's governance effectiveness depends on its understanding of what it is trying to achieve.

Frontline staff: governance in practice

What frontline staff own

Frontline staff — the people who directly use AI systems in their daily work — are the point at which governance either manifests or fails to manifest in practice. Every governance framework, every policy, every training program is ultimately tested by what frontline staff do when they sit down to work with an AI tool. This makes frontline staff governance actors, not merely governance subjects.

Frontline staff own three specific AI governance responsibilities.

The first is compliant use. Staff are responsible for using AI tools in ways that comply with institutional policy — providing inputs that are consistent with data governance requirements, applying the level of human review that policy specifies, maintaining the oversight practices that governance requires, and not using AI tools for purposes outside their designated scope. This is not a passive responsibility; it requires active knowledge of what policies require and genuine commitment to meeting them.

The second is judgment. Governance frameworks cannot specify every situation. Staff encounter edge cases, unusual outputs, and novel situations that policy does not directly address. In these cases, staff are responsible for exercising judgment — asking whether the AI output seems reliable, whether the situation is one where independent verification is appropriate, whether something unusual about the output warrants escalation. Governance frameworks support this judgment by providing principles and processes, but they cannot replace it.

The third is reporting. Staff are often the first people in the institution to observe AI system problems — outputs that seem wrong, patterns that appear unfair, situations where the AI is being used in ways it was not designed for. Governance depends on this observation reaching the people responsible for acting on it. Staff responsibility for reporting AI concerns — through whatever mechanism the institution has established — is a governance responsibility, not merely an employment obligation.

Supporting frontline governance

These responsibilities can only be met if staff are adequately supported. Governance that assigns significant responsibilities to frontline staff without providing the training, tools, and organizational support those responsibilities require is setting staff up to fail.

Training is the primary support mechanism — staff need to understand what the AI systems they use do, what their limitations are, what policies govern their use, and what to do when they encounter problems. Chapter 17 addresses AI literacy training in detail. The governance design question here is whether training is a genuine preparation for responsible use or a checkbox exercise — whether staff come away from training with the understanding they need to exercise their governance responsibilities, or merely with a completion record.

Beyond training, frontline governance requires clear and accessible reporting channels. Staff who observe AI problems need to know how to report them, to whom, and with what expectation of follow-up. If reporting channels are unclear, inaccessible, or perceived as unreliable — because reported concerns disappear without response or because raising concerns carries professional risk — staff will not use them, and the governance function will be deprived of the operational intelligence it needs.

Finally, frontline governance requires psychological safety: an institutional culture in which raising concerns about AI systems is seen as responsible professional behavior, not as obstruction, criticism of leadership, or sign of personal limitation. Staff who believe that raising AI concerns will be unwelcome, ignored, or held against them will not raise them. This is ultimately a culture and leadership question, but it has direct governance consequences.

Vendors: external partners in governance

What vendors own

AI vendors are not merely suppliers of technology; they are partners in governance, with specific responsibilities that institutional governance frameworks must address and that institutional contracts should make explicit.

Vendors own responsibility for the AI systems they provide at the level of design, training, and inherent capabilities. This includes the accuracy and reliability of the systems, the representativeness and quality of training data, the testing that was conducted before systems were made available, and the documentation that allows customers to understand what they are using and what its limitations are. Institutions cannot independently verify these things in most cases; they are dependent on vendor transparency and the contractual commitments that vendor transparency supports.

Vendors also own ongoing responsibility for maintaining the systems they provide: updating models, addressing identified performance issues, notifying customers of material changes, and maintaining the infrastructure that supports institutional deployment. When vendors make material changes to AI systems — updating models, changing data practices, modifying capabilities — institutions need to know, because those changes may affect the governance assessments and oversight arrangements that were established at deployment.

Vendors own responsibility for providing the information that institutions need to govern their use of AI systems. This includes making documentation available about system performance across demographic groups, providing sufficient access to audit system behavior, being transparent about data handling practices, and responding substantively to governance-related questions. Vendors who are unwilling to provide this information, or who respond to governance questions with generic assurances rather than specific documentation, are not fulfilling their part of the governance relationship.

The institution-vendor governance relationship

The relationship between institutions and vendors in AI governance is structured by the contract and by the practical dynamics of the business relationship. Both need to support genuine governance.

Contractually, the institution needs commitments that translate vendor governance responsibilities into enforceable obligations: performance standards with clear definitions and measurement methods, audit rights that allow independent verification of performance claims, data handling obligations that meet the institution's legal requirements, breach notification provisions that ensure timely disclosure of security incidents and material performance issues, and exit provisions that enable the institution to end the relationship and recover its data without prohibitive cost.

Practically, the institution needs a working relationship with vendor contacts who are accessible, knowledgeable, and empowered to address governance concerns. A vendor relationship in which governance questions are routed through a general support channel to staff who cannot engage with substantive questions is not a governance partnership; it is a service transaction.

Institutions should assess vendor governance responsiveness as an ongoing dimension of vendor management. Vendors who respond substantively to governance concerns, who proactively disclose relevant information, and who engage constructively with audit processes are demonstrating the kind of partnership that responsible AI deployment requires. Vendors who are evasive, dismissive, or contractually resistant to governance obligations are demonstrating something different — and institutions should factor that demonstration into their vendor relationship decisions.

How the roles work together

The seven roles described in this chapter are not independent governance actors. They are participants in an integrated governance system, and the system works when the roles connect effectively. Several key connection points deserve particular attention.

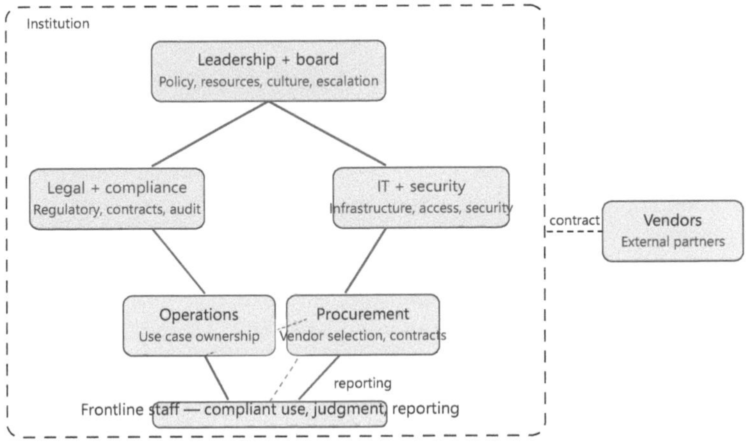

The intake connection: operations, legal, IT, and procurement

When an operational function proposes a new AI use case, the governance process requires coordinated input from multiple roles. Operations brings use case knowledge and organizational accountability. Legal assesses regulatory and legal risk. IT evaluates technical feasibility and security implications. Procurement manages vendor assessment and contract requirements. The intake and review process — described in Chapter 10 — is the mechanism that coordinates these contributions. For it to work, each function needs to understand its specific contribution to the review, the timeline within which that contribution is needed, and the decision authority that determines whether and how the use case proceeds.

The escalation connection: frontline staff, operations, and leadership

When frontline staff identify AI problems — errors, apparent bias, safety concerns, misuse — that information needs to travel upward through the organization to the people with authority and responsibility to act on it. This requires clear escalation pathways: staff need to know how to report concerns, operational leaders need to receive those reports and take them seriously, and the governance function needs to receive and act on escalated issues. The breakdown of escalation connections is among the most common causes of governance failure: problems that were observed by frontline staff never reached the people who could address them, because the escalation pathway was unclear, unused, or not functioning.

The vendor connection: procurement, legal, IT, and operations

The institution's relationship with AI vendors involves multiple functions, and coordination among them is essential. Procurement owns the commercial relationship. Legal owns the contractual and regulatory dimensions. IT owns the technical relationship. Operations owns the functional performance expectations. All four need to be engaged in vendor assessment before a relationship is initiated, and all four need channels for raising vendor performance concerns throughout the relationship. A vendor performance problem that operations is aware of but procurement has not been informed about cannot be addressed through the commercial leverage that procurement controls.

The monitoring connection: IT, operations, and governance

After AI systems are deployed, monitoring their performance requires data that IT collects, operational judgment about whether performance is acceptable, and governance oversight that synthesizes both. IT can provide technical metrics — system availability, processing volumes, error rates at a technical level. Operations can provide functional observations — whether the system is performing as expected from the perspective of the work it is supposed to support. Governance oversight integrates these inputs against the performance standards and oversight requirements that the governance framework established. None of these functions can do meaningful monitoring alone; the connection among them is what makes monitoring effective.

Role clarity in different institutional sizes

The role framework described in this chapter assumes a level of functional differentiation that is realistic for mid-sized and larger institutions but may require adaptation for smaller ones. A nonprofit with eight staff members does not have a chief compliance officer, a procurement department, and an IT security team. Its AI governance role structure will necessarily look different.

For smaller institutions, role consolidation is expected and appropriate. The executive director may hold leadership, legal oversight, and strategic responsibility simultaneously. A single operations manager may hold both operational and procurement responsibilities. A part-time IT consultant may cover both infrastructure and security roles. What matters is not that the roles are held by separate people but that the responsibilities associated with each role are clearly assigned, understood, and genuinely performed.

The governance design question for smaller institutions is: for each AI governance responsibility, who in this organization is accountable for it? If the answer to any governance responsibility is "no one," that is the gap to close. If the answer is "everyone," that is functionally equivalent to "no one" and also needs to be resolved by specific assignment.

For very small institutions — those where capacity constraints make even basic role assignments difficult — the governance framework can be simplified without being abandoned. The essential minimum is: someone reviews new AI tools before the institution uses them, someone is responsible for the institution's AI policy, and someone is the designated point of contact for AI-related concerns from staff. These three responsibilities can be held by a single person in a small organization. They represent the governance floor below which responsible AI use cannot be maintained.

The AI governance coordinator: a practical role

Many institutions find it useful to designate an AI governance coordinator — a specific person responsible for the administrative and coordination functions that keep the governance system running. This is not the same as an AI ethics officer, a chief AI officer, or a technical AI lead; it is a coordination role, appropriate for institutions that have governance responsibilities distributed across multiple functions and need someone to ensure that the connections among those functions work.

The AI governance coordinator's responsibilities typically include: maintaining the institution's AI inventory (the record of AI systems in use, described in Chapter 9); coordinating the intake and review process for new AI use cases (scheduling reviews, tracking status, distributing documentation); maintaining governance documentation (policies, review records, incident reports); organizing governance committee meetings and maintaining records of decisions; and serving as the first point of contact for staff with AI governance questions or concerns.

This role does not require technical expertise. It requires organizational skill, attention to detail, and enough familiarity with AI governance concepts to route questions and concerns to the right places. In smaller institutions, it can be a partial role — a few hours per week assigned to an existing staff member who has relevant administrative skills. In larger institutions, it may be a full-time position or a small team.

The AI governance coordinator role is not a substitute for the substantive governance responsibilities assigned to leadership, legal, IT, operations, and procurement. It is the connective tissue that keeps those substantive roles coordinated.

When responsibility is unclear: a decision rule

Despite the most carefully designed governance architecture, situations will arise in which it is unclear who is responsible for a specific AI governance question. The following decision rule is useful in those situations.

Ask first whether the question is primarily about regulatory compliance or legal risk. If yes, legal and compliance leads.

Ask next whether it is primarily about technical feasibility or security. If yes, IT leads.

Ask next whether it is primarily about vendor terms or vendor performance. If yes, procurement leads, with legal involvement for contractual issues.

Ask next whether it is primarily about the operational use of an AI system and its effects on the work of the institution. If yes, operations leads.

If the question is about institutional policy — what the institution should commit to, what values should govern AI use decisions, what level of risk is acceptable — it belongs at the leadership level.

If the question involves multiple dimensions simultaneously — a regulatory question with operational implications and contractual components — it needs a multi-function conversation rather than assignment to a single owner. The governance coordinator facilitates; no single function decides unilaterally.

This decision rule does not resolve every ambiguity, but it resolves most of them. The remainder are genuinely cross-functional questions that require the governance architecture to function as an integrated system — which is, ultimately, what governance is.

Responsibility as a living assignment

A final observation: governance responsibility is not a static assignment that can be made once and left unchanged. The AI landscape changes. Institutions adopt new tools. Regulatory requirements evolve. Organizational structures shift. The governance responsibilities described in this chapter need to be revisited regularly — at least annually and when significant changes in institutional AI use or the external environment occur — to ensure that they remain clearly assigned, understood, and genuinely performed.

The governance committee, described in the next chapter, is the mechanism for that review. Ensuring that AI governance responsibilities are current, appropriate, and actively owned is among the committee's most important ongoing functions.

Part II: Building the System

Chapter 6: Forming the Governance Team

From responsibility to structure

Chapter 5 described who is responsible for AI governance across institutional roles. This chapter addresses how those responsible parties are organized into a functioning governance team — the cross-functional group that coordinates AI governance activity, makes governance decisions, and ensures that the system described in this book actually operates rather than merely existing on paper.

Forming a governance team is not a bureaucratic exercise. It is the act of translating distributed governance responsibilities into a coherent institutional structure with clear authority, defined processes, and genuine accountability. An institution that has assigned governance responsibilities to individual roles but has no mechanism for those roles to coordinate, share information, make joint decisions, and hold each other accountable has responsibilities without a system. The governance team is what creates the system.

This chapter addresses every dimension of forming that team: the case for a formal structure, the design choices that determine whether the team will be effective, the membership that gives it the range it needs, the authority that gives it the power to act, the processes that make it functional, and the adaptations appropriate for institutions of different sizes. It closes with the practical steps of standing up a governance team from scratch — the first actions an institution should take once it has decided that governance requires an organized structure.

Why a team rather than a role

The first governance design question is whether AI governance requires a team at all, or whether it can be adequately managed by designating a single responsible person — an AI governance officer, a chief responsible AI officer, or a similar individual role. Some institutions take this approach, and for very small organizations it may be necessary. For most institutions, it is inadequate, for reasons that follow from the nature of AI governance itself.

AI governance is inherently multi-dimensional. As Chapters 3 and 5 established, AI governance requires legal and regulatory knowledge, technical assessment capability, operational judgment, procurement and contract expertise, and understanding of the institution's mission and the populations it serves. No single person combines all of these competencies at the depth that governance decisions require. An AI governance structure built around a single role will inevitably have blind spots in the dimensions where that person's expertise is limited.

AI governance is also inherently political in the institutional sense — it requires making decisions that affect different functions' autonomy and operational preferences. A single AI governance officer who tells an operational department that its proposed AI tool cannot proceed without additional review, or tells procurement that a vendor contract needs to be renegotiated, has only whatever organizational authority their role title confers. A cross-functional governance team that reaches the same conclusion has the combined authority of its members, which is much harder to dismiss or circumvent.

Finally, AI governance requires institutional legitimacy — the sense among staff that governance decisions reflect considered judgment by people who understand the institution's work, not arbitrary restrictions imposed by a distant function. A team whose members include people from the functions that are being governed has more legitimacy than a single function that governs others.

None of this means that an individual AI governance coordinator role is unnecessary. As described in Chapter 5, a coordination role is valuable. But it should support a team, not replace one.

Governance structure options

Before settling on a design, institutions should understand the range of structural options available to them. Three main patterns appear in institutional AI governance practice, each with different strengths and limitations.

The standing committee

The most common structure for institutional AI governance is a standing committee — a formally constituted group with defined membership, regular meeting cadence, documented terms of reference, and ongoing responsibility for AI governance across the institution. The standing committee reviews proposals, makes decisions, monitors performance, and escalates to leadership when required.

The standing committee's strength is continuity and authority. Because it is formal and permanent, it accumulates institutional memory, builds expertise over time, and has a stable identity within the organization that gives its decisions weight. Its limitation is resource intensity: committee members must invest ongoing time and attention, which can become burdensome if the committee's scope is too broad or its processes too heavy.

For mid-sized and larger institutions, a standing committee is generally the appropriate primary governance structure. The chapters that follow assume this structure as the default, with adaptations noted for smaller organizations.

The working group model

Some institutions establish AI governance as a working group rather than a standing committee — a time-limited group convened for specific purposes, such as developing the institution's AI policy, conducting a particular vendor assessment, or responding to an identified governance failure. Working groups are dissolved once their task is complete.

The working group model has the advantage of focus and flexibility: groups are formed with the specific expertise a task requires and dissolved when that task is done. Its limitation is discontinuity: institutions that rely solely on working groups have no persistent governance mechanism between tasks, which means that ongoing monitoring, ad hoc review needs, and emerging governance questions go unaddressed.

Working groups are most valuable as supplements to a standing committee — formed to address specific complex questions that exceed the standing committee's bandwidth — rather than as substitutes for it.

The distributed model

In some institutions, particularly large and decentralized ones, AI governance is distributed across business units or functions rather than centralized in a single committee. Each unit has its own AI governance processes, accountable to its own leadership, with a central coordination function providing standards, tools, and oversight without direct decision-making authority.

The distributed model has the advantage of proximity: governance decisions are made by people close to the operational contexts they affect. Its limitation is inconsistency: governance standards and practices may vary significantly across units, creating uneven protection for affected people and institutional risk that aggregates without any single function having visibility into the full picture.

For institutions that are large enough to require distributed governance, a hybrid model is generally most effective: unit-level governance for operational decisions, supported by central standards and oversight that ensure consistency and institutional-level risk visibility.

Membership: who belongs on the governance team

The membership of the AI governance team is among the most consequential governance design decisions. The team needs to be large enough to bring the range of perspectives that AI governance requires, small enough to function effectively as a decision-making body, and composed in a way that reflects genuine institutional commitment rather than nominal representation.

Core members

Core members are those whose participation is essential to every governance decision. They attend all meetings, vote on decisions, and are accountable for their function's governance contributions. The following roles should be represented as core members in most institutional AI governance teams.

A senior leadership representative — ideally the chief executive or a direct report with delegated authority — is essential for two reasons. First, it signals institutional seriousness. A governance team with no senior leadership engagement is a governance team that the institution's staff and vendors will treat as optional. Second, it provides the decision-making authority that operational and cross-functional governance decisions require. Some governance questions cannot be resolved at the working level; they need someone who can commit the institution.

Legal and compliance representation provides the regulatory and contractual expertise that governance decisions require. The appropriate person is someone with sufficient knowledge of applicable law to identify when AI use raises legal risk and to advise on how that risk can be managed, not merely a general counsel who attends meetings but does not engage substantively with AI-specific questions.

IT and information security representation provides technical assessment capability. This should be someone who understands AI systems at a sufficient level of technical depth to evaluate vendor claims, assess security implications, and translate technical information into terms relevant to governance decisions — typically a senior IT leader or an IT architect with specific AI knowledge.

Operations representation — from the functions that actually use or will use AI systems — provides the practical judgment about whether governance requirements are feasible, whether proposed AI systems would actually serve institutional purposes, and whether governance decisions are grounded in operational reality. In institutions with multiple distinct operational functions, operations representation may need to rotate or expand to ensure adequate coverage.

A data governance or privacy representative — which may be a role within legal, IT, or a dedicated function depending on the institution's structure — brings the specific expertise in data handling, privacy law, and information governance that AI's data-intensive character requires.

Extended members

Extended members participate in specific governance discussions where their expertise is relevant but do not attend every meeting. Their involvement is structured rather than standing — they are called in when the governance team is reviewing matters within their domain.

Human resources participation is relevant when AI governance decisions touch employment practices — hiring tools, performance management systems, workforce analytics. HR brings knowledge of employment law, workforce relations, and the practical implications of AI for employees.

Communications and public affairs participation is relevant when governance decisions have stakeholder communication dimensions — decisions about disclosing AI use to affected parties, responding to public inquiries about institutional AI practices, or managing the reputational dimensions of AI incidents.

Clinical or program leadership participation is relevant in institutions where AI is used in direct service delivery — healthcare, education, social services. Clinical or program leaders bring domain expertise that neither legal nor IT can supply: the professional standards, ethical frameworks, and practical wisdom that govern responsible practice in their fields.

Finance participation is relevant when governance decisions involve significant resource commitments — major AI investments, vendor contracts with substantial financial implications, or decisions about the allocation of governance resources.

The question of affected community representation

A governance design question that institutions increasingly face is whether the people most affected by AI decisions — patients, students, clients, employees, community members — should have a voice in AI governance. The case for inclusion is strong: governance decisions made without input from affected communities risk being technically compliant but substantively disconnected from the experiences of the people the institution serves.

Practical mechanisms for affected community voice in governance vary. Some institutions include patient advocates, student representatives, or community members as advisory participants in governance processes. Some establish formal consultation processes through which governance proposals are reviewed by affected community representatives before decisions are finalized. Some use surveys, focus groups, or regular feedback mechanisms to gather input without formal representation on the governance body itself.

The appropriate mechanism depends on the institution's type, the nature of its AI use, and its relationships with the communities it serves. What is not appropriate is treating affected community input as irrelevant to governance decisions. The people whose lives are most affected by institutional AI systems have legitimate standing to be heard in the governance processes that shape those systems.

Authority: what the governance team can actually do

A governance team without defined authority is a discussion group. The governance team's effectiveness depends entirely on the clarity and sufficiency of the authority it holds. Four dimensions of authority need to be defined explicitly.

Decision authority

The governance team needs clear authority to make specific categories of decisions, binding on the institution and its functions. The categories of decision that governance teams typically hold include: approving or declining proposed AI use cases (with conditions where appropriate); requiring modifications to existing AI deployments as a condition of continued use; directing investigations into AI system performance concerns; and recommending to leadership the suspension or termination of AI systems that present unacceptable risks.

For this authority to be real, it must be backed by institutional commitment: when the governance team approves a use case with conditions, those conditions must be complied with; when it declines a proposal, that decision cannot be overridden by a function head who simply proceeds anyway; when it directs an investigation, the investigation must be conducted. Governance authority that can be ignored or circumvented at the function level is not authority — it is advice.

The boundaries of governance team authority also need to be clear. Some decisions exceed what a governance team can make unilaterally — major institutional commitments, decisions with significant financial or legal implications, changes to fundamental institutional policy. For these, the governance team's role is to advise and recommend to senior leadership, not to decide independently. Defining both what the team can decide and what requires escalation is essential to its functioning.

Access authority

Governance team members need access to the information required to make governance decisions. This includes access to vendor documentation and contracts, to technical system specifications, to operational data about AI system performance, to legal assessments, to incident reports, and to any other information material to a governance question. Governance teams that lack access to relevant information cannot make informed decisions; they can only make decisions based on what they have been told by the parties whose practices they are supposed to be overseeing.

Access authority may require specific institutional commitments — policies that require functions to provide requested documentation to the governance team, contracts that give the institution audit rights that the governance team can exercise, IT systems that provide governance oversight access to performance data. These should be established when the governance team is formed, not negotiated case by case when information is needed.

Escalation authority

The governance team needs a clear pathway for escalating matters that exceed its decision authority to senior leadership or the board. This escalation pathway needs to be defined — who receives escalations, in what form, with what expectation of response, and on what timeline. A governance team that identifies a serious AI-related risk but has no clear pathway for bringing it to the attention of people who can act on it is not a functioning governance structure.

Escalation authority also implies a duty to escalate: governance team members should understand that identifying serious risks and failing to escalate them is a governance failure, not a conservative choice. The accountability that the governance role implies extends to accountability for escalation as well as for operational decisions.

Standard-setting authority

The governance team should have authority to establish and update the standards, templates, and processes that govern AI review and oversight across the institution — intake forms, review criteria, vendor questionnaires, monitoring frameworks, incident reporting protocols. This standard-setting function is what allows the governance team to systematize its work rather than approaching each governance question as if it were novel, and it ensures consistency across governance decisions over time.

Standard-setting authority is also what allows the governance team to respond to changing circumstances — new regulatory requirements, new categories of AI risk, new institutional AI use patterns — by updating standards rather than waiting for individual cases to expose the inadequacy of current standards.

Governance team processes: how the team actually works

Authority without process produces inconsistency. The governance team needs defined processes for its core functions — meeting, reviewing proposals, making decisions, monitoring, and reporting — that are documented, followed, and periodically reviewed for adequacy.

Terms of reference

The governance team's terms of reference — a single document that specifies its mandate, membership, authority, decision processes, meeting requirements, and reporting relationships — is the foundational governance document for the team itself. It should be formally approved by senior leadership, communicated to relevant institutional functions, and reviewed annually.

The terms of reference should address: the team's mandate (what it is responsible for governing); membership composition and how members are appointed and replaced; decision-making procedures (how decisions are made, what constitutes a quorum, how disagreements are resolved); the team's relationship to senior leadership and the escalation pathway; reporting requirements; and the process for amending the terms of reference.

A template for terms of reference is provided in Part V. The important point here is that terms of reference should be a genuine working document, not a ceremonial charter that is approved and filed. Members should have a current copy and refer to it when questions about the team's scope or processes arise.

Meeting cadence and structure

Regular meetings are the operational heartbeat of the governance team. The appropriate meeting cadence depends on the volume of AI governance work the institution generates, but a monthly standing meeting works well for most institutions. More frequent meetings may be needed during periods of high activity — when multiple intake reviews are in process, when significant vendor assessments are underway, or when an AI incident requires active governance engagement. Less frequent meetings may be appropriate for smaller institutions with modest AI use.

Meeting agendas should be structured around the governance team's core functions: review of pending intake proposals, updates on active governance matters, review of monitoring reports, discussion of emerging issues, and — at regular intervals — review of the team's own performance and the adequacy of its processes. Unstructured discussion without a fixed agenda tends to produce meetings that address whatever is most salient at the moment rather than the full range of governance responsibilities.

Meeting records should be maintained — not verbatim transcripts but records that document what was discussed, what decisions were made, what questions were escalated, and what follow-up actions were assigned. These records serve both accountability and institutional memory functions: they allow the team to track whether commitments were fulfilled, and they allow new members to understand the history and reasoning behind governance decisions.

Intake review process

The intake review process — the procedure through which proposed new AI use cases are submitted to the governance team, assessed, and decided — is the governance team's most frequent operational function. It is addressed in detail in Chapter 10; the governance team design questions here are about process rather than criteria.

The governance team needs a defined submission mechanism: a standard form or template that operational functions complete when proposing AI use cases (Chapter 25 provides a template), a clear submission pathway, and a designated person responsible for receiving and triaging submissions. Without a standard mechanism, proposals arrive in inconsistent forms, through ad hoc channels, and are difficult to track and compare.

The review process needs defined timelines: how long the governance team takes to complete a standard review, what the process is for expedited review when operational timelines require it, and when extended review is appropriate for complex or high-risk proposals. Timelines that are too long create pressure on operational functions to bypass the governance process; timelines that are too short produce superficial reviews.

The decision process needs to be clear: who votes, what constitutes approval, what conditions can be attached to approval, and how declined proposals can be resubmitted. Governance decisions that are perceived as arbitrary — cases where similar proposals receive different outcomes without clear explanation — undermine the legitimacy of the governance process.

Monitoring and reporting

The governance team needs regular access to information about the performance of AI systems the institution has deployed. This is what allows governance to be ongoing rather than episodic — a continuous function that maintains oversight of AI in operation, not only a review function that evaluates proposals before deployment.

The monitoring function requires two things from the governance team. First, it requires defining what will be monitored and how — establishing the performance metrics, oversight indicators, and incident reporting mechanisms that will produce the information the team needs. Chapter 16 addresses this in detail. The governance team's design task is to ensure that these monitoring requirements are specified and that the functions responsible for collecting monitoring data — IT, operations, the AI governance coordinator — understand and fulfill those responsibilities.

Second, it requires actually reviewing monitoring information when it is provided. Monitoring reports that are produced but not reviewed are governance theater. The governance team's meeting agenda should include a standing monitoring review item, and members should come to monitoring reviews having read the relevant reports and prepared to engage substantively with what they show.

Reporting upward — to senior leadership and the board — is a distinct governance team function. The governance team should produce regular reports (quarterly works well for most institutions) that summarize AI governance activity: proposals reviewed and their outcomes, active AI systems and their performance status, significant incidents and their resolution, emerging governance concerns, and any matters requiring leadership attention or decision. These reports should be factual and candid — including information about governance gaps and concerns, not only positive performance indicators.

Building the team: practical first steps

For institutions forming a governance team from scratch, the following sequence provides a practical starting point. It is not the only possible sequence, and institutions should adapt it to their specific circumstances and starting conditions.

Step one: secure leadership commitment

Before forming the team, secure explicit commitment from senior leadership that governance is a real institutional priority, that the team will have the authority it needs, and that leadership will support the team's decisions when operational functions push back. This commitment should be specific — covering the team's mandate, its authority to make binding decisions, and the resources allocated to support its work — not a general statement of support for responsible AI.

Leadership commitment is the foundation on which everything else rests. A governance team formed without genuine leadership backing will be ignored when its decisions are inconvenient, will be unable to secure the access and cooperation it needs, and will lose the engagement of its own members as they conclude that their participation does not make a difference.

Step two: identify and appoint core members

Using the membership framework described earlier in this chapter, identify the specific individuals who will serve as core members. Appointments should be made by senior leadership — not by functions appointing themselves — and should be accompanied by a clear briefing on what membership entails: the time commitment, the authority, the accountability, and the institutional significance of the role.

The people appointed to the governance team should be substantive participants in their functions, not junior staff nominated to reduce the burden on senior leaders. AI governance decisions require the authority and expertise of people who can commit their functions and whose judgment commands respect. Appointing people who lack that standing undermines the team's effectiveness from the outset.

Step three: draft and approve terms of reference

With core membership identified, draft the governance team's terms of reference. This document should be developed collaboratively with the team's founding members — not written by a single function and presented to others — so that members have genuine ownership of the governance structure they are operating within.

The terms of reference should be reviewed by legal counsel, approved by senior leadership, and communicated to relevant institutional functions. The approval and communication steps are not formalities; they are the acts that give the governance team its institutional legitimacy.

Step four: conduct an AI inventory

Before the governance team can begin reviewing new proposals, it needs to understand what AI systems the institution already has in use. Many institutions that have never done this exercise are surprised by what they find — tools that departments have been using for years without governance attention, vendor systems with AI features that were not recognized as such, and AI capabilities embedded in enterprise software that no one has specifically evaluated.

The AI inventory process is described in Chapter 9. For governance team formation purposes, the key point is that the inventory should be among the first substantive tasks the team undertakes, because it defines the scope of what the team is responsible for overseeing and reveals any immediate governance gaps that need to be addressed.

Step five: develop the initial governance toolkit

With the inventory complete and the scope of governance responsibility clear, the team should develop the initial toolkit that will support its work: the intake form for new proposals, the risk screening criteria, the vendor review questionnaire, the monitoring dashboard template, and the incident report template. Templates for each of these are provided in Part V of this book and should be adapted for the institution's specific context.

Developing these tools as a team — rather than delegating tool development to a single function — builds shared understanding of what governance processes are trying to accomplish and why specific requirements exist. The tool development process is itself a governance education exercise.

Step six: establish the meeting rhythm and begin operations

With tools in hand, establish the regular meeting cadence, schedule the first six months of meetings, and begin operating. The team's first meetings will inevitably be somewhat tentative — governance processes that look clear on paper often encounter ambiguities and edge cases in practice. This is expected and appropriate. The team should treat its early operational experience as a learning opportunity, documenting the ambiguities and edge cases it encounters and updating its processes to address them.

The governance team is not complete when it is formed. It is complete when it is functioning — and functioning means meeting regularly, reviewing proposals, monitoring performance, escalating concerns, and improving its own processes based on experience. Governance is built in operation, not in design.

Sustaining the team over time

Forming a governance team is substantially easier than sustaining one. Governance teams that are formed with genuine commitment sometimes lose momentum as the institutional environment changes, as founding members rotate out, as AI governance feels less urgent after an initial period of activity, or as the team's processes become routine and its work less visible.

Several practices support sustained governance team effectiveness.

Annual reviews of the terms of reference ensure that the team's mandate, membership, and processes remain appropriate as the institution's AI use evolves. A team whose terms of reference were written when the institution used AI primarily for administrative tasks may need to be substantially revised when the institution begins using AI in clinical or programmatic settings.

Member rotation that is managed, not accidental, maintains team effectiveness across leadership transitions. When a core member leaves their role, their governance seat should transfer to their successor as a formal institutional appointment, with a structured handover that maintains governance continuity. Governance knowledge that exists only in the heads of specific individuals is a governance vulnerability.

Regular reporting to senior leadership maintains the organizational visibility that keeps governance team work consequential. Leaders who receive regular governance reports, who ask questions about governance performance, and who respond to governance recommendations signal to the broader institution that governance matters — which in turn keeps governance team members engaged and operational functions compliant.

Periodic effectiveness reviews — honest assessments of whether the governance team is actually doing its job — are the most important sustainability practice of all. The questions are direct: Are all proposed AI use cases going through the intake process, or are some proceeding without review? Is monitoring information being reviewed and acted on? Are incidents being reported and addressed? Are governance team members genuinely engaged, or are meetings becoming formalities? Honest answers to these questions reveal whether governance is functioning as a system or decaying into ritual. Governance teams that ask and answer them honestly, and act on what they find, remain effective. Those that do not, do not.

Governance team design for smaller institutions

For small institutions — those with limited staff, constrained resources, and relatively modest AI use — the governance team framework described in this chapter requires adaptation without abandoning its substance.

A small nonprofit with ten staff members cannot form a six-person cross-functional committee with formal terms of reference, monthly meetings, and dedicated coordination support. But it can designate a governance lead — typically the executive director — with formal responsibility for AI governance decisions; establish a simple review process for new AI tools that involves at least one additional perspective (a board member with relevant expertise, an external advisor, a legal resource); create a minimal but real policy document; and establish a basic reporting mechanism that staff can use to raise AI concerns.

This scaled-down structure is real governance, not governance in name only, if it is actually used — if new AI tools actually go through the review process, if staff actually know how to raise concerns, and if the governance lead actually engages with what they find. A small institution with simple, genuinely used governance processes is better governed than a large institution with elaborate, routinely bypassed governance architecture.

The scaling principle is this: reduce the formality and complexity of governance processes in proportion to institutional size, but maintain the substance — review before adoption, monitoring in operation, escalation when problems arise, and accountability for outcomes. The forms governance takes can be simplified; the functions it serves cannot be eliminated.

Chapter 7: Principles for Responsible AI

Why principles matter in governance

Every governance decision rests on a foundation of values, whether those values are explicit or not. When a governance team reviews a proposed AI use case and concludes that it requires additional safeguards before approval, that conclusion reflects a judgment about what matters — fairness to the people affected, protection of their privacy, adequacy of human oversight. When a procurement officer insists on audit rights in an AI vendor contract, that insistence reflects a judgment about accountability. When a frontline worker escalates a concern about an AI system's outputs, that escalation reflects a judgment about what responsible practice requires.

The question is not whether institutional AI governance is guided by values. It always is. The question is whether those values are explicit, shared, and coherent — or implicit, inconsistent, and unexamined. Implicit values produce unpredictable governance: different decision-makers applying different unstated standards, producing outcomes that vary with the person rather than the principle, and generating no institutional learning about what responsible AI use means in practice.

Explicit principles solve this problem. They give governance teams a shared vocabulary for discussing difficult cases. They give staff a basis for understanding why governance requirements exist and what they are trying to protect. They give affected communities a basis for holding institutions accountable to stated commitments. And they give institutions a standard against which their own AI governance practice can be evaluated.

This chapter describes seven principles for responsible AI governance: fairness, transparency, safety, privacy, accountability, security, and human dignity. These are not the only possible principles, and institutions should adapt the language and emphasis to their own context. But they represent the core commitments that responsible AI governance requires across institution types, and each has direct operational implications that the chapters following this one will translate into specific processes and practices.

The chapter addresses each principle in terms of what it means, why it matters, what it demands in practice, and where it most frequently fails. It then addresses how principles work together — and what to do when they appear to conflict.

Fairness

What it means

Fairness in AI governance means that AI systems treat people equitably — not necessarily identically, but without unjustified differential treatment based on characteristics that are irrelevant to the purpose the system serves. An AI system that produces accurate results for some demographic groups and inaccurate results for others is not fair, regardless of its overall accuracy rate. An AI system that makes decisions on the basis of factors correlated with race, gender, or other protected characteristics — even without explicitly using those characteristics — is not fair, regardless of technical design intentions.

Fairness is not a single concept but a family of related concepts, and the relationships among them are sometimes in tension. Equal treatment — applying the same process to everyone regardless of characteristics — is one conception of fairness. Equal outcomes — producing results that do not systematically disadvantage any group — is another. Equal accuracy — performing at the same level across demographic groups — is a third. Equal error rates across groups — ensuring that the costs of AI errors are not concentrated in particular populations — is a fourth. These conceptions do not always point in the same direction, and governance requires clarity about which conception of fairness is most relevant to a given use case.

In most institutional AI contexts, the most operationally significant conception of fairness involves differential impact: whether the AI system produces outcomes that disproportionately advantage or disadvantage identifiable groups, and whether any such differential is justified by factors legitimately relevant to the system's purpose. A clinical risk model that produces higher false-negative rates for patients of color — missing actual risk in those patients at higher rates than for white patients — is not fair. A hiring model that produces lower scores for candidates from certain universities is not fair if those universities' credentials are not genuinely predictive of performance. A benefits eligibility system that produces higher denial rates for applicants from certain zip codes is not fair if those zip codes are not genuinely relevant to eligibility.

Why it matters

Fairness matters first because unfair AI systems cause real harm to real people. When an AI system makes or influences a consequential decision — about employment, healthcare, benefits, education, credit, or any other domain of life — unfairness in that system translates directly into disadvantage for the people it affects. The employee who is screened out by a biased hiring tool, the patient whose risk is missed by a poorly calibrated diagnostic model, the student whose work is incorrectly flagged by a biased plagiarism tool — these are not statistical abstractions. They are individuals whose circumstances are meaningfully worsened by a system that treated them unfairly.

Fairness matters also because institutions have legal and ethical obligations that AI systems must honor. Anti-discrimination law in most jurisdictions prohibits practices that produce unjustified disparate impacts on protected groups, whether those practices involve human judgment or algorithmic systems. Professional ethical frameworks in healthcare, education, law, and social services include obligations of equitable treatment that apply to AI-assisted practice as much as to unassisted practice.

And fairness matters because institutions that use unfair AI systems are failing their missions. A nonprofit whose stated mission is to serve a particular underserved community and whose AI intake system systematically disadvantages members of that community is failing its mission through technology. A healthcare provider whose commitment is to equitable care and whose clinical AI performs differently across racial groups is failing its commitment through technology. The alignment between institutional mission and AI system behavior is a fairness question, not only a legal and ethical onc.

What it demands

The fairness principle demands active attention at every stage of the AI governance lifecycle. Before adoption, it demands asking whether the proposed AI system has been tested for differential performance across relevant demographic groups, what those tests found, and whether any identified differentials are acceptable given the use case. During deployment, it demands monitoring outcomes across groups to detect disparate impacts that pre-deployment testing may not have revealed. When disparities are found, it demands investigation, response, and either remediation or discontinuation.

Fairness also demands institutional honesty about the limits of what can be known. Pre-deployment bias testing provides evidence about system behavior on test data; it does not guarantee absence of bias in deployment against a different population or under different conditions. Monitoring provides evidence about patterns in deployment; it requires sufficient data about identifiable groups to be statistically meaningful, which creates challenges for institutions that serve diverse but relatively small populations. The fairness principle requires not only doing what can be done but acknowledging uncertainty about what cannot be fully assessed.

Where it most frequently fails

Fairness governance most frequently fails at the monitoring stage. Institutions conduct pre-deployment bias assessments — often because vendors provide them — and treat those assessments as sufficient. Ongoing monitoring of outcomes across demographic groups in actual deployment is less common, partly because it requires data infrastructure and analytical capacity that not all institutions have, and partly because it requires acknowledging that a deployed system may have problems that were not identified before deployment.

The second most common failure is accepting vendor bias assessments at face value. Vendor documentation of bias testing typically describes testing on the vendor's own evaluation data, using the vendor's own testing methodology, with disclosure limited to what the vendor chooses to share. This documentation may be genuine and adequate, or it may be incomplete and optimistic. Governance that treats vendor bias documentation as sufficient without independent validation or meaningful scrutiny is governance that has outsourced its fairness obligation to the entity with a commercial interest in approval.

Transparency

What it means

Transparency in AI governance means that institutions are open — with the people affected by AI systems, with oversight bodies, and internally — about what AI they use, how it works, what it can and cannot do, and what role it plays in decisions that affect people's lives. It means not using AI in ways that are hidden from those affected by it, not representing AI outputs as human judgments, and not obscuring the basis on which consequential decisions are made.

Transparency operates at several levels. Internal transparency means that the people within the institution who are responsible for AI governance have access to the information they need — including from vendors — to make informed governance decisions. This is the transparency dimension addressed in the vendor due diligence and audit rights provisions of governance frameworks. External transparency means that the people affected by AI-assisted decisions have the information they need to understand the basis of those decisions and to seek review when they believe an error has been made. Systemic transparency means that the institution's practices are documented and accountable to external oversight — regulators, accreditors, funders, and the public.

Transparency does not mean unlimited disclosure of technical system details. Many AI systems involve proprietary designs and training methods that are legitimately confidential. Transparency does not require vendors to disclose the architecture of their models, and it does not require institutions to make their internal AI governance documents publicly available. What it requires is disclosure of the information that affected parties need — not every technical detail, but enough to understand what AI is doing in a situation that concerns them and to exercise their rights with respect to it.

Why it matters

Transparency matters for governance because accountability depends on it. An institution cannot be held accountable for AI systems that no one outside the institution knows it is using. The people affected by AI-assisted decisions cannot exercise meaningful recourse if they do not know that AI was involved, do not know what role it played, and have no way to understand why it produced the outcome it did. Oversight bodies cannot oversee what they cannot see.

Transparency also matters because it disciplines institutional behavior. When institutions know that their AI practices will be visible — to the people they serve, to regulators, to the public — they have stronger incentives to ensure those practices meet the standards they publicly claim. Governance that operates in the dark tends toward complacency; governance that operates in the light tends toward accountability.

Beyond discipline, transparency serves the people AI systems affect in a more direct way. When a patient learns that an AI system influenced their treatment recommendation, they can bring that information to their clinical relationship — questioning, seeking second opinions, engaging with the recommendation as something to be evaluated rather than accepted. When a job applicant learns that AI screening shaped the review of their application, they can seek review, provide additional information, or challenge criteria that seem irrelevant to their qualifications. Transparency enables agency.

What it demands

The transparency principle demands that institutions disclose AI use to affected parties in meaningful ways. Meaningful disclosure is not a footnote in terms of service. It is clear, accessible communication about what AI is being used, what it does in the relevant context, and what rights affected parties have with respect to it. The appropriate form and depth of disclosure varies by context — disclosing to patients that an AI tool assisted in reviewing their scan is different from disclosing to job applicants that AI scored their application — but the standard of meaningfulness applies in both cases.

Internally, the transparency principle demands that governance teams have access to the information they need about AI systems, including from vendors. Governance teams that make decisions based on incomplete information are not exercising genuine governance; they are ratifying vendor representations. Audit rights, documentation requirements, and independent performance assessments are the operational forms of the transparency principle at the institutional level.

Transparency also demands honesty about uncertainty and limitation. An institution that presents AI outputs as more reliable than they are, that overstates the accuracy or objectivity of AI systems to affected parties, or that conceals identified limitations is violating the transparency principle even if it discloses that AI was used.

Where it most frequently fails

Transparency most frequently fails in the external dimension — disclosure to affected parties. Many institutions use AI in contexts where affected people have no idea AI was involved, where the fact of AI use is disclosed only in legal documents that few people read, or where disclosure is technically present but practically inaccessible. The norm of AI non-disclosure in many institutional contexts is so widespread that departing from it can seem unnecessary — "everyone uses these tools and no one discloses." That norm is not a governance standard; it is a collective failure of transparency that governance should correct.

The second common failure is internal opacity about vendor systems. Governance teams that have no meaningful access to information about how vendor AI systems work, that have not negotiated audit rights, and that are evaluating AI tools based on vendor marketing materials rather than documented performance data are operating in a state of internal transparency failure. They cannot govern what they cannot see, and what they cannot govern they cannot make accountable.

Safety

What it means

Safety in AI governance means that AI systems do not cause foreseeable physical, psychological, or material harm to the people they affect, and that when harm is possible, appropriate safeguards are in place to prevent, detect, and respond to it. It means that AI systems used in consequential contexts are evaluated for their potential to cause harm before deployment, monitored for harm-related failures during operation, and subject to clear incident response processes when failures occur.

Safety is context-dependent. The safety requirements appropriate for an AI system used in clinical decision support are different from those appropriate for an AI system used to draft internal communications. Governance must therefore approach safety in terms of the specific harm potential of specific use cases, not through generic standards that apply the same requirements regardless of context.

Safety also encompasses indirect harms — harms that arise not from direct AI action but from AI-assisted decisions or AI-generated information that leads humans to act in ways that cause harm. A clinical AI tool that produces recommendations contributing to a harmful treatment decision is a safety concern even if the AI did not directly administer the treatment. An AI chatbot deployed in a mental health context that responds inappropriately to expressions of crisis is a safety concern even if the chatbot did not cause the crisis. Safety governance must account for the chain of causation between AI outputs and human outcomes, not only for direct AI-caused harms.

Why it matters

Safety matters because harm to people is the most direct way that AI governance failure translates into institutional failure. When AI systems used in healthcare, child welfare, mental health, crisis support, physical safety, or any other domain where human welfare is directly at stake perform in ways that cause harm, the consequences for affected individuals can be severe and irreversible. No governance framework, however well-designed in other respects, can be considered adequate if it does not prioritize preventing foreseeable harm.

Safety matters also because the consequences of safety failures extend beyond the immediate harm. A safety failure reveals institutional priorities — what risks were deemed acceptable, whose wellbeing was given adequate weight, what level of oversight was considered sufficient. When safety failures occur, they are not only operational failures; they are failures of institutional judgment that reflect on the organization's values.

What it demands

The safety principle demands risk-proportionate governance: the rigor of safety assessment, the stringency of deployment requirements, and the intensity of ongoing monitoring should all scale with the potential for harm. A proposed AI use case with significant potential to cause physical harm should receive more thorough safety evaluation than one whose potential for harm is limited and reversible.

Safety demands defined minimum performance thresholds — not just "as good as the best available" but "good enough to be used safely in this context." For some applications, particularly in clinical and safety-critical contexts, the minimum threshold may be quite high. For others, where human review is robust and errors are easily corrected, it may be lower. The key is that the threshold is established explicitly and is calibrated to the harm potential of the use case, not set by default at whatever the vendor's system achieves.

Safety also demands clear incident response processes. AI safety failures will occur. The question is whether the institution is prepared to detect them quickly, respond appropriately, minimize ongoing harm, and learn from the failure to prevent recurrence. Institutions that have no incident response process are not governing safety; they are hoping that nothing goes wrong.

Where it most frequently fails

Safety governance most frequently fails at the pre-deployment stage through inadequate contextual assessment. Institutions conduct performance testing that evaluates accuracy and reliability in general terms but does not specifically assess failure modes relevant to the deployment context. A system that performs well on general benchmarks may still fail in specific situations — particular patient presentations, particular student circumstances, particular crisis scenarios — that are precisely the situations where safety matters most. Pre-deployment testing needs to specifically examine failure modes, not just overall performance.

The second common failure is treating safety as a vendor responsibility. Vendors may conduct safety testing on their systems, but that testing is conducted on the vendor's evaluation data, for the vendor's conception of safety, without knowledge of the specific institutional context in which the system will be deployed. Safety in context requires institutional assessment, not only vendor certification.

Privacy

What it means

Privacy in AI governance means that AI systems handle personal information in ways that respect the reasonable expectations of the people it concerns, comply with applicable legal requirements, and serve the purposes for which information was collected rather than expanding into uses that people did not anticipate or consent to. It means that AI deployments do not collect more personal information than their purpose requires, do not retain it longer than necessary, do not share it beyond what people have reason to expect, and do not use it in ways that expose people to harm.

Privacy in the AI context extends beyond the collection and storage of personal information to include inferences about people — conclusions that AI systems draw from data that was not itself sensitive but that, in combination or through analysis, reveals sensitive characteristics. An AI system that infers a person's health conditions from their consumer purchase history, or their sexual orientation from their browsing patterns, or their political beliefs from their social connections, is processing sensitive personal information even if no sensitive information was explicitly provided. Privacy governance must account for these inferential dimensions, not only for explicit data handling.

Privacy also encompasses the use of personal information in AI training. When institutions use records about real people — patient records, student records, client records, employee records — to develop or customize AI systems, the privacy implications of that use must be addressed. The people whose information is used in training did not necessarily consent to that use, and the purposes for which their information is now being processed may differ significantly from the purposes for which they provided it.

Why it matters

Privacy matters because it is the foundation of autonomy — the capacity of people to control information about themselves, to shape their own narratives, and to engage with institutions without the exposure that uninvited disclosure creates. When institutions use AI in ways that violate privacy, they are not only violating legal requirements; they are undermining the trust relationship between the institution and the people it serves, which is particularly corrosive for institutions whose relationships depend on personal disclosure — healthcare, mental health, social services, education.

Privacy matters also because privacy violations create concrete risks of harm. Unauthorized disclosure of health information can affect employment, insurance, and relationships. Exposure of financial information can enable fraud. Revelation of immigration status, sexual orientation, political beliefs, or religious practice in contexts where those disclosures invite discrimination or violence can have severe consequences for affected individuals.

What it demands

The privacy principle demands data minimization — using only the personal information that is genuinely necessary for the AI system's purpose, not collecting or retaining information on the grounds that it might be useful. It demands purpose limitation — using personal information for the purposes for which it was collected, not expanding into new uses without fresh assessment of privacy implications. And it demands protection appropriate to the sensitivity of the information — stronger technical and organizational safeguards for more sensitive data categories.

Privacy also demands transparency about data practices, which connects it to the transparency principle: people should understand what information about them is being processed by AI systems, for what purposes, and under what conditions. And it demands individuals' rights — the ability to access information about themselves, to correct errors, and in many jurisdictions to contest or limit certain forms of automated processing.

Where it most frequently fails

Privacy governance most frequently fails at the vendor assessment stage — institutions adopt AI tools without adequately understanding what data those tools collect, how it is handled, and whether it is used for model training or other purposes beyond the stated scope. Standard vendor contracts often include data handling provisions that are unfavorable to institutions and the people they serve; governance that accepts those provisions without review is accepting privacy risks by default.

The second common failure is staff behavior with respect to AI inputs. Policies that specify what information staff may and may not enter into AI systems are only as effective as the training and monitoring that support them. Staff who use AI drafting tools to prepare communications containing patient information, or AI research tools to query sensitive client data, without understanding the privacy implications of doing so are creating privacy risks that policy alone cannot prevent.

Accountability

What it means

Accountability in AI governance means that when AI systems produce outcomes — including harmful outcomes — there are identifiable people and institutions answerable for those outcomes, and that being answerable has real consequences. It means that the diffusion of responsibility across vendors, algorithms, automated processes, and institutional structures does not result in no one being responsible for what AI systems do. And it means that institutions that use AI have the documentation, oversight processes, and responsive mechanisms to demonstrate — not merely assert — that they have governed AI responsibly.

Accountability is the principle that gives the others operational force. A commitment to fairness that is not backed by anyone accountable for ensuring fairness is not a governance commitment; it is an aspiration. A transparency requirement that is never enforced because no one is accountable for enforcement is not a governance requirement; it is a suggestion. Accountability is what converts principles from statements of intent into standards of practice.

Accountability also has a retrospective dimension: when things go wrong, accountability means identifying what happened, why, who was responsible, and what will be done differently. This retrospective function is not about punishment — though in serious cases it may involve consequences — but about learning and improvement. Institutions that treat AI failures as occasions for determining accountability in order to learn are better governed than those that treat them as occasions to minimize and move past quickly.

Why it matters

Accountability matters because the people affected by AI systems are entitled to recourse. When an AI system contributes to an outcome that harms someone — a denied benefit, a missed diagnosis, an unfair evaluation — that person is entitled to understand what happened, to seek correction if an error occurred, and to have their harm acknowledged. Accountability is what makes this recourse possible: without it, affected parties face systems that made consequential decisions affecting their lives and that no one is willing to explain, own, or correct.

Accountability matters also because it is the mechanism through which governance improves. Institutions that hold themselves accountable for AI governance performance — that measure whether governance processes are working, that investigate when they fail, and that make changes based on what they find — develop governance systems that get better over time. Institutions that are not accountable for governance performance have no mechanism for improvement other than external crisis.

What it demands

Accountability demands role clarity — specific people in specific roles responsible for specific governance functions, as described in Chapter 5. It demands documentation — records of governance decisions, the reasoning behind them, the information they were based on, and their subsequent outcomes. It demands monitoring — processes for identifying when AI systems are not performing as intended, not governed as required, or producing outcomes inconsistent with institutional commitments. And it demands response — actual action when accountability requires it, not merely acknowledgment.

Accountability also demands willingness to be held accountable by external parties — regulators, affected communities, oversight bodies — and the transparency that makes external accountability possible. An institution that is accountable only to itself is not fully accountable.

Where it most frequently fails

Accountability governance most frequently fails through diffuse responsibility — the pattern described at the opening of Chapter 5, in which everyone assumes someone else is responsible and nothing gets owned. The governance design response is explicit role clarity and documented authority. When accountability is assigned to specific people, accountability failures are identifiable. When it is diffuse, they are invisible.

The second common failure is accountability that applies to others but not to leadership. When frontline staff are held accountable for compliance with AI governance requirements but the governance processes that those requirements are embedded in are never evaluated or improved, accountability is asymmetric in ways that undermine its legitimacy. Genuine accountability extends to the governance function itself — the governance team is accountable for whether governance is working, leadership is accountable for whether governance has the resources and authority it needs, and the institution as a whole is accountable for the AI practices it sustains.

Security

What it means

Security in AI governance means that AI systems and the data they process are protected against unauthorized access, manipulation, misuse, and failure — and that the institution's AI-related security posture is actively managed rather than assumed. It encompasses both the security of AI systems themselves and the security implications of using AI systems that connect to external vendors, process sensitive institutional data, and introduce new attack surfaces into institutional technology environments.

Security in AI contexts has dimensions that traditional cybersecurity frameworks do not fully address. AI systems can be manipulated through adversarial inputs — carefully crafted data designed to cause the system to behave in unintended ways. Language models can be induced through prompt injection to reveal information they should not, follow instructions embedded in content they process, or override safety constraints built into their design. AI systems trained on data that has been deliberately corrupted — data poisoning — may behave in systematically incorrect ways that are difficult to detect. These attack vectors are specific to AI systems and require specific governance attention alongside traditional security measures.

Security also encompasses the data security of AI vendor relationships. When institutions transmit personal or sensitive data to AI vendor systems, they are extending the security perimeter of their data governance to include the vendor's systems, practices, and security posture. A vendor data breach is an institutional data breach for the purposes of legal and reputational consequence. Governance must address vendor security as an extension of institutional security, not as a separate matter the vendor handles independently.

Why it matters

Security matters because insecure AI systems create risks to the people whose information they process — risks of exposure, of manipulation, and of harm from AI systems that have been compromised or deceived. A healthcare AI system that is successfully manipulated could produce clinical recommendations that harm patients. An AI system used in financial services that is compromised could facilitate fraud. A chatbot whose safety constraints are bypassed through prompt injection could produce harmful content in contexts where vulnerable people encounter it.

Security matters also because AI security failures can be silent. A compromised AI system may continue to appear to function normally while producing subtly altered outputs — recommendations slightly skewed, classifications slightly biased, information slightly inaccurate. Unlike obvious system failures, security compromises that operate below the threshold of detection can cause harm over extended periods before being identified. This makes proactive security governance particularly important.

What it demands

The security principle demands that AI tools undergo information security assessment before adoption — evaluation of vendor security practices, data transmission and storage security, access controls, and AI-specific security risks. It demands access controls that limit who within the institution can use AI systems and in what ways, reducing the attack surface from internal misuse and error. It demands monitoring for anomalous AI system behavior that might indicate security compromise. And it demands vendor contractual requirements for breach notification — commitments that the vendor will promptly disclose security incidents that may have affected institutional data.

Security also demands that staff understand AI-specific security risks. Staff who understand that AI systems can be manipulated through their inputs, that sensitive information provided to AI tools may be accessible to vendors, and that seemingly helpful AI outputs can be the product of adversarial manipulation are better equipped to use AI systems securely than those who approach AI as a simple tool with no security implications.

Where it most frequently fails

Security governance most frequently fails through the treatment of AI security as equivalent to traditional software security. AI-specific risks — adversarial inputs, prompt injection, data poisoning, model extraction — are not addressed by standard cybersecurity controls designed for conventional software. Organizations that extend their existing security frameworks to AI without modification are likely to have gaps in their security posture that are not visible in standard security assessments.

The second common failure is inadequate attention to vendor security. AI vendors often have access to more sensitive institutional data than any other vendor category, because AI systems process information in real time as part of core institutional operations. Yet vendor security assessment in many institutions is no more rigorous for AI vendors than for software vendors with much more limited data access. Security governance proportionate to risk requires proportionately rigorous vendor security assessment for AI systems that handle sensitive data.

Human dignity

What it means

Human dignity in AI governance means that AI systems treat the people they affect as ends in themselves — as individuals with inherent worth, complexity, and rights — rather than as data points, optimization targets, or problems to be processed efficiently. It means that AI use in institutions does not reduce people to the characteristics that AI systems can observe and quantify, does not substitute algorithmic assessment for the human relationship that institutional care and service require, and does not treat efficiency of processing as a value that overrides the quality of the human experience.

Human dignity is the most philosophically substantial of the principles in this chapter, and it is the most difficult to operationalize. It does not translate as directly as the other principles into specific process requirements. But it is also the most fundamental: it provides the normative grounding for all the other principles. Fairness matters because people have equal dignity and deserve equal treatment. Transparency matters because people have the dignity of knowing what affects them. Safety matters because people's wellbeing has inherent worth. Privacy matters because people have the dignity of controlling information about themselves. Accountability matters because people who are harmed deserve acknowledgment and recourse. Security matters because people's vulnerability to harm deserves protection.

Human dignity in AI governance also has a specific practical dimension: the preservation of genuine human relationship in contexts where AI might otherwise substitute for it. When people interact with institutions during moments of vulnerability — seeking healthcare, applying for benefits, working through a crisis, navigating a complex legal or financial situation — they are not only seeking information or a decision. They are seeking to be seen and treated as human beings. AI systems that are efficient but cold, accurate but inflexible, capable but without the capacity to recognize what a person's situation requires cannot fully serve the human need in these moments. Governance must ensure that AI use enhances rather than diminishes the human dimensions of institutional service.

Why it matters

Human dignity matters in AI governance because the absence of dignity sensitivity produces AI deployments that are technically compliant with every other principle but nonetheless wrong. An AI system that is fair, transparent, safe, privacy-protective, accountable, and secure can still treat people in ways that fail to respect their complexity, their context, and their humanity. A benefits system that is accurate and unbiased but processes human hardship as a classification problem, without mechanism for human judgment about individual circumstances, is efficient but not dignified. A clinical AI that produces statistically accurate recommendations but is deployed in ways that remove the patient from meaningful participation in their care is effective but not humane.

Human dignity matters also because the absence of dignity sensitivity produces governance that focuses entirely on measurable harms and neglects harms that are real but harder to quantify. The indignity of being reduced to a data profile, the dehumanization of having a consequential decision about one's life made entirely by an automated system, the erosion of meaningful human relationship in institutional contexts — these are harms that dignity-sensitive governance must acknowledge even when they do not fit neatly into categories like bias measurement or accuracy assessment.

What it demands

The human dignity principle demands that governance teams ask not only whether AI systems perform acceptably but whether they are deployed in ways consistent with the human experience they affect. This means evaluating not only technical performance but the quality of human encounter that AI-assisted processes produce — whether affected people are treated with respect, whether they have access to human judgment when they need it, whether the institution's use of AI enhances or diminishes its capacity for genuine human service.

Human dignity demands that AI systems not be the sole basis for decisions that have profound effects on people's lives, and that humans with authority to exercise judgment on behalf of affected people be genuinely available — not as a nominal escalation option but as an accessible reality. It demands that AI use in interactions with vulnerable populations be specifically evaluated for its impact on the human dimensions of those interactions, not only its technical performance.

Human dignity also demands institutional reflection on the values that AI adoption serves. When AI is adopted primarily to reduce costs by reducing human contact, governance should ask whether that reduction is consistent with the institution's obligations to the people it serves. Efficiency is a legitimate value; it is not an unlimited one.

Where it most frequently fails

Human dignity governance most frequently fails through the gradual erosion of human interaction that AI deployment can produce — not through any single decision to remove human judgment from a process, but through accumulated small decisions that together progressively reduce the human dimensions of institutional service. Each individual step may be justified on efficiency or accuracy grounds; the cumulative effect may be an institution that is technically well-governed by every other standard but that has ceased to treat the people it serves with the fullness of human recognition they deserve.

The second common failure is treating human dignity as too abstract to govern. The other six principles in this chapter have relatively clear operational implications: fairness can be measured, transparency can be assessed, safety can be evaluated, privacy can be protected, accountability can be assigned, security can be tested. Dignity is harder to measure, which leads governance teams to treat it as aspirational rather than operational. The governance response is to build dignity assessment into use case review — asking, for any proposed AI deployment, what the human experience of this system will be, whether that experience is consistent with the institution's obligations and values, and whether there are dimensions of human relationship that this deployment would diminish in ways that should not be accepted.

How principles work together

The seven principles described in this chapter are not independent commitments that can be addressed sequentially or treated as separate checklists. They form an integrated normative framework, and governance that applies them requires attending to their relationships, including the tensions among them.

Some relationships among the principles are straightforwardly complementary. Transparency supports accountability — you cannot be held accountable for what is invisible. Safety supports dignity — people cannot be treated with respect if they are exposed to preventable harm. Privacy supports dignity — people's autonomy is undermined when their information is used without their knowledge or consent. These complementary relationships mean that governance investments that strengthen one principle tend to strengthen others.

Some relationships involve genuine tension. Transparency and privacy can conflict: making AI systems and their operation more transparent may require disclosing information about individuals whose privacy that disclosure affects. Safety and efficiency can conflict: the oversight requirements that robust safety governance demands reduce the speed and scale advantages that AI systems offer. Fairness and accuracy can conflict in specific technical configurations: adjusting models to produce equal error rates across demographic groups may in some cases reduce overall accuracy. These tensions are real and should be acknowledged rather than resolved by pretending one principle is always paramount.

The governance response to principled tension is not to prioritize principles in a fixed hierarchy — declaring, for example, that safety always trumps efficiency or that privacy always trumps transparency. Different tensions require contextual judgment about which considerations are most weighty in specific circumstances. What governance should establish is a process for that judgment: explicit deliberation by the governance team, drawing on the perspectives that different roles bring, reaching reasoned conclusions that can be documented and explained.

V

visualize

From principles to practice: embedding values in governance processes

The real test of principles is not whether they are stated but whether they shape decisions. An institution that articulates seven principles for responsible AI and then makes governance decisions without reference to them has principles in name only. The governance infrastructure described in the chapters that follow — intake and risk screening, vendor review, testing, monitoring, incident response — is the machinery that translates principles into decisions.

Each governance process should be explicitly connected to the principles it serves. The intake form (Chapter 25) should ask how a proposed AI use case implicates each relevant principle and what measures will be taken to honor them. The vendor questionnaire (Chapter 26) should include questions that probe vendor practices against each principle. The testing checklist (Chapter 27) should include assessments linked to specific principles. The monitoring dashboard (Chapter 29) should track indicators relevant to principle compliance in operation.

This explicit connection between principles and processes serves two purposes. First, it ensures that governance decisions are actually informed by principled reasoning rather than ad hoc judgment. Second, it creates a documentation trail that demonstrates principled governance to external parties — regulators, auditors, affected communities — when demonstration is required.

Principles also need to be embedded in governance culture, not only in governance processes. The governance team's discussions should reference principles explicitly. When a proposal is declined, the reasons should be stated in terms of which principles it failed to meet and why. When a monitoring report reveals a concern, the analysis should connect that concern to the principles at stake. Over time, this principled reasoning builds institutional vocabulary for AI governance that staff throughout the organization can share and apply in their own work.

Adapting principles to institutional context

The seven principles described in this chapter are intended as a framework that institutions adapt rather than adopt wholesale. Different institutional contexts will weight principles differently, define them in ways specific to their mission and regulatory environment, and encounter tensions among them in forms particular to their work.

A hospital's articulation of the safety principle will emphasize clinical risk and patient welfare in ways specific to healthcare. A school's articulation of the dignity principle will emphasize the developmental vulnerability of children and the particular obligations of educational institutions. A government agency's articulation of the accountability principle will emphasize democratic accountability and citizens' rights in ways specific to public sector obligations. A nonprofit serving vulnerable populations will bring all seven principles to bear with awareness of the specific vulnerabilities of the people it serves.

Adapting principles is not weakening them. It is making them usable — translating abstract commitments into specific standards that governance teams can apply to real decisions in real institutional contexts. The adaptation process itself is a governance exercise: bringing together the members of the governance team, drawing on their different areas of expertise, and working through what each principle means in the institution's specific context produces the shared normative understanding that effective governance requires.

What adaptation must not become is avoidance — treating principles as flexible enough to be satisfied by whatever the institution is already doing, or interpreting them in ways that eliminate their requirements whenever those requirements create friction. Principles that impose no demands are not principles; they are decorations. The test of principled governance is whether the principles ever require the institution to do something difficult — to decline a useful tool because it fails the fairness standard, to invest in oversight that reduces efficiency because it is required for safety, to disclose AI use to affected parties even when non-disclosure would be easier. Principles that pass only easy cases are not governing; they are ratifying.

Chapter 8: Writing the AI Policy

The policy as the institution's public commitment

An AI policy is the document through which an institution translates its governance principles into operational requirements. It is the written record of what the institution has decided about AI use — what is permitted and what is not, who is responsible for what, what processes must be followed, and what happens when things go wrong. It is the reference document that staff consult when they have questions about AI use, that governance teams apply when reviewing proposals, that legal counsel cites when assessing compliance, and that affected communities can hold the institution to when they have concerns.

A good AI policy is not a philosophical statement. It is not a list of aspirations. It is not a summary of risks. Those things belong elsewhere — in the principles chapter, in strategic communications, in training materials. A policy is a set of requirements: specific, actionable, enforceable obligations that govern real behavior in real institutional contexts. The test of any policy provision is whether a staff member who reads it knows what they are required to do, a manager who relies on it can determine whether a staff member has complied, and a governance team member can use it as the basis for a governance decision.

This chapter describes what every institution's AI policy should include, how each component should be drafted, what distinguishes an effective policy from an ineffective one, and how the policy should be developed, approved, implemented, and maintained over time. It addresses the full policy lifecycle — from the initial drafting process through communication, training, implementation, and the periodic revision that keeps policy current as the institutional and technological environment changes.

Chapter 24 provides a starter AI policy that institutions can adapt. This chapter provides the understanding necessary to adapt it intelligently — to know why each component exists, what it is trying to accomplish, and how to modify it for institutional context.

Before drafting: four foundational questions

Before a word of policy is written, four foundational questions should be answered. Institutions that skip this preparatory work produce policies that are generic, disconnected from institutional reality, or impossible to implement. Time spent on these questions is governance investment, not delay.

What AI is the institution actually using?

A policy that governs AI in the abstract, without reference to the specific tools and use cases the institution actually has, will be a policy that staff cannot connect to their daily work. Before drafting, conduct or review the AI inventory described in Chapter 9. Identify what AI tools are currently in use, by which functions, for what purposes, and under what conditions. This inventory provides the empirical foundation on which policy requirements should be built — the specific tools and use cases that need to be addressed, the gaps in current practice that policy needs to close, and the risk concentrations that warrant particular governance attention.

What legal and regulatory requirements apply?

The AI policy exists within a legal and regulatory environment that varies significantly by jurisdiction, sector, and institutional type. A hospital's AI policy operates within healthcare privacy law, professional licensing requirements, and clinical standards. A school's policy operates within student privacy law, disability accommodation requirements, and academic integrity standards. A government agency's policy operates within administrative law requirements, freedom of information obligations, and due process standards. Legal and compliance counsel should review the applicable legal framework before policy drafting begins, identifying mandatory requirements that the policy must incorporate and constraints on what the policy can legitimately require.

What is the institution's risk tolerance?

Policy requirements should be calibrated to the institution's actual risk tolerance — the level of AI-related risk the institution is prepared to accept in exchange for the operational benefits AI tools offer. An institution that serves highly vulnerable populations, or that operates in a highly regulated sector, or that has experienced significant AI-related problems may have a lower risk tolerance than one in a lower-stakes context. Risk tolerance affects how restrictive the acceptable use provisions should be, how intensive the review requirements for new AI use cases should be, and what level of oversight is required for AI systems already in operation. Governance leadership should make this calibration explicit before drafting begins, rather than discovering through the drafting process that different stakeholders have incompatible assumptions about how strict the policy should be.

Who needs to be involved in drafting?

An AI policy drafted by a single function — legal, IT, or a governance coordinator — and presented to others for approval will lack the operational grounding, technical accuracy, and cross-functional legitimacy that effective policy requires. Drafting should involve, at minimum, representatives from legal and compliance, IT and information security, operations, and senior leadership. For institutions that serve specific communities — patients, students, clients — drafting should also involve perspectives from those communities, whether through direct participation, representative consultation, or structured feedback processes. The drafting process is itself a governance exercise: the conversations it requires among different functions build the shared understanding of what governance means in practice that no subsequent training can fully replicate.

Structure: what the policy should contain

An AI policy for an ordinary institution should contain nine substantive components, in addition to standard policy administration elements. Each component addresses a distinct governance question. Together they constitute a complete governance framework in written form.

Component one: purpose and scope

The policy opens with a clear statement of its purpose — what it is trying to accomplish — and its scope — who and what it applies to.

The purpose statement should be specific about what the policy governs and why. A generic statement like "this policy governs the responsible use of artificial intelligence" provides no orientation. A specific statement like "this policy establishes requirements for how staff use AI tools in their work, how new AI tools are evaluated before adoption, and how AI systems are monitored and managed once deployed, in order to protect the people we serve, meet our legal obligations, and uphold our institutional values" tells the reader what the policy addresses and what it is trying to protect.

The scope statement answers three questions. First, who does the policy apply to — all staff, contractors, vendors operating within the institution's systems, volunteers? Most institutions should apply their AI policy to all people acting on behalf of the institution, not only employees. Second, what AI tools does it cover — all AI tools used for institutional purposes, including personal devices used for work, or only tools on institutional systems? Third, what does the policy define as AI for its purposes — and this definition matters considerably. A policy that defines AI narrowly may inadvertently exclude tools that create significant governance risk. A policy that defines AI so broadly that it covers basic automation and spell-checking will be unworkable. The definition should cover the meaningful category: systems that use machine learning or similar techniques to generate outputs, make predictions, provide recommendations, or take actions that affect people, institutional processes, or institutional decisions.

Component two: principles

The policy should state the principles that govern AI use — the values the institution commits to upholding through its AI governance practices. Chapter 7 addresses these principles in detail. The policy statement of principles should be concise — a paragraph each, not a chapter — but substantive enough that the principles can serve as interpretive guides when specific policy requirements are ambiguous or when novel situations arise that specific provisions do not address.

The principles section is also the component of the policy that connects it to the institution's broader mission and values. AI governance does not exist in isolation; it exists in the context of the institution's commitments to the people it serves and the values by which it operates. Making that connection explicit in the policy helps staff understand why governance requirements exist — not as compliance obligations imposed from outside but as expressions of institutional values that staff themselves hold.

Component three: acceptable and prohibited uses

This is the operational heart of the policy — the component that staff most frequently need to consult and that governance teams most frequently apply. It specifies what uses of AI are permitted, what uses are prohibited absolutely, and what uses require review and approval before proceeding.

The acceptable use provisions should describe the categories of AI use the institution explicitly permits without additional review — typically uses that are low-risk, involve publicly available tools, do not process personal information, and do not produce outputs that are acted on without human review. Examples might include using AI writing assistants for drafting that is reviewed and revised by staff, using AI translation tools for internal communications, or using AI scheduling tools for internal calendar management.

The prohibited use provisions should be explicit and specific. Vague prohibitions — "do not use AI in ways that are harmful" or "do not misuse AI tools" — are not enforceable and do not provide the guidance staff need. Specific prohibitions — "do not use AI tools to generate communications to clients or patients that are sent without review by a staff member," "do not enter personally identifiable patient information into AI tools that are not covered by our data processing agreements," "do not use AI to make final hiring decisions without human review of AI outputs by the hiring manager" — tell staff exactly what they cannot do.

The prohibited uses section should address several categories that apply across almost all institutional contexts. AI systems should not be used to make final, unreviewable decisions about matters that significantly affect people's rights, access to services, employment, or welfare. Personal information about people the institution serves should not be entered into AI tools that are not covered by appropriate data processing agreements. AI tools should not be used to generate content that impersonates or misrepresents real people. Staff should not represent AI-generated outputs as their own original work in contexts where that representation would be material — such as academic submissions, professional certifications, or regulatory filings. AI tools that have not been reviewed and approved through the institution's governance process should not be deployed for institutional purposes.

The conditional use provisions address the middle category — uses that are permitted, but only with specific safeguards, oversight arrangements, or prior approval. This is the largest and most important category for most institutions. It includes uses where the risk level warrants governance review before proceeding, where the use involves personal information and requires specific data governance conditions, where the use produces outputs that affect people and requires specific human oversight arrangements, or where the use is in a regulated context that requires legal assessment. The conditional use section should specify what conditions apply and, where conditions involve a review process, what that process is.

The structure of acceptable, prohibited, and conditional uses should be specific enough to guide decisions but organized to avoid the trap of trying to enumerate every possible use case. The right level of specificity is categorical — describing categories of use and the considerations that determine which category they fall into — rather than exhaustive. An exhaustive enumeration will always be incomplete; a categorical framework can be applied to novel cases.

Component four: roles and responsibilities

The policy should state clearly who is responsible for what in AI governance. Chapter 5 provides the detailed responsibility framework; the policy should incorporate the key assignments at a level of specificity sufficient for accountability.

This component should name or describe specific roles rather than using generic language. "The governance team is responsible for approving new AI use cases" is more useful than "appropriate oversight will be exercised over AI adoption." "Department heads are responsible for ensuring their staff complete AI literacy training" is more useful than "training will be provided to relevant staff." "The AI governance coordinator maintains the AI inventory" is more useful than "AI systems will be tracked."

The roles component should also address decision authority — who makes which governance decisions, what decisions require governance team approval, and what decisions can be made at the operational level within defined parameters. Without clear decision authority, the policy creates a framework that cannot be implemented because no one knows who has the authority to implement it.

Component five: the review and approval process

The policy should describe the process by which new AI use cases and new AI tools are reviewed and approved before adoption. This is the governance team's primary intake function, described in Chapter 10.

The policy description of the review process should address: who must initiate a review request and how; what information must be provided in the review request; who conducts the review and in what timeframe; what criteria determine whether a use case is approved, approved with conditions, or declined; what happens when a request is declined; and whether there is an expedited process for time-sensitive needs.

The policy should make clear that the review and approval process is mandatory — that AI tools cannot be adopted for institutional use without going through it. This is a frequent governance failure point: review processes that are nominally required but in practice optional, because no one enforces the requirement and staff who find useful tools simply start using them. The policy should state explicitly that staff who adopt AI tools without authorization may face disciplinary consequences, which gives the requirement practical force.

The policy should also clarify what does and does not require formal review. Not every new use of an existing approved tool requires a fresh review; the review applies to the tool and its defined use scope, and use within that scope by different staff members does not require individual approval. But a material change in how an approved tool is used — applying it to a new category of personal information, using it to support a different type of decision, deploying it in a different operational context — should trigger a new review.

Component six: data governance requirements

The policy should specify how AI systems may process, store, transmit, and retain data, with particular attention to personal information and other sensitive categories.

The data governance component should address: which categories of information may and may not be entered into AI systems; what data processing agreements or contract provisions must be in place before personal information is processed by vendor AI systems; what data retention and deletion requirements apply to AI-processed data; and how data subjects' rights — access, correction, deletion, objection to automated processing — are honored in AI contexts.

For institutions that handle particularly sensitive categories of information — health information, information about minors, financial information, information about vulnerable populations — the data governance provisions should be correspondingly specific about what those categories require. A general prohibition on entering sensitive information into unapproved AI tools is a starting point; specific guidance about what "unapproved" means and what counts as "sensitive" gives that prohibition operational meaning.

The data governance component should also address the specific question of AI training data: whether and under what conditions the institution's data may be used to train or improve AI models — the institution's own systems if it develops custom AI, and vendor systems if vendors seek to use institutional data for training purposes. Most institutions should require explicit institutional approval before any operational data is used for AI training purposes, and should ensure that vendor contracts reflect this requirement.

Component seven: human oversight requirements

The policy should specify when and how human oversight of AI outputs is required — establishing the oversight standards that protect against the hallucination, overreliance, and automation bias risks described in Chapter 3.

The oversight component should distinguish among categories of AI use by the level of oversight required. For low-risk uses — AI assistance with tasks where errors are easily corrected and consequences are minimal — a general expectation of staff review may be sufficient. For moderate-risk uses — AI assistance with tasks where outputs influence decisions that affect people but where errors are detectable and correctable — specific review requirements may be appropriate, such as a requirement that AI-generated communications to clients be reviewed and approved by a staff member before sending. For high-risk uses — AI assistance with decisions that significantly affect people's access to services, welfare, employment, or healthcare — the policy should require specific oversight arrangements: independent human assessment before the AI recommendation is reviewed, documented human decision-making authority, clear escalation processes, and audit trails.

The policy should also address the distinction between genuine and nominal oversight — making clear that the oversight requirement is substantive, not procedural. A requirement that "a staff member must review AI outputs" that in practice means a quick scan before accepting the AI's recommendation is not the oversight the policy intends. The policy should specify enough about what adequate review looks like that staff understand what is actually required.

This component is also where the policy should address decision rights — the categories of decision that may not be made by AI systems, or may not be made primarily on the basis of AI outputs, without human authority. Decisions that significantly affect individual rights, welfare, or circumstances should generally require human decision authority, with AI providing input rather than determination.

Component eight: incident reporting and response

The policy should specify how AI-related incidents are identified, reported, escalated, and managed. Chapter 19 addresses incident response in detail; the policy component provides the framework within which those detailed processes operate.

The incident component should define what constitutes a reportable AI incident. The definition should be broad enough to capture the range of AI problems that governance needs to know about — not only dramatic failures but also patterns of unexpected output, potential bias concerns, privacy near-misses, safety-adjacent situations, and staff concerns about AI system behavior. A narrow incident definition that captures only obvious failures will mean that many governance-relevant situations go unreported.

The policy should specify who receives incident reports — typically the AI governance coordinator, with escalation to the governance team for significant incidents — what the reporting mechanism is, and what the institution commits to doing in response to reports. Staff who report AI concerns need to know their reports will be taken seriously and acted on. Incident reporting mechanisms that accept reports and produce no visible response will be underused, depriving the governance function of the operational intelligence it depends on.

The policy should also address non-retaliation explicitly: staff who report good-faith AI concerns are protected from adverse consequences for doing so. This protection is essential to creating a culture where reporting is the norm rather than the exception.

Component nine: training and compliance

The policy should address training requirements — what AI literacy training staff are expected to complete and by when — and compliance expectations, including the consequences of policy violation.

Training requirements should be specific about who must complete what training on what timeline. A general statement that "staff will receive AI training" is not a policy requirement; a specific requirement that "all staff who use AI tools in their work must complete the institution's AI literacy training program within 60 days of its availability and within 30 days of joining the institution" is. Chapter 17 addresses what effective AI literacy training should contain; the policy component establishes the training obligation.

The compliance section should address what happens when policy requirements are not met. This does not require elaborate disciplinary frameworks, but it does require being clear that policy compliance is expected and that non-compliance has consequences. The form those consequences take will depend on the institution's human resources framework and the severity of the violation — minor inadvertent violations may warrant additional training; deliberate circumvention of review requirements or misuse of AI tools may warrant more serious consequences. The policy should give enough guidance that the nature of consequences is predictable, even if the specific response to any individual situation requires managerial judgment.

Drafting principles: what makes policy effective

Understanding what a policy should contain is necessary but not sufficient. Effective policy requires attention to how it is written. Several drafting principles distinguish policies that actually govern from policies that exist primarily as documents.

Specificity over aspiration

Every policy provision should be specific enough that a staff member can determine what it requires of them. Aspirational language — "we will use AI responsibly," "AI should serve our values," "we are committed to fair AI" — has no place in operational policy. It belongs in mission statements, values documents, and communications. In policy, it creates the illusion of governance without the substance.

The test for specificity is this: can a reasonable staff member who reads this provision determine what they are required to do in the situations it addresses? Can a manager determine whether a staff member has complied? If not, the provision needs to be more specific or, if it cannot be made specific, reconsidered for its place in the policy.

Active voice and clear obligation

Policy provisions should be written in active voice with clear statements of obligation. "Staff must obtain governance team approval before deploying AI tools for institutional purposes" is clear. "Governance team approval should be obtained prior to the deployment of AI tools" is weaker — "should" suggests recommendation rather than requirement. "It is important that AI tools be approved before deployment" is weaker still and introduces the passive construction that obscures who is responsible.

The language of obligation in policy — "must," "is required to," "shall" — should be consistent and used only when the provision is genuinely mandatory. If a provision is a recommendation rather than a requirement, it belongs in guidance documentation rather than policy. Mixing mandatory and advisory language in the same document creates confusion about which provisions are enforceable.

Definitions that reflect actual use

The policy should define key terms — AI, AI system, approved AI tool, AI output, personal information, incident — with precision sufficient for the definitions to guide interpretation. Definitions that are too narrow will exclude the tools and situations governance needs to cover. Definitions that are too broad will capture things governance is not trying to manage, creating unnecessary friction and encouraging staff to look for ways around the policy.

Definitions should be based on the actual tools and use cases the institution encounters. If the institution uses large language models, decision support systems, and automated workflow tools, the definition of AI should clearly encompass all three. If the institution's context makes certain definitional questions particularly significant — for example, whether AI-powered features in standard productivity software are covered by the policy — those questions should be directly addressed.

Proportionate requirements

Policy requirements should be proportionate to the risks the uses they govern create. A policy that applies the same intensive review process to an AI scheduling tool and to a clinical decision support system is not well-calibrated. A policy that exempts trivial AI uses from all governance requirements while imposing extensive requirements on high-risk uses is both more effective and more likely to be complied with than one that applies uniform requirements regardless of risk.

Proportionality also means that the policy should not be longer or more detailed than necessary. Every provision that is added to a policy is a provision that must be understood, complied with, and enforced. Long policies are less read, less understood, and less complied with than focused ones. The discipline of keeping a policy to what is essential is itself a governance virtue.

Consistency with operational reality

Policy provisions should describe processes and requirements that are actually feasible for the institution to implement. A policy that requires governance review within 48 hours is not feasible for an institution whose governance team can only meet monthly. A policy that requires specific technical monitoring capabilities the institution does not have is not operational. A policy that assumes staff expertise the institution has not provided is setting staff up to fail.

This does not mean that policy requirements should be limited to what the institution is already doing. Policy is partly aspirational in the sense of establishing higher standards than current practice — that is how governance improves practice. But requirements should be feasible given the institution's realistic capacity, taking into account the resources that will be allocated to governance. If a provision requires resources or capabilities the institution does not currently have, it should be accompanied by a plan to develop them, with a realistic timeline.

The policy development process

A policy that is developed without genuine multi-stakeholder involvement, no matter how well-drafted, will lack the institutional legitimacy and operational grounding that effective governance requires.

The development process matters almost as much as the resulting document.

Drafting

The initial draft should be developed by a small working group that includes legal and compliance, IT and information security, operations, and senior leadership. The working group should begin from the AI inventory — understanding what the institution is actually doing — and work outward from there, identifying the governance gaps that policy needs to close and the specific requirements that address those gaps.

The working group should consult Chapter 24's starter policy as a reference, adapting its provisions for institutional context rather than adopting them wholesale. The adaptation process is important: provisions that are understood — whose rationale the drafting team has worked through — are more likely to be implemented effectively than provisions that are copied without comprehension.

Consultation

Before the draft is finalized, it should be shared with the people who will be affected by it — staff who use AI tools, operational leaders whose functions it will constrain, and where possible people from the communities the institution serves. The consultation should be genuine: not a final review that makes cosmetic changes but an opportunity for substantive feedback that can improve the policy.

Consultation serves several governance purposes. It identifies provisions that are impractical, unclear, or inconsistent with operational reality before those provisions create compliance problems. It builds understanding of why governance requirements exist, which improves compliance and reduces the culture of workaround that poorly understood requirements invite. And it builds ownership — staff who have been consulted about the policy they are asked to follow are more likely to take it seriously than those who have had it imposed without explanation.

Legal review

Before finalization, the policy should be reviewed by legal counsel specifically for compliance with applicable law and consistency with existing institutional policies. This review should address both the minimum requirements that law imposes — provisions that must be included — and constraints that law creates — provisions that may not be appropriate or may require qualification in the institution's legal context.

Legal review is not the same as legal drafting. A lawyer who drafts the entire policy from scratch may produce a legally precise document that is practically unusable. Legal counsel should review a practically grounded draft, not write one.

Approval and communication

The policy should be formally approved at the appropriate level of institutional authority — typically senior leadership, with board notification where appropriate. The approval process gives the policy its institutional standing: a policy approved by leadership signals institutional seriousness in ways that a document circulated by a working group does not.

Communication of the policy to staff should be planned rather than incidental. A policy sent by email with a note to review it is not communicated; it is transmitted. Effective communication explains not only what the policy requires but why — the values it expresses, the problems it addresses, and the ways it supports the institution's mission. Chapter 18 addresses stakeholder communication about AI; many of the same principles apply to communicating the policy to internal audiences.

Implementation: making the policy work

A policy that exists as a document but does not shape behavior is not functioning governance. Implementation is the work of turning a document into a system — creating the processes, training, monitoring, and enforcement that make the policy's requirements real.

Training

The policy should be incorporated into existing training programs and should be the subject of specific AI literacy training as described in Chapter 17. Staff who do not know what the policy requires cannot comply with it. Training that addresses not only what the policy requires but why it exists — the harms it prevents, the values it upholds, the interests of the people it protects — produces more meaningful compliance than training that treats policy as a set of rules to be memorized.

Process implementation

Each policy requirement that involves a process — the review and approval process, the incident reporting process, the data governance process for AI — needs operational infrastructure: forms, tracking systems, review timelines, designated responsible parties. The process chapters in Part II and Part III of this book provide the detail needed to build this infrastructure. The policy itself specifies the requirements; the processes specify how those requirements are met.

Monitoring compliance

The governance team needs mechanisms for monitoring whether the policy is being complied with — not only whether incidents are being reported or review processes are being followed but whether AI tools are being used in ways consistent with policy requirements. Chapter 16 addresses monitoring in detail. For policy compliance specifically, monitoring should include periodic reviews of AI tool use across the institution, spot-checks of oversight practices in operational functions that use AI significantly, and review of any patterns in incident reports that suggest systematic compliance gaps.

Enforcement

Enforcement of AI policy requirements is primarily a management function, not a governance team function. The governance team establishes requirements and monitors compliance; managers hold staff accountable for meeting those requirements within their teams. The governance team needs channels for escalating significant compliance concerns to the appropriate management level, and leadership needs to reinforce consistently that policy compliance is expected and that non-compliance has consequences.

Enforcement should be consistent. Selective enforcement — applying consequences for some violations and not others, or applying them more rigorously to some functions than others — undermines the policy's legitimacy and creates the impression that compliance is optional. Governance teams and managers should aim for consistency in how violations are addressed, adapting consequences to severity while ensuring that comparable violations receive comparable responses.

Keeping the policy current

An AI policy written in 2024 and not revised since will not adequately govern AI use in 2026. The rate of change in AI technology, regulatory requirements, and institutional AI use is high enough that policies require regular review and revision to remain effective.

The governance team should conduct a formal policy review at least annually, asking whether the policy's provisions remain adequate given changes in the institutional AI landscape, the regulatory environment, and the governance team's accumulated experience with implementing the policy. Annual review does not necessarily mean annual revision — if circumstances have not changed significantly, a review that confirms the policy remains adequate is itself a governance act. But the review should be substantive: a genuine assessment of adequacy, not a formality that produces automatic reconfirmation.

The governance team should also establish a process for triggering off-cycle policy review when circumstances warrant. Triggers might include: a significant AI-related incident that reveals a gap in current policy provisions; adoption of a new category of AI that the current policy does not adequately address; significant changes in applicable law or regulation; or a material change in the institution's use of AI that makes existing provisions disproportionate in either direction.

When the policy is revised, the revision history should be documented and staff should be notified of material changes with explanation of what changed and why. The communication discipline that applies to the initial policy applies equally to revisions — staff need to understand not only that the policy has changed but how and for what reason.

The policy in relation to other governance documents

The AI policy is the central governance document, but it is not the only governance document. It exists in relationship to a set of supporting documents that provide more detailed guidance on specific governance processes.

The AI inventory (Chapter 9) is an operational document, not a policy document — it records what AI systems the institution uses, but it does not set requirements. The intake form (Chapter 25) implements the review and approval process the policy requires. The vendor questionnaire (Chapter 26) implements the vendor due diligence requirement. The testing checklist (Chapter 27) implements the pre-deployment testing requirement. The incident report template (Chapter 28) implements the incident reporting requirement. The monitoring dashboard (Chapter 29) implements the monitoring requirement.

Together with the policy, these documents constitute the institution's AI governance framework. The policy provides the requirements; the supporting documents provide the processes through which requirements are met. Each should reference the others — the policy should describe the intake process and note that the intake form implements it; the intake form should reference the policy provisions it gives effect to. This cross-referencing helps staff navigate the governance framework and reinforces the coherence of the overall system.

The relationship between the AI policy and the institution's other policies — its data privacy policy, its acceptable use of technology policy, its record-keeping policy, its conflict of interest policy — also needs to be managed. In some cases, AI policy provisions will be specific applications of existing policy principles and should be consistent with them. In other cases, AI use creates novel governance questions that existing policies do not address, and the AI policy provides governance that supplements rather than duplicates existing frameworks. Where there is potential for conflict or confusion between the AI policy and existing policies, the AI policy should address the relationship explicitly.

What the policy cannot do alone

A final caution is essential. Policy is a necessary component of AI governance, but it is not sufficient on its own. A well-drafted policy that is not enforced, not trained on, not backed by processes that implement its requirements, and not embedded in a governance culture that takes it seriously is a document, not a governance system.

The chapters that follow — on the AI inventory, intake processes, vendor review, data governance, human oversight, testing, deployment, monitoring, training, and communication — describe the system that gives policy its operational meaning. Each of those elements is necessary. The policy gives them direction; without them, the policy has nowhere to go.

The institution that has an AI policy and nothing else has started governance. The institution that has built the system the policy describes is doing governance. That distinction — between starting and doing — is what the rest of Part II and Part III of this book is about.

Chapter 9: Mapping AI Use Across the Organization

The governance blind spot

There is a question that governance teams in institutions that have never conducted an AI inventory almost universally answer incorrectly: how many AI systems is your organization currently using?

The typical initial answer is a small number — the tools that leadership approved, the systems that IT manages, the software that was explicitly purchased as AI. The actual answer, discovered through systematic inventory, is almost always substantially larger. It includes AI features embedded in productivity software that staff use daily. It includes standalone tools that individual departments or staff members adopted informally without institutional approval. It includes AI capabilities that vendors added to existing software through product updates, with no announcement beyond a changelog entry that few people read. It includes AI tools that staff use on personal devices for work purposes because they find them helpful and have no reason to think they require approval.

This gap between perceived and actual AI use is the governance blind spot. It is not evidence of bad intentions. It is the predictable result of AI becoming embedded in everyday software and accessible as a consumer product at the same time that most institutions lacked any systematic way of tracking AI adoption. The blind spot is common; it is not acceptable as a permanent condition. Governance that does not know what it is governing cannot govern.

The AI inventory — a systematic record of every AI system the institution uses, plans to use, or has recently stopped using — is the instrument that closes the blind spot. This chapter describes how to create that inventory, what it should contain, how to keep it current, and how to use it as the foundation of the broader governance system.

What an AI inventory is and is not

An AI inventory is an operational record, not a policy document. Its purpose is factual: to establish and maintain an accurate picture of what AI systems the institution uses, in what contexts, under what governance conditions, with what risk profiles, and subject to what oversight arrangements. It is the empirical foundation on which governance decisions are made — the document that allows the governance team to know, at any time, what it is responsible for overseeing.

An inventory is distinct from a policy, which sets requirements. It is distinct from a risk register, which tracks risks. It is distinct from a vendor registry, which tracks vendor relationships. It draws on all of these and feeds into all of them, but it is its own thing: a structured record of AI systems in use, organized to support governance oversight.

The inventory should be comprehensive — covering all AI systems used for institutional purposes, not only those that have gone through a formal adoption process. This inclusiveness is precisely what makes it valuable. An inventory that records only formally approved AI systems is a record of governance compliance, not a picture of institutional reality. The governance value of the inventory depends on its accuracy, and accuracy requires capturing AI use wherever it actually occurs, including uses that predate the governance framework or that circumvented it.

The inventory should be maintained — updated continuously rather than compiled periodically and allowed to become stale. An AI inventory that was accurate six months ago and has not been reviewed since is a snapshot of a previous state, not a current governance tool. Maintaining the inventory requires processes and responsibilities as well as a document, which this chapter addresses.

Why the inventory matters beyond compliance

Institutions sometimes approach the AI inventory as a compliance exercise — something required by governance frameworks or regulators that must be completed to demonstrate due diligence. This framing misses what the inventory is actually for.

The inventory matters because governance without it is blind. A governance team that does not know what AI systems the institution uses cannot monitor their performance, cannot ensure that oversight requirements are being met, cannot assess the institution's aggregate AI-related risk, cannot respond effectively when an AI-related incident occurs, and cannot make informed decisions about new AI adoption. The inventory is not a deliverable to be produced and filed; it is a living instrument that the governance function relies on to operate.

The inventory matters because it enables resource allocation. Governance resources — staff time, budget, committee attention — are limited. An accurate inventory allows the governance team to prioritize: which systems present the greatest risk and therefore deserve the most intensive ongoing oversight? Which uses are low-risk and can be managed with lighter-touch governance? Which vendors represent the greatest dependency and therefore warrant more attention in relationship management? Without the inventory, these prioritization questions cannot be answered systematically.

The inventory matters because it enables institutional learning. As the governance team accumulates experience reviewing AI systems and observing their performance in operation, the inventory becomes a record of that learning — what risk assessments found, what monitoring revealed, what incidents occurred and how they were resolved. This institutional memory is lost when governance is purely ad hoc. The inventory preserves it.

The inventory matters because it enables honest communication with external parties. When a regulator asks what AI systems the institution uses in a regulated function, when an accreditor asks about AI governance practices, when an affected community asks what AI is influencing decisions about them, the inventory provides the factual foundation for a complete and accurate answer. Institutions that cannot answer these questions accurately because they do not know what AI they are using are in a worse position — both in terms of external relationships and internal credibility — than those that have done the work of finding out.

Scope: what belongs in the inventory

The first practical question in building an AI inventory is scope: what counts as AI for inventory purposes? This is not an abstract definitional question; it has real consequences for which systems the inventory covers and therefore which systems governance oversight reaches.

The inventory should cover AI systems that use machine learning, neural networks, large language models, or similar techniques to generate outputs, produce predictions, provide recommendations, classify inputs, or take actions that affect institutional operations, decisions, or the people the institution serves. This definition is broad enough to capture the meaningful category of AI while excluding basic automation — rules-based systems, simple conditional logic, standard database queries — that does not present the distinctive risks that AI governance is designed to manage.

Within this broad category, the inventory should include several distinct types of AI deployment.

Standalone AI tools are applications whose primary or notable function is AI — dedicated AI writing assistants, standalone AI research tools, AI-powered image or document processing systems, and similar purpose-built AI applications. These are usually the easiest to identify because they are marketed and understood as AI.

AI features in existing software are AI capabilities embedded within broader software platforms — AI writing assistance in word processing software, AI-powered search in enterprise systems, AI-generated insights in analytics platforms, AI scheduling in calendar tools, AI transcription in meeting platforms. These are frequently overlooked in inventory exercises because the host software is not thought of as AI, even when AI features are actively used. For inventory purposes, the relevant unit is not whether the entire software system is AI but whether AI features are in use and create governance-relevant risks.

Vendor-provided AI in enterprise systems covers AI that vendors have incorporated into institutional management software — AI capabilities in electronic health record systems, learning management systems, human resources information systems, customer relationship management software, and similar enterprise platforms. These systems often include AI features that institutions did not specifically purchase or choose — features added as product updates that the institution may not have evaluated specifically as AI.

Custom or internally developed AI covers any AI systems the institution has built or customized using AI development frameworks, API services, or data science tools. These are more common in larger institutions with technical staff, but they are increasingly accessible to smaller organizations through low-code and no-code AI development platforms.

AI used by vendors on the institution's behalf covers cases where vendors use AI in performing services for the institution — an outsourced HR function that uses AI in processing applications, a benefits administrator that uses AI in claims processing, a facilities management company that uses AI in maintenance scheduling. The institution may not directly use these AI systems, but it is responsible for decisions and outcomes they produce.

Conducting the initial inventory

The initial AI inventory — the process of identifying what AI systems the institution currently uses — typically reveals considerably more than expected and requires more systematic effort than a single request for information. The following approach works well for most institutions, with adaptations for scale.

The documentation review

Begin with the documentary record: software licenses, vendor contracts, IT asset registers, procurement records, and budget documentation. This review identifies AI tools that have been formally procured and paid for. It will not capture informal AI use, but it establishes a baseline and often surfaces AI deployments that IT and governance leaders were not aware of at the level of detail the inventory requires.

During the documentation review, pay particular attention to vendor contracts for enterprise software systems. Many enterprise software vendors have added AI features to existing products; the contracts governing those products may reference AI capabilities, data processing arrangements for AI, or AI-specific terms that reveal AI deployments not otherwise tracked. A review of data processing agreements — the contracts that govern how vendors handle the institution's data — is particularly revealing, as these documents often describe AI processing that occurs in connection with vendor services.

Surveys and interviews

No documentation review will capture the full scope of AI use. Much institutional AI use is informal — individuals or teams that have found useful tools and started using them without a formal adoption process. Reaching this informal use requires asking the people who are actually doing the work.

A survey distributed to all staff — ideally brief, specific, and framed to make honest response easy — should ask what AI tools people use in their work, for what purposes, how frequently, and whether they use them on institutional systems or personal devices. The framing matters: surveys that ask about "AI tools" may receive narrow responses from staff who do not identify the tools they use as AI. More specific prompting — asking about AI writing assistants, chatbots, AI search tools, AI image tools, AI transcription, and similar categories — typically surfaces more complete responses.

Interviews with department heads and operational managers provide richer context than surveys and often surface AI uses that staff surveys miss — tools used at the team level rather than individually, AI capabilities in systems that managers rely on, and planned AI adoptions that have not yet been implemented but that governance should be aware of.

IT can contribute a technical perspective: reviewing network traffic logs for connections to known AI service endpoints, analyzing software installation records, and interviewing IT staff who support specific functions and have visibility into what tools those functions use.

The discovery meeting

For institutions of moderate to large size, a structured discovery meeting — bringing together representatives from each major operational function to discuss AI use in their areas — is one of the most effective initial inventory methods. It has the advantage of surfacing context that surveys miss, enabling cross-functional comparison that reveals inconsistencies and gaps, and building the shared awareness of institutional AI use that governance requires.

The discovery meeting should be framed constructively: the goal is to understand what AI use actually exists, not to identify compliance violations or create problems for staff or departments that have been using tools informally. Staff and departments are more likely to be forthcoming when the inventory exercise is presented as necessary for governance improvement rather than as an audit with punitive implications.

Vendor verification

After the initial documentation review and staff consultation, verify the picture with key vendors. Ask vendors of existing enterprise systems whether their products include AI features, what those features do, and how they handle data. Ask vendors of software platforms whether AI capabilities have been added since the institution's last review. Ask outsourced service providers whether they use AI in performing services for the institution.

Vendor verification often surfaces AI use that neither documentation review nor staff surveys identified, because vendors may have added AI features to existing products without specific institutional notification, or staff may not be aware that systems they use include AI capabilities.

What the inventory record should contain

For each AI system identified, the inventory should record a standard set of information sufficient to support governance oversight. The following fields constitute a minimum; institutions may add fields specific to their governance requirements or regulatory context.

Identification fields

Every inventory entry needs enough information to identify the system unambiguously: the name of the AI system or tool, the vendor or developer, the version or model in use if applicable, and a brief description of what the system does. The description should be specific enough to distinguish this system from others — not "AI writing tool" but "AI writing assistant used by communications staff to draft donor communications, grant reports, and social media content."

The entry should also record when the system was adopted, who in the institution is responsible for it (the operational owner), and what governance status it has — whether it has been through the institution's review and approval process, when that review occurred, and what its current governance standing is.

Use and context fields

The inventory should record how the AI system is used — what specific tasks it performs, in what operational contexts, by which staff or functions, and with what frequency. This contextual information is essential for risk assessment and governance oversight; an AI tool that produces suggestions staff occasionally consult is a different governance matter than the same tool whose outputs are systematically incorporated into operational records.

The record should document whether the system is used to make or influence decisions that affect people — patients, students, clients, employees, the public — and if so what those decisions are and how AI outputs relate to final decisions. This information identifies use cases where the governance protections for human oversight, fairness, and accountability are most relevant.

Data fields

The inventory should record what data the AI system processes: what categories of information it receives as inputs, what it retains, and what it produces as outputs. Particular attention should be given to whether the system processes personal information, what legal basis exists for that processing, and what data processing agreement governs the vendor's handling of institutional data.

The data record should also note whether institutional data is used in training or improving the AI model — either the institution's own model or the vendor's — and whether that use has been specifically assessed and approved.

Risk fields

Each inventory entry should include a risk assessment: the overall risk level of the use case (typically categorized as low, medium, or high, using the criteria described in Chapter 10), the specific risk categories most relevant to this use case (from the framework in Chapter 3), and any particular risk factors that informed the assessment.

The risk assessment is not a permanent fixture. It should be updated when significant changes occur — changes in how the system is used, changes in the population affected, material updates to the system by the vendor, or new information about system performance or risk that changes the assessment.

Oversight and compliance fields

The inventory should record what oversight arrangements are in place: what human review occurs before AI outputs are acted on, what monitoring is conducted, what incident reporting has occurred, and what governance conditions were attached to approval and whether those conditions are being met.

This section of the record is what allows the governance team to track governance compliance across all deployed AI systems — to know, at a glance, whether each system's oversight arrangements are current and adequate, and to identify systems that warrant follow-up.

Vendor and contract fields

The inventory should record key vendor information: the vendor's name and contact information, the governing contract and its key terms (including data handling provisions, audit rights, breach notification obligations, and contract expiration), and the institution's vendor relationship manager for this system.

This information connects the inventory to the institution's vendor management function and allows governance oversight of vendor compliance with contractual AI governance commitments.

Organizing and maintaining the inventory

The inventory is only as useful as it is accessible and current. A comprehensive inventory that exists in an unwieldy spreadsheet no one knows how to query, or that was accurate when created and has not been updated since, does not serve its governance purpose.

Format and access

The inventory should be stored in a format that is accessible to the governance team and AI governance coordinator, searchable and sortable to support different governance needs, and updatable without specialized technical skills. A shared spreadsheet or simple database works well for most institutions; more sophisticated governance management tools are available for larger organizations with more extensive AI portfolios.

The inventory should not be publicly available in its full form — it contains information about vendor relationships and system configurations that may be sensitive — but should be accessible to all governance team members, relevant operational leaders, and the AI governance coordinator. Some institutions create a summary view of the inventory — identifying categories of AI use without sensitive vendor or configuration details — that can be shared more broadly with staff and in some cases with external stakeholders.

Continuous update process

The inventory becomes stale immediately when changes occur and are not recorded. Keeping it current requires three things: a process for adding new entries when new AI tools are adopted, a process for updating existing entries when significant changes occur, and a process for removing or archiving entries when AI tools are discontinued.

The intake and approval process described in Chapter 10 provides the natural mechanism for adding new entries: every AI use case that goes through the intake process, when approved, should result in an inventory entry. The governance team or AI governance coordinator should create the entry at the time of approval, not as a separate subsequent task.

Updates to existing entries should be triggered by defined events: material changes in how a system is used, significant changes made by the vendor to the AI model or its capabilities, new data categories brought into the system's processing scope, significant monitoring findings, or incident reports related to the system. Operational owners — the staff members responsible for each AI system in the inventory — should be designated as responsible for notifying the AI governance coordinator when these events occur, with the coordinator updating the inventory record.

Periodic review — at minimum annually, as part of the governance team's annual review process — provides a systematic check on inventory currency. The annual review should involve reaching back out to operational functions to confirm that their inventory entries remain accurate, verifying with vendors that system capabilities and data handling practices have not changed in ways not previously notified, and assessing whether the risk assessments for existing entries remain appropriate.

The governance team's use of the inventory

The inventory is a working tool for the governance team, not a filing system. The governance team should actively use it in several distinct ways.

For oversight and monitoring, the inventory provides the list of AI systems the team is responsible for overseeing. Regular governance team meetings should include a review of the inventory — not a detailed examination of every entry, but a structured look at systems flagged for follow-up, systems whose monitoring has revealed concerns, and systems approaching key governance milestones such as contract renewal or scheduled performance review.

For risk assessment, the inventory allows the governance team to assess the institution's aggregate AI risk profile — the totality of AI-related risk across all deployed systems. This aggregate view reveals risk concentrations that individual use case reviews may not surface: if the institution has ten AI systems that all affect the same population, the cumulative impact on that population may be a governance concern even if each individual system is within acceptable risk parameters.

For regulatory compliance, the inventory provides the factual basis for responding to regulatory inquiries about institutional AI use. Regulatory frameworks that require disclosure or reporting of AI system use in regulated contexts — such as AI used in healthcare decisions, employment decisions, or credit determinations — require accurate institutional knowledge of what AI systems are in use and what decisions they affect. The inventory provides that knowledge.

For resource planning, the inventory allows the governance team to assess the governance workload ahead: how many systems need annual review, how many vendor contracts are expiring, how many monitoring reviews are due. This planning function is particularly important as AI use grows — governance resources that are adequate for the current inventory may not be adequate for a significantly expanded one, and the inventory provides the data needed to make the case for additional governance resource.

Common inventory challenges

Institutions that have conducted AI inventories reliably encounter several challenges that are worth anticipating.

Staff reluctance to disclose informal AI use

Staff who have been using AI tools informally — without institutional approval — may be reluctant to disclose that use in an inventory exercise, particularly if they are uncertain whether informal use constitutes a policy violation. The governance response is to conduct the inventory with a tone of genuine discovery rather than enforcement, and to make clear that the purpose of the exercise is to understand and improve governance, not to discipline staff for prior informal use.

Amnesty for prior informal use — a formal or informal commitment that staff who voluntarily disclose prior informal AI use in the context of the inventory exercise will not face disciplinary consequences for that prior use — significantly improves the completeness of inventory responses. The governance value of knowing about informal AI use substantially outweighs any disciplinary value of treating disclosure as an admission.

Vendor opacity about AI features

Some vendors are not forthcoming about whether their products include AI features, how those features work, or what data they process. This opacity may reflect competitive sensitivities about technical capabilities, concern about liability for AI performance, or simply inadequate internal documentation of AI features in complex software products.

Governance teams that encounter vendor opacity should treat it as a material governance concern — a vendor that cannot or will not describe what AI its products contain is not a vendor whose AI governance practices the institution can adequately oversee. Follow-up should be persistent and documented, and the opacity itself should be recorded in the inventory as a risk factor. If a vendor cannot provide adequate information about AI features affecting institutional data, the institution should consider whether those features should be disabled, whether the vendor relationship should be reconsidered, and what interim governance measures are appropriate.

Definitional disputes about what counts as AI

The inventory process frequently surfaces disagreements about whether specific tools or features constitute AI for inventory purposes. A rules-based recommendation engine: AI or not? A statistical model built with conventional methods: AI or not? Predictive text in email: AI or not?

Rather than resolving these definitional questions with bright-line rules, governance teams should apply a practical test: does this tool or feature create governance-relevant risks of the kinds described in Chapter 3 — bias, privacy violation, safety risk, hallucination, overreliance? If the answer is yes or possibly yes, it belongs in the inventory regardless of whether it fits a narrow definition of AI. The inventory's purpose is to support governance oversight of meaningful risks, not to satisfy a definitional exercise.

Managing a large and growing inventory

Institutions that use AI extensively may find that their inventory grows to a scale that is difficult to manage. A governance team responsible for overseeing dozens of AI systems cannot apply the same level of oversight attention to each; prioritization becomes essential.

Risk-based prioritization — applying more intensive oversight to higher-risk systems and lighter-touch oversight to lower-risk ones — is the governance response to inventory scale. The risk assessments in the inventory should inform the allocation of governance team attention, with periodic review ensuring that risk assessments remain current and that lower-risk classifications are not allowing meaningful governance concerns to go unaddressed.

Governance team structure may also need to adapt to inventory scale. Institutions with extensive AI portfolios may benefit from distributed governance arrangements — function-level governance for operational AI systems, with central governance oversight focused on higher-risk systems and institutional-level risk management — as described in Chapter 6.

The inventory as institutional self-knowledge

There is something more than administrative about the AI inventory. It is the institution's systematic account of its own AI-related actions — what it has chosen to do with AI, what risks it has accepted, what governance conditions it has applied, what oversight it has established. This account is the basis of institutional self-knowledge about AI, and institutional self-knowledge is the prerequisite for institutional accountability.

An institution that does not know what AI it uses cannot claim to be governing AI responsibly. An institution that has built and maintains an accurate inventory has done something real: it has established the factual foundation on which every other governance practice depends. The policies, review processes, vendor assessments, monitoring systems, and incident response procedures described in the chapters that follow are all more effective when they operate against an accurate picture of what is actually in use. The inventory is what makes that picture available.

Chapter 10: Intake and Risk Screening

The moment governance matters most

Of all the points in the AI governance lifecycle, the intake and risk screening stage is where governance has the greatest leverage. Before a tool is adopted, before workflows are redesigned around it, before staff are trained on it, before vendor contracts are signed, before data begins flowing into external systems — at that moment, the institution retains full freedom of decision. It can approve the use case with confidence, approve it with conditions that manage identified risks, require modification before proceeding, or decline it entirely. Every other governance intervention — monitoring, incident response, audit — addresses problems in systems already operating. Intake and risk screening is governance before problems exist, when prevention is still possible.

That leverage makes intake governance both the most valuable and the most contested part of any governance framework. Operational functions that want to move quickly resent review processes that create delay. Staff who have found useful tools resist being told they need to go through a process before using them. Vendors who want to sell resent scrutiny that makes the path to adoption longer. These pressures are real and should not be dismissed — governance processes that create unnecessary friction without corresponding benefit deserve to be streamlined. But the response to those pressures is to design intake processes that are proportionate, efficient, and genuinely useful — not to abandon them.

This chapter describes a complete intake and risk screening system: what triggers it, how it works, what it assesses, who is involved, how decisions are made, what documentation it produces, and how it connects to the broader governance framework. It addresses both the structure of the process and the substance of what good screening involves.

What triggers intake review

The first governance design question is what should trigger the intake process. If the trigger is too narrow — covering only formally procured, dedicated AI systems — large categories of institutional AI use will proceed without review. If the trigger is too broad — covering any digital tool with any automated feature — the intake process will be overwhelmed and its requirements will be circumvented as unworkable.

The intake process should be triggered by any of the following circumstances.

A staff member, team, or operational function intends to adopt a new AI tool for institutional use — including tools accessed through personal accounts, free-tier subscriptions, or informal arrangements, not only tools procured through formal purchasing processes. The informality of the adoption route does not reduce its governance implications.

A vendor of existing software has added AI features that the institution has not previously assessed, and staff are beginning to use or are considering using those features. The fact that the host software is already in use does not mean its new AI capabilities have been evaluated.

The institution intends to expand an already-approved AI use to a new operational context, a new population, or a new category of data that was not covered by the original approval. Changed use scope requires fresh screening because the risk profile may change materially with changed context.

The institution intends to develop, commission, or customize an AI system rather than adopt an existing one. Custom development often escapes intake review because it is perceived as internal rather than vendor-supplied; its governance requirements are if anything more extensive, not less.

A vendor notifies the institution of a material change to an AI system already in use — a model update, a change in data handling, a change in capabilities — that may affect the governance assessment. Material changes to approved systems require reassessment, not automatic continuation of existing approvals.

The institution is renewing a contract for an AI system that has not been reviewed under the current governance framework. Contract renewal is a governance checkpoint: an opportunity to assess whether the system's ongoing use remains appropriate and whether governance conditions need updating.

The intake process: an overview

The intake process moves through five stages: submission, preliminary triage, substantive screening, decision, and documentation. Each stage has defined inputs, outputs, responsible parties, and timelines. Together they constitute a complete governance review — proportionate in depth to the risk level of the use case, efficient enough to be workable in operational settings, and rigorous enough to provide genuine governance assurance.

The overall process is designed to take between one and four weeks for most use cases, with a faster track for low-risk proposals and a more extended timeline for complex or high-risk ones. These timelines are achievable when the governance function is adequately resourced and when the process is well-designed. They are not achievable when governance is an afterthought with no dedicated capacity.

Stage one: submission

The intake process begins when a staff member, team, or operational leader submits a request for review of a proposed AI use case. The submission is made through a standard intake form — the AI intake form provided in Chapter 25 — which collects the information the governance team needs to conduct its review.

What the intake form collects

The intake form is the primary document of the intake process. Its design determines both the quality of information available for screening and the burden placed on submitters. A form that asks for too little produces insufficient information for governance review; a form that asks for too much discourages submission and invites cursory responses.

The form should collect information in six areas.

Basic identification covers the essentials: who is submitting the request, what function or team they represent, what AI tool or system they are proposing to use, who the vendor is, and what the proposed implementation timeline is. This information establishes context and accountability.

Use case description asks the submitter to describe specifically what the AI system will do, in what operational context, for what purposes, and with what intended outcomes. This description should be specific enough that a reviewer unfamiliar with the submitter's function can understand what is being proposed. Vague descriptions — "using AI to improve efficiency" — are not adequate; specific ones — "using an AI tool to generate first-draft responses to standard member service inquiries, which staff will review and edit before sending" — are.

Population and impact asks who will be affected by the AI system — directly (people whose data it processes or about whom it makes recommendations) and indirectly (people who will receive communications generated with AI assistance, or decisions influenced by AI outputs). It asks whether affected people include members of vulnerable populations, whether they will be informed that AI is being used, and what mechanisms exist for them to seek human review if they have concerns.

Data description asks what information the AI system will process: what categories of data, what volume, what sensitivity classification, whether it includes personal information and of what types, whether any legally protected categories of data are involved, and whether the vendor's data handling practices have been reviewed. This section is where privacy risk first comes into view.

Oversight and integration asks how the AI system's outputs will be used: whether they inform human decisions or substitute for them, what review occurs before outputs are acted on, how the system integrates with existing workflows and institutional systems, and what happens when the system produces uncertain, unusual, or problematic outputs.

Vendor information asks about the vendor's AI governance practices: whether the vendor has provided documentation of system performance across demographic groups, what the vendor's data processing practices are, whether the institution has audit rights, and whether the proposed contract has been reviewed by legal counsel.

Submission acknowledgment and triage assignment

When a submission is received, the AI governance coordinator acknowledges receipt and assigns the submission for preliminary triage. The acknowledgment should be prompt — within one to two business days — and should confirm the submission has been received, provide an expected timeline for response, and identify who the submitter's primary contact is during the review process.

Prompt acknowledgment is not a formality. Submitters who hear nothing after submitting a request will either follow up repeatedly, consuming governance capacity, or proceed without approval on the assumption that silence implies consent. Neither outcome serves the governance function.

Stage two: preliminary triage

Preliminary triage is a rapid initial assessment — typically completed within two to three business days — that serves two purposes: determining the appropriate depth of review the use case requires, and identifying any obvious issues that warrant immediate attention before substantive screening begins.

Risk-level determination

The primary output of preliminary triage is a risk-level determination: low, medium, or high. This determination drives the subsequent review process — lower-risk use cases go through a streamlined review; higher-risk ones go through a more intensive process with more stakeholder involvement.

The risk-level determination should be based on a consistent set of criteria applied to every submission. The following framework provides a practical starting point that institutions should adapt to their specific context.

A use case is classified as *low risk* when all of the following apply: the AI system does not process personal information about the people the institution serves; its outputs are used only to assist staff with tasks that have no direct effect on anyone outside the institution; human review of outputs is built into the workflow with no possibility of outputs being acted on without staff review; the vendor is well-established with clear data handling practices; and the use case does not fall in any sector subject to specific AI-related regulation.

A use case is classified as *high risk* when any of the following apply: it uses AI to make or significantly influence decisions that affect individuals' access to services, employment, healthcare, education, housing, financial products, or legal treatment; it processes sensitive personal information including health data, financial data, information about minors, or legally protected characteristics; it involves AI in a context where errors could cause physical harm; it deploys AI in direct interaction with vulnerable populations; it involves AI with limited human oversight of individual outputs; the vendor's AI governance documentation is inadequate or unavailable; or it raises significant concerns under applicable law or regulation.

A use case is classified as *medium risk* when it falls between these categories — it processes personal information but not sensitive categories, it influences decisions without determining them, human oversight is present but not intensive, or some risk factors are present but not the most serious ones.

This framework will not resolve every case unambiguously, and triage will involve judgment. The governance coordinator who conducts triage should consult with at least one other governance team member — typically the legal representative and the IT representative — when the risk level is unclear, rather than making uncertain determinations alone.

Completeness check

Preliminary triage should also include a completeness check: does the intake form provide sufficient information to conduct substantive screening? Forms that are incomplete — vague use case descriptions, missing vendor information, inadequate data descriptions — cannot support substantive review and should be returned to the submitter with specific requests for additional information before screening proceeds.

Returning incomplete forms is preferable to proceeding with insufficient information. The governance function exists to make informed decisions; decisions made on incomplete information are not well-governed regardless of what they conclude.

Fast-track identification

Some low-risk use cases may be eligible for a fast-track review — a streamlined process that reaches a decision more quickly than the standard timeline. Fast-track eligibility criteria should be defined explicitly in governance procedures: typically, use cases that are clearly low-risk, involve established vendors with documented governance practices, process no personal information, and have clear human oversight built in.

Fast-track review should not be a rubber-stamp process. It should still involve substantive assessment of the submission; it simply does so more efficiently, with a smaller review group and a shorter timeline. The legitimacy of fast-track approval depends on the rigor of the criteria for fast-track eligibility and the consistency with which those criteria are applied.

Stage three: substantive screening

Substantive screening is the governance heart of the intake process. It is a systematic assessment of the proposed use case against the risk categories, governance principles, and institutional requirements that responsible AI use demands. Its depth and formality vary with risk level; its scope covers the same ground regardless of risk level.

Screening for the eight risk categories

Chapter 3 identified eight risk categories that institutional AI governance must address: bias and discrimination, privacy violations, safety failures, hallucination and unreliability, overreliance and automation bias, vendor lock-in, reputational harm, and legal exposure. Substantive screening assesses the proposed use case against each of these categories.

The screening is not a checklist exercise. Each category requires substantive judgment about the specific use case — not merely whether the risk exists in the abstract but how significant it is in this specific context, what mitigations are proposed or available, and whether the proposed use case as described is acceptable given identified risks.

Bias and discrimination screening asks whether the AI system could produce outputs that disadvantage identifiable groups, whether the vendor has documented performance across relevant demographic groups, whether the use case involves decisions that have disparate impact implications, and whether the oversight arrangements proposed are adequate to detect bias if it occurs. For high-risk use cases, screening should require specific bias testing documentation from the vendor and may require independent validation.

Privacy screening asks whether the data the system processes is proportionate to its purpose, whether the vendor's data handling practices meet the institution's legal obligations and policy commitments, whether affected individuals have been or will be informed of AI processing, and whether adequate data processing agreements are in place. Privacy screening should be conducted with direct involvement of legal counsel for any use case that processes personal information.

Safety screening asks whether the system could contribute to physical, psychological, or material harm, what the realistic failure modes are in the specific deployment context, whether minimum performance thresholds have been defined and documented, and whether oversight arrangements are sufficient to prevent failures from translating into harm. Safety screening for high-risk use cases in healthcare, child welfare, mental health, or similar domains should involve clinical or domain expert input.

Hallucination and unreliability screening asks what the accuracy characteristics of the system are, what independent validation of vendor accuracy claims exists, what categories of output are most susceptible to hallucination, and whether oversight requirements are calibrated to the reliability characteristics of the specific outputs. For generative AI systems, this screening should specifically address the institution's approach to output verification.

Overreliance screening asks whether the oversight arrangements proposed are designed to support genuine independent judgment rather than nominal review, whether staff will be trained on automation bias and the specific limitations of this system, whether the presentation of AI outputs to reviewers is designed to reduce anchoring effects, and whether override rates will be monitored. This screening is particularly important for use cases where AI recommendations will be visible to human decision-makers before those decision-makers have formed independent assessments.

Vendor lock-in screening asks whether the proposed contract includes adequate exit provisions and data portability requirements, what the institution's practical ability to switch vendors or discontinue the system would be if needed, whether the contract duration is appropriate given the institution's risk tolerance, and whether the degree of workflow integration proposed creates dependency risks. This screening should involve direct procurement involvement and, for significant contracts, legal review of exit provisions.

Reputational harm screening asks how the institution's stakeholders — staff, the communities served, funders, regulators, the public — would perceive this AI use if they became aware of it, whether the use is consistent with the institution's stated values, whether affected parties are being treated with the transparency the institution has committed to, and whether the use case could create media, regulatory, or community relations concerns. Reputational screening is partly a factual exercise and partly a judgment call about institutional values and stakeholder relationships.

Legal exposure screening asks what legal frameworks apply to this use case, whether the use case raises concerns under anti-discrimination law, data protection law, sector-specific regulation, or any other applicable legal framework, whether the vendor contract adequately allocates legal risk, and whether legal counsel has reviewed the use case. Legal screening should be conducted with direct involvement of legal counsel for any medium- or high-risk use case.

Principles assessment

In addition to risk category screening, substantive review should assess the proposed use case against the governance principles described in Chapter 7. The principles assessment asks whether the use case as proposed is consistent with each principle — fairness, transparency, safety, privacy, accountability, security, and human dignity — and identifies any principled concerns that are not fully captured by the risk category analysis.

The principles assessment is particularly useful for identifying concerns that cut across multiple risk categories or that reflect values dimensions the risk framework does not fully capture. A use case that passes individual risk screens but that involves AI making consequential decisions about people without adequate transparency to those people may have no single-category screening failure but may nonetheless fail the transparency and dignity principles in ways governance should address.

Vendor assessment

Substantive screening includes a specific vendor assessment component: a review of the vendor's AI governance practices, documentation, and contractual terms. The detailed vendor assessment framework is described in Chapter 11; the intake process includes a preliminary version of that assessment sufficient to inform the intake decision, with a more comprehensive vendor review conducted separately when the use case involves a new vendor relationship.

The intake vendor assessment should cover at minimum: whether the vendor provides adequate documentation of system performance including performance across demographic groups; whether the vendor's data handling practices are consistent with the institution's legal obligations; whether the proposed contract includes audit rights, breach notification obligations, adequate exit provisions, and appropriate liability terms; and whether the vendor's AI governance practices give the institution reasonable confidence in the system's ongoing reliability and the vendor's responsiveness to governance concerns.

Oversight adequacy assessment

Substantive screening should assess whether the human oversight arrangements proposed for the use case are adequate for its risk level. The detailed oversight design framework is described in Chapter 13; the intake assessment considers whether oversight is present, whether it is designed for genuine rather than nominal independence, and whether it is proportionate to the stakes of the decisions or outputs the AI system produces.

For high-risk use cases, oversight adequacy assessment should specifically examine: whether human reviewers will form independent assessments before reviewing AI outputs or will be anchored to AI recommendations; whether override mechanisms exist and are designed to be practically accessible; whether the volume of AI outputs to be reviewed is consistent with genuine review within operational constraints; and whether escalation pathways are clear and accessible.

Stage four: the governance decision

After substantive screening is complete, the governance team makes a decision on the proposed use case. There are four possible outcomes.

Approval

A use case is approved when screening finds that its risk profile is acceptable, its proposed oversight arrangements are adequate, its vendor and contractual provisions are sufficient, and it is consistent with the institution's principles. Approval should be documented with specific findings — what the review assessed, what it found, and why the use case is considered acceptable — not merely a notation that the use case was reviewed and approved.

Approval should also note any monitoring requirements specific to this use case: what performance indicators will be tracked, how frequently, and by whom. The inventory entry for the approved use case should be created at the time of approval, incorporating the information from the intake form and the screening findings.

Conditional approval

Many use cases that are acceptable in principle require modifications, additional safeguards, or specific conditions before they can be approved. Conditional approval is the appropriate outcome when the governance team finds that the use case can proceed but only with specific changes from what was proposed.

Conditions should be specific and actionable. A condition that says "oversight must be adequate" is not enforceable. A condition that says "AI outputs must be reviewed by a licensed clinician before being incorporated into patient records, and override decisions must be documented in the clinical record" is specific enough to be monitored and enforced.

The governance team should establish a process for confirming that conditions have been met before the use case goes live. Conditional approval that the operational function treats as unconditional — implementing the AI system without meeting the specified conditions — is a governance failure. Confirmation that conditions have been met should be a formal step in the process, with the inventory entry updated to reflect that conditions were specified and subsequently confirmed.

Declined with guidance

A use case is declined when screening finds that its risk profile is unacceptable and cannot be remedied through conditions, when proposed oversight arrangements are fundamentally inadequate, when vendor documentation or contractual terms are insufficient and cannot be adequately remediated, or when the use case raises principled concerns that outweigh its anticipated benefits.

Declining a use case is not a permanent prohibition. It is a determination that the use case as proposed is not acceptable — which may change if the submitter can address the concerns that prompted the decline. Declined use cases should therefore receive specific guidance: what concerns led to the decline, what would need to change for the use case to be reconsidered, and what the process is for resubmission.

Decline guidance should be constructive rather than simply prohibitive. The governance function's goal is responsible AI use, not restriction of AI use. A governance team that declines without explanation, or that declines proposals that could be made acceptable through modification, is not serving the institution's interests; it is creating adversarial relationships between governance and operational functions that will undermine governance effectiveness over time.

Deferred for further information

Sometimes substantive screening cannot be completed because insufficient information is available — the vendor has not provided adequate documentation, legal review has not been completed, or questions raised during screening require answers from the submitter. Deferral is appropriate when the information needed to make a sound governance decision is not yet available and can be obtained within a reasonable timeframe.

Deferred use cases should have a specific list of outstanding information needs, a timeline for providing them, and a scheduled governance team review once they are available. Deferral should not become a default outcome that allows difficult cases to be set aside indefinitely; the governance coordinator should actively manage deferred cases to ensure they resolve.

Stage five: documentation

Every intake review should produce a governance record — documentation that preserves the information considered, the assessment conducted, and the decision made. This documentation serves multiple governance purposes: it supports accountability, enables institutional learning, provides the audit trail that regulatory compliance may require, and protects the institution when governance decisions are later questioned.

The governance record for an intake review should include the original intake form as submitted, any supplementary information provided during the review process, notes from the substantive screening — what each risk category assessment found, what the principles assessment concluded, what the vendor assessment revealed — the governance decision with specific findings, and any conditions attached to approval or guidance provided with a decline. The record should be signed or authenticated by the governance team members who participated in the decision.

The governance record should be stored in the governance function's documentation system and linked to the corresponding inventory entry. It should be treated as a confidential institutional record — not publicly available but accessible to governance team members, legal counsel, and authorized oversight parties.

Process design for different risk levels

The five-stage process described above applies across all risk levels, but its implementation varies significantly between a low-risk fast-track review and a high-risk intensive review. The following describes the key differences.

Low-risk review

For low-risk use cases that meet fast-track criteria, the intake process can be completed by the AI governance coordinator and one or two governance team members — typically the legal representative and the IT security representative — without convening a full governance team meeting. The review focuses on confirming that the use case meets the criteria for low-risk classification, that the vendor's data handling practices are adequate, and that the proposed oversight arrangements are appropriate. Decision turnaround should be within five to seven business days of a complete submission.

Medium-risk review

Medium-risk use cases require full governance team review, including all core members. The substantive screening should be conducted by a subgroup — the AI governance coordinator coordinating contributions from legal, IT, and the relevant operations representative — with findings presented to the full team for decision. Legal review should be completed before the governance team meeting. Decision turnaround should be within two to three weeks of a complete submission.

High-risk review

High-risk use cases require the most intensive review process. In addition to full governance team engagement, high-risk reviews should involve relevant domain expertise — clinical leadership for healthcare AI, educational leadership for student-facing AI, social work leadership for client-affecting AI — and may require external consultation when the governance team lacks sufficient expertise in the specific risk domain. Legal review should be comprehensive, including review of vendor contracts and assessment of regulatory implications. The vendor assessment may require direct engagement with the vendor rather than documentation review only.

High-risk reviews may also require staged approval — conditional approval of a pilot deployment with defined evaluation criteria, before full deployment is approved. This staged approach allows high-risk use cases to build the evidence base for full approval while limiting risk during the initial phase. The pilot conditions should specify what the evaluation will assess, what evidence will support full deployment approval, and what would trigger discontinuation rather than expansion.

Decision turnaround for high-risk use cases should be within three to four weeks of a complete submission, with the possibility of extension when external consultation or additional vendor information is needed.

Handling pressure to bypass intake

In practice, the intake process will face pressure to be bypassed. Operational leaders who have identified a useful tool will want to move quickly. Vendors who have relationships with institutional leaders will seek to create deployment facts before governance review occurs. External events — a public health emergency, a competitive pressure, a funder requirement — will be cited as reasons why normal governance processes should not apply.

Some of this pressure reflects legitimate operational needs and should be addressed through well-designed expedited processes rather than governance circumvention. An expedited track that can produce a governance decision within days for time-sensitive cases, rather than weeks, removes much of the operational argument for bypassing review.

But some of this pressure reflects a simple preference for moving without governance scrutiny, dressed in operational language. The governance response to that pressure requires institutional backbone — the willingness of governance team members, and particularly governance team leadership, to hold the line on intake requirements even when that holding is uncomfortable.

Several practices support that backbone. First, leadership commitment to the intake process must be genuine and visible: leaders who personally comply with intake requirements, who support the governance team when it applies requirements to their functions, and who do not create special pathways for politically favored use cases send a message that intake is not optional. Second, the intake process must be efficient enough that compliance is not unreasonably burdensome. Third, the consequences of bypassing intake must be real: use cases that proceed without review should be identified through monitoring and should trigger a retrospective review, with appropriate consequences for the bypass.

The governance function that enforces intake requirements consistently — even under pressure, even for powerful stakeholders, even when it creates friction — is a governance function that is actually governing. The function that grants exceptions whenever they are requested is not governing; it is performing governance while achieving few of its purposes.

Intake for AI already in use

A specific intake challenge arises for AI systems that are already in use when the governance framework is established or when the inventory exercise reveals informal AI adoption that preceded governance. These systems are deployed, embedded in workflows, and actively depended on; they cannot simply be treated as new proposals.

The governance response to already-deployed AI that has not gone through intake review is a retrospective screening process: applying the intake framework to existing use cases to assess their risk profiles, identify governance gaps in their current operation, and establish the monitoring and oversight arrangements they should have had from the start.

Retrospective screening should be prioritized by risk level: high-risk systems should be reviewed first, medium-risk systems next, and low-risk systems last. The retrospective review follows the same substantive screening process as a prospective review, with the addition of an assessment of how the system has actually performed in operation — whether any incidents have occurred, what monitoring data exists, and what the operational experience reveals about the system's behavior in the institution's specific context.

Retrospective screening may find that some already-deployed systems should be modified, have conditions applied to their continued use, or in serious cases be discontinued. The governance team should approach these findings with a combination of firmness about governance requirements and sensitivity to operational disruption — particularly for systems that have become embedded in critical workflows. The goal is not to create operational crises but to ensure that all institutional AI use meets adequate governance standards, which may require transition periods and staged changes for systems with significant operational dependencies.

Connecting intake to the broader governance system

The intake process does not exist in isolation. It connects to every other component of the governance framework, and those connections should be explicit and maintained.

The intake process connects to the AI inventory: every approved use case creates an inventory entry, and the inventory record includes the intake findings. The intake process connects to vendor management: the vendor assessment component of intake feeds into the broader vendor relationship and the vendor questionnaire process described in Chapter 11. The intake process connects to testing and deployment: intake approval establishes the conditions that pre-deployment testing must validate and that deployment must honor. The intake process connects to monitoring: the oversight requirements and monitoring commitments established at intake become the baseline against which ongoing monitoring is conducted. And the intake process connects to incident response: the governance record from intake provides the context needed to understand and respond to incidents involving approved systems.

These connections are what make governance a system rather than a collection of independent processes. The intake process, well-designed and rigorously applied, is the entry point to a governance lifecycle that continues through the full arc of each AI system's use in the institution.

Chapter 11: Procurement and Vendor Review

The vendor relationship as governance relationship

When an institution uses an AI system provided by a vendor — which describes the overwhelming majority of institutional AI deployments — it enters a relationship that is simultaneously commercial, operational, legal, and ethical. The commercial dimension is familiar: the institution is purchasing a product or service and expects value in exchange for payment. The operational dimension is familiar too: the system needs to work reliably, integrate with existing workflows, and be supported when problems arise.

The legal and ethical dimensions are less familiar to most procurement processes, and they are where AI vendor relationships differ most significantly from conventional technology procurement. The institution that uses a vendor's AI system to make or influence decisions about the people it serves is not merely purchasing software. It is deploying a system that will affect real people in potentially consequential ways, under conditions the institution does not fully control, using a process the institution may not fully understand, with accountability that the institution cannot fully transfer regardless of what the vendor contract says.

This governance reality demands a procurement approach that goes substantially beyond standard technology vendor assessment. It requires asking questions that vendors may not be accustomed to answering, evaluating documentation that vendors may not routinely provide, negotiating contract provisions that vendor standard terms typically omit, and maintaining vendor relationships with ongoing governance engagement that most procurement frameworks do not contemplate.

This chapter describes that approach in full. It covers the vendor assessment process, the questions that assessment should ask, the red flags that should give institutions pause, the contract provisions that governance requires, and the ongoing vendor relationship management that responsible AI deployment demands. It is written for the people who do this work — procurement staff, legal counsel, governance team members, and operational leaders — and for the institutional leaders who need to understand what responsible AI procurement requires of their organizations.

The vendor assessment process: overview and timing

Vendor assessment for AI should occur at three points: during the selection process before a vendor is chosen, during contract negotiation before commitments are made, and on an ongoing basis throughout the vendor relationship. Each assessment point has a different purpose, involves different questions, and requires different institutional actors.

Pre-selection assessment — conducted when the institution is evaluating multiple vendors or assessing a proposed vendor before committing to engagement — focuses on whether a vendor's AI system is appropriate for the institution's use case and whether the vendor's governance practices are adequate. This is the stage at which the institution has the most leverage: it can choose not to proceed with a vendor whose documentation, practices, or responses to governance questions are unsatisfactory.

Pre-contract assessment — conducted during contract negotiation — focuses on whether the proposed contractual terms adequately protect the institution's governance interests. It involves legal review of vendor standard terms, negotiation of additional provisions, and confirmation that the contract reflects the governance commitments the vendor made during selection.

Ongoing assessment — conducted throughout the vendor relationship — focuses on whether the vendor is meeting its contractual and governance commitments, whether the AI system continues to perform as represented, and whether changes in the vendor's practices or system require governance reassessment. This ongoing engagement is what distinguishes a managed vendor relationship from a passive one.

Pre-selection assessment: what to ask and why

The pre-selection vendor assessment should be conducted through a combination of documentation review and direct engagement with vendor representatives. The vendor questionnaire in Chapter 26 provides a complete instrument for this assessment; this section explains the substantive questions the assessment should address and why each matters.

AI system performance and validation

The foundational governance question for any AI vendor is: how well does the system actually perform, and how do you know? Vendor marketing materials answer this question with impressive numbers — accuracy rates, efficiency gains, user satisfaction scores — that are typically derived from testing conditions chosen to present the system favorably. The governance assessment needs to go behind the marketing to understand what performance actually means in conditions relevant to the institution's use case.

Ask for documented performance metrics on evaluation data that resembles the institution's deployment context. A hiring AI vendor's accuracy data collected on a general evaluation set may not reflect how the system performs on candidates from the institution's actual applicant pool. A clinical AI vendor's diagnostic accuracy data collected at large academic medical centers may not reflect how the system performs in a community health setting. Ask specifically whether the vendor has conducted performance testing on data similar in composition and characteristics to the institution's own data, and if so, what those results showed.

Ask how performance was measured. Accuracy, precision, recall, and similar metrics all measure something real, but they measure different things, and the choice among them can materially affect how impressive the numbers look. A vendor that reports a 95% accuracy rate for a classification system is not necessarily providing as much information as it appears to, because the relevant question is not only how often the system is right overall but how often it is wrong in ways that matter — specifically, how often it produces false positives and false negatives in the institution's use case, and what the consequences of each type of error are.

Ask about performance across demographic groups. Chapter 3 established why this matters: AI systems trained on historical data frequently perform differently across racial, ethnic, gender, age, and disability groups in ways that translate into discriminatory outcomes. Ask the vendor specifically whether differential performance testing was conducted, what groups were assessed, what methods were used, and what the results were. A vendor that responds with generic assurances rather than specific documentation does not have adequate bias assessment to offer — which is itself a significant governance concern.

Ask about performance over time. AI systems can perform differently as the population they serve changes, as data patterns shift, as model updates are applied, or as the gap widens between training data and current deployment conditions. Ask how performance is monitored after deployment, whether the vendor provides performance reporting to customers, and what the vendor's practice is when post-deployment performance monitoring reveals a decline.

Data governance practices

Institutional AI systems process data — often large volumes of data, often including personal information about the people the institution serves. Understanding the vendor's data governance practices is not optional; it is a legal and ethical requirement for responsible procurement.

Ask what data the system collects from users and institutional inputs. The answer should cover both the information that users explicitly provide and any information the system collects passively — usage patterns, interaction logs, metadata, derived inferences. Systems that collect more than users are aware of create privacy risks that governance must address.

Ask what happens to institutional data after it enters the vendor's system. Does it stay within the vendor's system, or is it transmitted to third parties — subprocessors, cloud infrastructure providers, analytics partners? If it is transmitted, under what conditions, with what protections, and with what notification to the institution? AI vendor ecosystems are frequently complex, involving multiple layers of service providers; institutional data may travel farther and reach more parties than the primary vendor relationship suggests.

Ask explicitly whether institutional data is used to train or improve the AI model. This question is among the most consequential in AI vendor assessment, and the answer is often not what institutions expect. Many AI vendors include provisions in their standard terms that allow them to use customer data to improve their models; many customers sign these terms without understanding what they authorize. Ask whether the institution's data will be used for model training, under what conditions, whether that use can be opted out of, and what happens to institutional data that has already been used for training if the institution later requests its deletion.

Ask about the vendor's data retention and deletion practices. How long is institutional data retained? What triggers deletion? When the contract ends, what happens to institutional data in the vendor's systems? These questions are particularly important for institutions with obligations under data protection laws that include rights to data deletion — an institution that cannot ensure deletion of data in a vendor's systems may be unable to honor data subject rights.

Ask about the vendor's security practices for institutional data. What encryption is applied to data in transit and at rest? Who within the vendor organization has access to institutional data? What access controls and audit logging are in place? What is the vendor's history of data security incidents? Chapter 7's security principle requires that vendor security be assessed as an extension of the institution's own security posture.

Transparency and explainability

A vendor's willingness to provide information about how their AI system works is itself a governance indicator. Vendors that are forthcoming with documentation, that can explain their systems at multiple levels of technical and conceptual detail, and that respond constructively to governance questions are demonstrating the kind of partnership that responsible AI deployment requires. Vendors that are evasive, that respond to technical questions with marketing language, or that treat governance inquiries as obstacles are demonstrating something different.

Ask for documentation of how the AI system works. This documentation need not be proprietary technical specifications — which vendors legitimately protect as intellectual property — but should include enough description of the system's approach to allow governance assessment. What type of model does the system use? What data was it trained on, at what point in time, from what sources? What features does it use to produce outputs? What are its known limitations? This information does not require disclosure of proprietary architecture; it requires the kind of explanation that a thoughtful vendor should be able to provide to any customer using the system in a consequential context.

Ask what explainability capabilities the system provides. When the system produces an output — a recommendation, a classification, a risk score — can it explain the basis for that output in terms that are meaningful to the staff who will use it and to the people it affects? Explainability matters for governance because it affects the institution's ability to audit outputs for bias, to explain decisions to affected parties, and to fulfill due process obligations that may apply. A system that cannot explain its outputs cannot be adequately overseen.

Ask about the vendor's approach to system changes. When the underlying AI model is updated — retrained on new data, modified to improve performance, changed in response to identified problems — is the institution notified? What notice period is provided? What testing is conducted before updates are deployed? Does the institution have any control over whether and when updates are applied? Model updates can materially change system behavior, including introducing new performance disparities or changing the accuracy of outputs in ways that affect the institution's governance arrangements. Vendor change management practices are a governance matter, not only an operational one.

Governance and accountability practices

Ask what governance practices the vendor itself has for the AI systems it provides. Does the vendor have its own responsible AI principles, and can it demonstrate how those principles are implemented in practice rather than merely stated? Does the vendor conduct ongoing monitoring of deployed systems for bias and performance issues? Does the vendor have processes for receiving and responding to customer concerns about

AI system behavior? Does the vendor have an incident response process for AI-related problems?

Ask about the vendor's history with the AI system. Have there been significant performance failures, bias findings, or regulatory actions related to this system? How were they addressed? What changes were made? A vendor with a history of AI-related problems that was addressed responsibly — with transparent disclosure, genuine remediation, and demonstrable learning — may be a better governance partner than a vendor with a spotless record achieved by avoiding scrutiny rather than managing it well.

Ask how the vendor handles customer concerns about AI system performance. Is there a designated channel for governance-related inquiries? What is the vendor's commitment to response time? Who within the vendor organization is responsible for governance-related customer engagement? A vendor whose governance engagement is routed through a general support queue with no specialized capacity is not adequately organized for the governance partnership that responsible AI deployment requires.

Red flags: when to proceed with caution or not at all

Pre-selection assessment will surface information that ranges from reassuring to concerning. The following red flags should give governance teams serious pause — they do not necessarily preclude proceeding with a vendor, but each warrants careful attention and in many cases should trigger either negotiated remediation or a reconsideration of the vendor relationship.

Inability to provide bias testing documentation

A vendor that cannot or will not provide specific documentation of how their AI system performs across demographic groups has not conducted adequate bias testing, is unwilling to share results that may be unfavorable, or does not understand why this documentation matters. All three possibilities are governance concerns. The absence of bias testing documentation does not mean the system is biased; it means the institution cannot know whether it is, which is itself unacceptable for use cases that affect people in consequential ways.

The appropriate response to this red flag is to require specific documentation as a condition of proceeding. If the vendor cannot provide it within a reasonable timeframe, the governance team should treat the absence as a material deficiency and consider whether the use case can proceed at all without this information, or whether alternative vendors with better documentation are available.

Contractual refusal to allow audit

Vendors whose standard contracts include provisions that prohibit customer audits — direct assessments of AI system performance using the institution's own data and methods — are declining the kind of independent verification that governance requires. Vendor-provided performance documentation is necessary but not sufficient; governance that relies entirely on vendor self-reporting is not independent governance.

Audit rights do not require access to proprietary model architecture or training data. They require the ability for the institution to test system performance on relevant inputs and to assess whether outputs are consistent with the system's documented characteristics. A vendor that cannot accommodate this level of independent assessment should be approached with significant caution.

Broad data use rights in standard terms

Vendor standard contracts that include broad rights to use institutional data for model training or other vendor purposes — particularly rights that are difficult to opt out of, that apply retroactively to data already submitted, or that persist after contract termination — are incompatible with responsible governance of personal information. These provisions may appear in boilerplate terms as standard conditions the vendor presents as non-negotiable.

They are not non-negotiable for vendors who want institutional business and who are committed to responsible data practices. Institutions should require that data use rights be limited to what is necessary for service delivery, that model training use of institutional data require explicit opt-in consent, and that data submitted during the contract period be deleted or returned upon termination. Vendors who refuse these requirements after good-faith negotiation are demonstrating that their data practices are more important to them than customer governance requirements — which is itself a significant indicator.

No breach notification commitment

A vendor that will not commit to timely notification of security incidents affecting institutional data is a vendor that has either not thought seriously about its incident response obligations or is unwilling to accept accountability for them. Data breach notification is a legal requirement in most jurisdictions and an ethical obligation in all of them. A vendor contract that includes no breach notification provision, or that defines breach notification in terms so narrow as to be practically meaningless, is inadequate.

The red flag here is not that the vendor has a narrow definition of breach in its standard terms — that is common and expected. The red flag is a vendor that is unwilling to negotiate notification provisions that meet the institution's legal requirements and governance needs, which suggests a vendor that does not prioritize customer notification or that is concerned about its breach history.

Inadequate exit provisions

A vendor whose contract includes inadequate exit provisions — long notice periods for termination, no data portability commitments, provisions that make termination financially prohibitive except at contract expiration, or automatic renewal clauses that extend lock-in — is a vendor whose business interests conflict with the institution's governance interests. The ability to exit a vendor relationship when it is no longer appropriate is a governance requirement; a contract that makes exit prohibitively difficult is a contract that constrains governance.

Inadequate exit provisions are particularly concerning for AI systems that become deeply integrated into operational workflows, because the operational cost of exit grows with integration depth. The time to negotiate exit provisions is before integration occurs; after the system is embedded, the vendor's leverage is substantially higher.

Claims that their AI has been "audited" or "certified" as unbiased

Vendors that present certifications, audits, or claims of AI bias-free status as a substitute for specific performance documentation on demographic groups are using language that does not mean what customers may assume it means. No AI certification scheme currently provides the kind of comprehensive, context-specific bias assurance that institutional governance requires. A certification that a system meets certain technical specifications is not a certification that it produces fair outcomes in a specific deployment context. Governance teams should ask what specifically any claimed certification covers, what it does not cover, who conducted it, and what the methodology was.

This is not a red flag that should result in automatic disqualification — certifications may provide useful information even when their scope is limited. The red flag is a vendor that presents certification as a complete answer to bias concerns rather than one data point among several.

Dismissiveness toward governance questions

A vendor whose representatives respond to governance questions with impatience, condescension, or deflection — who treat governance inquiry as an obstacle to deal closure rather than a legitimate exercise of institutional responsibility — is a vendor that does not understand or prioritize the governance relationship that responsible AI deployment requires. This behavioral red flag is sometimes as informative as any specific documentation concern, because it reveals how the vendor will respond to governance concerns that arise during the relationship, not only during procurement.

Contract provisions: what governance requires

The AI vendor contract is the primary mechanism through which the institution's governance interests are protected in the vendor relationship.

Vendor standard contracts are designed to protect vendor interests; they need to be modified through negotiation to reflect institutional governance requirements. The following provisions are essential for AI vendor contracts; institutions should treat their absence from standard terms as a starting point for negotiation, not acceptance.

Performance standards and testing rights

The contract should specify performance standards for the AI system — not the vendor's general capability claims but specific, measurable performance commitments relevant to the institution's use case. These standards should address accuracy, reliability, availability, and where applicable performance across demographic groups.

Performance standards are only meaningful if they are measurable, and measuring them requires testing rights. The contract should give the institution the right to test system performance using its own data and methods, at reasonable frequency and with reasonable notice. It should also specify what happens when testing reveals that performance does not meet contracted standards — what remediation the vendor is obligated to provide, on what timeline, and what remedies are available to the institution if remediation is not achieved.

Testing rights should also cover the right to assess system performance after vendor updates. When a vendor updates the underlying AI model, the institution should be able to test whether performance characteristics have changed in ways that affect the governance assessment that supported original approval.

Data handling and processing

The contract must specify precisely what the vendor may do with institutional data. The specification should cover: what data the vendor collects, what processing is performed, where data is stored and in what jurisdictions, who may access it, under what conditions it may be transmitted to third parties, whether and under what conditions it may be used for model training or other purposes beyond service delivery, how long it is retained, and how it is deleted.

These provisions need to be consistent with the institution's legal obligations under applicable data protection law. In many jurisdictions, certain categories of personal data — health information, information about minors, sensitive personal characteristics — require specific contractual protections. Legal counsel should review data handling provisions specifically for compliance with applicable law, not only for general adequacy.

The contract should include a requirement that the vendor notify the institution before making material changes to its data handling practices — changes to subprocessors, changes to data location, changes to retention policies — with sufficient notice to allow the institution to assess the implications and if necessary seek alternative arrangements.

Audit rights

The contract should include explicit audit rights: the institution's right to conduct, or commission a third party to conduct, an assessment of the AI system's performance using the institution's own data and methods. Audit rights should specify the frequency with which audits may be conducted, the notice the institution must provide, the vendor's obligations in supporting the audit, and how audit findings are handled.

Audit rights should be broad enough to support meaningful governance oversight without being so broad as to be impractical. A right to conduct audits once per year, with 30 days' notice, using the institution's own test data, with the vendor providing reasonable technical assistance, is a practical and meaningful audit right. A right to audit that requires the vendor's prior approval for each audit, that limits audit scope to conditions of the vendor's choosing, or that gives the vendor control over audit methodology is not an audit right; it is the appearance of one.

Breach notification

The contract should specify the vendor's obligations when a security incident occurs that may have affected institutional data. Notification provisions should specify: what counts as a notifiable incident (the definition should be broad enough to capture the incidents the institution needs to know about), the timeline within which notification must be provided (typically 24 to 72 hours from the vendor's discovery of the incident), what information the notification must include, and what the vendor's obligations are for cooperating with the institution's incident response.

Breach notification provisions should meet or exceed the notification timeline the institution is legally required to provide to its own regulators and affected individuals. An institution that learns about a vendor data breach 30 days after it occurred, under a contract that allowed the vendor that long to notify, cannot meet a 72-hour regulatory notification requirement.

Liability and indemnification

The contract's liability and indemnification provisions determine who bears the financial consequences of AI system failures that cause harm. Vendor standard contracts typically include extensive liability limitations — caps on total liability, exclusions for consequential damages, disclaimers of all warranty for AI performance — that leave the institution bearing most of the risk.

The appropriate allocation of liability in AI vendor contracts is a legal question that counsel must assess in the specific institutional context. However, governance teams should understand the baseline risk allocation in vendor standard terms and should resist provisions that are entirely one-sided. A vendor that accepts no liability whatsoever for its AI system's performance — no matter how badly it performs, no matter what harm results — is a vendor whose incentives for ensuring system quality are exclusively reputational rather than financial. While liability allocation in AI contracts remains an evolving area, institutions should seek provisions that create at least some financial consequences for the vendor when systems fail to perform as represented or when vendor data governance failures cause harm.

Model change notification

The contract should require the vendor to notify the institution before making material changes to the underlying AI model. The definition of "material" should be specified: changes that affect system accuracy by more than a defined threshold, changes that affect performance across demographic groups, changes that affect what data the system processes or how it handles data, and changes to the system's capabilities or limitations.

Notification provisions should allow the institution sufficient time to assess whether the change affects the governance approval that supports current use — and if necessary to conduct testing, adjust oversight arrangements, or in extreme cases seek alternative solutions before the change takes effect. A notification period of 30 to 60 days before material model changes are deployed allows adequate governance response time for most institutions.

Termination and data return

The contract should specify the institution's right to terminate the relationship — with cause when the vendor fails to meet its obligations, and for convenience with reasonable notice. Termination for cause should be triggered by material and uncured performance failures, material breaches of data handling obligations, and situations where the AI system is found to be causing harm that the vendor refuses to remediate.

Upon termination, the contract should require the vendor to return institutional data in a usable format, to certify the deletion of institutional data from vendor systems, and to provide reasonable transition support to allow the institution to move to an alternative solution. The data return and deletion obligations should have a defined timeline and should not be conditioned on the institution's payment of additional fees.

Subprocessor management

Most AI vendors use subprocessors — third-party providers of cloud infrastructure, data analytics, security, and other services — that may have access to institutional data. The contract should require the vendor to disclose all subprocessors that will have access to institutional data, to impose equivalent data protection obligations on those subprocessors, to notify the institution before adding new subprocessors, and to give the institution the right to object to new subprocessors whose addition would create governance concerns.

Subprocessor management is frequently overlooked in AI vendor procurement, because the institutional relationship is with the primary vendor rather than with subprocessors. But the institution's data protection obligations extend to all parties that handle its data, and the contract should create a clear chain of accountability from the institution through the vendor to any subprocessors.

Contract negotiation: practical considerations

Understanding what contract provisions governance requires is one thing; negotiating to include them is another. Several practical considerations shape how AI vendor contract negotiation actually works.

Negotiating leverage and its limits

The institution's ability to negotiate favorable contract terms depends substantially on its leverage — which is primarily determined by the size and significance of the contract, the competitiveness of the vendor market for the specific AI capability, and the vendor's assessment of the institutional relationship's strategic value. Large institutions entering significant contracts with vendors for whom the relationship is commercially important have substantial negotiating leverage. Small institutions entering modest contracts with dominant vendors have limited leverage.

This reality does not mean small institutions should accept inadequate contract terms. It means they should understand which contract provisions are most essential for their governance requirements and focus negotiating effort there, rather than seeking perfection across all provisions. The essential provisions — data handling limitations, breach notification, termination rights, data return on termination — matter more than every possible governance-favorable provision. Prioritization is realistic; complete capitulation is not.

Some contract provisions that vendors present as standard and non-negotiable are in fact negotiable for customers who ask persistently and specifically. Many vendors have modified standard data use provisions for institutional customers who raised specific concerns; many have added breach notification provisions that were absent from standard terms; many have accepted audit rights provisions when customers requested them clearly and specifically. "This is our standard contract" is not always the end of negotiation; it is frequently the beginning of it.

Involving legal counsel appropriately

Legal counsel should be involved in AI vendor contract review and negotiation, but the nature of that involvement requires attention. General counsel who are experienced in commercial contracts may not have specific AI contract expertise; they may focus on familiar commercial law provisions and miss AI-specific governance provisions that are equally or more important. Institutions should either ensure their legal counsel is specifically briefed on AI governance contract requirements or seek counsel with AI contract experience.

Legal review should focus not only on whether individual provisions are legally adequate but on how the contract's provisions work together to create a governance framework. A contract whose individual provisions are each unobjectionable but that together create conditions of vendor opacity and institutional accountability without vendor accountability is not an adequate governance document. The totality of the contractual arrangement matters, not only the specific provisions.

Documenting negotiation outcomes

The negotiation process should be documented. When the institution requests specific provisions and the vendor accepts, modifies, or refuses, that exchange should be recorded. When provisions are removed, modified, or added from standard terms, the changes and the reasons for them should be documented. This documentation matters if disputes about contract interpretation arise later, and it also informs the institution's ongoing vendor risk assessment — knowledge of what the vendor accepted and refused in negotiation is relevant to assessing the vendor's governance orientation.

Ongoing vendor relationship management

Signing a contract with adequate provisions is not the end of vendor governance; it is the beginning of a relationship that requires active management. Several ongoing vendor management practices are essential to AI governance.

Regular performance review

Institutional governance does not relax after a vendor contract is signed. The governance team or its designated members should conduct regular reviews of vendor AI system performance — assessing whether the system continues to meet the performance standards contracted for, whether monitoring data reveals any patterns of concern, and whether any incidents have occurred that require vendor engagement.

For high-risk AI systems, performance review should occur at least quarterly. For medium-risk systems, semi-annual review is typically adequate. For low-risk systems, annual review in connection with the broader AI inventory review is generally sufficient. These reviews should be documented and should trigger escalation when performance concerns are identified.

Monitoring vendor communications

Vendors communicate with customers through release notes, product updates, terms of service changes, privacy policy updates, and various other channels. AI governance requires that someone in the institution is actually reading these communications and assessing their governance implications. A vendor that adds new AI features, changes data processing practices, updates subprocessor lists, or modifies AI model behavior through a product update has communicated a material governance-relevant change; missing that communication is a governance failure.

The AI governance coordinator or IT function should be designated to receive and review vendor communications related to AI systems in the institution's inventory, with a process for escalating communications that have governance implications to the governance team.

Exercising audit rights

Audit rights that are contracted for but never exercised are not governance; they are the theoretical possibility of governance. Institutions should plan to exercise audit rights at reasonable intervals — not necessarily annually for every system, but at least when there is specific reason to verify performance, when the vendor has made material system changes, or when monitoring data suggests performance concerns.

Audits should be planned and conducted by people with the relevant technical and domain expertise to assess what the audit reveals. An audit that consists of reviewing vendor-provided documentation is not an independent audit; it is documentation review. A meaningful audit tests system performance on the institution's own data using the institution's own methods or those of an independent assessor.

Managing vendor relationship escalation

When governance concerns arise in a vendor relationship — performance that falls below contracted standards, data handling practices that raise questions, system changes that were not adequately notified, or responses to institutional concerns that are inadequate — the institution needs a defined process for escalating and managing those concerns.

Escalation should move from operational contact to vendor account management to vendor leadership as concerns remain unresolved. The institution's procurement and legal functions should be engaged when concerns reach a level of seriousness that may require formal notice of breach, contract remedies, or transition planning. Governance escalation processes should be defined in advance rather than improvised when concerns arise.

Contract renewal as governance checkpoint

Contract renewal is one of the most important governance checkpoints in the vendor relationship lifecycle. At renewal, the institution has maximum leverage — the threat of non-renewal — and the opportunity to reassess both the vendor relationship and the contractual terms. The governance team should treat contract renewal not as an administrative formality but as a substantive governance review: has the vendor met its contractual commitments? Has system performance been adequate? Are the contractual provisions still appropriate given current governance requirements? Are the data handling, notification, and exit provisions still adequate given current legal requirements and the institution's governance framework?

Renewal should not be automatic. It should require a positive governance determination that continued use is appropriate and that contract terms remain adequate. Contracts that auto-renew without governance review are not subject to governance at renewal — they are subject to inertia.

Special considerations for different vendor types

AI vendor relationships vary significantly by the type of vendor and the nature of the AI system being provided. Several vendor types require governance approaches with specific adaptations.

Large enterprise AI platform providers

The largest AI platform vendors — providers of foundation models, AI development platforms, and AI-integrated enterprise software suites — typically operate at a scale that gives them significant negotiating leverage relative to most institutional customers. Their standard contracts may be difficult or impossible to modify in many provisions; their data handling practices may be governed by platform-wide policies rather than customer-specific contracts.

Governance of relationships with large platform vendors requires realistic assessment of what can and cannot be negotiated, and compensating governance measures where contractual provisions cannot be made adequate. If a large platform vendor's terms permit data use for model training and this cannot be negotiated out, the governance response may be to limit what data is entered into the platform rather than accepting unrestricted data flow. If audit rights cannot be contractually obtained, the governance response may be to rely on third-party assessments of the platform's performance rather than independent institutional audits.

Institutions should be clear-eyed about what governance they can actually maintain with large platform vendors and should factor that assessment into decisions about which use cases are appropriate for those platforms. High-risk use cases that require robust audit rights and stringent data handling commitments may not be appropriate for platforms whose standard terms do not support those governance requirements.

Niche and specialized AI vendors

Smaller, specialized AI vendors — providers of specific clinical AI tools, sector-specific decision support systems, or purpose-built AI applications — typically have more flexibility to negotiate contract terms and more specific documentation of AI system performance in relevant contexts. They also typically present different governance risks: less financial stability, less mature data security practices, greater risk of acquisition by larger companies whose governance practices may differ, and potentially less investment in ongoing AI governance.

Governance of niche vendor relationships should specifically address vendor stability: what happens to the institution's data and the service relationship if the vendor is acquired, goes out of business, or significantly changes its business model? Contract provisions that protect the institution's interests in the event of vendor acquisition or discontinuation — including data portability rights, service continuity commitments, and source code escrow for high-dependency systems — are particularly important for niche vendor relationships.

Vendors providing AI as a component of broader services

Some AI vendor relationships arise not through direct procurement of AI tools but through service relationships where the vendor uses AI in delivering services on the institution's behalf — an outsourced benefits administrator that uses AI in claims processing, a staffing firm that uses AI in candidate screening, a facilities management company that uses AI in maintenance scheduling.

These relationships present a specific governance challenge: the institution may not think of them as AI vendor relationships at all, even though AI is affecting outcomes the institution is responsible for. Governance of service provider AI requires asking, in every significant service relationship, whether the vendor uses AI in performing services for the institution, and if so what AI systems, for what purposes, and with what governance practices.

Service provider contracts should include provisions equivalent to those for direct AI vendor contracts when AI is used in performance of the services — data handling commitments, performance standards for AI components, notification of AI system changes, and the institution's right to assess AI performance as part of service quality review.

Procurement as governance infrastructure

The vendor assessment and contract management practices described in this chapter are governance infrastructure — the institutional capacity that makes it possible to use AI responsibly in a world where most AI capability comes through vendor relationships. Building this infrastructure requires investment: developing procurement staff expertise in AI governance requirements, creating vendor assessment processes that can be applied consistently, building legal expertise in AI contract provisions, and establishing ongoing vendor management practices that extend beyond contract signing.

That investment has a return that is both protective and operational. Institutions with mature AI vendor governance avoid the category of harm that arises from vendor relationships entered without adequate assessment. They have contractual protections that give them recourse when vendor systems fail. They have audit capabilities that allow independent verification of vendor performance claims. And they have vendor relationships that are genuinely governed — where the vendor knows that governance standards will be enforced and responds accordingly.

The institution that treats AI vendor procurement as a governance exercise, not merely a commercial one, is building the foundation for responsible AI use at scale. The institution that treats it as standard technology procurement is accepting risks that standard technology procurement was not designed to manage.

Chapter 12: Data Governance for AI

Data as the substrate of AI governance

Every governance concern addressed in this book has a data dimension. Bias originates in training data. Privacy violations occur when data is mishandled. Safety failures often trace to data quality problems. Hallucination arises partly from gaps and errors in the data on which models were trained. Vendor lock-in is compounded when institutional data is held in formats or systems that make exit difficult. Legal exposure frequently crystallizes around data protection failures. The principles of fairness, transparency, accountability, and human dignity are all compromised when data about people is used in ways they did not anticipate, did not consent to, or cannot understand.

Data governance for AI is not a separate discipline from AI governance; it is AI governance applied specifically to the data dimension of AI systems. It addresses the full lifecycle of data in AI contexts: how data is collected and sourced, how its quality is assessed and maintained, how consent is obtained and honored, who can access it and under what conditions, how long it is retained, how it is deleted, and how sensitive categories of information receive the heightened protection they require.

This chapter addresses each of these dimensions in turn. It is written for the institutional leaders, operations staff, legal counsel, IT professionals, and governance team members who must together manage data governance for AI — people who need to understand not only the technical and legal requirements but the values and practical reasoning that make those requirements necessary.

Why AI creates distinctive data governance challenges

Institutions that have existing data governance frameworks — policies governing how personal information is collected, used, and protected — sometimes assume that those frameworks extend naturally to AI. In many respects they do: the principles of data minimization, purpose limitation, and individual rights apply to AI just as they apply to conventional data processing. But AI creates several data governance challenges that conventional frameworks were not designed to address, and that require specific attention.

Data as a training asset, not only an operational input

In conventional data governance, data is primarily an operational input: information that is processed to produce a service or decision, and then retained for a period consistent with the purpose for which it was collected. In AI contexts, data is also a training asset: a resource whose value extends beyond any individual transaction because it is used to build, improve, and validate AI models.

This additional role creates governance complications. Data collected for one purpose — providing a service, making a decision, recording a transaction — may be subsequently used for a fundamentally different purpose: training an AI model that will be used across a much broader range of contexts. The people whose data is used in training typically did not anticipate this use when they provided their information. Many data protection frameworks restrict the use of personal data to the purposes for which it was originally collected; using operational data for AI training may require fresh assessment of legal basis, fresh consideration of whether affected individuals should be informed, and in some cases fresh consent.

Institutions that develop or customize AI systems using their own data face these questions directly. Institutions that use vendor AI systems face them indirectly: vendor contracts that permit use of customer data for model training are authorizing a use of institutional data — and the personal information it contains — that the institution may not have specifically assessed or that affected individuals may not have anticipated.

Inference and the creation of new sensitive data

Conventional data governance manages the data that institutions explicitly collect. AI systems create new data: inferences drawn from existing data that may be more sensitive than the inputs from which they were derived. A language model that processes a staff member's emails may infer political views, health conditions, or family circumstances that the staff member never disclosed. A predictive model trained on patient encounter data may infer undiagnosed conditions, medication adherence patterns, or social circumstances beyond what any individual record contains.

These inferences are data governance matters even though the institution did not collect the inferred information explicitly. If an AI system produces inferences about individuals that are stored, acted on, or shared, those inferences are personal data subject to the same governance obligations as explicitly collected information — and may be subject to heightened obligations if the inferences fall into sensitive data categories.

Data quality as a governance variable

In conventional data governance, data quality is primarily an operational concern: poor-quality data produces poor operational outcomes, which creates management incentives for quality improvement. In AI contexts, data quality is also a governance variable: the quality of training data determines the quality of model outputs, which determines whether governance commitments to fairness, accuracy, and safety can be met.

A model trained on incomplete, inconsistent, or systematically biased training data will produce outputs that reflect those data quality problems — and the outputs may be difficult to distinguish from outputs produced by a model trained on high-quality data. This means that data quality governance is not only about operational performance; it is about whether the institution can actually honor its commitments to the people AI systems affect.

Data flows in distributed AI systems

Conventional data governance typically addresses data flows within relatively well-defined institutional boundaries. AI deployment often involves complex data flows across multiple parties: the institution, the AI vendor, the vendor's subprocessors, cloud infrastructure providers, and potentially other third parties. Personal data about the people the institution serves may traverse this entire ecosystem in the course of a single AI-assisted transaction — entering the institution's system, being processed by the vendor's AI model, passing through cloud infrastructure, being logged for model improvement purposes, and being retained in multiple locations across multiple parties.

Governing these distributed data flows requires visibility into the entire ecosystem, contractual obligations that extend from the institution to every party in the chain, and monitoring that confirms the flows are operating as governed and not as assumed.

Data quality: the governance foundation

Data quality governance for AI addresses whether the data that AI systems use — both training data and operational data — is accurate, complete, representative, and fit for the purposes to which it is put.

Why data quality is a governance matter

The connection between data quality and governance outcomes is direct. An AI system trained on inaccurate data learns inaccurate patterns. A model trained on incomplete data has blind spots — it performs well on the cases that training data covered and poorly on the cases it did not. A model trained on data that is not representative of the population it will serve performs differently across demographic groups in ways that may be discriminatory in effect.

Data quality problems in training data are particularly insidious because they are embedded in the model rather than present in the data itself. Once a model has been trained, the data quality issues that shaped its behavior are no longer visible in the training data — they are expressed as model outputs that may look plausible and authoritative even when they reflect historical errors, gaps, or biases. Detecting and addressing training data quality problems requires proactive governance before and during training, not only evaluation of model outputs after the fact.

Dimensions of data quality relevant to AI governance

Data quality governance should assess several distinct dimensions that each have specific governance implications.

Accuracy refers to whether data correctly represents the real-world entities and events it describes. Inaccurate data in training sets teaches models incorrect patterns. Inaccurate data in operational inputs produces incorrect model outputs. The consequences of inaccuracy depend on the use case: in a clinical AI system, training data that contains coding errors may produce models that misclassify conditions; in a hiring AI system, training data with incorrect performance ratings may produce models that reward or penalize characteristics that were not actually related to performance.

Completeness refers to whether data includes the full range of information that it purports to represent. Systematic gaps in training data — certain populations underrepresented, certain time periods missing, certain outcome categories not recorded — produce models that have corresponding gaps in their capabilities. A model trained on complete data about some groups and incomplete data about others will perform differently across those groups, producing the differential performance that fairness governance is designed to prevent.

Consistency refers to whether data is recorded in uniform ways across different sources, time periods, and collectors. Inconsistent data — the same entity described differently in different records, the same outcome coded differently across time periods, the same concept measured in incompatible ways across different institutional contexts — creates noise in training data that reduces model performance and may produce outputs that reflect recording inconsistencies rather than real-world patterns.

Currency refers to whether data reflects current conditions rather than outdated patterns. Models trained on historical data reflect historical conditions; when the world has changed significantly, historically trained models may produce outputs that are accurate for a past state but not for the current one. Currency matters particularly in contexts where conditions change rapidly — a fraud detection model trained on pre-pandemic fraud patterns may perform differently in a post-pandemic fraud environment; a clinical risk model trained on pre-treatment-advance data may underestimate risk for conditions that have improved treatment options.

Representativeness refers to whether training data includes adequate representation of the populations, contexts, and conditions the model will encounter in deployment. This dimension is the most directly connected to bias and fairness governance: models trained on non-representative data will perform differently across the underrepresented groups, precisely because the model has less information about those groups to learn from.

Data quality governance practices

Governance teams should require that vendors provide documentation of training data quality assessments — specifically addressing representativeness across relevant demographic groups, accuracy validation methods, and known data quality limitations. This documentation is essential for the bias risk assessment that intake screening requires and for the ongoing monitoring that responsible deployment demands.

For institutions that develop or customize AI systems using their own data, internal data quality governance is directly applicable. Before institutional data is used for AI training, it should be assessed for completeness, accuracy, consistency, and representativeness across relevant groups. Data quality assessments should be documented and should inform decisions about whether the data is adequate for the intended training purpose.

Operational data quality governance — ensuring that inputs to deployed AI systems are accurate and consistent — is equally important. An AI system that produces accurate outputs given high-quality inputs may produce unreliable outputs given degraded or inconsistent inputs. Governance should include processes for monitoring input data quality as part of ongoing AI system oversight.

Data retention: how long is long enough, and when is it too long

Data retention governance for AI addresses how long data — training data, operational data, AI outputs, and audit logs — should be kept before deletion, and what requirements govern the transition from retention to deletion.

The tension at the heart of retention governance

AI data retention governance involves a fundamental tension. Longer retention supports some governance purposes: audit logs that capture AI system decisions over extended periods enable historical analysis of patterns; retained training data supports model validation and retraining; operational data retained over time enables monitoring of performance trends. Longer retention conflicts with other governance purposes: data protection principles of data minimization and storage limitation require that personal data not be retained beyond the period necessary for the purpose for which it was collected; longer retention increases the security risk surface and the consequences of a breach; and the rights of individuals to have their data deleted cannot be honored if data is retained indefinitely.

Resolving this tension requires defining retention periods that are adequate for legitimate governance purposes — including audit, monitoring, and accountability — while meeting legal minimums and the commitments the institution has made to the people whose information it holds.

Retention categories and appropriate periods

AI data governance should distinguish among several categories of data, each with different retention considerations.

Training data used to build or customize AI models presents the most complex retention question. Training data that includes personal information should be retained only as long as needed for model development and validation purposes; once a model has been trained and validated and the training data is no longer needed for those purposes, personal information in training data should be deleted or anonymized. The practical challenge is that model debugging and retraining may require access to training data for extended periods; governance should establish a maximum retention period for personal information in training data that is long enough to support legitimate technical purposes but not indefinite.

Operational inputs — the data that users provide to AI systems in the course of using them — should typically be retained no longer than is necessary for the specific operational purpose the AI system serves. For many use cases, operational inputs need not be retained at all after the AI-assisted task is complete; the task output and any required audit log can be retained without retaining the specific inputs. When operational inputs do need to be retained — for example, to support audit of AI-assisted decisions — the retention period should be defined by the audit or accountability purpose rather than by default.

AI outputs — the recommendations, classifications, scores, summaries, and other outputs that AI systems produce — should be treated as data governance matters in their own right, not only as technical results. When AI outputs are incorporated into institutional records — clinical records, personnel files, case management records, student files — they become part of those records and are subject to the retention rules that govern them. When AI outputs are used transiently — a draft that is either revised and used or discarded — they may not need to be retained at all. Governance should be specific about which AI outputs are incorporated into records and therefore subject to record retention requirements.

Audit logs — records of AI system activity, including what inputs were processed, what outputs were produced, what decisions were made, and what oversight actions were taken — should be retained for a period consistent with the institution's accountability and audit purposes. For high-risk AI systems, audit log retention should be long enough to support any investigation of alleged discrimination or other harm — typically several years, and in some jurisdictions the applicable statute of limitations period for relevant claims.

Model artifacts — the trained models themselves, including model weights and configuration — are a retention consideration for institutions that develop or customize AI systems. Models may need to be retained for debugging, audit, and regulatory purposes even after they have been replaced by newer versions. However, models that have been replaced should eventually be archived or deleted; indefinite retention of outdated model versions creates security and compliance risk without proportionate governance benefit.

Legal retention requirements

Retention periods must be consistent with applicable legal requirements, which in AI contexts may include both general data protection requirements — which typically require deletion of personal data when it is no longer necessary for the purpose for which it was collected — and sector-specific requirements that mandate retention of records for minimum periods. These requirements may pull in opposite directions: data protection law may require deletion while a sector-specific regulatory framework requires retention.

Resolving these tensions requires legal analysis specific to the institutional context. The resolution typically involves retaining data for the legally required period in a form that limits its use to the purposes that justify retention — audit compliance, regulatory reporting, legal hold — rather than treating retention as authorization for ongoing operational use.

Consent: the foundation of legitimate data use

Consent governance for AI addresses whether the institution has adequate legal and ethical basis for the data uses that AI systems require, and specifically whether individuals whose data is used in AI systems were adequately informed and where necessary gave meaningful consent.

The legal basis question

Data protection law in most jurisdictions requires that personal data be processed on a recognized legal basis — consent, contractual necessity, legal obligation, vital interests, public task, or legitimate interests. The appropriate legal basis for AI processing depends on the specific processing activity, the category of data, and the applicable legal framework.

Consent is not always the appropriate legal basis, and in some contexts it is not available as a basis at all. An institution that processes employee personal data in AI-assisted HR systems cannot typically rely on employee consent as its legal basis because employee consent is not freely given — employees cannot realistically refuse to consent to data processing by their employer without risking their employment. Healthcare institutions that process patient data for clinical AI purposes may be able to rely on the legal basis of treatment provision or vital interests rather than consent in many circumstances.

However, consent — or its absence — is always a governance consideration even when it is not the formal legal basis. The ethical commitment to transparency and human dignity requires that the institution consider whether affected individuals know that AI systems are processing their data, whether they have meaningful opportunity to raise concerns, and whether the processing is consistent with reasonable expectations given the context in which they provided their information.

When consent is required

Consent is most clearly required when AI processing involves sensitive categories of personal data — health information, biometric data, data about minors, data about racial or ethnic origin, political opinions, religious beliefs, sexual orientation, or other categories that receive heightened protection under applicable law. Many data protection frameworks require explicit consent for processing of these categories in the absence of another specifically recognized legal basis. AI systems that process these categories must have their consent and legal basis assessed by legal counsel before deployment.

Consent is also most clearly required when AI processing involves uses that individuals would not reasonably anticipate based on the context in which they provided their information. The concept of contextual integrity — the idea that information flows appropriately when they match the norms of the context in which information was originally shared — provides a useful governance heuristic. Medical information shared with a healthcare provider for treatment purposes flows appropriately when used for clinical care; it may not flow appropriately when used to train a commercial AI model that will be used across multiple institutions for purposes the patient did not know about.

Obtaining meaningful consent

Where consent is required, the institution must ensure that it is obtained in a form that meets legal requirements and ethical standards. Meaningful consent is specific — the person knows what data is being processed, by what systems, for what purposes, and with what outcomes. It is informed — the person has sufficient understanding of the relevant facts to make a genuine choice. It is freely given — the person can decline without disproportionate consequences. And it is revocable — the person can withdraw consent and have their data deleted or processing ceased.

AI-specific consent challenges arise frequently. Large language model tools that process anything a user types create consent challenges because the scope of data processing is not well-defined in advance — users cannot specifically consent to every category of information that might appear in their inputs. AI systems that collect data through automated means — processing records, analyzing documents, monitoring activities — create consent challenges because the collection is not visible to the individuals whose data is being collected. AI training data consent creates challenges because training data is often collected for one purpose and later repurposed for training in ways that were not disclosed at the time of collection.

Governance responses to these challenges include: designing AI tools to minimize collection of unnecessary personal information, providing clear and accessible disclosures of how AI systems use information, building opt-out mechanisms where required by law or appropriate to the context, and specifically assessing the legal basis for any AI use case that involves repurposing previously collected data.

Consent in vendor relationships

Institutions that use vendor AI systems must ensure that their use of those systems is consistent with the consent and disclosures they have provided to the people whose data is processed. A healthcare institution that has obtained patient consent to use of their health information for treatment cannot extend that consent to authorize a vendor's use of the same information for AI model training without additional disclosure and, where required, additional consent.

Vendor contracts should reflect the limits of the institution's legal basis for data processing. If the institution can only process patient data on the basis of treatment provision, the vendor contract must restrict vendor data use to purposes consistent with that basis and must prohibit uses — including model training — that exceed it.

Access control: who can touch what

Access control governance for AI addresses who within the institution — and within the vendor ecosystem — can access the data that AI systems use, the outputs they produce, and the systems themselves.

The access control challenge in AI systems

Conventional access control governance typically addresses access to defined data stores — databases, file systems, records — by defined users or roles. AI systems create access control challenges that do not fit neatly into this framework. A large language model that a staff member uses for drafting effectively gives that staff member access to the model's training knowledge, which may include patterns derived from data the institution considers restricted. A predictive model that produces risk scores effectively makes certain inferences about individuals accessible to whoever can query the model, regardless of whether those individuals' underlying data is separately controlled.

AI systems also create access control challenges at the inference level: access to an AI model may enable reverse-engineering of information about training data even without direct access to the training data itself. A model that was trained on personally identifiable data may be queried in ways that recover identifiable information about specific individuals who appeared in the training data — a phenomenon known as model inversion or membership inference. Access controls that adequately protect the training data directly may not adequately protect it against recovery through AI queries.

Role-based access principles

AI data access governance should be organized around role-based access principles: access to data — training data, operational data, AI outputs, audit logs — should be granted based on the minimum information necessary for a specific role to perform its legitimate functions, not on the basis of general organizational rank or convenience.

Governance teams should assess, for each AI system in the inventory, who has access to what data in connection with that system: who can query the system and receive outputs, who can view the training data, who at the vendor can access institutional data processed by the system, and who can view audit logs of system activity. This access mapping should be documented and reviewed periodically, with access rights adjusted as roles and operational needs change.

Access controls should be technically enforced, not merely policy-stated. A policy that says only authorized users should query a high-risk AI system is not access control; it is guidance. Access controls that technically restrict system queries to authenticated users with appropriate roles — enforced by the system itself rather than relying on user compliance with policy — are actual access control.

Vendor access governance

Vendor access to institutional data is among the most significant access control challenges in AI governance. When an institution uses a vendor AI system, it is inherently granting the vendor access to operational inputs — the data that users provide — and potentially to stored data if the system retains inputs. In addition, vendor technical staff may have access to institutional data for purposes of system maintenance, debugging, model training, and technical support.

Governance of vendor access should address: what data vendor staff can access, under what circumstances, with what justification requirement, and with what logging of access events. Vendor contracts should specify that vendor staff access to institutional data is restricted to what is necessary for defined service delivery purposes, that access is logged and auditable, and that the institution has the right to request access logs. For systems processing highly sensitive data, vendors should commit to specific technical controls that limit staff access — encryption arrangements that prevent plaintext data access by vendor staff, data compartmentalization that limits the scope of any individual access event.

Insider threat considerations

Access control governance should account for insider threat: the risk that individuals with legitimate access — staff, vendors, contractors — use that access in ways that are not authorized or appropriate. AI systems that process sensitive personal information are attractive targets for insider misuse because their outputs can reveal patterns across many individuals without requiring access to individual records.

Monitoring for anomalous access patterns — queries that are unusually broad, unusually targeted at specific individuals, or inconsistent with the user's role — is an access control governance measure that supports detection of insider misuse. For high-risk AI systems, audit logging of all queries should be implemented with monitoring for anomalous patterns.

Sensitive information: heightened protection in AI contexts

Certain categories of information are recognized across legal frameworks and ethical traditions as requiring heightened protection because of the particular harms that their mishandling can cause. Data governance for AI must address how AI systems handle sensitive categories and what additional requirements apply.

Categories requiring heightened protection

Health and medical information creates heightened protection requirements across virtually all jurisdictions. In the United States, HIPAA governs the handling of protected health information by covered entities and their business associates; AI vendors that process PHI on behalf of healthcare institutions must execute Business Associate Agreements and meet HIPAA's security and privacy requirements. Similar frameworks apply in most other jurisdictions. AI systems used in clinical contexts — diagnostic support, treatment recommendation, risk stratification, care coordination — will almost inevitably process health information, and their governance must specifically address the legal requirements applicable to that information.

Information about minors receives heightened protection in most jurisdictions, including specific regulatory frameworks governing the collection and use of children's online data. Educational institutions using AI in student-facing contexts must comply with FERPA in the United States, which restricts disclosure of student educational records; many other jurisdictions have equivalent requirements. AI systems used in school contexts — adaptive learning systems, student risk identification tools, behavioral monitoring systems — must be assessed specifically for compliance with applicable student privacy frameworks.

Financial information — account data, payment information, credit information, financial records — is subject to sector-specific regulatory requirements in most jurisdictions. AI systems used in financial contexts must be assessed against applicable requirements including PCI-DSS for payment card data, the Gramm-Leach-Bliley Act in the United States, and equivalent frameworks elsewhere.

Biometric data — facial images used for recognition, fingerprints, retinal scans, voice prints — is subject to heightened protection in a growing number of jurisdictions, including specific state laws in the United States. AI systems that use biometric data for identification or authentication must be assessed specifically against applicable biometric data frameworks, which in some jurisdictions include specific consent and retention requirements.

Data about legally protected characteristics — racial or ethnic origin, political opinions, religious beliefs, sexual orientation, gender identity, disability status — receives special category status under data protection frameworks in many jurisdictions, requiring specific legal basis for processing and heightened security protections. AI systems that process or infer these characteristics require specific legal assessment.

De-identification and anonymization

A common approach to using personal information in AI training while managing privacy risk is de-identification or anonymization: removing or altering identifying information so that the data can no longer be attributed to specific individuals. This approach has genuine value but also significant limitations that governance must account for.

True anonymization — processing data in a way that makes re-identification impossible — is technically much harder to achieve than is commonly assumed, particularly with AI training data. AI models trained on supposedly anonymized data can in some cases recover identifying information about individuals in the training data through model inversion techniques. Datasets that appear fully anonymized can be re-identified by combining them with other datasets. The legal standard for anonymization — whether data has truly been anonymized such that data protection law no longer applies — varies across jurisdictions and may be harder to meet in AI contexts than conventional ones.

De-identification that falls short of full anonymization — pseudonymization, for example — reduces privacy risk without eliminating it. It does not exempt data from data protection law in most jurisdictions; pseudonymized data remains personal data under most frameworks. It should be understood as a risk reduction measure rather than a compliance solution.

Governance should approach de-identification claims with healthy skepticism: vendor representations that data is anonymized should be assessed against the specific technical methods used, the specific dataset characteristics, and current understanding of re-identification risk for that type of data. A blanket claim that a dataset is "de-identified and therefore not personal data" is not adequate governance; a specific technical assessment of re-identification risk, conducted by qualified assessors, is.

The aggregation problem

Even when individual data elements are not sensitive in isolation, their combination in AI systems may create sensitive profiles. A dataset that contains no individually sensitive fields may nonetheless reveal health conditions when patterns across fields are analyzed by AI; a dataset that contains no location data may nonetheless reveal home address patterns through transaction data; a dataset that contains no demographic data may nonetheless reveal racial or ethnic characteristics through patterns in names, zip codes, and behavioral data.

Governance of sensitive information in AI contexts must attend to the aggregation problem: the tendency of AI systems to combine non-sensitive data elements in ways that produce sensitive inferences. Use cases that involve AI analysis of large datasets should be assessed not only for the sensitivity of individual data elements but for the sensitivity of the patterns and inferences the AI might extract from their combination.

Data governance for the full AI lifecycle

The data governance dimensions addressed in this chapter — quality, retention, consent, access control, and sensitive information — apply at different points in the AI lifecycle and require different governance practices at each point.

At the design and development stage — when AI systems are being built or customized using institutional data — data governance focuses on training data quality, representativeness, and legal basis for training data use. This is the stage at which foundational decisions about data governance are made; problems embedded here are typically much harder to address after the model has been trained.

At the procurement and vendor assessment stage — when institutions are evaluating AI vendors — data governance focuses on understanding vendor data practices and negotiating contractual protections. This is the stage at which the institution's contractual data governance rights are established; failing to negotiate adequate terms at this stage leaves the institution with limited options later.

At the deployment stage — when AI systems are first put into operation — data governance focuses on confirming that operational data flows are consistent with the governance arrangements established during procurement, that access controls are technically implemented, and that staff understand data governance requirements relevant to their use of the system.

During ongoing operation, data governance focuses on monitoring compliance with retention and access policies, confirming that vendor data practices remain consistent with contractual commitments, and reviewing the adequacy of consent and legal basis arrangements as data uses evolve.

At the end of the system's life — when an AI system is decommissioned or a vendor relationship ends — data governance focuses on ensuring that institutional data is returned or deleted, that vendor certifications of deletion are obtained, and that audit logs and other records required for ongoing accountability are retained according to defined schedules.

Building data governance capacity

Data governance for AI requires institutional capacity that many organizations have not yet developed. The following capabilities are foundational to the practices described in this chapter and should be treated as governance investments rather than optional enhancements.

A data inventory — a record of what data the institution holds, in what systems, subject to what governance requirements — is the data governance equivalent of the AI inventory described in Chapter 9. Without knowing what data exists and where, data quality assessment, retention management, access control, and sensitive data identification cannot be conducted systematically.

Data classification — a framework for categorizing data by sensitivity level and applying corresponding governance requirements — is the foundation of proportionate data governance. Without classification, governance must treat all data as if it were the most sensitive, which is impractical, or must assess each governance question on a case-by-case basis, which is inconsistent. A practical classification scheme — typically three to four tiers from public to highly sensitive — with defined governance requirements for each tier is sufficient for most institutions.

Legal counsel with data protection expertise — either in-house or accessible through an advisory relationship — is essential for the legal basis assessments, consent framework development, and regulatory compliance analysis that AI data governance requires. General counsel who are not specifically expert in data protection may miss AI-specific data governance requirements that are increasingly significant in regulatory expectations and enforcement activity.

Staff training on data governance requirements — specifically on what data may and may not be entered into AI systems, what the institution's legal obligations regarding personal data are, and how to recognize and report data governance concerns — is the mechanism through which data governance policy translates into actual practice. Governance policies that staff do not understand cannot be complied with.

Data governance as an expression of institutional values

The practical requirements of data governance — retention schedules, access control matrices, consent frameworks, de-identification standards — can make data governance feel technical and procedural. It is worth stepping back to recognize what those requirements are actually for.

Data governance for AI is ultimately about honoring the relationship between the institution and the people it serves. People who share health information with a healthcare provider, educational records with a school, financial information with a bank, or personal circumstances with a social services organization are trusting that institution to use their information for the purposes for which it was provided and to protect it from uses they did not anticipate. When AI systems use that information in ways that affect those people — influencing their care, their opportunities, their access to services — the institution has an obligation to ensure that the data on which those systems operate is handled in ways that honor that trust.

This is why data quality matters: poor-quality data produces AI systems that do not work well for the people they affect. It is why retention limits matter: holding data indefinitely creates risks to the people it concerns that are not justified by corresponding benefits to them. It is why consent matters: people whose information is used in AI systems they did not know about, for purposes they did not anticipate, have been treated as data subjects rather than as people with interests in how their information is used. It is why access controls matter: unlimited access to personal information creates conditions for misuse that undermine the trust the institution depends on. And it is why sensitive information receives heightened protection: certain information, if misused, can cause harm that is severe, lasting, and personal in ways that call for the strongest available governance protections.

Data governance is governance on behalf of people, not governance of data. That distinction keeps the practical requirements from becoming ends in themselves and connects them to the values they are designed to serve.

Part III: Using AI Responsibly

Chapter 13: Human Oversight and Decision Rights

The irreplaceable function

There is a version of AI governance that treats human oversight as a concession to institutional anxiety — a friction-generating requirement that slows down the efficiency gains AI promises, maintained until trust in AI systems is sufficient to reduce or eliminate it. This version is wrong in its premise and dangerous in its implications.

Human oversight in AI-assisted processes is not a transitional accommodation. It is a permanent governance requirement whose justification is not distrust of technology but the nature of institutional accountability, the complexity of human circumstance, and the limits of what any automated system — however capable — can be authorized to determine about people's lives without human answerable authority in the loop.

An AI system that recommends a treatment, scores a job candidate, assesses a child's welfare situation, or determines a benefit eligibility is not making a decision in the way a human decision-maker makes one. It is producing an output based on learned patterns. The output may be accurate, helpful, and efficiently produced. It may be better, on average, than unaided human judgment on certain dimensions of the task. But it is not accountable in the way human decisions must be in institutional contexts. It cannot explain itself in terms that honor the complexity of the specific person and situation before it. It cannot bring moral judgment to the question of what a human being in a specific set of circumstances is entitled to expect from an institution that holds power over their circumstances. It cannot be asked — and cannot answer — why.

Human oversight is what preserves these capacities in AI-assisted processes. It is what keeps institutional decision-making accountable, explainable, and subject to the moral reasoning that consequential decisions about people require. This chapter describes what genuine human oversight means in practice: when it is required, what it must accomplish to be meaningful, how decision rights should be allocated between humans and AI, and how institutions should design the workflows, training, and accountability structures that make oversight real rather than nominal.

The spectrum of human-AI decision arrangements

Before addressing when human oversight is required and what it must consist of, it is useful to map the full range of arrangements through which humans and AI systems can relate to decisions. These arrangements exist on a spectrum from full human authority to full AI authority, with numerous meaningful gradations between them.

At one end, *human-only decisions* involve no AI input: a human decision-maker exercises judgment based entirely on their own knowledge, experience, and information-gathering. This arrangement is increasingly rare in institutional contexts as AI tools become available, and it is not necessarily the gold standard — human-only decisions are subject to their own forms of error, bias, and inconsistency. But it remains the appropriate arrangement for categories of decision where the values and contextual sensitivity required exceed what any AI-assisted process can adequately support.

AI-informed decisions involve AI providing information, analysis, or perspective that a human decision-maker can consider alongside other inputs. The AI has no formal role in the decision; it is one source among many. The human exercises independent judgment and is not presented with an AI recommendation as such — they may receive AI-processed data, AI-generated summaries, or AI-conducted analysis, but not a recommendation that frames the decision in terms the human is expected to accept or override.

AI-recommended decisions involve AI generating a specific recommendation that the human decision-maker reviews and may accept, modify, or reject. The recommendation creates an anchor for the human's assessment. This is the most common arrangement in institutional AI deployment — clinical decision support, hiring AI, risk scoring, fraud detection — and the arrangement most vulnerable to automation bias, because the human is placed in a reactive relationship to the AI recommendation rather than an independent one.

AI-driven decisions with human review involve AI making decisions that take effect unless a human intervenes to prevent or modify them. The human is not reviewing before the decision is made but after; their role is exception management rather than decision-making. This arrangement is appropriate for lower-stakes, high-volume decisions where post-hoc human review provides adequate governance, but it is inadequate for higher-stakes decisions where the human review needs to occur before effect.

AI-driven decisions without human review represent full automation: AI makes decisions that take immediate effect without human involvement in individual cases. This arrangement is appropriate for a narrow category of low-stakes, reversible, high-volume operational decisions, and inappropriate for any decision that significantly affects a person's circumstances, rights, or access to services.

The governance task is to ensure that the level of human oversight actually applied to each AI use case is appropriate for its risk level, stakes, and the nature of the decisions it produces — and that the oversight arrangements in place are genuine rather than nominal.

When human oversight is required: the decision rights framework

Decision rights governance addresses which decisions humans must make, which AI may make, and which require a defined collaboration between them. The framework presented here organizes this governance question around four criteria: consequence, reversibility, individuation, and accountability.

Consequence: the stakes of the decision

The most fundamental criterion for human oversight requirements is the consequence of the decision — what is at stake for the person or people affected. Decisions that significantly affect people's access to healthcare, employment, education, housing, financial services, legal treatment, or social services carry consequences substantial enough to require human authority in the decision.

The consequence criterion is not binary. It scales along dimensions of severity and scope. A decision that affects whether a person receives a service they urgently need is more consequential than one that affects their optional enrollment in an additional service. A decision that affects many aspects of a person's circumstances over an extended period is more consequential than one with a single limited effect. A decision that is difficult for the affected person to challenge or reverse is more consequential than one that can easily be reviewed and corrected.

Governance teams should assess the consequence of AI-assisted decisions specifically — not in the abstract but as they occur in the institution's specific operational context. A risk score that is used to prioritize outreach carries different consequences than the same score used to determine eligibility. A recommendation that staff members treat as advisory carries different consequences than one they treat as effectively determinative. The consequence criterion requires understanding not only what the AI system does but what it actually causes in the workflows it inhabits.

Reversibility: can errors be corrected

The second criterion is reversibility: if the AI system makes an error, can the error be corrected before it causes harm, and how difficult is that correction? Decisions whose errors are easily detected and corrected — flagged for review, appealed by the affected party, identified through monitoring — can tolerate somewhat less intensive human oversight than decisions whose errors are difficult to detect or whose effects are difficult to reverse.

Irreversibility takes several forms in institutional AI contexts. A decision that removes a person from a service or denies them access to a benefit may have immediate practical effects that persist even if the decision is later reversed: the benefit was not received when it was needed, the service was interrupted, the opportunity was missed. A decision recorded in a file or record that is shared across systems or time may have downstream effects that are difficult to trace and correct. A decision communicated to the affected person in terms that create expectations may be practically difficult to unwind even if the formal decision is reversed.

Governance should be more conservative about AI authority — requiring more human involvement, at earlier points in the decision — for decisions whose errors are more difficult to correct. The precautionary logic is straightforward: when errors are easily corrected, the cost of allowing AI authority and discovering an error through correction is low. When errors are difficult to correct, that cost may be very high.

Individuation: does the decision require specific contextual judgment

The third criterion is individuation: whether the decision requires specific assessment of the individual person and their particular circumstances, as distinct from pattern-matching against statistical regularities in historical data.

AI systems are fundamentally statistical: they produce outputs based on learned patterns in training data, applied to the features of the current input. This approach is well-suited to decisions where general patterns are reliably predictive of individual cases and where individual circumstances do not substantially deviate from population-level patterns. It is less well-suited to decisions where individual circumstances deviate significantly from population-level patterns, where the relevant features of the situation are not quantifiable in the data the AI processes, or where the decision requires attending to aspects of the person's humanity that are not captured in the data.

Clinical medicine involves frequent individuation: a patient may be statistically high-risk for a condition but have specific features of their presentation that change the clinical judgment. Social services involves frequent individuation: a family that scores poorly on a risk instrument may have specific strengths or contextual factors that experienced professional judgment would weigh significantly. Employment decisions involve individuation: a candidate who does not match the profile of past successful employees may have specific capabilities or perspectives that make them exceptionally valuable for a specific role.

When decisions require genuine individuation — when getting the right answer for this person requires attending to specifics that statistical patterns cannot capture — human judgment is not merely a compliance requirement. It is the only means by which the right decision can be reached. Governance should protect human judgment at precisely these points rather than treating them as inefficiencies to be optimized away.

Accountability: who can be held responsible

The fourth criterion is accountability: whether the institution can meet its accountability obligations for the decision without human authority. Some decisions carry accountability requirements — legal, ethical, professional, or democratic — that cannot be met by AI systems alone.

In healthcare, clinical decisions are governed by professional accountability frameworks that require human clinicians to be responsible for decisions about patient care. In legal contexts, decisions with legal consequences typically require human actors with legal authority and accountability. In government contexts, administrative decisions often require human decision-makers who can be accountable to administrative law review. In employment contexts, decisions that create or terminate legal relationships require human authority.

Beyond formal legal requirements, accountability to affected individuals requires that someone can explain a decision, acknowledge an error, and take responsibility for correction. AI systems cannot do these things in the way that human institutional actors can. When affected individuals need to understand why a decision affecting them was made, to challenge it, to provide additional information, or to hold someone accountable for an error — these needs can only be met by human decision-makers with genuine authority and genuine accountability.

The four categories of human oversight requirement

Applying the decision rights framework produces four categories of oversight requirement, each with specific operational implications.

Category one: mandatory human decision authority

Some decisions must be made by a human, with AI providing supporting information or analysis but not a recommendation that the human is expected to accept or override. This is the highest level of human oversight requirement and applies when all four decision rights criteria are satisfied: the decision is highly consequential, its errors are difficult to reverse, it requires genuine individuation, and it carries accountability requirements that cannot be met without human authority.

Examples include: initial determinations of benefit eligibility that significantly affect a person's access to essential services; decisions to remove a child from their home or to alter a custody arrangement; decisions to initiate involuntary treatment or detention; decisions to terminate employment for cause; and decisions with significant legal consequences for specific individuals.

For these decisions, AI may have a role — producing analysis, surfacing relevant information, identifying patterns that should be brought to the decision-maker's attention — but the decision itself must be made by a human with appropriate authority, and that human must form their judgment independently of any AI recommendation. Governance frameworks for this category should ensure that AI does not present recommendations to the decision-maker in a form that would anchor their judgment before independent assessment is formed.

Category two: human approval required before effect

Many decisions can be made with AI generating a recommendation, but must receive explicit human approval before taking effect. This arrangement is appropriate when the decision is consequential and requires human accountability, but where human reviewers can genuinely evaluate AI recommendations rather than needing to form fully independent assessments.

Examples include: approval of AI-recommended treatment plans, before communication to the patient; approval of AI-generated determinations about program eligibility, before notification to the applicant; approval of AI-scored hiring decisions, before candidates are advanced or rejected; and approval of AI-flagged fraud or compliance concerns, before any enforcement action is initiated.

For this category, the critical governance question is whether the approval process is designed to produce genuine review or nominal review. The design principles that support genuine review are addressed in detail later in this chapter. The key requirements are that reviewers have access to the information they need to evaluate the recommendation, that they are empowered to modify or reject it, and that the volume and time pressure of review do not make genuine assessment practically impossible.

Category three: human monitoring and intervention authority

Some AI-assisted processes can operate with AI making decisions or taking actions, subject to human monitoring that detects anomalies and human authority to intervene when needed. This arrangement is appropriate for higher-volume, lower-stakes decisions where post-hoc monitoring provides adequate governance, or for processes where individual decisions are less consequential but aggregate patterns require human oversight.

Examples include: AI-assisted routing of service requests, with human monitoring for routing errors or patterns of concern; AI-generated draft communications, with human review at a sampling rather than individual level; AI-conducted preliminary screening that narrows but does not determine case handling; and AI-powered monitoring systems where alerts require human assessment before action is taken.

For this category, governance must specify what the monitoring covers, who conducts it, at what frequency, and what constitutes an anomaly that requires intervention. The risk in this category is that the interval between an AI error and human detection allows harm to accumulate before correction occurs. Monitoring design should minimize that interval for higher-consequence errors.

Category four: AI authority within defined parameters

For a limited category of decisions — those that are low-stakes, highly reversible, subject to clear rules rather than judgment, and not significantly individuated — AI can have authority to act without individual human review, subject to governance through parameter-setting and exception identification rather than decision-level oversight.

Examples include: scheduling, routing, and logistics optimization where individual errors are quickly identified and easily corrected; filtering and categorization tasks where the AI is making preliminary organizational decisions rather than consequential ones; content classification that is subject to human appeal and correction; and automated quality checks that flag issues for human attention rather than making final determinations.

For this category, governance focuses on parameter definition — establishing the boundaries within which AI authority operates, the conditions under which cases are escalated out of AI authority into human review, and the monitoring that confirms the AI is operating within its parameters. Human oversight is not absent; it is expressed at the level of governance design and monitoring rather than at the level of individual decisions.

Designing for genuine oversight: the seven principles

The difference between meaningful and nominal oversight is primarily a design question. The following principles guide the design of human oversight processes that actually deliver the governance they are intended to provide.

Principle one: independence before anchoring

The most damaging feature of poorly designed oversight processes is that they present the AI recommendation before the human reviewer has formed an independent assessment. When a reviewer sees the AI's conclusion first, that conclusion anchors their subsequent evaluation: they are no longer assessing the situation independently and then comparing their assessment to the AI's; they are assessing whether there is sufficient reason to deviate from the AI's assessment. These are different cognitive tasks, and they produce different outcomes. The first is independent review; the second is a check on the AI that gives the AI the benefit of the doubt by default.

Governance should require, for any use case in Category One or Category Two, that human reviewers form at minimum a preliminary assessment of the key question before they are shown the AI recommendation. This does not require elaborate pre-review processes; it may mean simply that reviewers document their initial clinical impression, their own assessment of an applicant's qualifications, or their preliminary risk assessment before accessing the AI recommendation. The act of forming and documenting an independent view, however preliminary, creates cognitive separation between the reviewer's judgment and the AI's output.

Principle two: access to the right information

Human reviewers cannot exercise meaningful oversight if they only see the AI's output. Meaningful review requires access to the underlying information the AI processed — or a representative sample of it — and to information about the AI's typical performance and known limitations in the type of case under review.

Governance frameworks should specify what information human reviewers must have access to when reviewing AI outputs in each oversight category. For clinical decision support, this includes access to the patient's clinical record, not only the AI's recommendation. For hiring AI review, this includes access to the candidate's actual application materials, not only their AI-generated score. For benefit eligibility review, this includes access to the applicant's documentation and circumstances, not only the AI's eligibility determination.

Reviewers should also have access to explanations of why the AI produced the output it did — what features of the input most strongly influenced the recommendation, what patterns in training data support the conclusion. Where AI systems cannot provide this explanation, governance should note that limitation as a constraint on the quality of oversight that can be achieved.

Principle three: practical authority to deviate

Reviewers who nominally have authority to override AI recommendations but who face practical obstacles to exercising that authority are not genuinely empowered. Practical authority requires that override be procedurally easy — requiring no more documentation than would be required to accept the recommendation, routing through no more approval layers, and attaching no implicit or explicit professional or reputational risk.

Governance should assess the practical obstacles to override in each oversight context. If overriding an AI recommendation requires a staff member to complete additional documentation, escalate to a supervisor, or defend their judgment in a way that accepting the recommendation does not require, the practical authority to deviate is limited even if formal authority is unrestricted. Governance frameworks should actively work to remove these asymmetries.

Where institutional culture treats AI recommendations as presumptively correct — where staff who override them are implicitly expected to justify themselves while those who accept them are not — governance should directly address that culture through explicit policy, leadership communication, and training that reinforces the normalcy and value of independent professional judgment.

Principle four: manageable oversight volume

Genuine review takes time. A human reviewer who is expected to review 200 AI recommendations per hour is not genuinely reviewing them; they are scanning and accepting, with insufficient time for the independent assessment that meaningful oversight requires. Volume requirements that make genuine review impossible are a governance failure even when they arise from resource constraints rather than deliberate circumvention.

Governance should establish maximum review volumes for different oversight categories, calibrated to the time that genuine review of each case type requires. These maximums should be established before deployment, not after monitoring reveals that reviewers are overwhelmed. When operational demands require review volumes that exceed what genuine oversight can accommodate at current staffing, the governance response is to either increase reviewer capacity or reduce the volume of AI-assisted cases — not to accept nominally overseen high-volume processing as adequate governance.

Principle five: structured escalation pathways

When reviewers encounter AI outputs that are unusual, uncertain, or raise concerns they cannot resolve within their authority, they need clear pathways to escalate. Escalation should be procedurally simple, culturally normalized, and functionally effective — cases escalated for review should receive review from someone with appropriate expertise and authority, within a timeframe that does not create backlogs that discourage escalation.

Governance frameworks should define escalation pathways specifically: what types of concerns warrant escalation, to whom, through what mechanism, within what timeframe, and with what expected follow-up. Generic escalation guidance — "consult a supervisor if you have concerns" — is not a functional escalation pathway. Specific guidance — "if an AI output seems inconsistent with the clinical presentation in a way you cannot explain, document your concern in the clinical record, flag the case for attending review, and notify the department AI liaison" — is.

Principle six: documentation of review and deviation

Oversight processes should produce documentation: records that capture what the human reviewer assessed, what the AI recommended, and what the human decided — including whether they accepted, modified, or rejected the AI recommendation and in the latter cases why. This documentation serves several governance purposes: it creates an audit trail for accountability; it provides data for monitoring override rates and patterns; it supports investigation of specific AI-related concerns; and it enables institutional learning about the circumstances in which AI recommendations are most and least reliable.

Documentation requirements should be proportionate to the stakes of the decision. For high-consequence decisions in Category One, detailed documentation of the reviewer's reasoning is appropriate. For lower-stakes Category Two decisions at high volume, lighter documentation — a structured record of the AI recommendation, the reviewer's decision, and a coded reason for deviation if any — is more proportionate and more practically sustainable.

Principle seven: monitoring override rates

The rate at which human reviewers deviate from AI recommendations — the override rate — is one of the most important governance indicators for oversight processes. An unusually low override rate may indicate automation bias: reviewers deferring to AI recommendations without genuine independent assessment. An unusually high override rate may indicate that the AI system is not performing adequately for the use case. Both patterns warrant investigation.

Governance frameworks should specify the expected range of override rates for different oversight contexts — not a specific target, which would create perverse incentives, but a range below which investigation of automation bias is triggered and above which investigation of AI system adequacy is triggered. Override rates should be monitored at the individual, team, and institutional levels, and significant deviations from expected ranges should prompt governance team review.

The accountability assignment: who is responsible for what

Human oversight requires clear accountability assignments: for any AI-assisted process in which human oversight is required, specific people in specific roles must be accountable for the quality of that oversight.

The operational accountability owner is the person whose professional authority is engaged by the decision — the clinician who approves a treatment recommendation, the hiring manager who approves a candidate selection, the eligibility worker who approves a benefit determination. This person is accountable for the quality of their individual review decisions, for the exercise of genuine independent judgment, and for escalating when they encounter situations that require it.

The supervisory accountability owner is the person responsible for oversight of a team of operational accountability owners — the department head, the service manager, the supervising clinician. This person is accountable for ensuring that the oversight environment — volumes, training, escalation culture, documentation practices — supports genuine rather than nominal review, and for detecting and addressing patterns that suggest nominal review is occurring.

The governance accountability owner is the governance team, responsible for the adequacy of oversight arrangements across AI-assisted processes, for monitoring override rates and other oversight quality indicators, and for updating oversight requirements when monitoring reveals inadequacy.

These accountability assignments should be explicit — documented in governance frameworks and communicated to the people who hold them — not assumed. The accountability gap described at the opening of Chapter 5 arises precisely when oversight accountability is diffuse: when everyone assumes someone else is responsible for ensuring oversight quality and no one is actually checking.

Special circumstances: when oversight arrangements need to flex

Standard oversight arrangements are designed for standard conditions. Several circumstances require specific adaptations.

High-volume operational contexts

In high-volume operational contexts — where AI systems support hundreds or thousands of decisions per day — individual decision-level human review may be impractical for lower-stakes decisions. Governance frameworks for these contexts should employ sampling strategies: requiring intensive review of a statistically meaningful sample of AI-assisted decisions rather than all of them, with mechanisms for cases outside the sample to escalate to human review if anomalies are detected.

Sampling strategies must be designed carefully. Samples should be random or systematically representative, not convenience samples of easy cases. Sample sizes should be sufficient to detect meaningful performance patterns within a reasonable statistical confidence level. And sampling strategies should not reduce oversight for the highest-consequence cases: even in high-volume contexts, decisions above a defined consequence threshold should receive individual review rather than being included in the sampling population.

Emergency and time-pressured contexts

Healthcare, emergency services, and similar contexts involve situations where the time available for review is severely compressed. Governance frameworks for these contexts must balance the genuine time pressure of emergency decision-making against the requirements of meaningful oversight.

Emergency contexts are not grounds for abandoning oversight; they are grounds for having designed oversight that can function quickly. Pre-approved protocols that specify how AI recommendations should be used in defined emergency categories — when to accept rapidly, when to deviate based on specified clinical or operational criteria, what documentation should be completed as soon as time permits — can provide governance-adequate oversight in time-pressured situations without requiring deliberative review that emergency conditions do not permit.

Novel situations outside AI training distribution

AI systems perform less reliably on inputs that differ significantly from their training data — what is technically described as out-of-distribution inputs. Human reviewers may encounter AI outputs that seem inconsistent with the situation, that the system has classified in ways that do not fit standard patterns, or where the AI's apparent confidence seems disproportionate to the complexity of the case.

Oversight frameworks should specifically address novel situations: directing reviewers to be particularly skeptical of AI recommendations when the situation they are assessing does not fit familiar patterns, when the AI's explanation of its output references features that seem irrelevant to the specific case, or when the AI's confidence is high in a situation the reviewer recognizes as genuinely complex. Anomalous AI outputs in novel situations should be treated as candidates for escalation by default rather than as cases where the reviewer should assume the AI has captured something they missed.

Situations involving vulnerable populations

When AI-assisted decisions affect people who are in positions of vulnerability — people in crisis, people with significant cognitive or communication disabilities, children, people who are acutely ill — oversight requirements should be more conservative than standard frameworks specify. Vulnerable populations are less able to detect AI errors, less able to seek correction, and more likely to be harmed by decisions that do not adequately account for their specific circumstances.

Oversight for decisions affecting vulnerable populations should be designed with the assumption that affected individuals may not be able to self-advocate and that the institution therefore bears a heightened obligation to ensure that human judgment is genuinely brought to bear on their circumstances. For these populations, the individuation criterion is almost always satisfied — their specific circumstances typically require attention that statistical patterns cannot provide — which places their cases in the highest oversight category.

Building the oversight culture

Technical oversight design — the workflows, documentation requirements, escalation pathways, and monitoring systems — is necessary but not sufficient. Effective human oversight also requires an institutional culture that values and supports genuine human judgment.

The culture dimensions of oversight include: leadership communication that treats human judgment as essential rather than as a friction-generating burden; performance management that assesses quality of oversight rather than only speed and volume; training that builds both AI literacy and professional confidence in applying independent judgment; and incident analysis practices that treat cases where AI errors were not caught by human review as learning opportunities rather than failures to be concealed.

Building this culture requires consistent, visible effort over time. Individual governance team actions — requiring documentation of deviations, monitoring override rates, providing feedback to operational leaders about oversight quality — are the building blocks. Leadership communication that explicitly values meaningful oversight, that acknowledges the tension between efficiency and oversight quality, and that is clear about the institution's priority when those values conflict is what orients the culture around oversight as a value rather than a compliance exercise.

The limits of oversight design

A final note of honesty about what oversight design can and cannot achieve. The oversight frameworks described in this chapter are the best available governance tools for the challenges they address. They are not perfect solutions.

Automation bias is a deep and persistent cognitive phenomenon; even reviewers who have been trained about it and who operate in oversight environments designed to reduce it will still exhibit it to some degree. Volume pressures will sometimes exceed what governance frameworks define as manageable; operational reality creates constraints that governance ideals do not always accommodate. AI systems will sometimes encounter situations for which no oversight design can fully compensate for fundamental limitations in what the AI can be expected to do well.

These limitations are reasons to be honest about what oversight governance achieves — not to abandon the attempt but to be clear-eyed about what it does and does not guarantee. Human oversight of AI systems is not a guarantee against error; it is the institutional mechanism through which errors are made less likely, detected more reliably, corrected more promptly, and held accountable more effectively than they would be without it. That is what oversight is for, and it is a significant and genuine contribution to responsible AI use even when it falls short of perfection.

Chapter 14: Testing Before Deployment

The last best opportunity

Testing before deployment is the last point in the AI governance lifecycle at which the institution has full freedom of decision without operational disruption. Once an AI system is live — once workflows have been redesigned around it, staff have been trained on it, vendor relationships have been formalized, and affected people have begun interacting with it — the cost of discovering a fundamental problem rises sharply. Governance problems identified in testing can be addressed by modifying conditions, requiring vendor changes, or declining to deploy. The same problems discovered after deployment require remediation under operational pressure, with affected people already exposed to whatever harm the problems produce.

This asymmetry makes pre-deployment testing among the most consequential governance investments an institution can make. Testing done well is expensive in time and attention but cheap relative to the costs of deploying systems that fail in ways testing would have revealed. Testing done poorly — superficially, hastily, or focused on the wrong dimensions — provides false assurance that is more dangerous than acknowledged uncertainty, because it leads institutions to deploy with confidence they have not earned.

This chapter describes what comprehensive pre-deployment testing for institutional AI systems should involve: what dimensions of system performance must be evaluated, what methods should be used, who should conduct different aspects of testing, what standards should govern test design and result interpretation, what documentation testing should produce, and how testing findings should inform the deployment decision. It is a chapter for people who will commission, conduct, oversee, or use the results of AI testing — which in different ways includes governance teams, operational leaders, IT staff, legal counsel, and the external evaluators that some testing requires.

What testing is and is not

Before describing what testing should cover, it is worth being clear about what testing does and does not establish.

Testing establishes that, under defined conditions with defined inputs of defined characteristics, an AI system produced outputs with defined properties. It provides evidence — which may be strong or weak, depending on test design — that the system behaves in ways consistent with the institution's governance requirements. Well-designed testing on representative data provides genuine grounds for deployment confidence. Poorly designed testing on favorable data provides false assurance that should not inform deployment decisions.

Testing does not establish that an AI system will perform identically in deployment as it performed in testing. The inputs a deployed system encounters may differ from test inputs in ways that affect performance. The operational context — the workflows, the staff using the system, the integration with other institutional systems — may create conditions that were not represented in testing. Vendor model updates may change system behavior after testing. And the populations that the system serves in deployment may differ from the populations represented in test data.

These limitations are not arguments against testing; they are arguments for honest assessment of what testing establishes and for building ongoing monitoring (Chapter 16) that extends the governance function into deployment. Testing provides pre-deployment assurance; monitoring provides post-deployment verification. Both are necessary; neither substitutes for the other.

Testing also does not establish that a system meets governance standards in contexts other than those tested. An AI hiring tool tested for bias against applicants with certain characteristics provides evidence about performance on those characteristics, not about performance on characteristics that were not specifically assessed. A clinical AI tested for accuracy in diagnosing a specific condition provides evidence about performance on that condition, not about performance on adjacent conditions the system might also encounter. Scope limitations in testing are among the most important things to document and communicate to governance decision-makers.

Who should test

Before addressing what to test and how, governance should resolve who should conduct testing. The answer is not simple, because different testing functions require different kinds of expertise and independence, and the appropriate testing structure depends on the use case, the risk level, and the resources the institution can bring to bear.

Vendor-conducted testing

Vendors typically conduct their own testing before releasing AI systems, and they provide documentation of that testing — accuracy assessments, performance metrics, bias evaluation results — as part of the information they share with prospective customers. This documentation is a necessary starting point for pre-deployment governance but is not sufficient on its own.

Vendor testing is conducted on the vendor's evaluation data, using the vendor's testing methodology, with the vendor's interests in the results. Vendors are not necessarily acting in bad faith when they conduct testing; most are genuinely trying to understand and represent their systems' performance. But the structural reality is that vendors have commercial incentives to present their systems favorably, and testing methodologies can be chosen in ways that produce favorable results without being technically dishonest. The test data may not be representative of the institution's specific deployment context. The metrics reported may highlight dimensions where the system performs well and omit dimensions where it performs less well.

Institutional governance should review vendor testing documentation critically — assessing methodology, data representativeness, metric appropriateness, and scope completeness — but should not treat it as a substitute for independent institutional assessment.

Institution-conducted testing

Institutions should conduct their own testing of AI systems before deployment, using their own data and their own testing methodology. Institutional testing has the advantage of relevance: test data drawn from the institution's actual operational context will more accurately predict deployment performance than vendor evaluation data that may not resemble institutional reality.

The depth and formality of institutional testing should be proportionate to the use case risk level. For high-risk systems — clinical AI, AI used in benefit determinations, AI used in employment decisions — institutional testing should be systematic, documented, and conducted by people with relevant technical and domain expertise. For medium-risk systems, institutional testing may be less formal but should still be structured and documented. For low-risk systems, a lighter-touch assessment — confirming that the system behaves as expected in the institution's specific operational context — may be adequate.

Institutional testing capacity varies enormously across institution types. A large healthcare system with a dedicated analytics team has very different testing capacity than a small nonprofit with limited technical staff. Governance frameworks should define testing requirements that are proportionate to risk while being realistic about institutional capacity, and should provide practical guidance on how to conduct testing at different levels of technical sophistication.

Independent third-party testing

For the highest-risk AI use cases — systems that make or significantly influence decisions with major consequences for vulnerable populations, systems operating in highly regulated contexts, systems where bias or safety failures could cause serious harm — independent third-party testing provides governance assurance that neither vendor nor institutional testing can fully provide.

Independent testing means testing conducted by evaluators who have no commercial relationship with the vendor, no operational stake in the deployment decision, and sufficient technical expertise and methodological independence to produce reliable assessments. Third-party AI auditors, academic researchers, and specialized testing organizations offer different forms of independent assessment capability.

Third-party testing is expensive and takes time. Its governance value for high-risk systems justifies that cost; its value for lower-risk systems may not. The governance decision about when to require independent testing should be based on explicit risk level assessment, with high-risk systems and those where institutional testing capacity is inadequate receiving independent evaluation.

Domain expert involvement

Technical testing establishes whether AI systems perform accurately, consistently, and fairly on defined metrics. It does not establish whether they perform appropriately in the context of professional practice — whether a clinical AI recommendation is clinically sensible, whether a social work risk assessment captures the factors that experienced practitioners recognize as relevant, whether an educational AI assessment aligns with pedagogical judgment about what matters.

Domain expert involvement in testing is therefore necessary alongside technical evaluation for any AI system operating in a professional practice context. Clinicians should assess clinical AI outputs for clinical appropriateness. Social workers should assess social risk AI outputs against professional judgment. Educators should assess educational AI outputs against pedagogical standards. The integration of technical and domain expert evaluation is what allows testing to assess both whether the system does what it is designed to do technically and whether what it is designed to do is appropriate for the context in which it will operate.

The five dimensions of pre-deployment testing

Comprehensive pre-deployment testing evaluates AI systems across five dimensions: accuracy, bias, robustness, safety, and security. Each dimension addresses different aspects of system performance that governance requires, and each requires specific testing methods and standards.

Dimension one: accuracy and reliability testing

Accuracy testing establishes how well an AI system performs on its primary function — how accurately a classification model classifies, how reliably a prediction model predicts, how factually correct a language model's outputs are for the use case at hand.

Establishing appropriate accuracy standards

Before conducting accuracy testing, governance must establish what accuracy standard the use case requires. This standard should be determined by the consequences of errors in the specific deployment context, not by the system's available capabilities or by vendor benchmarks.

The appropriate accuracy standard varies enormously across use cases. A clinical AI tool that contributes to diagnosis of a serious condition may need to achieve a sensitivity above a defined threshold — high enough that the acceptable false-negative rate reflects clinical judgment about the consequences of a missed diagnosis. A hiring AI tool that produces an initial screen before human review may need to achieve false-negative and false-positive rates low enough that qualified candidates are not systematically excluded and the human reviewer is not overwhelmed by poor recommendations. A document summarization tool whose outputs are always reviewed by a staff member may need to achieve only sufficient accuracy that the staff member's review time is not consumed correcting errors.

The standard should be defined before testing begins and should not be adjusted after testing reveals what the system actually achieves. Post-hoc standard adjustment — setting the acceptance threshold at whatever the system achieved — is not governance; it is rationalization. If the system does not achieve the pre-defined standard, the governance response is to address the gap — through vendor remediation, additional oversight requirements, or declining to deploy — not to lower the standard.

Accuracy testing methods

Accuracy testing should be conducted on a test dataset that is representative of the inputs the system will encounter in deployment. Representativeness means that the test data should resemble deployment data in the characteristics that affect system performance: the demographic composition of the people represented, the time period from which data is drawn, the operational context from which cases were collected, and the distribution of case types and complexity.

For institutions with sufficient operational data, the test dataset should be drawn from the institution's own historical records — a held-out validation set from institutional data that was not used in model training. This approach maximizes relevance and minimizes the risk that test performance will diverge from deployment performance due to data distribution differences.

Accuracy testing should produce metrics relevant to the specific use case, not only overall accuracy rates. For classification systems, this means sensitivity, specificity, positive predictive value, and negative predictive value — and the governance decision about which metric to prioritize should reflect which type of error is more consequential in the deployment context. For prediction systems, this means calibration assessment — whether the system's probability estimates reflect actual event rates — as well as discrimination metrics. For generative AI systems, this means factual accuracy assessment for factual claims and appropriate evaluation of output quality for non-factual tasks.

Confidence calibration testing — assessing whether the system's expressed confidence in its outputs accurately reflects their actual reliability — is particularly important for systems where confidence scores influence human oversight decisions. A system that expresses high confidence in outputs that are frequently incorrect may direct human oversight away from precisely the outputs that most need it. Calibration assessment requires comparing expressed confidence distributions to actual accuracy rates across confidence levels, typically through reliability diagrams or calibration curves.

Consistency testing assesses whether the system produces similar outputs for equivalent inputs. Many AI systems — particularly large language models — exhibit sensitivity to superficially minor input variations, producing different outputs in response to questions that are semantically equivalent but phrased differently. For use cases where consistency matters — comparative assessments, standardized scoring, applications of defined criteria — consistency testing should verify that the system's outputs are stable across reasonable input variations.

Establishing baseline comparisons

Accuracy testing results are most informative when compared against meaningful baselines. Three baselines are most useful for institutional governance.

A simple rule-based baseline — what accuracy a simple rules-based decision process would achieve on the same test data — establishes whether the AI system provides improvement over non-AI alternatives. An AI system that does not outperform a simple rules-based approach on the dimensions that matter may not justify the governance complexity it introduces.

A human performance baseline — what accuracy trained human decision-makers achieve on the same test cases — contextualizes AI accuracy in terms that matter for oversight design. An AI system that is substantially less accurate than trained human judgment presents different governance considerations than one that is substantially more accurate, and both present different considerations than one that is roughly equivalent.

A vendor-claimed baseline — comparing institutional test results to the vendor's documented performance claims — assesses whether the vendor's representations are accurate in the institution's specific deployment context. Significant divergence between vendor claims and institutional test results is a major governance concern that must be investigated and resolved before deployment.

Dimension two: bias and fairness testing

Bias testing evaluates whether the AI system performs differently across identifiable demographic groups in ways that could constitute discrimination or produce unjust differential outcomes. It is the testing dimension most directly connected to the fairness principle and the most frequently under-tested in institutional AI deployments.

What bias testing must address

Effective bias testing requires making deliberate choices about which groups to assess, which performance metrics to use, what threshold of differential performance is acceptable, and what the governance response is when unacceptable differentials are found. These choices are not purely technical; they reflect values about what fairness requires in the specific use case.

The groups to assess should include, at minimum, the demographic groups that are most relevant to the risks of discriminatory impact in the specific use case: racial and ethnic groups, gender, age groups, and where relevant disability status, national origin, and other protected characteristics. The selection of groups should reflect the context of the use case — a hiring tool should assess differential performance by race, gender, and age at minimum; a clinical risk tool should assess differential performance by race and ethnicity at minimum given the known patterns of differential clinical AI performance.

The metrics for assessing differential performance must be chosen with care, because different fairness metrics can produce different conclusions about whether a system is fair, and in some cases a system that meets one fairness criterion cannot simultaneously meet another. The most commonly assessed metrics include demographic parity (whether the system produces positive outcomes at the same rate across groups), equalized odds (whether the system's true positive and false positive rates are equal across groups), and predictive parity (whether positive predictions have the same precision across groups). Governance teams should understand which metrics are most relevant to their use case — the choice is a values judgment about what kind of fairness is most important, not a technical question.

Conducting bias testing

Bias testing should be conducted on a test dataset that includes adequate representation of the groups being assessed. Bias testing on a dataset that severely underrepresents a group — having only a handful of cases from a population the system will serve extensively — provides insufficient statistical power to detect meaningful performance differences for that group. Sample sizes for bias testing should be large enough to detect meaningful performance differences at appropriate confidence levels for each group assessed.

Statistical testing should accompany bias testing results. A performance difference between groups may be large enough to be statistically significant — meaning it is unlikely to be due to random sampling variation — without being large enough to be practically significant in governance terms. Conversely, a difference that appears large in a small sample may not be statistically significant. Governance should require both statistical significance testing and practical significance assessment: reporting the size of performance differences, their statistical confidence intervals, and an explicit assessment of whether the differences are large enough to constitute a governance concern.

Intersectional testing — assessing performance across combinations of demographic characteristics rather than each characteristic independently — is methodologically demanding but often reveals bias patterns that single-characteristic analysis misses. A clinical AI that performs comparably across racial groups and comparably across gender groups may still perform significantly worse for women of color than for any other demographic combination. Intersectional testing should be conducted where test dataset size allows, with acknowledgment of the limitations when adequate intersectional sample sizes cannot be achieved.

The threshold question

Governance must define, before testing, what level of differential performance is acceptable. This is not a question that testing itself can answer; it is a governance judgment that testing results are evaluated against.

The appropriate threshold depends on the use case, the severity of the differential, and the available alternatives. For use cases with high stakes — clinical decisions, benefit eligibility, employment — even modest performance differentials may be governance concerns that require vendor remediation. For lower-stakes use cases with robust human oversight, somewhat larger differentials may be acceptable if oversight is designed to catch and correct them.

The threshold definition should be explicit in governance documentation before testing begins, should be developed with legal counsel who can assess applicable legal standards, and should not be set simply at whatever differential the test results happen to show. If testing reveals differentials that exceed the pre-defined threshold, the governance response should be specific: require vendor remediation, implement additional oversight for affected groups, limit the use case scope, or decline to deploy.

Dimension three: robustness testing

Robustness testing evaluates how an AI system performs under conditions that deviate from the optimal conditions under which it typically performs — degraded inputs, unusual cases, edge cases outside the typical distribution, and inputs that are designed to challenge the system.

Types of robustness to test

Input variation robustness tests whether the system produces consistent outputs when inputs vary in ways that should not materially affect the output. For language models, this includes testing whether equivalent questions phrased differently produce consistent answers. For clinical AI, it includes testing whether clinically equivalent cases described with different documentation styles produce consistent outputs. For classification models, it includes testing whether minor formatting variations in inputs change classification outcomes.

Edge case performance tests how the system handles inputs that are at the margins of its intended scope — unusual cases that fall at the boundaries of the categories the system was trained to handle, or cases that combine features in ways that are rare in training data. Edge cases are important governance tests because they often reveal system limitations that are invisible in standard accuracy testing, and because the people most affected by edge case failures may be those whose circumstances are most unusual — precisely the people whose individuation the fairness and dignity principles require attention to.

Distributional shift robustness tests how system performance changes when the deployment data distribution differs from the training data distribution. When an AI system trained on one population is deployed with a somewhat different population — a different age distribution, a different geographic catchment, a different referral pattern — performance may degrade in ways that are not visible in standard accuracy testing on training-distribution data. Distributional shift testing involves deliberately constructing test sets that differ from training distribution in relevant ways and assessing performance degradation.

Temporal robustness tests whether system performance is stable over time, specifically whether performance on data from different time periods shows concerning trends. AI systems may perform differently on older versus more recent data if the patterns in data have shifted over time. For systems that will be deployed over extended periods, temporal robustness testing provides evidence about whether performance can be expected to remain stable or whether decay should be anticipated and planned for.

Degraded input robustness tests how the system handles imperfect inputs — documents with formatting issues, records with missing fields, inputs with data quality problems that may occur in operational contexts. Real-world operational data is rarely as clean as evaluation datasets; governance needs to understand how system performance degrades when input quality is less than optimal.

Robustness testing methods

Robustness testing often involves deliberate perturbation of test inputs — systematically varying inputs along dimensions of interest to assess performance sensitivity. For language models, this may involve paraphrasing test questions, changing the order of presented information, or modifying formatting. For structured data models, it may involve systematically varying individual features to assess their impact on outputs.

Robustness testing should be informed by knowledge of the operational context — the specific ways in which deployment inputs may differ from test inputs, the specific edge cases that operational experience suggests are likely to arise, and the specific distributional characteristics of the institution's population that may differ from the vendor's evaluation population. Domain experts should contribute to robustness test design, identifying the case types and input variations that are most governance-relevant in the specific operational context.

Dimension four: safety testing

Safety testing evaluates whether an AI system could cause physical, psychological, or material harm in the deployment context, and whether the safeguards built into the system and the deployment design are adequate to prevent foreseeable harms.

Defining safety for the use case

Safety testing must begin with explicit definition of what safety means in the specific use case — what harms are possible, how they could occur, and what their severity and likelihood are. This definition is not a technical exercise; it requires domain expertise, ethical judgment, and genuine engagement with the circumstances of the people the AI system will affect.

For clinical AI, safety definition involves clinical expertise: identifying the specific failure modes that could contribute to patient harm, the conditions under which AI errors might propagate into clinical decisions, and the specific populations or case types where errors would be most consequential. For AI used with vulnerable populations — children, people in crisis, people with disabilities — safety definition involves understanding those populations' specific vulnerabilities and the specific ways AI failure could compound rather than address them. For AI used in high-stakes administrative decisions, safety definition involves understanding what happens to people when the decisions are wrong and how quickly and easily errors can be detected and corrected.

Safety testing without explicit safety definition produces testing that may miss the most governance-relevant failure modes. Governance teams should require that safety definition documentation be completed before safety testing begins and should review that documentation for completeness and realism — specifically asking whether the defined failure modes reflect genuine understanding of the deployment context or whether they reflect only the failure modes that are easy to test.

Safety testing methods

Failure mode testing involves deliberately constructing test inputs designed to elicit the specific failure modes identified in the safety definition. For a clinical AI, this means presenting cases representative of the specific clinical presentations where false negatives or inappropriate recommendations would be most harmful. For a crisis support chatbot, this means presenting inputs representative of the expressions of acute distress where inappropriate responses could contribute to harm.

Boundary testing involves identifying and specifically testing the boundaries of the system's intended scope — cases that are at the edge of the situations the system is designed to handle, where performance may be less reliable. Boundary testing is particularly important for safety because the most dangerous failures often occur precisely at the boundaries of system capability.

Stress testing involves presenting the system with high volumes of inputs, rapid sequences of queries, or unusual combinations of conditions to assess whether performance degrades under conditions that may arise in operational deployment. For systems that will operate at significant volume, stress testing provides evidence about whether performance characteristics observed in standard testing are stable under load.

Adversarial safety testing — deliberately constructing inputs designed to elicit unsafe outputs — is particularly important for generative AI systems deployed in contexts where harmful outputs could cause direct harm to users. For AI deployed in mental health contexts, for example, adversarial safety testing should include inputs specifically designed to elicit responses that could harm someone in crisis. For AI deployed in contexts where safety constraints need to remain robust, adversarial testing should attempt to bypass those constraints through the kinds of manipulative inputs that real users might construct.

The human oversight safety interaction

Safety testing should specifically test the interaction between system performance and the human oversight design — not just how the system performs in isolation but how the system performs in the workflow context in which it will be deployed, including the human review processes that are supposed to catch AI errors.

This interaction testing might involve presenting AI outputs to human reviewers under simulated operational conditions and assessing whether reviewers catch errors that safety testing identified in the system — specifically whether automation bias reduces the effectiveness of human oversight for the kinds of errors safety testing reveals. If testing shows that reviewers consistently fail to catch the specific failure modes identified in safety analysis — accepting AI outputs that safety tests showed were problematic — that finding is a safety governance concern that requires design response before deployment.

Dimension five: security testing

Security testing evaluates whether the AI system has security vulnerabilities that could be exploited to cause harm — through unauthorized access to data the system processes, through manipulation of system behavior, or through attacks that compromise system integrity.

AI-specific security vulnerabilities

AI systems present security vulnerabilities that are distinct from those of conventional software and that require specifically targeted security testing. Chapter 7 introduced several AI-specific security concerns; pre-deployment security testing should specifically assess each of them.

Adversarial input testing — also called adversarial attack testing — evaluates whether carefully crafted inputs can cause the AI system to produce incorrect or harmful outputs. For image classification systems, adversarial images can be constructed that appear normal to human viewers but that cause misclassification. For text classification systems, adversarial text can be constructed that appears normal but that evades detection. For language models, adversarial inputs — prompt injection attacks — can be constructed to override system instructions, extract restricted information, or produce harmful outputs. Security testing should attempt to construct adversarial inputs of the types most relevant to the deployment context and assess system robustness against them.

Data extraction testing evaluates whether the system can be queried in ways that extract training data — including personally identifiable information about individuals in the training set. Model inversion attacks and membership inference attacks are techniques by which adversaries can recover information about training data from model outputs. For AI systems trained on sensitive personal information, testing should assess vulnerability to these attack types.

Prompt injection testing is specifically relevant for language model systems — testing whether instructions embedded in content the system processes can override system-level instructions or cause the system to take actions outside its intended scope. For AI systems that process external content — documents, emails, web content — prompt injection is a significant security concern that requires specific testing.

Access control testing evaluates whether the system's access controls function as designed — whether users without authorization can access system capabilities or data, whether data for one user can be accessed by another, and whether administrative functions are adequately protected. Access control testing should be conducted by security specialists using standard penetration testing methods adapted to the AI system context.

Security testing standards

Security testing for AI systems should be conducted by information security professionals with AI security expertise, or by information security generalists who have been specifically briefed on AI security vulnerabilities and who have access to AI security testing methodologies. Standard penetration testing that does not specifically address AI vulnerabilities will not adequately assess AI system security.

Security testing results should be assessed against defined security requirements — not against a general standard of "adequately secure" but against specific requirements appropriate to the sensitivity of the data the system processes and the severity of the harm that security failures could cause. High-risk AI systems processing sensitive personal information should meet higher security standards than low-risk systems processing non-sensitive data.

Security vulnerabilities identified in testing should be disclosed to the vendor if they are in vendor-provided systems, and the vendor's response — whether they address identified vulnerabilities and on what timeline — should inform the deployment decision. Significant unresolved security vulnerabilities should prevent deployment, not be accepted as residual risk.

The testing process: from design to deployment decision

Testing across the five dimensions described above is not a single event but a process — a sequence of activities from test design through result interpretation to deployment decision. The following describes the governance-adequate testing process.

Test plan development

Before any testing begins, a test plan should be developed that specifies: what the testing will assess and on what dimensions, what datasets will be used and how they were selected and validated, what success criteria will be applied to each dimension, who will conduct each component of testing, what the testing timeline is, and how testing results will be documented and reviewed.

The test plan should be reviewed and approved by the governance team before testing begins. This review ensures that the plan is adequately comprehensive, that success criteria have been appropriately established, and that the governance team has committed to the standards against which results will be evaluated. A test plan reviewed after the fact — after results are known — is susceptible to the temptation to set standards that the results happen to meet.

For high-risk systems, test plan review should include input from legal counsel (assessing whether the planned testing will provide adequate evidence of compliance with applicable legal standards), domain experts (assessing whether the planned testing will surface the failure modes most relevant to the deployment context), and information security (assessing whether security testing is adequately designed for the system type and deployment context).

Data collection and validation

Test datasets are the foundation of testing quality. Their collection and validation deserves as much governance attention as the testing itself. Governance teams should require documentation of how test datasets were assembled — what sources they were drawn from, what selection criteria were applied, what representativeness was assessed, and what known limitations exist.

Test data validation should confirm that the data is representative of the deployment context in the dimensions that matter for each testing dimension. For accuracy testing, this means that the distribution of case types and complexity resembles the deployment distribution. For bias testing, this means that the demographic composition of the test population adequately represents the groups to be assessed. For robustness testing, this means that edge cases are included at frequencies that allow meaningful assessment.

Data validation should also confirm that test data does not include data used in training. Testing a system on data it was trained on produces accuracy results that overestimate deployment performance, sometimes dramatically. This contamination — called data leakage — is one of the most common and consequential testing errors; governance must explicitly require and verify that test data is held out from training.

Testing execution and documentation

Testing execution should follow the test plan — not improvised in ways that diverge from the approved methodology — with documentation of what was done, what inputs were used, what outputs the system produced, and what metrics resulted. This documentation supports both governance accountability and institutional learning: future testing can draw on documented methodology and results to assess whether performance is changing over time.

Anomalies discovered during testing — results that do not fit expected patterns, system behaviors that were not anticipated, testing errors that require correction — should be documented and assessed rather than dismissed. Some anomalies are testing artifacts; others are genuine governance signals. The appropriate response is to investigate rather than ignore.

Result interpretation and governance review

Testing results require interpretation — translation from raw metrics to governance assessments. This interpretation requires both technical knowledge and governance judgment, and it should be conducted by people who have both rather than delegated entirely to either technical staff or governance staff alone.

Result interpretation should address: whether results meet the pre-defined success criteria for each testing dimension; what the results reveal about the system's behavior in ways that governance needs to understand beyond pass/fail determinations; what limitations of the testing itself affect how confidently the results can be extrapolated to deployment; and what the results imply for oversight requirements, monitoring priorities, and risk management in deployment.

The governance team should review testing results and their interpretation before making the deployment decision. This review should be substantive — the governance team should understand what was tested, what results were found, what limitations the testing has, and what residual risks remain after testing — not a formality in which a testing summary is approved without genuine engagement.

The deployment decision

Testing results inform but do not determine the deployment decision. The governance team makes the deployment decision based on the full picture: testing results, risk assessment, oversight design, vendor assessment, legal review, and the institution's values and risk tolerance.

Testing results that meet all pre-defined success criteria support but do not require deployment. The governance team retains authority to decline deployment or require additional conditions even when testing results are technically satisfactory, if other governance considerations warrant that outcome.

Testing results that fail to meet pre-defined success criteria on one or more dimensions do not automatically preclude deployment if the governance team determines that specific conditions — enhanced oversight, monitoring requirements, use case scope limitations, vendor remediation — can adequately manage the identified deficiencies. But the governance team should be rigorous about the conditions it requires and the assurance it needs that those conditions will be met before deployment proceeds. Deployment with conditions that are not actually implemented is not conditional deployment; it is deployment with false assurance.

For use cases where testing results reveal significant deficiencies that cannot be adequately managed through conditions, the governance response is to decline deployment and require vendor remediation before resubmission. The institution's willingness to decline deployment when testing reveals significant governance concerns is what gives the testing process its teeth.

Pilot deployment as extended testing

For some use cases — particularly those at the higher end of the medium-risk category, where full-scale deployment seems premature but where the deficiencies that would preclude deployment have not been found — a structured pilot deployment can serve as extended pre-deployment testing in a controlled operational environment.

A pilot deployment differs from full deployment in scope — limited to a defined operational unit, a defined population, or a defined use case subset — and in monitoring intensity — with more intensive monitoring than would be required for full deployment, specifically designed to test whether performance in the operational environment is consistent with pre-deployment testing results.

A pilot deployment is not a soft launch. It requires all the governance preparations that full deployment would require — completed intake review, vendor assessment, oversight design, staff training, incident response procedures — but applies them at reduced scale with heightened monitoring. The pilot has defined evaluation criteria: what evidence, over what period, would support expansion to full deployment, and what evidence would trigger discontinuation.

Pilot results should be reviewed by the governance team before a deployment expansion decision is made. The expansion decision requires positive governance affirmation — evidence from the pilot that performance in the operational context is consistent with pre-deployment testing results — not merely the absence of significant incidents during the pilot period.

Testing documentation and institutional learning

The documentation produced by pre-deployment testing has value beyond the immediate deployment decision. It contributes to institutional learning about AI governance, provides the evidentiary basis for accountability if deployment problems arise later, and creates the baseline against which ongoing monitoring can assess performance change.

Test documentation should be stored as part of the governance record for each AI use case, linked to the corresponding inventory entry, and retained for a period consistent with the institution's accountability and audit obligations. For high-risk systems, test documentation should be retained for at least as long as the system is in operation, and for a further period sufficient to support any investigation of harm that might arise from deployment.

Systematic review of test documentation across multiple AI deployments — identifying patterns in where testing revealed deficiencies, which vendor types or system categories have the most concerning performance profiles, which testing methods have been most revealing — builds institutional learning that improves future testing design and governance decision-making.

The testing minimum for institutions with limited capacity

Some institutions — particularly small nonprofits, small government agencies, and other resource-constrained organizations — lack the technical capacity to conduct the comprehensive testing described in this chapter. The governance question for these institutions is not whether to test but what testing is achievable within their capacity that still provides meaningful governance assurance.

For institutions with limited technical capacity, testing should prioritize: reviewing vendor-provided performance documentation with specific attention to demographic performance differentials; conducting a structured assessment of a sample of system outputs using the domain expertise that institutional staff possess; verifying that the system behaves as described in operational scenarios representative of actual use; and assessing whether the vendor is responsive to governance questions in ways that support confidence in ongoing relationship governance.

This limited testing does not provide the same governance assurance as comprehensive testing across the five dimensions. The governance team should document that limitation explicitly — acknowledging the residual uncertainty that limited testing leaves — and should compensate through more intensive ongoing monitoring, more conservative deployment scope, and more conservative oversight requirements than would be needed if comprehensive testing had been conducted.

Limited testing capacity is a governance resource issue that institutional leadership should address. The governance investment in testing capacity — building staff skills, engaging external assessors for high-risk systems, developing testing methodologies — is justified by the risk reduction and accountability it enables.

Chapter 15: Safe Deployment in Daily Operations

From tested to deployed: the transition that changes everything

Testing establishes what an AI system can do under defined conditions. Deployment establishes what it actually does under operational ones. Between these two states lies a transition that is more consequential than institutions typically recognize — a moment when a system that performed well in controlled evaluation enters the complexity, variability, and unpredictability of real institutional life.

The transition matters because operational conditions differ from test conditions in ways that matter for governance. Real users interact with systems differently than testers do — less systematically, more creatively, and often in ways that surface failure modes that structured testing did not anticipate. Real data has quality problems that test data was cleaned to avoid. Real workflows create pressures and patterns that were not represented in test scenarios. Real affected people — patients, students, clients, applicants — have circumstances and needs that the system's design did not fully anticipate.

None of this means deployment is inadvisable for systems that passed pre-deployment testing. It means that deployment itself is a governance activity, not merely an operational one, and that how deployment is conducted — the speed, scope, oversight intensity, and monitoring design of the rollout — is a governance decision with real consequences for the institution and the people it serves.

This chapter addresses how to deploy AI systems safely and responsibly in daily institutional operations. It covers the principles that should guide deployment design, the staged rollout approach that is the single most important structural choice for most institutional AI deployments, the operational preparations that must be complete before any deployment begins, the staff support that deployment requires, the communication obligations deployment creates, and the governance monitoring that distinguishes genuine deployment oversight from wishful thinking that everything is working because nothing has obviously gone wrong.

The staged rollout: why gradual deployment is a governance requirement

The most important structural choice in AI deployment is whether to deploy all at once — turning on the system for the institution's full operational scope simultaneously — or gradually, expanding scope in stages as evidence accumulates that the system is performing adequately in practice.

For almost every institutional AI deployment of any significance, staged rollout is not merely preferable. It is a governance requirement. The reasoning is straightforward and worth stating explicitly.

Every AI system that passes pre-deployment testing carries residual uncertainty about deployment performance. Testing, however comprehensive, cannot fully predict how a system will behave when it encounters the full range of real operational inputs, when it is used by staff with varying levels of training, when it is integrated with institutional systems in their actual configurations, and when it affects the full diversity of the people the institution serves. This residual uncertainty is not a reason to avoid deployment; it is a reason to deploy in ways that limit the consequences of discovering that deployment performance diverges from test performance.

Staged rollout limits those consequences by limiting scope. When deployment begins at small scale, discovery of a significant performance problem — a bias pattern that testing did not reveal, a failure mode that emerges in specific operational conditions, an interaction with institutional data that produces unexpected outputs — affects a limited population and a limited workflow. Correction can occur before the problem scales. The same discovery in a full-scale deployment affects the entire operational scope simultaneously, requires remediation under full operational pressure, and may have already caused harm to a significant number of people before it is identified.

Staged rollout also produces the operational learning that full-scale deployment requires. The early stages of deployment are when institutions learn how their staff actually use AI systems, which aspects of the deployment design are working and which need adjustment, what monitoring is revealing about real-world performance, and what governance conditions need to be modified before expansion. This learning is only possible if early deployment is monitored intensively enough to produce it — which is part of what staged rollout governance requires.

Designing the staged rollout

A staged rollout is not simply deployment at reduced scale. It is deployment at reduced scale with defined evaluation criteria, intensive monitoring, and explicit decision points at which evidence from earlier stages is assessed before expansion to later stages. The following describes the governance design of a well-structured staged rollout.

Defining stages

The stages of a rollout should be defined before deployment begins, as part of the deployment plan that governance approval covers. Each stage should specify: the operational scope of the stage (which functions, which staff, which populations, which use cases are included), the duration of the stage, the monitoring that will be conducted during the stage, the evaluation criteria that must be met for expansion to the next stage, and the conditions that would trigger rollback rather than expansion.

The number of stages is not fixed; it depends on the risk level of the use case, the institution's confidence from pre-deployment testing, the complexity of the operational context, and the institution's capacity for intensive monitoring. A staged rollout for a high-risk system in a complex operational context might have four or five stages spanning several months. A staged rollout for a medium-risk system in a simpler context might have two stages spanning a few weeks. A low-risk system that passed testing with confidence might be deployed in a single stage with enhanced monitoring for a defined initial period before transitioning to standard monitoring.

The design principle is that each stage should provide enough evidence — about real-world performance, about staff use, about effects on affected people — to make the expansion decision with confidence. Stages that are too short or too small to produce meaningful evidence are not providing governance value; they are creating the appearance of staged rollout without its substance.

Stage one: the controlled pilot

The first deployment stage should be the most controlled: the smallest scope, the most intensive monitoring, the most experienced and prepared staff, and the most closely managed operational conditions. Its purpose is not to provide representative operational experience — it is too small for that — but to confirm that the system behaves in the operational environment as testing predicted, to identify any significant deployment issues before they affect a larger population, and to refine the operational design before expansion.

Stage one scope should be defined to minimize risk while providing meaningful evidence. In most institutional contexts, this means selecting an operational unit whose staff are among the most experienced with the use case, whose workload is representative but not at peak volume, and whose leadership is engaged with governance and capable of supporting intensive monitoring. The population affected by stage one should be identifiable so that any problems discovered can be addressed for those specifically affected.

Stage one monitoring should be more intensive than any subsequent stage. Monitoring in stage one should produce daily or at minimum weekly governance reporting — not because daily problems are expected but because the purpose of stage one is precisely to detect problems early, and that detection requires high-frequency observation. Governance team members should review stage one monitoring reports personally, not through summary, and should be prepared to make rapid decisions if monitoring reveals significant concerns.

Stage one duration should be long enough to observe the system across the range of operational conditions it will encounter — different staff shifts, different case mixes, different workflow pressures. For most institutional contexts, two to four weeks is a reasonable minimum. For systems that will be used in contexts with significant seasonal or cyclical variation, longer stage one periods may be needed to observe representative conditions.

Expansion stages

Each subsequent stage expands the deployment scope based on evidence from the preceding stage. The expansion decision is a governance decision, not a project management milestone. It requires positive governance affirmation — evidence that earlier stage performance is adequate — not merely the absence of serious incidents.

Expansion stage design should address: how scope will be expanded (which additional functions, populations, or use cases will be included), what monitoring will be conducted during the expansion stage, what the evaluation criteria for further expansion are, and how the governance function will remain engaged as the deployment grows.

As deployment scales, the monitoring that was intensive in stage one typically becomes less intensive — there are simply too many transactions to monitor every one at scale. This is expected and appropriate; the transition to standard monitoring levels is itself a governance decision that should be explicitly made at a defined stage, not simply allowed to occur as operational volume increases and intensive monitoring becomes impractical.

The governance function should remain meaningfully engaged throughout expansion stages, even as monitoring intensity decreases. Governance engagement at expansion stages includes: reviewing aggregated monitoring reports, assessing whether performance at larger scale is consistent with earlier stage performance, ensuring that staff support and training are adequate for the expanded scope, and confirming that escalation pathways are functioning.

Steady-state deployment

Full deployment — the steady state in which the AI system operates at its intended scope with standard operational monitoring — is reached when all deployment stages have been completed with satisfactory results. At this point, the deployment transitions from an active rollout to an ongoing operation subject to the monitoring and review processes described in Chapter 16.

The transition to steady state should be explicitly documented — governance records should reflect when full deployment was reached, what evidence supported that determination, and what the ongoing monitoring requirements are. The transition is not a point at which governance attention withdraws; it is a point at which governance transitions from intensive rollout oversight to standard operational oversight.

Pre-deployment operational preparations

A staged rollout can only be safe if the operational preparations that responsible deployment requires are complete before any stage begins. Testing and governance approval are necessary but not sufficient; the following preparations must also be complete.

Technical integration verification

Before deployment, IT must verify that the AI system is correctly integrated with the institutional systems it interacts with — that data flows are functioning as designed, that access controls are correctly configured, that the system is receiving the input data it needs and producing outputs in the form institutional workflows require, and that fallback procedures work when the AI system is unavailable.

Integration verification should specifically confirm that the data the system receives in the operational environment is consistent with the data it was tested on — that format, quality, and content match test assumptions. Integration problems that cause the system to receive different data than expected can produce performance degradation that would not be predicted from testing results.

Technical integration verification should produce documented sign-off from IT before deployment proceeds. For high-risk systems, this sign-off should specifically address AI-relevant integration considerations — not only that the technical integration works but that the data flowing into the AI system is consistent with governance requirements.

Staff training completion

Staff who will interact with an AI system — as direct users, as reviewers of AI outputs, as supervisors of users, or as escalation recipients for AI-related concerns — must have completed appropriate training before deployment begins, not as an aspiration but as a deployment prerequisite.

The content of AI literacy training is addressed in Chapter 17. For deployment purposes, the governance question is whether completion of required training should be verified before deployment, and the answer is yes. Deploying an AI system to staff who have not completed required training is deploying with inadequate oversight. The oversight design established in governance approval assumes that staff have the training needed to exercise it; if they do not, the oversight design is not operative.

Training completion verification should be appropriate to the scale of the deployment. For small-scale stage one deployments, individual completion records for specific staff are practical and should be required. For larger-scale deployments, institutional training completion rates with specific requirements for direct users may be more appropriate. In either case, the governance record should document what training was required, what completion was verified, and when verification occurred.

Escalation pathway confirmation

The escalation pathways established in governance approval — how staff report AI concerns, who receives those reports, who is responsible for investigating and responding to them — must be operationally active before deployment begins. Governance should confirm that:

The AI governance coordinator or designated escalation recipient is aware that the system is being deployed, knows what the system does, and is prepared to receive and act on escalation reports. Staff know how to escalate — both technically (what channel or form to use) and culturally (that escalation is expected and welcomed, not a sign of failure). Supervisors know what to do with escalated concerns — whether to handle them directly, refer them to the governance coordinator, or elevate to governance team attention. Response time commitments for escalations are defined and the people responsible for meeting them are aware of their obligations.

Escalation pathway testing — a simulation in which a test escalation is submitted and the response process is observed — is a practical way to verify that pathways are functioning before live deployment. For high-risk systems, this testing should be required. For other systems, it is good practice even when not required.

Fallback procedures

Fallback procedures define what happens when an AI system is unavailable — due to technical failure, scheduled maintenance, vendor outage, or governance-directed suspension. Before deployment, these procedures must be defined, documented, and known to the staff who will need to use them.

Fallback procedures should address specifically how the work the AI system supports will be done in its absence. For some uses — AI assistance with drafting, AI-powered search, AI scheduling support — fallback is simply reverting to the pre-AI workflow. For uses where AI has been more deeply integrated — where workflows have been redesigned around AI outputs, where staff have become accustomed to AI support for tasks they previously handled differently — fallback may require more specific planning.

The adequacy of fallback procedures is a governance matter because AI availability is not guaranteed and AI suspension may be a governance response to a discovered problem. An institution whose operations are deeply dependent on an AI system and that has no adequate fallback is an institution whose governance options are constrained — because suspending the system creates operational disruption that may make governance-directed suspension practically difficult to execute.

Incident response readiness

Before deployment, the incident response process for the AI system should be operationally ready. This means that incident response procedures are documented (Chapter 19 provides detailed guidance), responsible parties know their roles, and the documentation mechanisms — the incident report template, the logging systems, the communication protocols — are in place.

Incident response readiness is not something to establish after an incident occurs. The purpose of having it in place before deployment is precisely to avoid the situation of managing an incident while simultaneously establishing how to manage it — a combination that guarantees poor incident management.

Operational design: embedding governance in daily practice

Deployment is not only a technical process of making a system available. It is an operational design process — establishing the workflows, norms, and practices through which the AI system will be used day to day in ways that honor the governance commitments made in the approval process.

Workflow integration design

The AI system's role in institutional workflows must be explicitly designed, not left to emerge organically from staff experimentation. Workflow integration design addresses: where in the workflow AI outputs appear, how they are presented to staff, what staff are expected to do with them, what documentation of AI use is required, and how the workflow handles situations where AI outputs are unusual, uncertain, or incorrect.

Workflow design should implement the oversight requirements established in governance approval. If approval conditions require that AI outputs be reviewed by a specific role before being acted on, the workflow must make that review step explicit and unavoidable — not merely recommended but structurally embedded so that proceeding without review requires deliberate circumvention rather than passive omission.

Workflow design should also attend to the presentation of AI outputs to human reviewers. As Chapter 13 established, the way AI outputs are presented significantly affects whether human review is genuine or nominal. Workflow designs that present AI outputs before reviewers have access to underlying information, that present AI confidence scores in ways that create unwarranted authority, or that make deviation from AI recommendations cumbersome will produce nominal oversight even when reviewers are well-intentioned. Governance should review workflow designs specifically for these features.

Documentation practices

Daily operations should include documentation of AI use — records that capture, at a level appropriate to the use case risk level, that AI was used, what it produced, and what human judgment was applied to its outputs. This documentation serves accountability, supports monitoring, and enables investigation when concerns arise.

The required documentation depth should be specified in governance approval and translated into specific practices in workflow design. For high-risk use cases — AI contributing to clinical decisions, benefit determinations, employment actions — documentation should specifically record the AI output, the human reviewer's assessment, and the action taken. For lower-risk uses, documentation may be lighter — a notation that AI assistance was used, or aggregate records rather than case-by-case logging.

Documentation requirements create staff burden, and governance should be realistic about what documentation practices are sustainable in operational contexts. Requirements that are theoretically correct but practically impossible to maintain will be abandoned, producing documentation gaps that are worse than streamlined documentation that is actually kept. Governance team and operational leaders should work together to define documentation practices that meet governance requirements and are operationally feasible.

The daily review habit

For AI systems in active deployment, daily operational practice should include brief attention — by supervisors and operational leads, not necessarily by the governance team — to how the system is performing and whether any concerns have arisen. This is not formal monitoring; it is the operational awareness that allows problems to surface before they accumulate.

Daily review habits might include: a brief check of the previous day's AI output logs for obvious anomalies; a standing question in daily team huddles about whether any staff noticed unexpected AI behavior; a review of any escalation reports submitted since the last check. These practices do not require significant time; they require the institutionalization of awareness that AI system performance is something to pay attention to rather than assume.

Staff support during deployment

Staff experience in the early stages of AI deployment significantly affects both the quality of governance in practice and the long-term acceptance of governance requirements. Staff who feel well-supported during deployment are more likely to follow governance procedures, escalate concerns appropriately, and use AI systems in ways consistent with their intended design. Staff who feel unsupported — who encounter problems they do not know how to handle, who receive conflicting guidance, or who feel exposed when AI systems produce unexpected results — may develop workarounds that circumvent governance or avoidance behaviors that undermine the operational benefits deployment was supposed to provide.

The first-week experience

The first week of deployment deserves specific governance attention. It is when staff encounter the gap between training and operational reality — when the system they practiced with in training meets the specific, unpredictable circumstances of their actual work. Problems that training did not prepare them for, questions that training did not answer, and uncertainty about whether specific situations warrant escalation are all concentrated in the first week.

Governance should ensure that first-week support is specifically provided: that staff have a designated point of contact for operational questions about the AI system, that that contact is responsive and available during operational hours, and that the threshold for reaching out is explicitly set low — staff should understand that they are expected to ask questions during the first week, and that doing so is not a sign of inadequate preparation but the normal process of learning operational practice.

For stage one deployments, first-week check-ins — structured conversations with each user about their experience, what questions they have, and what they observed about the system's behavior — are a valuable governance practice. They surface early operational learning while it is still early enough to inform deployment design before expansion.

Ongoing operational support

Beyond the first week, staff need ongoing access to support as their operational experience with the AI system evolves. Support should address several distinct needs: technical questions about system behavior, questions about governance procedures, uncertainty about when to escalate, and feedback about aspects of the system's performance that are not meeting operational needs.

Support mechanisms should be proportionate to the scale and risk level of the deployment. For large-scale high-risk deployments, a dedicated AI support function — staffed by people who know both the AI system and the governance requirements — may be appropriate. For smaller or lower-risk deployments, designated AI liaison roles within operational teams, with a clear escalation pathway to the governance coordinator, may be sufficient.

Support should not be confused with substituting for appropriate escalation. Staff who encounter AI system behavior that raises governance concerns should be supported in escalating those concerns — not reassured that the system is working as designed if it is not, and not discouraged from escalating by support contacts who are more interested in resolving questions than in identifying genuine governance issues.

Feedback collection

Staff operational experience is a governance information resource. The people using AI systems every day observe performance patterns, use conditions, and operational impacts that monitoring systems may miss — because monitoring typically captures structured data about system outputs, while staff experience captures the qualitative texture of how the system behaves in practice.

Structured feedback collection — through brief periodic surveys, through standing agenda items in team meetings, or through facilitated after-action conversations — translates staff experience into governance intelligence. Feedback should specifically ask about: observed AI behaviors that seem unusual or concerning, situations where the system's outputs did not match operational expectations, aspects of the workflow design that are creating friction, and suggestions for improvements to how the system is used.

Feedback collection is only valuable if it is acted on. Staff who provide feedback and observe no response will stop providing it. Governance should establish a feedback loop — not necessarily addressing every suggestion but acknowledging feedback received, communicating what has been done with it, and explaining when feedback has not resulted in changes and why.

Communicating with affected people

When AI systems influence decisions or services that affect people outside the institution — patients, students, clients, benefit applicants, employees — those people have a right to know that AI is involved and, in most contexts, to understand what role it plays. Chapter 18 addresses stakeholder communication in detail; deployment is the moment at which those communications must be operationally implemented.

Disclosure at the point of service

Disclosure of AI use should occur at or before the point at which AI begins to influence what affected people experience. For clinical AI, this means before or at the clinical encounter where AI is being used. For hiring AI, this means as part of the application process communication. For benefit eligibility AI, this means as part of the intake communication.

Disclosure does not require technical explanation. It requires honest, accessible communication about the fact that AI is involved, what role it plays, and what rights affected people have with respect to it. "We use AI tools to help our staff review applications more efficiently. Our staff review all AI outputs before making decisions. If you have questions about how your application was reviewed, you can contact [designated contact]" is a disclosure that meets these requirements. A footnote in terms and conditions that requires a law degree to interpret does not.

Deployment operations should confirm that disclosure mechanisms are in place and functioning before deployment begins and should include disclosure adequacy in the monitoring framework for the deployment. If disclosure is supposed to occur through specific materials or channels and monitoring reveals it is not actually reaching affected people, that is a governance concern requiring operational response.

Rights and recourse

Affected people's rights with respect to AI-assisted decisions — the right to explanation, the right to request human review, the right to appeal or challenge — must be operationally accessible, not merely formally available. Deployment should establish specific mechanisms through which affected people can exercise these rights: designated contacts, accessible processes, defined response timelines, and staff who are equipped to respond to rights requests.

For high-risk AI use cases — systems that significantly affect access to services, employment, healthcare, or other consequential domains — rights and recourse mechanisms should be specifically tested before deployment: confirming that requests for explanation can be fulfilled meaningfully, that requests for human review are routed correctly and responded to within defined timelines, and that appeal processes are functioning.

Monitoring from day one

Monitoring is addressed comprehensively in Chapter 16; its deployment dimension deserves emphasis here. The monitoring framework for an AI system should not be established after deployment — it should be operational from the first day of deployment, including during stage one when the monitoring should be most intensive.

Day-one monitoring readiness means that: the monitoring metrics defined in governance approval are being collected, dashboards or reporting mechanisms are functioning, the people responsible for reviewing monitoring data know they are responsible and are receiving it, and escalation processes for monitoring alerts are operational.

A specific deployment monitoring practice that is often overlooked is the baseline establishment during stage one. Before full deployment, the system's behavior is unknown in operational conditions. Stage one monitoring should specifically be designed to establish operational baselines — the distributions of outputs, the rates of key events, the patterns of staff behavior — against which subsequent monitoring can assess whether anything is changing. Baselines established in stage one become the reference points against which monitoring in subsequent stages detects meaningful divergence.

The governance team should define what deviations from baseline would trigger governance review. These thresholds should be defined explicitly — not left to the judgment of whoever is reviewing monitoring data — so that governance response is triggered consistently when conditions warrant it. A monitoring system whose escalation thresholds are implicitly defined by the comfort level of the person reviewing reports is not well-governed.

When to pause or stop: the deployment suspension criteria

A deployment that is underway can be paused or stopped. Governance frameworks that do not include explicit criteria for when suspension is warranted — and processes for acting on those criteria — leave the institution without a defined governance response to the most serious deployment problems.

Suspension criteria should be established before deployment begins, as part of the deployment plan. The following circumstances should typically trigger immediate suspension consideration:

A safety-related incident — an event where the AI system may have contributed to physical, psychological, or material harm to a person the institution serves — should trigger immediate governance review, with suspension as the default pending investigation unless the governance team affirmatively determines that continued operation is appropriate under enhanced monitoring.

Discovery of significant bias — monitoring evidence or incident reports revealing that the system is producing differential outcomes across demographic groups at a level that was not identified in pre-deployment testing and that is not adequately managed by current oversight arrangements — should trigger suspension consideration. Whether suspension is warranted depends on the severity of the differential, the use case stakes, and whether immediate operational modifications can adequately manage the concern pending remediation.

Vendor notification of a material system change that has not been reviewed by the governance team should trigger at minimum a hold on expansion and a governance review before continued deployment. If the change is material enough to affect the governance assessment that supported deployment, suspension pending reassessment may be warranted.

Discovery of a significant security vulnerability should trigger immediate escalation to IT and governance leadership, with suspension as the default pending security assessment if the vulnerability could expose institutional data or enable manipulation of system behavior.

Staff behavior patterns that indicate systematic governance non-compliance — override rates that suggest automation bias is eliminating the human oversight that governance approval assumed, escalation rates near zero in a context where escalations should be occurring regularly, documentation patterns indicating that required review is not occurring — should trigger governance review of oversight design and potentially deployment pause pending redesign.

The process for suspension decision should be rapid — the governance team or designated governance team members with authority should be reachable on short notice for suspension decisions — and should produce a documented record of what triggered suspension consideration, what the governance review found, and what decision was made with what rationale.

Steady-state transition: what changes and what does not

When a staged rollout is complete and the AI system transitions to steady-state operation, several things change and several things do not.

What changes: monitoring intensity decreases from the heightened level of staged deployment to the standard ongoing monitoring level defined for the use case. Deployment governance attention — the specific governance team engagement with active rollout decisions — transitions to standard periodic review. The deployment plan is closed and replaced by the ongoing governance record for the system.

What does not change: the governance obligations associated with the AI system's operation, the oversight requirements that governance approval established, the escalation pathways and incident response readiness, the disclosure and rights mechanisms for affected people, and the accountability for system performance. Steady state is not a graduation from governance; it is a transition to a different phase of governance — operational oversight rather than active rollout — that is no less real for being less visible.

The governance team should explicitly mark the transition to steady state — with a governance record entry noting when full deployment was reached, what evidence supported that determination, and what the ongoing governance requirements are. This marking ensures that the transition is a deliberate governance act rather than something that happens by default when rollout activities have stopped. Governance by default — governance that operates only when something is actively happening and withdraws when things seem stable — is not adequate governance for systems that continue to affect people every day in steady-state operation.

Deployment as governance in action

The practices described in this chapter — staged rollout, thorough operational preparation, staff support, affected party communication, day-one monitoring, explicit suspension criteria — are governance in its most operational form. They are not bureaucratic additions to what would otherwise be a purely technical deployment process; they are the means by which governance commitments made in policy, validated in testing, and operationalized in oversight design actually take effect in the daily work of the institution.

Safe deployment is governance made visible: the point at which the institution's stated commitments to the people it serves — to fairness, transparency, safety, privacy, accountability, security, and human dignity — either are or are not honored in the actual conduct of operations. The distance between governance documents and governance reality is crossed, or not crossed, here.

Institutions that deploy AI carefully — who plan their rollouts, prepare their staff, communicate with affected people, monitor from the start, and are willing to pause when monitoring reveals problems — are institutions that are governing AI rather than merely hoping it works. That distinction is what this book is about, and deployment is where it most concretely manifests.

Chapter 16: Monitoring and Ongoing Review

The governance that never stops

Every governance activity described in this book so far — principles development, policy writing, intake screening, vendor assessment, testing, deployment planning — is preparation for the moment when an AI system begins operating in the institution's daily work. That preparation is necessary. It is not sufficient. The moment deployment begins, governance enters a new phase that is less visible than the activities that preceded it but no less essential: ongoing monitoring and review.

Monitoring is governance sustained over time. It is the institutional practice of watching what deployed AI systems actually do — not what they were designed to do, not what testing suggested they would do, but what they are doing right now, with real inputs, in real workflows, affecting real people. It is the mechanism through which the gap between governance assumptions and operational reality is discovered, assessed, and addressed.

Without monitoring, governance is provisional. The intake review, the vendor assessment, the pre-deployment testing, the oversight design — all of these are based on predictions about how a system will behave in deployment. Those predictions may be well-founded, but they are predictions, and predictions fail. AI systems behave differently in operational conditions than in testing. Vendor model updates change system behavior. The population the system serves shifts in ways that affect performance. Staff use patterns evolve, sometimes in ways that undermine oversight design. Data quality changes. Operational pressures create shortcuts. Over time, a system that was well-governed at deployment drifts from the conditions that justified its governance approval.

Monitoring is what converts the governance system from a point-in-time assessment to a continuous assurance function. It is what allows institutions to know — on an ongoing basis, not only at the moment of deployment — that the AI systems they operate are performing as required, that oversight is functioning, that affected people are not being harmed in ways governance did not anticipate, and that the institution can account for what its AI systems are doing.

This chapter describes what institutional AI monitoring requires: what to monitor, how to monitor it, who is responsible for monitoring, how to organize monitoring information for governance use, how to identify when monitoring reveals problems, and how to conduct the periodic reviews that complement continuous monitoring with deeper governance reassessment.

What monitoring must cover: the four surveillance domains

AI system monitoring should cover four distinct domains, each of which addresses different aspects of system governance. These domains are not independent — problems in one typically manifest in others — but they require different monitoring approaches and generate different kinds of governance intelligence.

Domain one: technical performance

Technical performance monitoring tracks the operational characteristics of the AI system itself: how accurately it performs, whether its behavior is consistent, whether its performance is changing over time, and whether it is operating within the technical parameters that governance approval established.

The specific metrics in technical performance monitoring depend on the system type and use case. For classification systems, relevant metrics include accuracy, sensitivity, specificity, positive predictive value, and negative predictive value — tracked over time to detect changes from baseline. For prediction systems, relevant metrics include calibration — whether expressed probabilities match actual event rates — and discrimination metrics. For generative AI systems, relevant metrics include factual accuracy rates for fact-check-able outputs, output consistency across equivalent inputs, and refusal rates for requests that fall outside appropriate scope.

Beyond output quality metrics, technical performance monitoring should track operational performance: system availability and uptime, response time distributions, error rates at the infrastructure level, and any anomalies in system behavior that might indicate technical problems or security incidents. These metrics are primarily IT monitoring responsibilities, but they belong in the governance monitoring framework because technical failures have governance implications — a system that is unavailable when decisions need to be made, or that produces errors that staff cannot identify as errors, is a governance failure as well as a technical one.

Technical performance monitoring should be continuous or near-continuous — producing data at sufficient frequency to detect meaningful changes before they have accumulated into significant harm. For high-risk systems, daily metric calculation is appropriate. For medium-risk systems, weekly metrics are generally adequate. For lower-risk systems, monthly metrics may suffice. The key principle is that the monitoring interval should be short enough that a meaningful performance change is detected while the affected population is still small enough for effective remediation.

Domain two: fairness and demographic performance

Fairness monitoring tracks whether the AI system is performing consistently across the demographic groups that governance and legal frameworks require equal treatment for, and whether any differential performance is within the bounds that governance approval established as acceptable.

Fairness monitoring requires data about the demographic characteristics of the people affected by the AI system — which means that the monitoring infrastructure must include mechanisms for collecting this data in a way that is legally appropriate, operationally practical, and analytically adequate. This is often the most technically and logistically challenging aspect of AI monitoring, and it deserves specific planning attention.

The metrics for fairness monitoring mirror those used in pre-deployment bias testing (Chapter 14): performance rates across demographic groups, differential error rates, disparate impact ratios for outcome distributions.

What changes between testing and monitoring is the data source — monitoring uses operational data rather than test data — and the statistical challenge of detecting meaningful differentials in real-time data that may arrive in smaller volumes and less structured forms than test datasets.

Statistical power is a persistent challenge in fairness monitoring. Detecting a meaningful performance differential between demographic groups requires sufficient numbers of cases from each group to achieve statistical confidence. For institutions that serve relatively homogeneous populations, or that make relatively few decisions per period, the sample sizes available for fairness monitoring may be insufficient to detect modest performance differentials at high confidence. Governance frameworks should acknowledge this limitation explicitly — documenting what sample sizes are available, what differentials can be detected at what confidence levels, and what this implies for the institution's ability to monitor fairness adequately. Where sample sizes are inadequate for statistical detection of meaningful differentials, more conservative human oversight requirements may be appropriate to compensate.

Fairness monitoring should be reported to the governance team at defined intervals — for high-risk systems, at least quarterly — with specific attention to any trends toward increasing differential performance over time. Gradual drift in fairness metrics is as concerning as sudden changes, but it is easier to miss without explicit trend analysis. Monitoring reports should present fairness metrics not only as current snapshots but as trend lines, allowing the governance team to identify concerning directions before they reach alarming levels.

Domain three: operational use and oversight quality

Operational monitoring tracks how the AI system is actually being used in daily operations — specifically whether staff are using it in ways consistent with governance requirements, and whether the human oversight arrangements established at deployment are functioning as designed.

The most governance-critical operational metrics involve human oversight quality. As Chapter 13 established, the difference between meaningful and nominal oversight is primarily visible in behavior patterns rather than in formal compliance with oversight procedures. Override rates — the proportion of AI recommendations that human reviewers modify or reject — are the primary oversight quality indicator. Escalation rates — the proportion of AI outputs that are elevated to additional review rather than handled at the front-line level — provide complementary information. Documentation compliance rates — the proportion of AI-assisted decisions that are documented in the manner governance requires — indicate whether the record-keeping that supports accountability is being maintained.

These metrics require interpretation in context. As Chapter 13 noted, a very low override rate may indicate automation bias — reviewers deferring to AI recommendations without genuine independent assessment — or it may indicate that the AI system is performing well and reviewers have learned through experience that its recommendations are reliable. A very high override rate may indicate that the AI system is not meeting operational needs, or that reviewers are systematically second-guessing a system whose recommendations are actually sound. The governance significance of these metrics depends on the context, the history, and the comparison to expectations.

Monitoring should therefore include qualitative assessment alongside quantitative metrics. Periodic conversations with operational leaders and frontline staff — about how the AI system is working in practice, what challenges staff are encountering, whether oversight feels genuine or perfunctory, and whether the escalation culture is healthy — provide interpretive context that numbers alone cannot supply.

Volume and distribution monitoring tracks whether the AI system is being used at the expected scale, for the expected purposes, by the expected users. Anomalies in volume — sudden increases or decreases in use, unexpected concentration of use in specific time periods, use by staff who were not trained or designated for the system — may indicate governance compliance problems, operational issues, or changes in use scope that have not been assessed by the governance function.

Domain four: harm and complaint signals

Harm and complaint monitoring tracks the signals that may indicate the AI system is causing problems for the people it affects — the patients, students, clients, applicants, or employees whose circumstances are influenced by AI-assisted decisions.

These signals come from multiple sources. Incident reports — submitted through the incident reporting mechanism described in Chapter 19 — are the most direct harm signals. Complaints — received through whatever channels affected people use to raise concerns about institutional service — may reference AI-related problems even when the person does not know AI was involved. Appeals — requests for human review of decisions, formal grievances, or other formal recourse mechanisms — may cluster in ways that indicate AI performance problems affecting specific populations or decision types. Litigation or regulatory inquiries may signal problems that have reached the threshold of formal legal action.

Harm and complaint monitoring requires that the institution has defined what counts as an AI-related complaint or harm signal, how such signals are to be recorded and categorized, and who is responsible for reviewing them and escalating governance-relevant patterns to the governance function. Without this definitional and process infrastructure, harm signals may arrive in the institution through various channels and never reach the governance function in a form that allows pattern recognition.

Pattern recognition in harm and complaint signals is particularly important. Individual complaints may be dismissed as outliers. Patterns of complaints from similar populations, about similar outcomes, in similar time periods are governance signals that require investigation. The governance function should receive regular reporting on complaint and incident patterns — not only on the volume of individual complaints but on whether patterns are emerging that suggest systematic problems.

Drift: the slow failure mode

Of all the things that monitoring tracks, drift — the gradual degradation of AI system performance or governance compliance over time, in ways that are difficult to detect in any individual measurement but significant in accumulated effect — is the most important and the most frequently overlooked.

Drift occurs through multiple mechanisms. Model drift happens when the statistical relationship between the inputs the AI system receives and the appropriate outputs changes over time, so that a model calibrated on historical data becomes progressively less accurate as the world it was calibrated on diverges from the world it currently serves. Population drift happens when the characteristics of the population the system serves change in ways that move them away from the distribution the model was trained on. Behavioral drift happens when staff use patterns evolve — shortcuts, workarounds, changed workflows — in ways that undermine the oversight design established at deployment. Data quality drift happens when the inputs to the AI system change in quality, completeness, or consistency in ways that degrade output quality without any change in the model itself.

Each of these drift types produces gradual performance deterioration that is invisible in any single measurement but significant over time. A system that was 92% accurate at deployment and is 84% accurate two years later did not fail suddenly; it drifted. The governance significance of that drift — whether it is acceptable given the use case requirements, or whether it represents a performance decline that requires remediation — cannot be assessed without the baseline and trend data that continuous monitoring provides.

Monitoring for drift

Drift detection requires comparing current performance to a defined baseline and assessing whether the deviation is within acceptable bounds. The baseline should be established during the deployment phase (Chapter 15), using the performance characteristics observed during stage one and early full deployment. The acceptable deviation bounds should be defined explicitly — in governance documentation, before deployment — so that drift detection triggers are not set retrospectively at whatever level happens to have been observed.

Trend analysis — examining performance metrics not as individual data points but as time series — is the primary drift detection tool. A metric that is within acceptable bounds today but has been declining consistently for six months may warrant governance attention even if the current level is technically acceptable, because the trend indicates it will become unacceptable without intervention.

Statistical process control methods — tools from quality management practice that distinguish between normal variation and signals of systematic change — are useful for drift detection in AI monitoring. Control charts that plot performance metrics over time with upper and lower control limits derived from baseline variation make it visually and statistically clear when performance is drifting outside the range that normal operational variation would explain.

Governance should define, for each monitored AI system, what trend patterns trigger governance review even when no individual measurement exceeds defined thresholds. A performance metric declining steadily over five consecutive reporting periods, even if still within the acceptable range, is a pattern that warrants investigation — not because the current situation is unacceptable but because the trajectory suggests it will become unacceptable without action.

The monitoring infrastructure

Monitoring requires infrastructure — the technical systems, data pipelines, reporting mechanisms, and human processes through which monitoring data is collected, processed, and made available for governance review. Building this infrastructure is a governance investment that must be planned for, not assumed to exist.

Data collection

The foundation of monitoring is data collection: ensuring that the events and transactions that monitoring needs to track are captured in a form that allows analysis. For AI systems, this means logging AI inputs and outputs, recording human reviewer decisions and override events, capturing complaint and escalation submissions, and tracking demographic characteristics of affected people where governance requires fairness monitoring.

Data collection should be designed before deployment, not retrofitted after. Systems that are deployed without logging capabilities are not monitorable in the ways governance requires; adding logging infrastructure after deployment may require system modifications that carry their own governance implications. The data requirements of monitoring should be specified in the deployment plan and confirmed as part of pre-deployment preparation.

Data collection must be consistent with data governance requirements (Chapter 12): logs that capture personal information must be subject to appropriate access controls and retention policies, must be consistent with the legal basis for processing, and must not create new privacy risks in the course of generating governance intelligence. The monitoring data infrastructure is itself subject to data governance.

Dashboards and reporting

Monitoring data should be organized into governance-ready reporting — dashboards, scheduled reports, or both — that present monitoring information in forms that allow governance review without requiring direct analysis of raw data. Dashboards that are technically sophisticated but practically unread are not governance infrastructure; they are technical infrastructure that governance has failed to use.

Governance-ready reporting should present monitoring metrics at the level of detail appropriate for each audience. Governance team members need summary metrics and trend indicators — information sufficient to assess whether significant concerns exist and to direct attention to areas warranting closer review. Operational leaders need operational metrics — information about how the system is performing in their specific function and whether oversight practices are meeting requirements. IT needs technical metrics — information about system availability, error rates, and performance characteristics at the infrastructure level.

Reporting frequency should be matched to monitoring interval and governance review cadence. If technical performance is monitored daily, daily summary reports should be available to the AI governance coordinator, with governance team review of weekly summaries. If fairness metrics are calculated monthly, monthly reports should be available for governance team review. The reporting cadence should ensure that monitoring information reaches governance review within a timeframe that allows meaningful response — not so frequently that governance is overwhelmed with data, not so infrequently that problems have accumulated significantly before governance sees them.

Automated alerting — notifications triggered when monitoring metrics exceed defined thresholds — reduces the reliance on governance team members proactively reviewing reports to detect problems. Alert thresholds should be defined explicitly, tested before deployment, and calibrated to generate meaningful signals rather than noise. Alert systems that generate too many notifications will be ignored; alert systems that generate too few will miss genuine governance signals. Calibration of alert thresholds is an ongoing process that should be reviewed periodically as the system accumulates operational history.

Governance review cadence

Monitoring data must be reviewed by governance team members, not merely collected. The review cadence — how frequently the governance team examines monitoring information — should be defined in the governance framework and should be appropriate to the risk level of the system.

For high-risk systems, governance team review of monitoring information should occur at least monthly, with the AI governance coordinator reviewing at higher frequency and escalating to governance team attention when monitoring signals warrant it. For medium-risk systems, quarterly governance team review is generally adequate, with the coordinator reviewing monthly. For lower-risk systems, semi-annual review may be sufficient.

Governance team review of monitoring should be substantive — members should come to monitoring reviews having read the relevant reports and prepared to engage with what they show. A governance team that approves monitoring reports without examining them is not exercising oversight; it is performing the administrative act of review without its substance. Governance culture should treat monitoring review as consequential work, not as a routine confirmation that nothing is wrong.

Recognizing problems: from signal to response

Monitoring generates signals. Governance converts signals into assessments and responses. This conversion requires judgment — the ability to distinguish meaningful signals from noise, to assess the significance of observed patterns, and to determine what governance response is proportionate to what monitoring reveals.

Distinguishing noise from signal

Not every monitoring anomaly is a governance concern. AI systems produce variable outputs; performance metrics fluctuate with case mix, seasonal variation, and operational variation that is normal and expected. The governance challenge is distinguishing fluctuations that are within the range of normal variation from changes that reflect genuine performance shifts warranting governance attention.

Statistical methods — particularly control chart approaches and hypothesis testing — provide principled ways to make this distinction. A metric that moves outside its statistical control limits is providing a signal that the change is unlikely to be due to normal variation alone. A metric that has crossed a threshold once may be noise; a metric that has crossed the same threshold in multiple consecutive periods is more likely to be a signal.

Domain expertise also contributes to signal assessment. A clinical informaticist reviewing a clinical AI monitoring report may recognize patterns that are clinically significant without meeting statistical thresholds — specific case types or patient populations where performance changes have clinical meaning that aggregate statistics obscure. This is why monitoring review should involve domain expertise alongside technical expertise, particularly for high-risk systems in professional practice contexts.

The problem escalation protocol

When monitoring reveals a potential concern — a metric that has crossed a threshold, a pattern that warrants investigation, a signal from complaint data that suggests systematic harm — the governance response should follow a defined protocol rather than being improvised.

The protocol should specify: who makes the initial assessment of whether a monitoring signal requires governance escalation, what information should be gathered before escalation to characterize the concern adequately, who receives the escalated concern, on what timeline, and what initial responses are within the authority of the receiver versus what requires governance team involvement.

A practical escalation protocol for most institutions has three levels. The first level — assessment by the AI governance coordinator — applies to all monitoring signals that exceed defined thresholds. The coordinator reviews the signal, gathers contextual information, and determines whether it requires governance team attention or can be addressed operationally. The second level — governance team notification — applies to signals that the coordinator assesses as potentially significant: possible bias patterns, performance changes that exceed acceptable bounds, unusual complaint clusters, or operational compliance concerns. The third level — governance team urgent meeting — applies to signals that may require immediate action: potential safety concerns, evidence of significant harm to affected people, or security-related monitoring signals.

This protocol should be documented, distributed to all relevant parties, and tested periodically to confirm it functions as designed. An escalation protocol that has never been tested may have gaps — unclear handoffs, unresponsive contacts, ambiguous thresholds — that only become apparent when an actual escalation is needed.

Periodic review: the scheduled governance reassessment

Continuous monitoring detects changes as they occur. Periodic review — scheduled, structured reassessment of deployed AI systems at defined intervals — serves a different governance purpose: stepping back from the continuous data stream to ask whether the overall governance picture for a system remains adequate, whether the assumptions that supported governance approval still hold, and whether any changes in institutional context, regulatory requirements, or AI development practice require governance attention.

Annual review: the standard governance checkpoint

Every AI system in the institutional inventory should undergo annual governance review — a structured reassessment that addresses the following questions.

Has the system's performance over the past year been within the parameters that governance approval established? Annual review should include a comprehensive analysis of the year's monitoring data: performance trends, fairness metric history, oversight quality patterns, complaint and incident patterns. The goal is not to reconfirm that individual measurements were within bounds but to assess the overall performance picture — whether the system is behaving as governance approval anticipated and whether any concerning patterns have developed.

Have the use case, scope, or operational context changed in ways that affect the governance assessment? Use cases evolve. A system approved for a specific operational scope may have been gradually extended to additional uses without triggering a formal review, because each individual extension seemed minor. The annual review is an opportunity to examine whether the current actual use of the system matches the use case that was assessed and approved.

Have the vendor's practices, system capabilities, or contractual commitments changed in ways that affect governance? Annual review should include a check of vendor communications, model update notifications, contract status, and any changes to the vendor's governance practices or product documentation.

Have applicable legal or regulatory requirements changed in ways that require governance response? The regulatory environment for AI is developing rapidly; requirements that did not exist at the time of the original governance approval may now apply. Annual review should include a legal and compliance check against current requirements.

Has the governance framework itself evolved in ways that require reassessment of existing deployments? As the governance team develops its AI policy, refines its standards, and accumulates experience, the standards it applies to new approvals may differ from those applied to existing systems. Annual review should assess whether existing systems would meet current governance standards and should require updates where they would not.

The annual review should produce a governance record — a documented assessment of the system's ongoing compliance with governance requirements, any concerns identified, any changes required, and any conditions attached to continued use. This record should be incorporated into the system's governance file and should inform the governance team's overall assessment of the institution's AI risk profile.

Triggered review: when circumstances require unscheduled reassessment

In addition to scheduled annual reviews, governance should define triggers for unscheduled reviews when circumstances change in ways that may affect the governance assessment.

Vendor notification of a material model update is a trigger for review. Material updates — changes to the model's training data, architecture, or output characteristics — may change the system's performance in ways that affect the governance approval. The review should assess whether the updated system still meets governance requirements or whether testing, oversight adjustments, or other governance responses are needed.

Significant monitoring findings — a monitoring signal that escalated to governance team attention — should trigger a focused review of the affected dimension of the system's governance. If monitoring reveals a potential bias pattern, the triggered review should specifically examine fairness metrics in depth and assess whether the finding represents a genuine governance concern requiring remediation or an artifact of statistical variation.

Regulatory or legal developments that specifically affect the use case should trigger legal review and governance reassessment. New guidance from a regulatory agency about AI in the relevant sector, new legislation affecting AI use in the institution's domain, or enforcement actions against other institutions for similar AI uses are all triggers for reassessment of whether current governance remains adequate.

Institutional changes that affect the use case — a merger, a significant change in the population served, a material change in the operational context — should trigger assessment of whether the changed context affects the governance picture.

Staff turnover in key oversight roles should trigger reassessment of whether oversight is functioning as governance approval assumed. When the specific people who have been exercising oversight of an AI system change, there is no guarantee that their successors will exercise oversight with the same quality. Triggered review of oversight quality following significant turnover is a governance best practice.

Monitoring program governance: who owns what

Monitoring is a distributed function — different people and functions contribute different aspects of the overall monitoring picture. The governance framework should specify these contributions explicitly.

The AI governance coordinator is responsible for: maintaining the monitoring framework, collecting and organizing monitoring reports from contributing functions, reviewing monitoring data at defined intervals, identifying signals that require governance team escalation, and maintaining the documentation of monitoring findings and responses.

IT is responsible for: technical performance monitoring, availability and infrastructure metrics, security monitoring, and providing technical data in formats that the monitoring framework requires.

Operational leaders are responsible for: oversight quality monitoring within their functions, reporting operational observations about AI system behavior, ensuring that escalation mechanisms are accessible to frontline staff, and providing qualitative context for quantitative monitoring data.

The governance team is responsible for: reviewing monitoring reports at defined intervals, making governance decisions when monitoring reveals concerns, updating monitoring requirements when governance review suggests current monitoring is inadequate, and ensuring that the overall monitoring program is providing the governance intelligence that responsible AI operation requires.

Vendors are responsible for: providing performance reporting as specified in vendor contracts, notifying the institution of material system changes, disclosing security incidents promptly, and cooperating with institution-initiated audits and assessments.

Using monitoring to improve governance

Monitoring is not only a detection function — it is a learning function. The data that monitoring generates, analyzed thoughtfully over time, provides governance intelligence that can improve the overall quality of the institution's AI governance.

Monitoring data from existing deployments should inform the governance team's assessment of proposed new AI use cases. If monitoring of a deployed clinical AI system reveals that performance varies significantly by documentation style, that finding is relevant to the governance assessment of other clinical AI systems the institution may consider. If monitoring reveals that escalation rates are consistently near zero in a specific operational context despite AI systems that cannot be perfect, that finding suggests an oversight culture problem that is relevant to governance of any AI deployment in that context.

Monitoring data should feed the annual review of the AI policy. If monitoring consistently reveals specific types of governance concerns — vendor notification failures, oversight quality problems in high-volume contexts, fairness monitoring limitations due to sample size — those patterns suggest policy provisions that may need strengthening or operational requirements that need clarification.

The governance team should cultivate a practice of explicit learning from monitoring — periodic discussions that ask not only what monitoring reveals about specific systems but what patterns across the monitoring portfolio reveal about governance strengths and weaknesses. This meta-level monitoring — monitoring the monitoring, assessing the governance system's overall performance — is how governance programs improve over time rather than merely persisting at their initial quality level.

The relationship between monitoring and audit

Monitoring and audit serve related but distinct functions. Monitoring is continuous and operational — it tracks AI system performance in real time, flags concerns as they arise, and provides the ongoing situational awareness that governance requires. Audit is periodic and evaluative — it assesses whether the governance system as a whole is functioning as designed, whether monitoring is adequate, and whether governance documentation reflects actual practice.

The audit function is addressed in Chapter 22. The relationship between monitoring and audit deserves mention here: monitoring generates the data that audit draws on, and audit assessments of monitoring adequacy shape the governance team's investment in monitoring improvement. Governance that monitors without auditing may be generating data about AI systems that it is not using adequately to improve governance. Governance that audits without monitoring has nothing meaningful to audit — it can assess whether governance processes exist but not whether they are detecting what they are supposed to detect.

Monitoring and audit together constitute the assurance function of AI governance: the ongoing institutional practice of confirming that AI systems are doing what governance requires, that governance processes are functioning as designed, and that the institution can account for its AI governance with confidence rather than hope.

When monitoring reveals that governance has failed

Monitoring will sometimes reveal that AI systems are not performing as governance approval assumed, that oversight is not functioning as designed, or that affected people have been harmed in ways governance was supposed to prevent. These findings are governance failures — situations where the governance system did not prevent a harm it was designed to prevent.

Governance failures revealed by monitoring are not merely operational problems. They are accountability events that require governance response: honest assessment of what went wrong and why, appropriate remediation for affected people, improvement of governance processes to prevent recurrence, and in some cases public acknowledgment of what occurred.

The governance team should approach monitoring-revealed failures with the combination of honesty and constructiveness that genuine accountability requires. Honest acknowledgment that governance did not perform as required — that monitoring data shows bias that testing missed, that oversight quality metrics indicate nominal rather than genuine review, that a harm that governance was supposed to prevent occurred — is the beginning of improvement. Defensive minimization of monitoring findings, or retroactive reinterpretation of monitoring data to avoid uncomfortable conclusions, is the beginning of governance deterioration.

The institution that responds to monitoring-revealed governance failures by investigating thoroughly, remediating diligently, and improving its governance processes genuinely is building governance capability that compounds over time. The institution that responds by minimizing findings and protecting its own record is building governance complacency that will compound into larger failures. Monitoring provides the evidence; the institution's response to that evidence determines what kind of governance it actually has.

Chapter 17: Building AI Literacy

The gap between having tools and using them well

Institutions that deploy AI systems without adequately preparing the people who interact with them have built governance infrastructure on an unstable foundation. Policies, intake processes, vendor contracts, testing protocols, oversight designs — all of these are governance investments that depend for their effectiveness on human beings who understand what AI systems are, what they can and cannot do, why governance requirements exist, and what their own responsibilities are when AI is part of their work.

That understanding is AI literacy. It is not technical expertise. The staff member who processes benefits applications does not need to understand transformer architecture to use an AI decision support tool responsibly. The clinical manager who oversees AI-assisted triage does not need to understand gradient descent to exercise meaningful oversight. The board member who receives AI governance reports does not need to understand training data pipelines to ask the right accountability questions. What each of these people needs is accurate, proportionate understanding — enough to do their job in the AI-augmented environment responsibly, enough to recognize when something is wrong, and enough to know what to do when it is.

The gap between what most institutional staff currently understand about AI and what responsible AI use requires them to understand is significant and growing. AI capabilities are expanding faster than institutional learning programs. The tools that staff encounter in their daily work are more capable, more consequential, and more governance-relevant than the tools they were trained for. And the stakes of this literacy gap are not merely operational — they are governance stakes, because governance commitments that staff do not understand cannot be honored in practice.

This chapter describes what institutional AI literacy programs should accomplish, what they should cover for different audiences, how they should be structured, how their effectiveness should be assessed, and how they should be maintained as AI capabilities and institutional use evolve. It is a chapter about organizational learning — about how institutions build the human capacity that governance requires.

What AI literacy is and is not

Before describing what AI literacy programs should contain, it is important to be clear about what AI literacy means in the institutional governance context — and what it does not mean.

AI literacy is not technical training. The goal is not to turn institutional staff into AI engineers, data scientists, or machine learning practitioners. The goal is to give people sufficient understanding of how AI systems work, what their characteristics are, and what responsible use requires to enable them to do their jobs well and exercise their governance responsibilities effectively. This is a much more achievable goal than technical training, and it is the right goal for the vast majority of institutional staff.

AI literacy is not vendor training. Vendors provide product training — how to use specific tools, how to navigate specific interfaces, how to interpret specific outputs. Product training is useful and necessary, but it is not governance literacy. A staff member who knows how to use an AI screening tool efficiently but does not understand what bias means, why oversight is required, or when to escalate a concern is product-trained but not literacy-trained. Product training typically serves vendor interests — efficient tool use, feature adoption, positive product perception — while governance literacy serves institutional interests and the interests of the people the institution serves. Both are needed; neither substitutes for the other.

AI literacy is not a one-time compliance exercise. Many institutional training programs approach AI literacy as a box to be checked — a module to be completed, a signature to be obtained, a completion record to be filed. Compliance training has its place, but AI literacy that consists only of a compliance exercise will not build the genuine understanding that governance requires. People who complete an AI literacy module without achieving the understanding it is supposed to convey have a completion record but not literacy. The goal of AI literacy programs is changed understanding and changed behavior, not completed training records.

AI literacy is a functional capacity — the ability to work with AI systems in ways that serve the institution's mission and governance obligations, recognize situations that require escalation or special care, apply governance principles in daily practice, and contribute to the collective organizational learning that improves governance over time. This functional definition means that literacy success is measured by what people can do, not by what they have sat through.

The literacy audiences: different people need different things

AI literacy is not one-size-fits-all. Different institutional roles interact with AI in different ways, bear different governance responsibilities, and require different kinds of understanding. A well-designed AI literacy program addresses the specific needs of each audience rather than delivering identical content to everyone and hoping it sticks.

Board and senior leadership

Senior leaders and board members need AI literacy that supports their governance and oversight roles — not operational knowledge of how to use specific AI tools but strategic and governance understanding of what AI means for the institution.

The board and senior leadership audience needs to understand: what AI the institution is using and why; what the most significant risks associated with institutional AI use are; what governance structures are in place and whether they are adequate; what questions they should be asking to exercise meaningful oversight; what regulatory and reputational exposure institutional AI use creates; and how to recognize when AI governance is functioning well versus when it is performing adequacy without achieving it.

This audience typically has limited time for training and may be skeptical of training framed as introductory or basic. Effective leadership AI literacy programs are framed around governance and strategic questions rather than technical orientation. They use concrete cases — real examples of institutional AI successes and failures — rather than abstract concepts. They create space for genuine engagement and questioning rather than one-way information delivery. And they connect AI governance directly to the leadership and oversight responsibilities that participants are already accountable for.

The appropriate format for board and senior leadership AI literacy is typically not a training module but a facilitated session — a working meeting at which governance questions about institutional AI are addressed through structured discussion, case analysis, and Q&A with governance specialists. Annual facilitated sessions, updated with current information about the institution's AI activities and the evolving external environment, are appropriate for most governance bodies. Supplementary briefings when significant AI-related developments occur — a new AI deployment, a significant AI-related incident, a major regulatory development — keep leadership understanding current between annual sessions.

Governance team members

The governance team bears specific responsibility for institutional AI governance decisions, and its members need AI literacy that is more substantive than leadership literacy while remaining non-technical. Governance team members need to understand AI well enough to conduct meaningful intake reviews, assess vendor claims critically, evaluate testing documentation, interpret monitoring reports, and make governance decisions that are genuinely informed rather than formally adequate.

Governance team literacy should cover: how AI systems work in plain language (building on Chapter 4 of this book), the specific risk categories that governance must address (Chapter 3), the principles that should guide governance decisions (Chapter 7), the specific processes the governance team owns (Chapters 10, 11, 14, 16), and how to recognize red flags in vendor claims, test documentation, and monitoring data.

Governance team members should also develop specific expertise in the domains most relevant to the institution's AI use. A governance team member from the legal function needs AI literacy that connects to their legal expertise — AI law and regulation, contractual AI governance. A governance team member from clinical leadership needs AI literacy that connects to clinical expertise — clinical AI performance, clinical AI risk, clinical oversight design. The combination of governance framework knowledge and domain expertise is what makes governance team members effective at their function.

Initial governance team AI literacy training — when the team is formed or when new members join — should be substantial: a program of several hours that covers the governance framework, the institution's specific AI uses, and the governance responsibilities of the team. This initial training should be supplemented by ongoing development: regular governance team discussions of AI governance topics, invited presentations from technical experts, and review of significant developments in AI governance practice and regulation.

Managers and supervisors

Managers and supervisors occupy a critical position in AI governance: they are the link between institutional governance requirements and frontline practice. They are responsible for ensuring that their teams comply with governance requirements, for creating the oversight culture that governance depends on, for receiving and acting on escalations from frontline staff, and for providing the qualitative assessment of AI system performance that quantitative monitoring alone cannot supply.

The manager and supervisor literacy audience needs to understand: what AI systems their teams use and what governance requirements apply; what good oversight practice looks like and how to support it; how to recognize compliance problems — override rates that suggest automation bias, escalation patterns that suggest cultural barriers to reporting — and what to do about them; how to respond to staff concerns about AI performance; and what their responsibilities are if AI-related incidents occur.

Manager and supervisor training should be specifically practical — focused on the situations that managers actually encounter in their roles, the decisions they need to make, and the conversations they need to have with their teams. Scenario-based training — presenting managers with realistic situations and asking how they would respond — is particularly effective for this audience because it develops judgment as well as knowledge.

Manager training should also specifically address the cultural dimensions of AI governance oversight. Managers who unconsciously signal that override rates should be low, that escalation is unwelcome, or that compliance with governance documentation requirements is optional will undermine governance regardless of what governance policy says. Training that makes these cultural dynamics explicit — that helps managers understand how their behavior shapes their team's governance culture — is among the most governance-valuable elements of management AI literacy programs.

Frontline staff who directly use AI systems

Frontline staff who use AI tools in their daily work are the human beings through whom governance commitments are or are not honored in practice. They are the people who exercise or fail to exercise meaningful oversight, who escalate or fail to escalate concerns, who document or fail to document AI use as required, and whose judgment in AI-assisted decisions is the primary human governance protection for the people the institution serves.

Frontline staff AI literacy must be closely connected to specific tools and specific workflows — generic AI literacy that does not connect to the actual tools and situations staff encounter will not transfer to practice. The training should cover: what the specific AI tools they use do and how, what those tools' known limitations are, what governance requirements apply to their use, what good oversight practice looks like for their specific role, when and how to escalate concerns, and what documentation is required.

The most governance-critical literacy elements for frontline staff are those that support genuine oversight: understanding automation bias and why independent judgment matters, knowing what kinds of AI outputs to be particularly skeptical of, understanding when a situation is unusual enough to warrant escalation, and having the professional confidence to deviate from an AI recommendation when their judgment calls for it. These elements should receive explicit emphasis in frontline training, not be buried in a broader curriculum.

Frontline training should be role-specific wherever possible. The AI literacy needs of a nurse using a clinical decision support tool differ from those of a benefits eligibility worker using an AI screening system, which differ from those of a teacher using an AI grading assistant. Generic training that does not address role-specific situations will feel irrelevant and will not build the role-specific judgment that governance requires. Where resources permit, frontline training should be tailored to specific roles and specific tools.

Staff who do not currently use AI but might

AI is expanding throughout institutional operations. Staff who do not currently use AI systems may encounter them — through vendor updates to existing software, through departmental adoption of new tools, through institutional rollouts that extend existing systems — without specific preparation. This audience needs foundational AI literacy: understanding what AI is in plain terms, what risks it presents, what governance exists, and how to identify and respond to AI use in their work context.

Foundational literacy for this audience is primarily about awareness — enough understanding that staff who encounter AI in their work recognize it as something that has governance implications, know that institutional policy applies, and know how to find out what requirements apply to a specific situation. It is not about deep operational knowledge of tools they are not yet using.

Core literacy content: what everyone should know

Despite the audience-specific variations described above, certain AI literacy content is foundational — sufficiently important for institutional AI governance that every staff member who encounters AI in their work should understand it. The following constitute the core curriculum for institutional AI literacy.

What AI actually is and how it works

Institutional staff should have a basic accurate mental model of what AI systems are and how they work — not technical detail but enough conceptual understanding to avoid the misconceptions that cause governance failures.

The most important conceptual understanding for institutional governance is the distinction between pattern recognition and reasoning. AI systems recognize patterns in training data and apply those patterns to produce outputs; they do not reason about situations the way humans do, do not have goals or intentions, and do not understand context in the way humans understand it. This distinction matters for governance because it explains why AI systems fail in the ways they do — not through malice or error in any human sense, but through the application of learned patterns to situations where those patterns do not fit.

Connected to this is the concept of training data and its role in determining AI behavior. Staff who understand that AI systems learn from historical data — and that historical data reflects historical human behavior, including historical human biases — understand why fairness is a governance concern rather than merely a technical one. This understanding does not require knowing anything about machine learning algorithms; it requires only the intuition that a system that learned from biased history will produce biased outputs.

Staff should also understand that AI outputs are probabilistic rather than deterministic — that the same input can produce different outputs, that expressed confidence is not the same as actual accuracy, and that AI systems do not know when they are wrong. These properties explain why verification matters, why human oversight is not optional for consequential uses, and why treating AI outputs as authoritative is a governance failure.

The concept of hallucination and its implications

Hallucination — the production of fluent, confident, factually incorrect outputs by language model AI systems — is among the most practically consequential AI concepts for institutional staff to understand. Staff who do not understand hallucination will treat AI-generated text as reliable and will incorporate AI errors into institutional records, communications, and decisions without realizing they are doing so.

AI literacy should convey three things about hallucination. First, it is a structural feature of how language models work, not a bug that better systems have eliminated. Second, it is not detectable from the output — hallucinated text looks exactly like accurate text, and AI systems do not flag their own hallucinations. Third, the appropriate response is verification — treating AI-generated factual claims as claims to be checked, not as facts established.

The practical implication of hallucination literacy for frontline staff is specific: any AI-generated content that contains factual claims — citations, statistics, descriptions of specific events, statements about specific people, legal or regulatory references — should be verified against authoritative sources before being incorporated into institutional records, communications, or decisions. Staff who understand hallucination know why this verification requirement exists; staff who do not will treat it as bureaucratic friction.

Automation bias and its governance implications

Automation bias — the tendency to defer to automated recommendations at rates that exceed their actual reliability — is the cognitive phenomenon that makes human oversight governance both necessary and fragile. Staff who have not been specifically educated about automation bias will exhibit it without knowing they are doing so, believing that they are exercising genuine judgment when they are actually deferring to AI recommendations.

AI literacy about automation bias should accomplish three things. First, make the phenomenon visible: staff should know what automation bias is, that it affects virtually everyone who works with automated systems, and that it affects them regardless of their training, expertise, or awareness of the phenomenon. Second, explain why governance cares: automation bias is the mechanism through which nominal oversight replaces genuine oversight, which is why governance requires oversight designs that structurally counteract it. Third, provide practical counterstrategies: forming a preliminary judgment before reviewing an AI recommendation, deliberately seeking reasons the AI might be wrong, treating a high AI confidence score as a reason for extra scrutiny rather than reduced scrutiny.

This content is most effectively taught through demonstration — showing participants the phenomenon in action, using exercises where they observe their own deferral patterns — rather than through lecture. Participants who have experienced automation bias in a training context rather than merely heard about it are more likely to recognize it in operational contexts.

What the institution's AI governance requirements are

Staff need to understand, specifically and practically, what governance requirements apply to their AI use. Abstract awareness that governance exists is not functional literacy; the ability to answer the question "what do I need to do before using this AI tool for this task" is functional literacy.

The governance requirements content of AI literacy programs should cover: what the institution's AI policy requires in terms that connect to staff's actual work, what the process is for getting a new AI tool reviewed, what data governance restrictions apply to what they might enter into AI systems, what human oversight is required for what types of AI-assisted decisions, how to escalate a concern about AI performance, and what documentation of AI use is required.

This content should be taught in connection with specific examples from the institution's operational context, not in abstract terms. "You may not enter patient information into AI tools that are not covered by our data processing agreements" is more useful and more likely to be remembered than "data governance applies to AI system inputs." The specificity and the connection to real practice is what makes governance requirements content functional rather than merely informational.

How to recognize and respond to AI problems

Staff who encounter AI system behavior that concerns them — outputs that seem wrong, patterns that seem unfair, situations where the AI is being used in ways it was not designed for — need to know what to do. Literacy that covers AI risks but does not tell staff what to do when they observe those risks in practice is incomplete.

The practical content here covers: what kinds of AI behavior should concern a staff member, how to document a concern effectively, what the escalation process is, and what staff can expect in response to a report. The message that training should send is clear: reporting AI concerns is expected, supported, and valuable. Staff who observe concerning AI behavior and do not report it are not doing their jobs fully; staff who report concerns are contributing to governance in the way their role requires.

Program structure: how to build AI literacy effectively

Understanding what AI literacy should cover is necessary but not sufficient. Effective AI literacy programs require thoughtful design of how content is delivered, how learning is reinforced over time, how effectiveness is assessed, and how programs adapt as the AI landscape and institutional use evolve.

Learning design principles

Several learning design principles are particularly important for AI literacy programs.

Relevance to actual work. AI literacy content that feels abstract or disconnected from participants' actual work will not transfer to practice. Training should be built around the specific AI tools, workflows, and situations that participants actually encounter. Where the institution has multiple distinct operational contexts, AI literacy programs should be customized for each rather than using a single generic curriculum.

Active learning over passive transmission. Lecture-based AI literacy — delivering information to passive recipients — builds awareness but not capability. Active learning approaches — case analysis, scenario-based exercises, simulations of oversight situations, discussion of real institutional examples — build judgment and decision-making capacity. The goal of AI literacy is not that participants can recall information; it is that they can apply understanding to novel situations.

Learning from failure, not only from success. AI literacy programs that present only good examples of AI use and good governance practice do not prepare staff for the situations where AI fails and governance is tested. Programs should include realistic cases of AI failures — bias incidents, hallucination in operational use, automation bias in oversight contexts, governance process failures — and should engage participants in analyzing what went wrong and what would have prevented it. The emotional salience of failure cases makes them more memorable than success cases; the analytical engagement of determining what went wrong builds practical judgment.

Psychological safety in learning. AI literacy content includes challenging topics — human cognitive limitations like automation bias, governance failures like inadequate oversight, risks like bias and privacy violations — that can feel threatening to staff who are responsible for the functions where these failures occur. Training that is experienced as accusatory or evaluative will produce defensiveness rather than learning. Program design should establish a learning environment in which participants feel safe examining difficult topics, acknowledging their own limitations, and asking questions without fear of being seen as inadequate.

Application supported by coaching. Even well-designed training rarely produces lasting behavior change without follow-up support. AI literacy programs should include mechanisms for supporting application — manager coaching conversations, peer discussion groups, governance coordinator Q&A sessions — that help participants translate training learning into operational practice. These support mechanisms are often more valuable for sustained behavior change than the initial training itself.

Format options and their appropriate uses

Different AI literacy formats are appropriate for different audiences, different content types, and different institutional resource contexts.

Instructor-led facilitated sessions are most appropriate for governance team members, managers, and senior leaders — audiences where interactive discussion, tailored examples, and live Q&A add significant value over asynchronous options. Facilitated sessions allow trainers to respond to participants' specific questions, to use examples from the institution's actual AI context, and to develop the shared understanding that governance team functioning requires. Their disadvantage is resource intensity: they require skilled facilitators and scheduled participation.

E-learning modules are appropriate for foundational literacy content that needs to reach large numbers of staff efficiently and that can be completed on individual schedules. Well-designed e-learning can include interactive elements — quizzes, decision scenarios, branching narratives — that support active learning. Their limitation is the difficulty of incorporating institution-specific content, the absence of the Q&A interaction that clarifies misunderstanding, and the tendency toward passive consumption even with interactive elements.

Microlearning — short, focused content delivered in small units — is appropriate for ongoing literacy maintenance and for targeted updates when specific content needs to be communicated quickly. A five-minute video on a specific AI concept, a brief case study shared with the governance team before a monthly meeting, a one-page guidance document on a specific governance situation — these microlearning elements reinforce foundational literacy and keep staff current on evolving issues without requiring the time investment of longer training programs.

Practical simulation and role play is particularly valuable for content that involves judgment under realistic conditions — oversight exercises where participants practice reviewing AI outputs and making override decisions, escalation scenarios where participants practice identifying and reporting AI concerns, governance review simulations where governance team members practice conducting intake assessments. Simulation-based learning builds the specific capabilities that governance requires in ways that passive learning formats cannot.

Peer learning communities — groups of staff from similar roles who discuss AI governance topics regularly — build distributed governance capability and create the social infrastructure that supports escalation culture. Peer learning is not a replacement for structured training but a supplement that sustains learning over time and builds the collective practice intelligence that no training program can fully provide.

Sequencing and timing

AI literacy programs should be sequenced to provide foundational understanding before role-specific depth, and to time delivery in connection with actual AI use rather than as a separate preparatory exercise.

Foundational literacy — the core concepts described earlier — should be provided to all staff as part of onboarding and before staff encounter AI systems in their work. Providing foundational literacy only after staff are already using AI is providing it too late; the misconceptions and unsafe practices that literacy is designed to prevent may already have established themselves.

Role-specific literacy — the operational knowledge specific to each staff member's role — should be provided before or concurrent with the introduction of specific AI tools and workflows. Pre-deployment training, timed to occur in the weeks immediately before an AI system goes live, is more effective than training that occurs months earlier and has become stale by the time it is relevant, or training that occurs after deployment and must catch up with already-established practices.

Refresher training — updates to core literacy content and reinforcement of governance requirements — should occur annually for staff who use AI regularly, and whenever significant changes occur: new AI tools adopted, significant governance incidents, significant updates to AI policy, or significant developments in the external AI landscape that affect institutional governance.

Connecting literacy to governance processes

AI literacy should be explicitly connected to the institution's governance processes rather than presented as standalone content. Staff who understand governance policy in the abstract but cannot connect it to the specific intake process, the specific escalation pathway, or the specific documentation requirement are not operationally literate.

Training curricula should include specific, practical exercises in using governance tools: completing an intake form for a hypothetical AI use case, submitting a practice escalation report, reviewing a sample monitoring dashboard, and identifying what monitoring signals would warrant governance attention. These exercises build operational familiarity with governance processes alongside conceptual understanding of governance principles.

Training should also introduce staff to the people in governance roles — the governance coordinator, the relevant governance team members, the designated escalation contacts — so that governance processes are connected to real, accessible people rather than abstract institutional functions. Staff who know who to call with an AI governance question are more likely to make that call than staff who know only that an unspecified governance function exists.

Assessing literacy effectiveness

AI literacy programs that are not evaluated for effectiveness are programs that may be generating completion records without generating the understanding and behavior change they are designed to produce. Assessment is what converts training investment into governance value.

Knowledge and understanding assessment

Knowledge assessment — quizzes, knowledge checks, scenario responses — measures whether participants have understood the content delivered. Well-designed knowledge assessment should test the application of understanding to novel situations, not recall of content covered in training. A quiz that asks "what is automation bias" tests recall; a scenario that asks "a clinical staff member mentions that they have never overridden the AI recommendation in three months of use because they trust the system — what governance concern does this raise and what would you do about it" tests application.

Knowledge assessment results should be reviewed not only for individual completion but for patterns that reveal program design problems. If a significant proportion of participants cannot answer questions about a core literacy concept, that finding suggests the concept was inadequately taught, not that participants failed to learn. Program revision based on assessment patterns is how literacy programs improve over time.

Behavior and practice assessment

Knowledge assessment alone does not establish that training has changed behavior. Behavior assessment — examining whether staff are actually using AI systems in ways consistent with governance requirements — is the more governance-relevant measure of literacy effectiveness.

Behavior assessment draws on the monitoring data described in Chapter 16: override rates that indicate whether oversight is genuine, escalation rates that indicate whether concerns are being reported, documentation compliance that indicates whether required records are being maintained. Connecting monitoring data to literacy program outcomes — examining whether behavior metrics improve following training, whether functions that have completed refresher training show better oversight quality metrics than those that have not — allows institutions to assess whether training is producing the governance behavior it is designed to produce.

Qualitative behavior assessment — observation of AI-assisted work, conversations with staff about their AI use practices, review of AI-related decisions and escalations — provides depth that quantitative metrics cannot. Governance coordinators and operational leaders who regularly check in with staff about AI governance practices are conducting informal behavior assessment that informs program improvement.

Governance impact assessment

The ultimate measure of AI literacy program effectiveness is governance impact: whether the institution's AI governance is stronger because of the literacy program than it would be without it. This is difficult to measure directly, but several indicators provide evidence.

Escalation quality — whether escalations from frontline staff are governance-relevant, well-documented, and appropriately framed — indicates whether staff understand what warrants escalation and how to report it effectively. Poor escalation quality may indicate literacy gaps in what kinds of AI behavior are governance-relevant and how to document concerns.

Governance process compliance — whether intake requirements are being followed, whether review processes are producing substantive rather than perfunctory assessments, whether oversight documentation is adequate — indicates whether governance requirements are understood and taken seriously. Systematic non-compliance patterns may indicate literacy gaps in what compliance requires or why it matters.

Reduction in governance-related incidents over time — fewer instances of AI use that violated policy, fewer monitoring signals of inadequate oversight, fewer complaints from affected people about AI-assisted decisions — provides evidence that literacy program investment is translating into governance improvement, though this evidence is always confounded by multiple factors that affect governance quality simultaneously.

Staying current: AI literacy in a rapidly evolving landscape

AI is changing faster than any static training curriculum can track. An AI literacy program designed in 2023 will be partially outdated in 2025 and significantly outdated in 2027. Maintaining AI literacy program currency is a governance responsibility, not merely an administrative one.

Content update cycles

Core AI literacy content should be reviewed and updated at least annually. Review should address: whether the foundational conceptual content remains accurate given developments in AI capabilities and AI research, whether the governance process content reflects current institutional policy and processes, whether the regulatory and legal content reflects current and emerging requirements, and whether the case examples used in training are current and representative of the AI landscape staff actually encounter.

Content updates should be prioritized by governance relevance: changes that affect what governance requires of staff — new policy provisions, new regulatory requirements, new AI tools in institutional use — warrant faster updates than conceptual content that remains broadly accurate. The governance team should maintain a list of AI literacy content that requires updating when governance developments occur, so that updates are triggered by relevant events rather than only by calendar review.

Responding to AI developments

Major AI developments — significant new AI capabilities, major AI governance incidents at other institutions, significant regulatory developments — may warrant urgent literacy responses outside the normal update cycle. The governance team should establish a process for rapid literacy response: how will the institution communicate with staff about a significant AI development that has governance implications for their work, what channels will be used, what content will be included, and what follow-up is expected?

This rapid response capacity is particularly important for AI safety and security developments. If a major vulnerability in a widely used AI system is discovered, if a significant AI governance failure at a peer institution reveals a risk that the institution's current practices do not adequately address, or if regulatory guidance significantly changes what is required — staff need to be informed and given guidance quickly, not through the next scheduled training cycle.

Building an AI-literate organization over time

The goal of AI literacy programs is not only to train current staff but to build an organization that develops AI literacy as a collective capability — where AI governance knowledge is distributed, where governance culture is self-reinforcing, and where the institution becomes more capable of responsible AI use over time rather than maintaining a baseline of literacy through repeated training.

This organizational literacy goal requires attention to culture alongside training: recognizing and valuing staff who exercise good governance judgment, creating organizational stories about good governance practice that transmit values through the institution, developing governance expertise in staff who have demonstrated aptitude and interest, and building AI governance into performance expectations and professional development pathways rather than treating it as a compliance requirement disconnected from career growth.

An institution with a genuine AI-literate culture — where staff understand why governance matters, feel ownership of governance commitments, and contribute to governance improvement through their daily practice — is an institution whose governance is qualitatively different from one that merely has a training program. Building that culture is the long-term goal of AI literacy investment, and it requires patience, consistency, and genuine institutional commitment rather than any single training program.

The institutional investment in literacy

AI literacy programs require investment — of time, money, and institutional attention. That investment is sometimes resisted on the grounds that training is overhead, that staff are already stretched, or that the benefits are difficult to quantify directly. These objections are understandable but mistaken.

The cost of inadequate AI literacy is paid in governance failures — in AI systems that cause harm because oversight was nominal, in bias that went undetected because staff did not know what to look for, in incidents that escalated to serious harm because no one knew to escalate a concern, in institutional reputation damage because governance commitments were not honored in practice. These costs are real and significant; they are simply difficult to attribute directly to literacy inadequacy rather than to the proximate event that made them visible.

The investment in AI literacy should be understood as what it actually is: the human dimension of the governance infrastructure investment. Intake processes without staff who understand why they exist will be circumvented. Oversight designs without staff who understand automation bias will be nominal. Escalation pathways without staff who know how to use them will be empty. The governance architecture described throughout this book is only as effective as the people who operate it, and the people who operate it are only as effective as their understanding of what they are doing and why.

That understanding — the AI literacy that this chapter describes — is not background to governance. It is governance, in its most human form.

Chapter 18: Communicating with Stakeholders

The obligation to speak clearly

When an institution uses AI in ways that affect people — when AI influences a clinical recommendation, shapes a hiring decision, determines a benefit eligibility outcome, personalizes educational content, or routes a service request — those people have a legitimate interest in knowing that AI was involved, understanding what role it played, and having meaningful ways to raise questions or concerns. This interest is not contingent on whether the AI system performed well or poorly. It exists because transparency is a condition of trust, and trust is the foundation of the relationship between institutions and the people they serve.

Yet communication about AI in institutional contexts is poorly practiced almost everywhere. The dominant norm in most sectors is non-disclosure: AI is used without specific acknowledgment, affected parties are not told that automated systems influenced decisions about them, and public statements about AI are either vague affirmations of responsible intentions or defensive responses to problems that have already surfaced publicly. This norm is not legally adequate in many jurisdictions, not ethically adequate under the transparency and dignity principles described in Chapter 7, and not strategically adequate for institutions that wish to maintain the trust of their stakeholders as AI use grows.

This chapter describes how institutions should communicate about AI — with employees, with the people they serve (patients, students, clients, customers), with the public and media, and with regulatory bodies and oversight entities. It addresses the principles that should guide AI communication, the different requirements that different stakeholder relationships create, the specific situations that require specific communication approaches, the formats and channels that reach different audiences effectively, and the mistakes that undermine communication even when the underlying governance is sound.

Why communication is a governance function, not a PR function

Before addressing what AI communication should contain, it is important to address how institutions typically approach it — and why that approach is inadequate.

Most institutional AI communication is designed and owned by communications or public affairs functions. This is appropriate for some aspects of AI communication — managing media relationships, crafting public statements, shaping organizational narrative. But when communications functions own AI communication without deep governance function involvement, the result is typically communication that is strategically optimized at the expense of substantive accuracy: language that is carefully crafted to project responsibility without committing to specific accountability, disclosures that are technically present but practically inaccessible, and public statements that describe AI governance aspirations rather than governance realities.

This approach fails stakeholders who need genuine information. It also fails the institution in the longer run, because the gap between communication and reality — the difference between what the institution says about its AI governance and what its AI governance actually consists of — is discoverable. When that gap is discovered, through a regulatory investigation, a journalistic inquiry, a litigation disclosure process, or a significant AI-related incident, the damage is compounded by the discovery that the institution's communications were misleading. The trust deficit created by discovering that AI governance communications were performance rather than substance is typically greater than the trust deficit that honest, imperfect communication would have created.

AI communication that serves governance purposes — and the institution's long-term interest — is substantive rather than performative, specific rather than generic, complete rather than selective, and honest about limitations rather than silent about them. It is owned jointly by governance and communications functions, with governance ensuring substance and accuracy while communications ensures accessibility and appropriate framing.

Principles for AI communication

The following principles should guide AI communication across all stakeholder contexts. They are grounded in the governance principles described in Chapter 7 and translated into communication-specific guidance.

Specificity over abstraction

Vague AI communication — "we use AI responsibly," "we are committed to ethical AI," "our AI systems are designed to serve your interests" — provides no information that stakeholders can use to understand what the institution is actually doing, what role AI plays in specific decisions that affect them, or what protections they have. These statements are not merely uninformative; they are actively misleading because they suggest a level of specificity and accountability that the vague language does not actually commit to.

Effective AI communication is specific: this system does this specific thing, in this specific context, with this specific role in decisions about you. Specificity requires knowing what the institution's AI systems actually do — which requires the AI inventory and governance infrastructure described in earlier chapters. Institutions that cannot communicate specifically about their AI use because they do not know specifically what their AI does have a governance problem that communication cannot solve.

Honesty about limitations

AI systems have limitations. They make errors. They may perform differently across demographic groups. They rely on human oversight that varies in quality. They are based on historical data that may not fully represent current conditions. Communicating as if institutional AI is perfect — or silently omitting mention of limitations — is dishonest and creates unrealistic expectations that make eventual failures more damaging.

Honest AI communication acknowledges limitations in accessible terms: "This system is one tool our staff uses to assist with clinical assessment. Like all AI systems, it can make errors, and our clinicians review its recommendations before making care decisions." This acknowledgment is not self-defeating; it accurately frames the human oversight that governs the AI use and sets realistic expectations that support trust rather than undermine it.

Honesty about limitations is also strategically sound. When the AI system does make an error that affects someone, the institution that communicated its limitations and human oversight from the beginning is better positioned than the institution that presented AI as fully reliable. The former's error is a known limitation; the latter's is a broken promise.

Accessibility and plain language

AI communication must be accessible to the people it is designed to reach. Technical language — references to model architectures, training data distributions, algorithmic parameters — does not serve people who do not have technical backgrounds. Legal language — drafted to limit liability rather than to convey meaning — does not serve people who need to understand their rights and options. Policy language — dense, comprehensive, written for institutional records — does not serve people who need to make quick practical decisions about their interactions with the institution.

Plain language for AI communication means using terms that people outside technical and legal fields understand, explaining AI concepts through concrete examples rather than abstract descriptions, avoiding jargon even when technical accuracy might seem to call for it, and testing communications with representative audience members to verify that intended meaning is actually conveyed.

The standard for accessibility should be: can the intended audience read this communication, understand what it says about the AI system, and know what it means for them? If not, the communication is not yet accessible regardless of how technically accurate or legally complete it may be.

Proportionality to stakes

AI communication requirements should be proportionate to the stakes of the AI use. An AI system that influences who receives a critical service, who is hired, who receives clinical care, or who is considered for housing requires more extensive disclosure and more accessible communication than an AI system that helps sort institutional emails. The proportionality principle means that communication investment should match the significance of the AI use for the people it affects.

Proportionality does not mean that low-stakes AI use requires no communication. It means that the form, depth, and accessibility of communication should scale with how much the AI matters for the people it affects. A brief acknowledgment that AI assists with a low-stakes administrative function may be adequate. Meaningful disclosure, explanation of rights, and accessible recourse information are required for AI that significantly affects consequential decisions about people's lives.

Timeliness

AI communication should reach people at the time it is relevant to decisions they can make. Disclosing AI use in terms and conditions that people sign before receiving services — documents that are typically not read in detail and that people must accept as conditions of service — is technically present but practically absent. Disclosure that reaches people at the point where AI is being used in ways that affect them, and that gives them meaningful opportunity to ask questions or seek alternatives before the AI-assisted process is complete, is substantive rather than nominal.

Timeliness also applies to communication when AI systems fail or when governance changes affect how AI is used. Prompt communication when AI-related problems occur, and proactive communication when significant changes to AI use are made, maintains trust better than reactive communication that reaches stakeholders after they have already been affected by changes they did not know about.

Communicating with employees

Employees are the most immediate audience for internal AI communication. They are the people who will use AI tools, exercise oversight, follow governance requirements, and in many cases directly interact with the people the institution serves on behalf of AI-assisted processes. Their trust in the institution's AI governance — and their willingness to engage with governance requirements genuinely rather than minimally — depends significantly on how the institution communicates with them about AI.

Before deployment: the introduction

When an institution deploys a new AI system that affects employees — whether as users of the system or as people whose work is affected by it — the introduction of that system should be accompanied by substantive communication. The communication should address: what the system does, why the institution is adopting it, what role it will play in employees' work, what governance requirements apply, what oversight the institution has in place, and how employees can raise questions or concerns.

This communication should go beyond operational instructions for using the tool. It should address the questions that employees who care about their work will naturally have: Is this system going to make my judgment less important? How do I know when to trust its recommendations? What happens if I think it's wrong? What are my responsibilities when I use it? What happens to the data I put into it?

Institutions that adopt AI systems without answering these questions — or that answer them only with reassurances rather than information — will find that employees develop their own answers, which may or may not be accurate, and may or may not support governance. Honest, complete introduction communication is an investment in the quality of operational governance.

Ongoing transparency

After initial deployment communication, institutions should maintain ongoing transparency with employees about AI systems in their work. This means communicating when AI systems change — when vendor updates alter system behavior, when governance conditions are modified, when monitoring has revealed concerns that are being addressed. It means sharing, in accessible terms, what monitoring shows about how AI systems are performing. And it means communicating when AI-related incidents have occurred and how they were resolved, which models the transparency and accountability that governance requires.

Ongoing employee transparency has a specific implication that institutions often miss: employees should not learn about significant AI-related developments in their institution from external sources — media coverage, regulatory disclosures, peer networks — before they hear from the institution. When employees learn that their institution has been using AI in ways they were not told about, or that an AI system they use has been found to have governance problems that were not communicated to them, the trust damage is compounded by the sense of having been kept in the dark. Proactive internal communication prevents this.

Employee rights and recourse

Employees whose work is affected by AI — including employees about whom AI systems produce assessments, recommendations, or decisions — have rights that internal communication must address. These rights vary by jurisdiction but may include: the right to know that AI was involved in employment decisions, the right to request human review of AI-assisted decisions, the right to explanation of how AI-assisted assessments were made, and in some jurisdictions specific rights under labor or employment law governing AI use in the workplace.

Internal communication should specifically address what employee rights apply in the institution's jurisdiction and context, how employees can exercise those rights, and what the institution's commitments are around human review of AI-assisted employment decisions. This communication is not only a legal compliance matter; it is an expression of the respect for employee dignity that the institution's governance principles require.

Communicating with the people institutions serve

The people most directly affected by institutional AI use — patients, students, clients, benefit applicants, customers — are the stakeholder group whose AI communication rights are most ethically significant and most frequently neglected. They are often in relationships of dependency or vulnerability with the institution, which makes the institution's communication obligations particularly strong and the consequences of non-disclosure particularly serious.

The disclosure obligation

Institutions that use AI in ways that influence decisions about the people they serve are obligated to disclose that use. This obligation has multiple grounds.

The legal ground is strongest in jurisdictions with specific AI disclosure laws — and those are growing. GDPR's Article 22 creates specific rights in relation to automated decision-making in the European Union. Several US states have enacted or are developing requirements for disclosure of AI use in employment, healthcare, and other contexts. Sector-specific regulatory frameworks increasingly address AI disclosure obligations.

The ethical ground applies even where legal requirements are not yet specific. The transparency and dignity principles established in Chapter 7 require that people know when AI is involved in processes that affect them. Being processed by an automated system without knowing it is a violation of dignity — of the sense that one is being treated as a person with a right to know, not as a data point being processed. This ethical obligation does not disappear when legal requirements are absent.

The trust ground is practical: institutions that use AI without disclosure are taking a risk with the trust relationships that their work depends on. When undisclosed AI use is discovered — and institutional AI practices are increasingly discoverable through regulatory investigations, media inquiries, and litigation — the discovery creates a trust deficit that is harder to recover from than the trust that proactive disclosure would have produced.

What disclosure should include

Disclosure of AI use to the people an institution serves should include, at minimum: the fact that AI is being used in the relevant process, a plain-language description of what the AI does and what role it plays in decisions or services, what data the AI uses, what the limitations of the AI system are, what human oversight is in place, and how the person can ask questions, request human review, or challenge an AI-influenced decision.

The disclosure does not need to be technically comprehensive. Patients do not need to know the architecture of a clinical AI system; they need to know that AI tools assist their clinical team, that their clinicians review AI recommendations, and that they can ask their clinician questions about how AI was used in their care. Students do not need to understand how an adaptive learning algorithm works; they need to know that their learning platform uses AI to personalize content, what data it uses to do so, and how they can opt out or request human assessment. The standard is informed awareness, not technical comprehension.

Disclosure format should be matched to context. A written notice in intake paperwork may be appropriate for healthcare settings. A brief verbal acknowledgment may be appropriate in service interactions. A clear notification in the digital environment may be appropriate for online services. The format should be chosen based on what will actually be noticed, read, and understood by the intended audience — not based on what is easiest for the institution to provide.

Explaining AI in accessible terms

The challenge of explaining AI to non-technical audiences is real but solvable. Several approaches consistently produce more accessible AI explanations.

Analogies to familiar processes help people understand AI without requiring technical knowledge. "The AI system works like a calculator that has learned from millions of previous cases to identify patterns that human reviewers might miss" is more accessible than "a machine learning model applies statistical pattern recognition to structured clinical data." The analogy is not technically precise, but it conveys the relevant functional understanding.

Explaining what the AI does rather than how it works keeps explanations grounded in what stakeholders need to know. "This system reviews your application and identifies factors that have historically predicted success in similar programs" tells an applicant what is relevant. A description of the machine learning algorithm used does not.

Explaining the human role clearly addresses the question that most concerns people: is a machine making decisions about me? "Our staff review the AI's assessment and make the final decision, taking into account your full application and any additional information you provide" answers this question directly and accurately.

Addressing what happens when the AI is wrong — and making the answer reassuring and specific — builds trust in ways that claiming AI accuracy cannot. "If you believe our AI assessment was incorrect or missed something important about your situation, you can request a full human review by contacting [specific contact] within [specific timeframe]" gives people a concrete recourse option.

Rights and recourse communication

Communication with affected people about AI must include accessible, specific information about their rights and how to exercise them. Rights that exist but that people cannot practically exercise are not meaningful. Rights that exist but that people do not know about are not meaningfully provided.

Recourse options should be communicated in terms that make action easy: a specific contact name or function, a specific communication channel, a specific timeframe, and a specific description of what will happen when recourse is sought. "You may request a human review of this decision by contacting our Client Services office at [phone/email] within 30 days. We will complete the review within 10 business days and notify you of the outcome in writing" is actionable. "You have the right to dispute automated decisions" is not, because it does not tell the person what to do to exercise that right.

Institutions should monitor recourse requests for patterns that indicate governance or communication problems. If a high proportion of affected people are requesting human review of a particular type of AI-assisted decision, that pattern may indicate that the AI system is not performing adequately, that communication has created unrealistic expectations, or that the affected population has specific concerns the governance framework has not addressed.

Communicating with the public

Institutional AI communication extends beyond direct stakeholders to the broader public — the communities institutions are embedded in, potential users of institutional services, civic organizations, advocacy groups, and the public generally. Public AI communication shapes institutional reputation, influences regulatory and legislative development, and contributes to the broader public understanding of AI that affects the environment in which all institutions operate.

Proactive public communication

Institutions should communicate proactively about their AI use rather than waiting for external pressure to compel disclosure. Proactive public communication — through annual reports, institutional websites, public governance summaries, and community engagement — demonstrates accountability and gives the institution control over the narrative of its AI governance rather than ceding that control to outside parties.

Proactive public communication should be substantive: describing what AI the institution uses, for what purposes, what governance it has in place, what oversight mechanisms exist, and what the institution's commitments are to the people it serves. It should be updated regularly — at minimum annually — to reflect the current state of institutional AI use rather than a historical snapshot.

Many institutions resist proactive public communication about AI because they fear scrutiny of AI practices that are less than perfect. This resistance misunderstands what the public typically expects of institutions: not perfection, but honesty, governance, and demonstrated commitment to improvement. A public communication that acknowledges the challenges of institutional AI governance, describes the governance systems in place, acknowledges known limitations, and commits to ongoing improvement is more trust-building than silence or generic assurances of responsibility.

Responding to public inquiries and scrutiny

When institutions face public inquiries about their AI use — from journalists, from community organizations, from advocacy groups, from members of the public — the communication response should be guided by the same principles that govern direct stakeholder communication: specificity, honesty, accessibility, and acknowledgment of limitations.

Defensive responses — denials, deflections, generic responsibility claims, or legal boilerplate — typically make situations worse. The institution that responds to a journalist's inquiry about AI use with "we are committed to responsible AI development and take privacy very seriously" has said nothing, has made no commitments, and has communicated implicitly that it is not willing to engage substantively with the question. The institution that responds with specific, accurate information about its AI use, its governance practices, and what it is doing to address identified concerns is demonstrating the accountability that builds rather than destroys credibility.

Institutions should have pre-prepared communication frameworks for common AI-related public inquiries — not scripted responses that eliminate genuine engagement but frameworks that organize the information commonly needed to respond accurately and accessibly to questions about AI use, governance, bias, privacy, and human oversight. Preparing these frameworks before they are needed allows communication teams to respond thoughtfully under the time pressure of media inquiries rather than improvising under pressure.

Communicating AI governance progress

Public communication should not be only defensive — responding to scrutiny or disclosing problems. It should also be affirmative — sharing governance progress, describing governance investments, and reporting on what the institution is learning about responsible AI use. Institutions that communicate openly about their governance journey — including what they have improved, what challenges remain, and what they are working on — build credibility and trust in ways that only reporting successes cannot.

AI governance reporting — a periodic public report that describes the institution's AI use, its governance framework, its monitoring findings, and its governance priorities — is a communication practice that leading institutions are beginning to adopt. These reports serve multiple purposes: they demonstrate accountability to affected communities, they signal seriousness to regulators, and they contribute to the development of governance norms that benefit the field as a whole. Institutions that produce genuine governance reports — as distinct from glossy responsibility brochures — are making a valuable contribution to the broader project of responsible institutional AI use.

Communicating with media

Media communication about AI deserves specific attention because it differs in important ways from communication with other stakeholders. Media inquiries typically occur under time pressure, in contexts where the institution does not control the framing, about topics that may be technically complex, with significant potential for misrepresentation in either direction.

Preparing for AI-related media engagement

Institutions should prepare for AI-related media engagement before they face it — not by developing defensive messaging but by building the internal communication infrastructure that allows accurate, confident responses to AI-related inquiries.

This preparation includes: designating and briefing spokespeople who are knowledgeable about institutional AI use and governance (not only communications staff but governance staff who can speak to governance substance), developing accurate factual summaries of the institution's AI use that can inform responses to common questions, establishing internal processes for rapid consultation between communications and governance functions when AI-related media inquiries arrive, and building communication team AI literacy that allows journalists' questions to be understood accurately and answered substantively.

Preparation also includes accepting that not all AI-related media coverage will be favorable. Institutions whose AI governance is genuinely strong have nothing to fear from accurate coverage; their preparation should focus on ensuring that coverage is accurate rather than on preventing coverage. Institutions whose AI governance has significant problems should address those problems before they become media issues rather than managing communications around them.

Responding to AI incident coverage

When AI-related incidents become public — when a governance failure, a bias finding, a data breach, or a harmful AI outcome receives media attention — the communication response should be guided by the same accountability principles that govern internal incident response.

Immediate response to AI incident coverage should: acknowledge the concern seriously without minimizing it, describe what the institution knows at this point (even if that is less than full clarity), describe what immediate steps are being taken, commit to a fuller account when more is known, and identify a specific point of contact for media inquiries.

The temptation in AI incident communication is to minimize — to describe a significant bias finding as "a technical issue we are addressing," to characterize a harmful AI outcome as "an isolated incident," or to respond to a governance failure with statements about the institution's general commitment to responsible AI. This minimization strategy consistently makes situations worse: it communicates that the institution does not understand the significance of what occurred, that it is prioritizing reputation management over accountability, and that its communications about AI governance cannot be trusted.

Honest acknowledgment — of what occurred, of its significance, of the institution's responsibility, and of what is being done — is both the ethical and the strategic right response. Institutions that respond to AI incidents with genuine accountability rather than reputation management consistently emerge from those incidents with more trust than they had before, because genuine accountability is itself a demonstration of the values that governance is supposed to embody.

Communicating with regulatory bodies and oversight entities

Regulatory bodies, accreditors, funders with oversight responsibilities, and other external oversight entities represent a distinct communication context with specific requirements, specific obligations, and specific stakes.

Regulatory communication obligations

Regulatory communication about AI is increasingly defined by specific requirements rather than only by general disclosure principles. Data protection authorities in many jurisdictions require notification of AI-related data breaches and may require prior consultation for high-risk AI processing. Healthcare regulators may have specific requirements for disclosure of AI use in clinical contexts. Financial regulators may require disclosure of algorithmic decision-making in credit and insurance contexts. Employment regulators may require disclosure of AI use in hiring and performance management.

Institutions must understand and comply with the specific regulatory communication requirements that apply in their jurisdictions and sectors. Legal counsel with regulatory expertise should advise on these requirements and should be involved in the development of regulatory communication frameworks before regulatory inquiries or incidents create urgency. Regulatory communication prepared thoughtfully in advance is substantially more effective than regulatory communication prepared under investigative pressure.

Proactive regulatory engagement

Beyond compliance with specific reporting requirements, institutions can benefit significantly from proactive regulatory engagement — building relationships with regulatory contacts before problems require them, participating in regulatory consultations about AI governance standards, and seeking regulatory guidance when uncertain about compliance in novel AI contexts.

Regulatory bodies that perceive institutional AI governance as genuine — as substantive commitment rather than compliance performance — are more likely to engage constructively when questions arise, to credit governance investments in their assessments, and to provide guidance that serves the institution rather than simply imposing requirements. This constructive relationship is built through the quality of regulatory communication: the accuracy, completeness, and proactive nature of what institutions share with regulatory bodies about their AI use and governance.

Proactive regulatory engagement includes being transparent about governance challenges, not only governance successes. A regulator who learns that an institution is struggling with a specific governance challenge from the institution's own proactive communication is in a very different posture than one who discovers the same challenge through an external complaint or investigation. The former creates an opportunity for constructive guidance; the latter creates an adversarial investigation context.

Responding to regulatory inquiries

When regulatory bodies make inquiries about institutional AI use — through formal investigations, compliance reviews, or informal information requests — responses should be accurate, complete, and prompt. Incomplete or inaccurate regulatory responses, even when the incompleteness or inaccuracy is inadvertent, create the appearance of concealment that is more damaging than honest disclosure of imperfect governance.

Regulatory inquiry responses should be developed with legal counsel involvement and with governance function involvement to ensure accuracy. Communications functions may support the format and presentation of responses but should not own the substance; governance functions understand the governance reality that regulatory responses must accurately describe.

Communication during and after AI incidents

AI incidents — when AI systems cause harm, when governance failures become visible, when AI-related complaints create institutional crisis — are communication challenges of the highest difficulty and highest stakes. They are also communication opportunities: how an institution communicates during and after an AI incident reveals more about its genuine governance values than any communication it makes in better circumstances.

Immediate communication

When an AI incident becomes known — whether through internal monitoring, through an affected party complaint, through media inquiry, or through regulatory notification — immediate communication to relevant stakeholders is required. The form of immediate communication depends on who the affected parties are and what the nature of the incident is, but the principles are consistent.

Immediate communication should acknowledge that an incident has occurred, describe its apparent nature as accurately as current knowledge allows, describe what immediate steps are being taken, and commit to further communication as more is learned. It should not wait for full investigation to be complete — waiting for complete information before communicating typically means that affected parties learn from secondary sources rather than from the institution. It should not minimize — describing a significant incident in terms that suggest it is less significant than it is damages trust more than honest acknowledgment of the situation's significance.

For incidents that may have caused harm to specific individuals, direct personal communication — not only institutional statements — should be provided as quickly as possible. A patient who may have received a suboptimal care recommendation because of an AI failure deserves a direct conversation with their care team, not a public statement. A benefits applicant whose application may have been incorrectly denied due to an AI error deserves a direct communication about what occurred and what will happen to address it, not a reference to a press release.

Investigation-period communication

During investigation of an AI incident, ongoing communication should update stakeholders on investigation progress, describe interim protective measures being taken, and provide any corrections to initial characterizations of the incident that emerge from investigation.

Investigation-period communication should maintain the tone of honest engagement that immediate communication established.

The investigation-period communication challenge is balancing the legitimate need to complete investigation before making definitive statements with the stakeholder need for ongoing information. Regular, brief updates — even when those updates primarily communicate that investigation is ongoing — are more trust-preserving than silence during investigation. Silence during investigation is typically interpreted as defensiveness or concealment, regardless of whether either is actually occurring.

Resolution communication

When AI incident investigation is complete and remediation has been determined, resolution communication should provide a full account of what occurred, what the investigation found, what harm was caused and to whom, what remediation is being provided to affected individuals, what systemic changes are being made to prevent recurrence, and what ongoing monitoring will be implemented.

Resolution communication should be specific enough to demonstrate genuine accountability. "We are making improvements to our AI governance" is not adequate resolution communication. "We found that our AI screening tool was producing false negatives at significantly higher rates for applicants over 50, we have suspended use of the tool pending redesign, we are reviewing all applications that were processed by the tool over the past 18 months and notifying affected applicants, and we are implementing an annual bias audit requirement for all AI tools used in hiring" is resolution communication that demonstrates accountability.

Resolution communication should also be honest about what remains uncertain or unresolved. Not all incidents have clean resolutions; some AI-related harms cannot be fully remediated; some governance improvements require time to implement; some questions about causation cannot be definitively answered. Honest acknowledgment of these limitations is more credible than claims of comprehensive resolution that overstate what the institution has achieved.

Building a communication infrastructure for AI governance

Effective AI communication across all the stakeholder contexts described in this chapter requires institutional communication infrastructure — the systems, processes, roles, and materials that allow the institution to communicate accurately, consistently, and efficiently about AI across diverse contexts and circumstances.

Core communication materials

Institutions should develop and maintain a set of core communication materials that can be adapted for specific contexts and audiences.

An institutional AI use summary — a plain-language description of what AI the institution uses, for what purposes, with what governance — is the foundational public communication document. It should be comprehensive enough to answer the questions most stakeholders would have, accessible enough to be read and understood without technical background, and current enough to reflect the institution's actual AI use rather than a historical snapshot. It should be publicly available on the institution's website and referenced in relevant communications.

Audience-specific disclosure materials — designed for patients, for students, for clients, for employees — adapt the core AI use summary for specific stakeholder contexts, emphasizing the information most relevant to each audience and including the rights and recourse information specific to each relationship.

A frequently asked questions resource — addressing the questions that stakeholders most commonly have about institutional AI use — serves both direct stakeholder communication and media inquiry response. Developing this resource requires genuine anticipation of what stakeholders want to know, not only what the institution wants them to know.

Communication templates for common AI-related situations — new AI deployment announcements, AI incident notifications, regulatory inquiry responses, employee AI policy communications — reduce the time required to produce accurate communications under pressure and ensure consistency in how institutional AI governance is described across different contexts and occasions.

Roles and responsibilities

Communication about AI is a joint responsibility of governance and communications functions. Governance functions ensure accuracy and substance; communications functions ensure accessibility, appropriateness, and strategic alignment. Neither function can produce adequate AI communication alone.

The governance team should designate a member or liaison responsible for supporting AI communication — reviewing communication materials for accuracy, providing governance information to communications staff responding to inquiries, and flagging communication needs to the governance team when AI developments require stakeholder communication.

Communications functions should develop AI-specific expertise — staff who understand the governance framework, the institution's AI use, and the common misconceptions and concerns that stakeholders bring to AI communication. This expertise cannot be improvised when AI-related communication situations arise; it needs to be built proactively.

Feedback mechanisms

Communication infrastructure should include mechanisms for receiving and responding to stakeholder feedback about AI communication. Were disclosure materials understood by the people they were designed to reach? Are recourse options being used, and are they working? Are media coverage and regulatory communications accurately reflecting institutional AI governance? What questions are stakeholders asking that current materials do not answer?

Feedback mechanisms might include structured feedback on disclosure materials, tracking of recourse requests and their resolution, review of media coverage and regulatory correspondence for accuracy gaps, and periodic stakeholder surveys or focus groups. This feedback loop is what allows AI communication to improve over time rather than remaining static as the AI landscape and stakeholder expectations evolve.

The communication standard: honest, accurate, and respectful

The standard to which institutional AI communication should be held is, ultimately, simple: honest, accurate, and respectful of the people it reaches.

Honest communication does not conceal what institutions are doing with AI, does not use technical complexity as a shield against accountability, and does not claim governance achievements that have not been made.

Accurate communication describes AI systems in terms that are technically correct, describes governance in terms that reflect governance reality rather than governance aspiration, and corrects errors when they are discovered rather than allowing inaccurate communications to stand.

Respectful communication treats its audiences as people with legitimate interests in the information being communicated, as capable of understanding that information when it is presented accessibly, and as entitled to make informed decisions about their relationship with the institution based on what they know.

These standards are not difficult to articulate. They are difficult to maintain when institutional interests create pressure toward self-protection, when legal counsel advises caution over transparency, when communications functions optimize for perception rather than substance, and when the easier path is to say less rather than more.

Governance is what creates and maintains the institutional discipline to meet these standards anyway — because governance is how institutions hold themselves accountable to the values they claim, including the value of honest communication about the AI systems that increasingly shape their work and affect the lives of the people they serve.

Part IV: When Things Go Wrong

Chapter 19: Incident Response and Escalation

When governance is tested

Every governance system is eventually tested by something going wrong. The quality of a governance framework is revealed not only in how well it prevents problems but in how effectively it responds when prevention fails. An institution whose AI governance consists primarily of intake review and policy documents, but that has no functional capacity to detect, investigate, escalate, and remedy AI-related failures, has built governance for the easy cases and left itself exposed for the hard ones.

AI incidents are not hypothetical. They happen at institutions of every type and size. Clinical AI systems produce recommendations that contribute to patient harm. Hiring AI tools screen out qualified candidates in ways that constitute discrimination. Benefit determination systems produce errors affecting thousands of people before anyone notices. Generative AI tools used by staff produce incorrect or inappropriate content that reaches clients, patients, or the public. AI systems are misused by staff in ways that violate privacy, compromise security, or produce harmful outputs. Vendors make undisclosed system changes that alter AI behavior in ways the institution did not anticipate and did not govern.

When these things happen — and they will happen, in any institution that uses AI extensively enough — the institution's response determines the consequences for the people who were harmed, the institution's accountability standing, its regulatory and legal exposure, and its long-term relationship with the communities it serves. A well-governed incident response converts a governance failure into a demonstration of governance values. A poorly governed incident response converts a containable problem into a crisis of institutional credibility.

This chapter describes what institutional AI incident response requires: how to define incidents, how to detect them, how to escalate appropriately, how to investigate effectively, how to remediate for affected people and institutional systems, how to communicate during and after incidents, and how to learn from incidents in ways that strengthen governance rather than merely surviving them.

Defining incidents: what requires a governance response

The first governance design question for incident response is scope: what constitutes an AI incident that triggers the institution's incident response process? The definition matters because it determines what gets surfaced to governance attention and what does not. A definition that is too narrow misses governance-relevant events; a definition that is too broad overwhelms the incident response function with events that do not require formal response.

The most useful definition for institutional AI governance purposes is functional: an AI incident is any event involving an AI system that has caused, may have caused, or creates meaningful risk of causing harm to people, legal or regulatory exposure for the institution, significant operational failure, or material breach of institutional governance commitments.

This definition captures four distinct incident categories, each of which warrants governance attention though not necessarily the same level of response.

Harm incidents

Harm incidents are events in which an AI system has directly or indirectly caused harm — physical, psychological, material, or dignitary — to one or more people. A clinical AI recommendation that contributed to a care decision resulting in patient harm. A hiring AI assessment that excluded a qualified candidate from consideration in violation of anti-discrimination requirements. A benefit eligibility AI that incorrectly denied an urgent benefit. A chatbot deployed in a crisis support context that responded inappropriately to expressions of acute distress. A fraud detection AI that froze the account of a legitimate customer in circumstances causing material hardship.

Harm incidents are the most serious incident category and warrant the most intensive governance response. They require not only investigation and system remediation but direct response to affected individuals — acknowledgment, apology, and where possible practical remedy for the harm caused.

Governance failure incidents

Governance failure incidents are events in which AI governance requirements were not followed — where policy was violated, where required processes were bypassed, where approved conditions were not met, or where institutional governance commitments were not honored. A staff member who adopted an AI tool for institutional use without going through the intake process. A department that deployed an AI system beyond its approved scope without governance review. A vendor that made a material system change without the notification its contract required. A monitoring function that failed to produce required reports for an extended period without anyone noticing.

Governance failure incidents may not have caused identifiable harm in a specific case, but they represent breakdowns in the governance system that prevent the institution from knowing whether harm occurred and create conditions for harm to occur undetected. They warrant investigation and governance system repair even when no specific harm is identified.

Near-miss incidents

Near-miss incidents are events in which harm was avoided or was minimal, but where the AI system's behavior, a staff member's response, or an operational circumstance reveals conditions that could produce harm if not addressed. An AI recommendation that a staff member overrode based on professional judgment, where investigation reveals the recommendation was incorrect in a way that could have caused harm if accepted. A monitoring alert that was triggered by an anomalous AI output pattern that, on investigation, suggests a performance problem that has not yet produced identifiable harm. A staff member who attempted to enter sensitive personal information into an AI tool whose data practices are inadequate, caught before submission.

Near-miss incidents are governance gold — opportunities to detect and address problems before they cause the harm that harder-to-miss incidents produce. Governance frameworks that only respond to realized harm miss the learning and prevention value that near-miss reporting provides. Institutions should explicitly define near-misses as reportable incidents and should cultivate a culture in which near-miss reporting is valued rather than dismissed as "nothing actually happened."

Misuse incidents

Misuse incidents are events in which AI systems were used deliberately in ways that are inconsistent with policy, ethical requirements, or the institution's governance commitments — regardless of whether that misuse caused identifiable harm in the specific instance. Staff members using AI tools to process personal information they are not authorized to process. Use of AI to generate content that misrepresents the institution or specific individuals. Circumvention of required oversight arrangements through deliberate workflow manipulation. Use of AI for purposes outside its governance-approved scope in ways that create risks the institution has not assessed.

Misuse incidents require both governance system response — investigating what occurred and addressing governance gaps that enabled misuse — and personnel response — addressing the behavior of the individuals involved through whatever personnel processes are appropriate. The governance response and the personnel response are distinct and should not be conflated; investigating an AI governance failure is not the same as disciplining an employee, and the two processes may require different expertise, different standards of evidence, and different confidentiality considerations.

Detection: how incidents become known

Incidents can only be responded to when they are known. Detection — the processes through which AI incidents come to governance attention — is therefore a foundational component of incident response capability. Detection failures are governance failures; incidents that occur but are not detected cannot be investigated, remediated, or learned from.

Detection through monitoring

The monitoring framework described in Chapter 16 is the primary systematic detection mechanism for AI incidents. Performance metrics that exceed defined thresholds, fairness metrics that show emerging differential patterns, anomalous output distributions, unusual complaint clustering, and other monitoring signals are the institutional nervous system for AI incident detection.

Effective monitoring-based detection requires that monitoring is genuinely active — that metrics are being collected, that reports are being reviewed, that alert thresholds are calibrated to detect meaningful signals, and that escalation from monitoring observation to governance attention follows a defined, functioning protocol. Monitoring infrastructure that generates data no one reviews does not provide detection capability; it provides the appearance of detection capability.

The specific monitoring indicators most likely to surface incident-related signals include: performance metric deterioration that exceeds baseline variation, fairness metric changes that suggest emerging bias, override rate changes that suggest shifts in oversight quality or system reliability, unusual complaint volume or clustering, and security monitoring anomalies.

Detection through staff reporting

Staff — the people who use AI systems, observe their outputs, and interact with the people affected by them — are often the first to notice AI problems. A clinical staff member who observes that an AI system is producing unusual recommendations. An eligibility worker who notices that a pattern of AI outputs seems inconsistent with the cases they know well. A communications staff member who recognizes that AI-generated content contains a factual error that would have reached clients without their review.

Staff reporting is one of the most valuable detection mechanisms available, but it only functions when staff know what to report, how to report it, and that reporting is valued and protected. Institutions with strong escalation cultures — where staff feel genuinely safe raising AI concerns and where those concerns receive genuine governance attention

— detect incidents earlier than those where staff are uncertain about what warrants reporting or fear professional consequences for raising concerns.

The training described in Chapter 17 should specifically prepare staff to recognize reportable AI events and to understand the reporting mechanism. The cultural elements described in Chapter 15 — making escalation easy and normal — are directly relevant to detection effectiveness. And the non-retaliation protections described in the AI policy (Chapter 8) are the foundation of the psychological safety that makes staff reporting reliable.

Detection through affected party complaints

People affected by AI-assisted decisions — patients, clients, students, applicants, employees — are another detection source. When an affected person raises a concern about a decision or experience that involved AI, that complaint is potentially an AI incident signal even when it is not specifically framed as an AI complaint.

Most affected people do not know whether AI was involved in decisions affecting them, and those who do know may not specifically connect their complaint to AI performance. Complaint handling processes should be designed to flag potential AI-related complaints for governance attention: complaints about decisions that were AI-assisted, complaints about content that was AI-generated, complaints about processes where AI was used, and complaints from populations where monitoring has shown elevated risk of differential AI performance.

Detection through external sources

AI incidents sometimes come to institutional attention through external sources: media coverage of AI failures at the institution or at peer institutions using similar systems, regulatory inquiries that reveal performance problems, litigation discovery that surfaces AI-related evidence, or research findings that identify problems with AI systems the institution uses.

External detection is the worst-case scenario for incident governance: it means the institution learned about a problem from outside rather than through its own governance systems. Externally detected incidents typically involve larger affected populations (because the problem persisted long enough to become externally visible), more serious governance consequences (because external detection suggests governance systems failed to function), and more complex communication challenges (because the institution is responding to a public situation rather than managing an internal one).

The appropriate response to externally detected incidents is the same as for internally detected ones — investigation, remediation, communication — but conducted under much more challenging circumstances. Governance frameworks that rely on internal detection working effectively, through robust monitoring and staff reporting, reduce the frequency of external detection events and limit their severity when they occur.

The escalation protocol: from observation to response

When a potential incident is detected — through any of the detection mechanisms described above — it must travel through a defined escalation pathway from initial observation to governance response. This pathway should be defined before incidents occur, not improvised when they do.

Level one: initial observation and documentation

When a staff member, monitoring system, or external source produces an observation that may constitute an AI incident, the first response is documentation and initial triage. The person who observes the potential incident documents what they observed — what the AI system did or did not do, what context surrounded the observation, what harm if any appears to have occurred or been avoided, and when the observation was made — and routes it to the designated escalation recipient.

Documentation at the initial observation stage does not require complete analysis or definitive characterization. It requires enough specificity that the next level of the escalation protocol can assess whether the observation warrants further investigation and at what priority. The incident report template in Chapter 28 provides a structure for this documentation.

The designated escalation recipient for initial observations is typically the AI governance coordinator, or in the coordinator's absence a designated backup. The escalation pathway should specify who receives initial reports, in what timeframe they should be acknowledged, and what their initial assessment responsibilities are.

Level two: initial assessment and classification

Upon receiving an incident report, the AI governance coordinator conducts an initial assessment: reviewing the documentation provided, gathering any immediately available additional information, and classifying the incident by type and apparent severity.

Initial classification addresses three questions: What type of incident does this appear to be — harm, governance failure, near-miss, or misuse? What is the apparent severity — how significant is the harm or risk that has occurred or been avoided? What is the urgency — does this require immediate action to prevent ongoing or escalating harm, or can it be investigated on a standard timeline?

Classification informs the subsequent escalation and response: the level of governance escalation required, the timeline for investigation, the immediate protective measures needed, and the communication obligations triggered.

Incident classification at this stage is preliminary and subject to revision as investigation proceeds. The governance coordinator should be explicit about the preliminary nature of initial classifications and should not treat initial classifications as definitive characterizations of what occurred.

Level three: governance team escalation

Incidents that meet defined criteria for governance team involvement should be escalated to governance team attention promptly — within hours for high-severity potential harm incidents, within one to two business days for lower-severity incidents. The escalation should provide the governance team with enough information to understand the apparent nature and severity of the incident, what immediate response has been initiated, and what governance team involvement is required.

The criteria for governance team escalation should be defined explicitly: events that may have caused significant harm, events that may create significant legal or regulatory exposure, events that reveal systematic governance failures rather than isolated incidents, events that may require immediate suspension of an AI system, and events that may require external communication. These criteria should err on the side of escalation — governance teams that are occasionally escalated unnecessary information are better positioned than governance teams that learn about significant incidents too late.

Governance team escalation does not always require an emergency meeting. The escalation protocol should specify what actions governance team members are expected to take at different escalation levels: reviewing the situation and providing guidance by communication for lower-severity incidents, convening an emergency meeting for highest-severity situations.

Level four: senior leadership and board escalation

The most serious incidents — those involving significant harm to multiple people, major regulatory exposure, significant reputational events, or situations that may require major institutional decisions — must reach senior leadership and in some cases the board. The escalation criteria for senior leadership involvement should be defined explicitly, with the governance team responsible for making the determination and for providing senior leadership with timely, accurate briefings.

Senior leadership escalation is not for every incident; it is for incidents whose significance exceeds what governance team authority can manage. The governance team should not delay senior leadership escalation for incidents that clearly warrant it — waiting for complete investigation, waiting for better news, or attempting to resolve situations internally that require leadership authority — because delay compounds the governance failure the incident already represents.

Investigation: understanding what happened and why

Once an incident has been detected, escalated, and assessed, investigation begins: the systematic effort to understand what occurred, why it occurred, who was affected, what the scope and severity of harm was, and what the contributing factors were in both AI system performance and institutional governance.

Investigation principles

Several principles should guide AI incident investigation to ensure that it produces the understanding governance requires.

Independence proportionate to severity. Investigation of minor incidents can be conducted by the functions most directly involved. Investigation of significant incidents — particularly those involving potential harm, potential regulatory exposure, or governance failures within a specific function — should involve people independent of the functions under investigation. This independence protects the integrity of findings and ensures that the investigation is not shaped by the interests of those whose practices are being examined.

Evidence before conclusion. Investigation should follow evidence to conclusions rather than beginning with conclusions and selectively collecting evidence. This is a discipline that is easier to state than to maintain — institutional pressures often create incentives to reach conclusions quickly, to characterize incidents in ways that minimize institutional culpability, or to frame investigation findings in terms that support preferred narratives. Governance should establish investigation practices that prioritize accuracy over speed and honest findings over comfortable ones.

Scope adequate to the question. The investigation scope should be adequate to answer the governance questions that the incident raises, not limited to what is convenient to examine. An incident that raises questions about potential systematic bias in an AI system cannot be adequately investigated by examining only the specific cases that triggered the incident report; it requires examining whether the apparent pattern is present more broadly. An incident that raises questions about governance process failures cannot be adequately investigated by examining only the AI system's performance; it requires examining the oversight and escalation processes that should have caught the problem earlier.

Documentation throughout. Investigation findings should be documented as they develop, not only in a final report. Documentation during investigation creates a record that supports accountability, enables subsequent review if investigation conclusions are challenged, and provides the institutional learning material that makes incidents governance education rather than merely governance trauma.

What investigation should determine

A complete AI incident investigation should determine the following.

What the AI system did. A precise technical account of the AI system's behavior in the incident — what inputs were processed, what outputs were produced, how those outputs compared to expected performance, and what technical explanation exists for the divergence.

What governance failed. An honest assessment of where the governance system failed — whether pre-deployment testing did not detect the problem the incident revealed, whether oversight arrangements were inadequate to catch the failure, whether monitoring was not configured to detect the relevant signal, or whether escalation was delayed or absent when it should have occurred. This assessment should examine each stage of the governance lifecycle at which the problem might have been caught but was not.

Who was affected and how. A determination of who was affected by the incident — how many people, what populations, what decisions or experiences were shaped by the AI failure — and what harm if any they suffered. For incidents involving potential bias, this determination requires demographic analysis of affected populations to assess whether harm fell disproportionately on specific groups.

What the contributing factors were. An analysis of the factors that contributed to both the AI failure and the governance failure — including system design choices, deployment decisions, oversight design, training adequacy, monitoring configuration, vendor performance, and institutional culture. Contributing factor analysis is what distinguishes investigations that produce governance learning from those that merely establish what happened.

What immediate remediation is required. A determination of what immediate steps are needed to prevent ongoing harm — system suspension, output review, direct outreach to affected individuals, immediate oversight changes — that may need to precede completion of the full investigation.

Working with vendors during investigation

When an incident involves a vendor-provided AI system, the investigation necessarily involves the vendor — obtaining the technical information needed to understand system behavior, understanding what changes the vendor made that may have contributed to the incident, and assessing whether the vendor met its contractual obligations. Vendor cooperation in investigation is a governance matter that the institutional contract should address.

Investigation communication with vendors should be factual and specific: describing the incident that has been observed, requesting specific technical information about system behavior, and asking specific questions about what the vendor did or did not do that is relevant to the investigation. Vendors who are evasive, who provide incomplete information, or who attempt to characterize incidents in ways that minimize their responsibility should be treated as governance concerns in themselves — non-cooperation with investigation is a relationship issue that governance and legal functions should address in parallel with the substantive investigation.

Documentation of vendor communication during investigation is important. Records of what the vendor was asked, what was provided, when, and what was not provided support both the investigation and any subsequent contractual or legal proceedings.

Immediate response: protecting people during investigation

Investigation determines what happened; immediate response addresses what is happening now. These are parallel activities, not sequential ones — immediate protective measures may be required before investigation is complete, precisely because investigation takes time and harm may be ongoing.

System suspension

When an AI incident suggests that an AI system may be causing ongoing harm, system suspension — stopping the system's operation while investigation and remediation proceed — should be considered immediately. The governance team should make suspension decisions based on the apparent severity and scope of ongoing harm, not on the operational disruption that suspension would cause.

Suspension decisions should be explicit: what system is being suspended, effective when, for what reason, with what expected duration, and who has authority to reinstate. Suspension should not occur informally — a system that is "quietly not being used for now" without formal governance documentation of the suspension creates ambiguity about governance status and may allow informal reinstatement without appropriate review.

For systems where suspension would cause significant operational disruption — clinical systems, critical service delivery systems — the suspension decision must weigh ongoing harm from continued operation against harm from suspension. This is a genuine governance dilemma in some cases, not a decision whose right answer is obvious. The governance team should make this decision explicitly, with full awareness of both risks, and should document the reasoning.

Outreach to affected individuals

When investigation identifies individuals who may have been harmed by an AI incident — who received incorrect clinical recommendations, who were incorrectly denied benefits, who were subject to discriminatory AI screening — the institution has an obligation to reach out to them directly and promptly.

Outreach to affected individuals should: acknowledge that a problem occurred with the AI system that was used in their care, service, or decision process; describe in accessible terms what the problem was; acknowledge honestly that they may have been affected; explain what the institution is doing to investigate and address the problem; offer whatever immediate practical remedy is available (a review of their case by a human expert, reinstatement of a wrongly denied benefit, a follow-up clinical assessment); and provide a specific contact for their questions and concerns.

This outreach is ethically required regardless of legal obligation. It is also typically legally required under data breach notification frameworks when the incident involves unauthorized data access, and is increasingly required under AI-specific regulations in various jurisdictions. The institution's legal counsel should advise on specific notification requirements; the institution's governance values should lead it to exceed minimum legal requirements in cases where affected people need and deserve direct communication.

Outreach to affected individuals is one of the hardest parts of incident response because it requires acknowledging institutional error directly to people who may have been harmed. Institutions that handle this well — with genuine acknowledgment, genuine apology when warranted, and genuine commitment to remedy — typically find that affected people's responses are more forgiving than feared. Institutions that handle it badly — with defensive language, minimization, or bureaucratic processes that obscure institutional accountability — consistently make situations worse.

Internal communication during incidents

When an AI incident is under active investigation and response, internal communication — to staff, to operational leaders, to governance team members not directly involved in response — should be managed carefully. Not all staff need to know all details of every incident; sharing incomplete information broadly can create confusion, create secondary governance problems through informal communication, and compromise investigation integrity.

Internal communication during incidents should be need-to-know: sharing what specific individuals need to know to fulfill their roles in incident response, to adjust their operational practices if needed, or to respond accurately to questions from affected individuals. A clear internal communication tree — specifying who should know what at each stage of incident response — prevents both the information vacuum that produces rumors and the information flood that produces confusion.

Remediation: fixing what broke

Investigation determines what happened. Immediate response addresses ongoing harm. Remediation — the systematic repair of both the harms that occurred and the governance conditions that allowed them — is the work that converts an incident from a failure into a governance improvement.

Remediation for affected individuals

Remediation for affected individuals should address, to the extent possible, the specific harm each person suffered. This remediation varies by incident type and by what is practically possible.

For clinical AI incidents, remediation may include a review of care decisions that were AI-assisted during the incident period, additional clinical assessment for patients who may have been affected, correction of medical records, and in cases of actual harm, engagement with whatever clinical error resolution processes apply.

For benefit or service determination incidents, remediation should include review of all determinations affected by the AI problem, correction of incorrect determinations, provision of benefits or services that were wrongly withheld, and where retroactive remedy is not fully possible, acknowledgment and explanation of what occurred.

For bias incidents, remediation must address both the individuals harmed by discriminatory AI outcomes and the systemic condition that produced those outcomes. Individual remediation — reviewing affected cases, correcting discriminatory determinations, contacting affected applicants or clients — and systemic remediation — fixing the AI system, changing oversight processes, implementing additional safeguards — are both required. Systemic remediation without individual remediation fails the specific people who were harmed; individual remediation without systemic remediation fails the people who will be harmed in the future if the underlying problem is not fixed.

Governance system remediation

The investigation's determination of what governance failed should drive governance system remediation: specific changes to governance processes, policies, oversight designs, monitoring configurations, vendor relationships, or training programs that address the contributing factors the investigation identified.

Governance system remediation should be specific and actionable. "Improving oversight processes" is not remediation; it is aspiration. "Requiring that clinical staff document their independent assessment before reviewing AI recommendations for the specific system involved in this incident, with compliance monitored monthly and reported to the governance team quarterly" is remediation — it addresses a specific governance failure with a specific, implementable, monitorable change.

The changes identified in governance remediation should be tracked to implementation: assigned to specific responsible parties, with defined timelines, and with verification that implementation has occurred before the incident is formally closed. Remediation commitments that are made but not implemented are governance failures in themselves.

Vendor remediation

When investigation reveals that vendor AI system performance contributed to an incident — through a system failure, an undisclosed system change, a data handling problem, or inadequate performance documentation — the institution must pursue vendor remediation in parallel with internal remediation.

Vendor remediation requests should be specific, documented, and framed in terms of the vendor's contractual obligations. The institution's legal counsel should be involved in vendor remediation engagement when the incident suggests contractual breach. The vendor's response to remediation requests — whether they are responsive, what remediation they commit to, whether they honor those commitments — should be documented and should inform the institution's ongoing vendor relationship assessment.

In cases where vendor remediation is inadequate — where the vendor is unwilling to address identified performance problems, where vendor system changes contributed to harm and the vendor is unwilling to accept responsibility, or where the vendor's conduct during the incident revealed governance partnership problems — the institution should consider whether the vendor relationship should continue and what contractual mechanisms are available to address vendor failures.

Post-incident review: learning from what happened

After investigation is complete and immediate remediation is underway, governance requires one more step: a structured post-incident review that extracts the learning from what occurred and uses it to strengthen governance.

The post-incident review process

The post-incident review should occur after the acute phase of incident response is complete — typically four to eight weeks after the incident, when investigation findings are documented, immediate remediation is initiated, and the governance team has enough distance from the incident to examine it analytically rather than reactively.

The review should address: what the incident reveals about the overall adequacy of the institution's AI governance — not only the specific governance failures identified in investigation but what systemic conditions made those failures possible; whether the incident response itself was adequate — whether detection was timely, escalation was appropriate, investigation was thorough, communication was effective; and what governance improvements beyond the specific remediation actions are warranted.

Post-incident review should involve the governance team and relevant subject matter experts, and should produce documented findings and recommendations. These findings and recommendations should be incorporated into governance improvement priorities and tracked to implementation like other governance commitments.

Learning that generalizes

The most governance-valuable post-incident learning extends beyond the specific incident to the question of what it reveals about the adequacy of governance across the institution's AI portfolio. If an incident reveals that monitoring for a specific type of AI failure was inadequate, the question is not only whether monitoring for that specific system should be improved but whether monitoring for all systems should be assessed for similar inadequacies. If an incident reveals that vendor contracts did not provide adequate notification and remediation rights, the question is not only whether that specific contract should be renegotiated but whether all AI vendor contracts should be reviewed for similar gaps.

Generalizing learning from incidents is what converts incidents from isolated failures into systemic governance improvement. The governance team should build this generalization practice into post-incident review: explicitly asking, for every incident finding, whether the finding reveals a condition that exists only in the context of this incident or that may be present more broadly.

Communicating incident findings and improvements

Post-incident communication — sharing what the institution learned from the incident and what improvements are being made — closes the accountability loop that incident response requires. This communication serves affected parties who deserve to know what the investigation found. It serves staff who benefit from knowing what governance improvements are being implemented and why. It serves the public and regulatory stakeholders who have legitimate interest in how the institution responds to governance failures.

Post-incident public communication should be calibrated to the significance and public visibility of the incident. For significant incidents that received public attention, a public account of investigation findings and governance improvements is appropriate. For lower-profile incidents, communication may be more limited but should still reach the relevant stakeholders — affected individuals, relevant regulatory contacts, and internal governance audiences.

The content of post-incident communication should reflect the investigation findings honestly, describe governance improvements specifically, acknowledge institutional accountability appropriately, and avoid the defensive framing that undermines trust. An institution that communicates about an incident in terms designed to minimize its culpability rather than to honestly account for what occurred is demonstrating that its governance is less mature than its communications would prefer to suggest.

Maintaining incident response readiness

Incident response capability does not exist by virtue of having an incident response policy. It exists when the people, processes, and infrastructure needed for effective response are operational and tested.

Regular readiness assessment

The governance team should assess incident response readiness at least annually: reviewing whether the incident detection mechanisms are functioning, whether escalation pathways are current and known to relevant staff, whether investigation capacity is adequate, whether communication materials are current, and whether the incident report template and documentation systems are accessible.

This assessment should involve actual testing of key components: submitting a test escalation report and verifying that it reaches the right people within the expected timeframe; reviewing whether current incident response documentation reflects current governance team membership and current AI system portfolio; and confirming that operational leaders know their roles in incident response.

Tabletop exercises

Tabletop exercises — structured simulations of AI incident scenarios in which governance team members and other relevant staff walk through how they would respond — are among the most valuable readiness investments an institution can make. They reveal gaps in escalation protocols, ambiguities in role assignments, and inadequacies in communication templates that only emerge when people attempt to apply the incident response framework to specific scenarios.

Tabletop exercises should use realistic scenarios drawn from the types of incidents most plausible given the institution's specific AI portfolio. A healthcare institution should exercise clinical AI failure scenarios. A social services institution should exercise benefit determination error scenarios. A hiring-intensive organization should exercise algorithmic discrimination scenarios. The scenarios should be specific enough to require concrete decisions — specific enough that participants cannot respond with generic process descriptions — and should include complications that force governance team members to engage with the difficult judgment calls that real incidents produce.

Tabletop exercise findings — the gaps and ambiguities they reveal — should be addressed through protocol updates, training revisions, or other governance improvements before the exercises are considered complete. An exercise that reveals gaps but produces no subsequent improvements has identified problems without solving them.

Incident response culture

Beyond processes and infrastructure, incident response capability depends on culture: an institutional culture in which incidents are treated as governance information rather than institutional embarrassments, in which staff feel safe reporting concerns without fear of professional consequences, and in which the leadership response to incidents is accountability rather than defensiveness.

This culture cannot be created by incident response policy alone. It is built through how leaders respond to incidents when they occur — whether they express genuine commitment to understanding what happened and preventing recurrence, or whether their primary concern is managing the institutional narrative. It is built through how the governance team treats incident reporters — whether staff who report concerns feel valued and protected, or whether they experience reporting as futile or professionally risky. And it is built through whether post-incident improvements are actually implemented — whether the institution learns from incidents in the ways its process commits to learning.

An institution that has genuinely built this culture — where incidents are surfaced promptly, investigated honestly, remediated thoroughly, and learned from systematically — is an institution whose AI governance is genuinely protecting the people it serves. That protection is the purpose for which the entire governance system described in this book exists. Incident response is where governance proves whether that purpose is real.

Chapter 20: Special Cases: Generative, Automated, and Agentic AI

Why some AI requires different governance thinking

The governance framework described in earlier chapters applies to all institutional AI use. The principles, intake processes, vendor assessment, testing requirements, oversight design, monitoring, and incident response described in Parts II and III are not optional for any AI deployment — they are the baseline of responsible institutional governance regardless of what type of AI system is involved.

But some categories of AI present governance challenges that the baseline framework, while necessary, does not fully address. Three categories in particular — generative AI, automated decision systems, and agentic AI — have characteristics that create governance dimensions requiring specific attention beyond what standard governance processes provide. These categories are not marginal or exotic; they are among the most widely deployed and rapidly growing categories of institutional AI use. Understanding their distinctive governance requirements is essential for any institution whose AI portfolio includes them.

This chapter addresses each category in turn: what it is, what makes it distinctive from a governance perspective, what the standard governance framework misses about it, and what additional governance measures its distinctive characteristics require. It closes by addressing situations where these categories overlap — generative AI that is also automated, agentic systems that use generative capabilities — because the intersections often create the most complex governance situations.

The chapter is placed in Part IV — "When Things Go Wrong" — not because these AI types are inherently more problematic than others, but because they are the categories most likely to challenge governance frameworks that were not specifically designed with them in mind, and because governance failures involving them tend to be particularly consequential.

Generative AI: the governance of creation

What generative AI is

Generative AI systems produce new content — text, images, audio, code, or other media — in response to human inputs. They include large language models used as chatbots or writing assistants, image generation systems, code generation tools, audio and video synthesis systems, and multimodal systems that combine several of these capabilities. They are, as of this writing, among the most rapidly adopted AI categories in institutional settings: used for drafting communications, generating reports, answering stakeholder questions, assisting with research, producing code, creating training materials, and performing countless other content creation and transformation tasks.

What distinguishes generative AI from other AI categories is the open-ended, creative character of its outputs. A classification model produces a label from a predefined set. A prediction model produces a probability estimate. A recommendation model produces a ranked list of options. Generative AI produces outputs whose content, form, and character are not predefined — the system constructs something new in response to each input, drawing on learned patterns in ways that can produce useful, creative, and appropriate outputs, or outputs that are incorrect, inappropriate, biased, harmful, or inconsistent with institutional values and obligations.

This open-ended character is what makes generative AI both genuinely useful — it can assist with a vast range of tasks that structured AI systems cannot address — and genuinely challenging for governance. The governance of a classification system can focus on whether its labels are accurate and fair, and those questions can be assessed against defined criteria. The governance of a generative system must address an unbounded space of possible outputs, some of which the institution would not anticipate in advance, across an unbounded range of potential uses that staff may discover and apply.

The hallucination problem in institutional context

Chapter 3 introduced hallucination — the production of fluent, confident, factually incorrect outputs — as a significant risk for generative AI systems. In the governance of generative AI specifically, hallucination deserves extended attention because it is not a peripheral failure mode; it is a structural feature of how these systems work, present in every institutional generative AI deployment, and requiring specific governance countermeasures.

The institutional significance of hallucination is amplified by the contexts in which institutions use generative AI. When a communications staff member uses an AI writing assistant to draft a letter to clients, a patient portal response, or a public statement, hallucinated content that is not caught in review may reach its audience and cause harm: incorrect medical information reaching a patient, incorrect regulatory guidance in a compliance communication, fabricated statistics in a public statement. When a researcher uses a generative AI tool to assist with literature synthesis, hallucinated citations or misrepresented study findings can corrupt institutional knowledge bases and decisions made from them. When staff use generative AI to answer questions from the people the institution serves, hallucinated answers may lead those people to make decisions based on false information.

The governance response to hallucination requires three elements operating together. Policy must specify which uses of generative AI require what level of verification — defining categories of output (factual claims, citations, statistics, regulatory references, descriptions of specific individuals) that must always be verified against authoritative sources before use, regardless of the use case. Training must build genuine understanding of hallucination among staff who use generative AI — not merely awareness that the phenomenon exists but practical ability to recognize high-risk output categories and to apply appropriate skepticism. And monitoring must track whether verification practices are being followed, through documentation reviews, output quality sampling, and incident patterns.

Prompt injection and manipulation

A security vulnerability specific to generative AI systems — and particularly to those that process external content as part of their operation — is prompt injection: the embedding of instructions in content the AI processes that are designed to override the system's intended behavior. When a language model processes a document, an email, a web page, or any other external content, that content may contain text crafted to function as instructions that the model interprets and follows rather than as content to be processed.

The implications for institutional governance are significant. A contract review AI that processes a vendor's contract may encounter prompt injection instructions embedded in the document. A customer service chatbot that processes customer-submitted content may be manipulated to produce responses that contradict institutional policy or reveal information it should not. A document summarization tool may be induced to produce summaries that misrepresent the content being summarized in ways the staff member reviewing the summary would not detect.

Governance of prompt injection risk requires: technical controls where available (some AI systems have architectural features that reduce prompt injection susceptibility), operational controls (not using generative AI to process untrusted external content in high-stakes contexts without specific safeguards), staff awareness (training that includes prompt injection as a security risk to be aware of), and monitoring for outputs that are anomalous in ways consistent with successful injection attacks.

Content appropriateness and institutional representation

Generative AI systems can produce content that is inappropriate, offensive, inconsistent with institutional values, or that appears to represent the institution in ways it has not authorized. When a staff member uses an institutional AI system — or a personal AI tool for institutional work — to produce content associated with the institution, the institution's governance must address what content is appropriate and what is not.

This governance challenge has several dimensions. Institutional voice: generative AI outputs should not be used as institutional communications without review and editing that ensures they reflect the institution's actual positions, values, and obligations — not merely the AI's pattern-based approximation of institutional communication. Sensitive topics: generative AI systems may produce outputs on sensitive topics — health conditions, financial circumstances, legal situations, political questions — that are incorrect, insufficiently nuanced, or inappropriate for the institutional context. Regulatory constraints: many institutional communications are subject to regulatory requirements about accuracy, completeness, and appropriate caveats; generative AI outputs may not meet these requirements without human review and revision.

The governance framework for content appropriateness should specify: what categories of institutional communication require human authorship rather than AI generation, what review and revision requirements apply before AI-assisted content is used as institutional communication, and what training is required for staff to recognize when AI-generated content is not appropriate for institutional use.

Chatbots deployed in direct service contexts

Chatbots — conversational generative AI systems deployed to respond to questions and requests from the people an institution serves — require particularly specific governance because they place generative AI in direct interaction with potentially vulnerable people, often with limited staff oversight of individual exchanges, and in contexts where inappropriate or incorrect responses can cause direct harm.

The deployment of chatbots in healthcare contexts raises specific governance concerns: a chatbot that provides health information must not produce outputs that substitute for professional medical advice without appropriate caveats, must not provide specific medical recommendations for individual circumstances, and must have clear mechanisms for escalating to human staff when interactions suggest urgent clinical need. The deployment of chatbots in mental health or crisis support contexts raises heightened concerns: a chatbot that responds inappropriately to expressions of acute distress may cause direct harm, and the governance requirements for this context must specifically address crisis recognition and escalation.

Governance of direct-service chatbots requires: system-level prompt design that establishes appropriate scope, tone, and safety behaviors for the chatbot's specific deployment context; testing that specifically probes the chatbot's behavior in sensitive and crisis-adjacent scenarios before deployment; monitoring of interaction patterns that may indicate the chatbot is operating outside its intended scope or producing harmful outputs; clear mechanisms for users to reach human staff; and disclosure to users that they are interacting with an AI system.

The disclosure obligation for chatbots is not negotiable. People interacting with institutional systems have a right to know whether they are communicating with a human or an AI. Chatbots designed to appear human — that deny being AI when asked, that use human names without disclosure that the system is AI-powered — violate the dignity and transparency principles that governance requires, and are in violation of emerging legal requirements in many jurisdictions.

Copyright and intellectual property

Generative AI systems are trained on large bodies of text, images, and other content whose copyright and intellectual property status is complex and contested. Outputs produced by generative AI systems may incorporate patterns learned from copyrighted material in ways that raise intellectual property concerns. And institutional use of generative AI — for drafting, creating, and publishing content — raises questions about the intellectual property status of AI-generated outputs and the institution's obligations regarding attribution, disclosure, and rights.

These questions are evolving rapidly in law and practice. Governance must monitor legal developments in this area and ensure that institutional AI use policies reflect current understanding of copyright obligations. At minimum, governance should require that institutions not use AI-generated content in ways that claim human authorship when that misrepresentation could be material — in academic submissions, in professional certifications, in regulatory filings, or in any context where the origin of content is legally or ethically significant.

Automated decision systems: the governance of consequential machinery

What automated decision systems are

Automated decision systems are AI systems that make or significantly determine decisions that affect specific people, with limited or no individual human review of each decision. They include: automated benefit eligibility determinations, automated credit scoring systems, automated fraud detection systems that take immediate account actions, automated hiring screening that determines who receives further consideration, automated insurance pricing systems, automated sentencing or parole risk assessment tools, and any other system whose outputs directly determine outcomes for individuals at a scale and speed that makes individual human review of each decision impractical or non-standard.

The defining characteristic of automated decision systems is not that they operate without any human involvement — most institutional automated decision systems involve humans in some capacity, whether in system design, parameter setting, exception handling, or periodic review. The defining characteristic is that individual decisions — each specific determination about each specific person — are made by the system rather than by a human exercising judgment about that specific person's circumstances.

This characteristic distinguishes automated decision systems from decision support systems, where human judgment is exercised on each case. A clinical AI that recommends a treatment and a clinician decides whether to follow that recommendation is a decision support system. A claims processing system that automatically approves or denies claims based on AI-assessed eligibility criteria, without individual human review of each determination, is an automated decision system. The governance requirements for these two categories differ substantially.

The due process dimension

Automated decision systems have a governance dimension that other AI categories do not share with the same intensity: the due process dimension. When a decision that significantly affects a person's life is made by an automated system rather than a human, the requirements of procedural fairness — notice, explanation, opportunity to contest, access to a human decision-maker — apply with particular force and are more difficult to honor.

The difficulty arises from the structural characteristics of automated decision systems. Notice that a decision was automated is straightforward to provide; notice that allows a person to meaningfully contest the decision is more demanding. Explanation of an automated decision — what factors led to this outcome — requires that the system be capable of providing explanation in terms the affected person can understand and that a human reviewer can assess for reasonableness. Opportunity to contest requires not only a formal appeal mechanism but one that is practically accessible, timely, and that provides genuine possibility of a different outcome rather than merely automated reconsideration by the same system.

Governance of automated decision systems must specifically address each element of due process: how notice of automated processing is provided, what explanation the system can offer and in what form, how individuals can contest decisions and through what mechanism, who has authority to override automated determinations and on what basis, and what review mechanisms are available for systematic patterns of complaint.

Legal requirements for these elements vary by jurisdiction, sector, and decision type. The European Union's GDPR Article 22 provides specific rights in relation to automated processing that significantly affects individuals. US legal frameworks address specific sector contexts — credit decisions, employment, housing — with varying requirements. Emerging AI-specific legislation in multiple jurisdictions is adding additional requirements. Governance must ensure that automated decision systems meet applicable legal requirements and should consider exceeding those requirements where the stakes of decisions warrant it.

Calibration and threshold governance

Automated decision systems typically operate through thresholds — score levels above or below which decisions are made. A credit scoring system approves applications above a score threshold and declines below it. A fraud detection system flags transactions above a risk threshold for intervention. A benefit eligibility system approves applications that meet score criteria and denies those that do not.

Threshold calibration — the process of setting these decision boundaries — is a governance matter, not merely a technical one. Threshold choices determine error rates and their distribution: a more restrictive threshold for benefit approval produces more false negatives (deserving people denied), while a more permissive threshold produces more false positives (ineligible people approved). These trade-offs are values questions — they reflect institutional judgments about which errors are more acceptable, which populations bear the cost of errors, and what the institution's risk tolerance is — that should be made by governance authority rather than default to technical optimization.

The governance of threshold calibration should require that: thresholds are set through a process that involves governance authority, not only technical staff; the error rate implications of threshold choices are documented, including differential error rates across demographic groups; threshold choices are reviewed periodically rather than set once and forgotten; and changes to thresholds are treated as material system changes subject to governance review.

Exception handling and human review pathways

Automated decision systems produce cases that fall outside their intended scope: cases whose circumstances are unusual, cases whose input data is incomplete or inconsistent, cases that present characteristics the training data did not adequately represent. These exception cases are precisely where automated decision systems are most likely to produce incorrect or inappropriate determinations, and where human judgment is most needed.

Governance of exception handling requires: explicit definition of what conditions trigger exception handling rather than automated determination; clear mechanisms for the system to identify and route exception cases; accessible pathways for affected individuals to request exception handling; and capacity — in terms of human resources and process design — to handle exceptions within timeframes that do not deny the timely service that affected people need.

The exception handling capacity must be genuine, not nominal. An exception handling process that requires affected people to navigate complex bureaucratic requirements, that provides no timeline for response, that routes exceptions to staff who are not equipped to exercise genuine independent judgment, or that effectively re-applies the automated system's logic through a human intermediary is not meaningful exception handling. It is the performance of process without the substance of human review.

Explainability requirements

The requirement that automated decisions be explainable — that individuals can understand, in accessible terms, why an automated system made the determination it did about them — is both a legal requirement in many contexts and an ethical requirement under the dignity and transparency principles.

Explainability governance requires that: the system's technical architecture is assessed for explainability capability before deployment — some AI approaches are inherently more explainable than others, and choosing between approaches should partly depend on explainability requirements; explanations are generated in forms that are accessible to non-technical affected parties, not in technical language that satisfies a formal requirement without conveying meaningful information; the accuracy of explanations is assessed — explanations that do not accurately reflect the system's actual decision logic are worse than no explanation because they misdirect contests and oversight; and explanation adequacy is monitored through the review of individual complaints and systematic assessment of whether explanations are enabling meaningful contest.

For institutions that use vendor-provided automated decision systems, explainability governance requires that vendor contracts specifically address explanation capabilities: what explanations the system can produce, in what form, for whom, and whether the institution has the right to require improvements in explanation quality if explanations prove inadequate in practice.

Cumulative impact assessment

A governance dimension specific to automated decision systems, particularly those operating at high volume across large populations, is cumulative impact: the aggregate effect of many automated determinations on the people and communities affected by them. Individual automated decisions may each be within acceptable error parameters while the cumulative effect of many such decisions creates patterns of systematic disadvantage that individual-level analysis does not reveal.

Consider a housing assistance eligibility system that correctly approves 90% of eligible applicants — a seemingly adequate accuracy rate. If the 10% incorrectly denied are disproportionately concentrated in specific demographic groups, if those groups' members also face other systemic disadvantages that make the loss of housing assistance particularly harmful, and if the system processes tens of thousands of applications annually, the cumulative impact on those groups may be substantial even if individual decisions seem reasonable.

Cumulative impact assessment requires: population-level analysis of automated decision outputs across demographic groups; assessment of whether error concentrations, while perhaps individually defensible, create patterns of systematic disadvantage at scale; engagement with affected communities about the experienced impact of automated systems, not only technical assessment of error rates; and governance processes that can identify and address cumulative impact concerns even when individual decision errors are within defined thresholds.

Agentic AI: the governance of autonomous action

What agentic AI is

Agentic AI systems are AI systems that take sequences of actions to accomplish goals — that operate with a degree of autonomy, pursue objectives over multiple steps, interact with external systems and environments, and in doing so produce consequences that extend beyond a single output produced in response to a single input. They include: AI systems that autonomously browse the web and compile information; systems that autonomously execute multi-step research tasks; systems that interact with other software to accomplish tasks; systems that schedule, email, purchase, or take other actions on behalf of human users; and more complex autonomous agents that pursue goals through sequences of actions with limited human involvement in individual steps.

Agentic AI represents a qualitatively different governance challenge from the AI categories previously discussed. Classification models, prediction models, recommendation models, and even generative AI produce outputs that a human can review before acting on them. The human is in the loop between AI output and real-world consequence. Agentic AI takes actions — it browses, it emails, it schedules, it purchases, it modifies files, it interacts with systems — and those actions have real-world consequences that may occur before any human reviews them. The loop between AI operation and real-world consequence does not include a systematic human review point; it includes, at most, human review of goals set at the beginning and results assessed at the end, with autonomous AI operation in between.

This compression of human oversight is what makes agentic AI governance distinctively challenging. The governance framework for all other AI types is organized around human review of AI outputs before those outputs affect the world. Agentic AI requires governance that anticipates what actions the AI might take, constrains the space of available actions, monitors actions as they occur rather than reviewing outputs after the fact, and provides recovery mechanisms for actions that have already occurred and produced unwanted consequences.

The scope of action problem

The fundamental governance challenge for agentic AI is that the institution deploying it must define, in advance, what actions the agent is permitted to take — because unlike a generative AI whose output a human reviews before acting on, the agent's actions occur autonomously. This requires answering questions that are much easier to ask than to answer: What should this agent be allowed to do? What actions are within its permitted scope? What actions, if taken autonomously, would create unacceptable risk?

The difficulty is that agentic systems are designed to accomplish goals through whatever actions are available to them, and the specific actions that will be needed to accomplish a goal are often not fully predictable in advance. An agent tasked with researching a topic may need to access websites, databases, and documents that cannot all be enumerated in advance. An agent tasked with scheduling meetings may need to contact external parties, access calendar systems, and compose communications that vary with each specific scheduling task. The pre-specification of permitted actions must be broad enough to allow the agent to accomplish its intended task while being specific enough to prevent the agent from taking actions outside its intended scope.

The governance response to the scope of action problem requires several elements. First, explicit permission architecture: defining what categories of action the agent is permitted to take, rather than relying on the agent to infer appropriate scope from its task description. An agent permitted to browse the web is not by that permission permitted to submit forms, create accounts, or make purchases unless those actions are specifically authorized. Second, hard constraints: technical limitations on the agent's action space that are enforced by the system rather than relied on through the agent's own judgment. An agent whose account credentials do not include the ability to make purchases cannot make purchases regardless of whether its task description would seem to authorize them. Third, scope monitoring: ongoing assessment of whether the agent's actions are within its intended scope, with alerts when actions are taken that are unusual, unexpected, or potentially outside permitted boundaries.

The irreversibility problem

Many of the actions that agentic AI systems take are irreversible or difficult to reverse. An email sent cannot be unsent. A database record modified may be recoverable through version history but creates complications if others have read or acted on the modified version. A purchase made may be reversible through refund processes but involves real-world transactions that have already been executed. A file deleted without backup is gone. An external commitment made on behalf of an institution — scheduling an event, agreeing to a term, initiating a service — may create real obligations even if the institution would not have made the commitment had it reviewed the action before it occurred.

The irreversibility problem is why the pre-deployment risk assessment for agentic AI systems must specifically inventory the irreversible or difficult-to-reverse actions available to the agent and establish governance requirements specific to each category. Actions that are easily reversible can be permitted under general oversight frameworks. Actions that are irreversible or consequential enough that their unauthorized occurrence would constitute a significant harm require specific controls: human authorization before the action, strict scope limitations that prevent the action without explicit authorization, or technical constraints that make the action impossible without deliberate human enabling.

For any agentic AI deployment, governance should require what might be called a consequentiality inventory: a systematic assessment of every category of action available to the agent, classified by reversibility and consequence, with specific governance requirements attached to each category. This inventory is the agentic equivalent of the pre-deployment testing required for other AI types — it is the systematic pre-assessment that allows governance to be designed rather than improvised after something consequential has already occurred.

The authorization and identity problem

When an agentic AI system takes actions on behalf of an institution — communicating with external parties, interacting with vendor systems, executing transactions — those actions represent the institution. The external parties receiving an email from an institutional AI agent are receiving a communication that they may treat as authoritative institutional communication. The vendors processing a transaction initiated by an AI agent are processing what appears to be a legitimate institutional transaction. The governance question is: what authority has the institution actually delegated to the AI agent, and what constraints on that authority have been established?

The authorization governance for agentic AI requires explicit documentation of what the agent is authorized to do on the institution's behalf, analogous to the authorization documentation that would accompany a human employee's authority to commit institutional resources. This documentation should specify: what classes of commitment the agent can make without human authorization, what thresholds above which human authorization is required, what external parties the agent is authorized to interact with, and what representations the agent is permitted to make about the institution.

The identity governance for agentic AI requires that external parties interacting with an AI agent know they are interacting with an AI agent rather than a human. The same principle that requires disclosure of chatbot identity to direct service users applies to agentic systems interacting with external parties: people and organizations interacting with institutional AI agents should not be led to believe they are interacting with a human when they are not.

Monitoring actions in real time

For non-agentic AI, monitoring is largely retrospective: reviewing outputs after they are produced, assessing whether performance is within bounds, detecting patterns that indicate problems. For agentic AI, retrospective monitoring is insufficient because the consequences of AI actions may occur before retrospective review is possible. Monitoring for agentic AI systems must be real-time or near-real-time — observing actions as they occur, not only reviewing a log of actions that have already taken their effect.

Real-time action monitoring for agentic AI requires: comprehensive logging of agent actions at sufficient granularity to support oversight — not only what the agent did but what it considered doing, what information it accessed, what decisions it made at each step of its operation; alerting mechanisms that flag unusual or potentially out-of-scope actions for human review as they occur rather than after the fact; and human oversight capacity that can respond to alerts promptly enough to intervene before irreversible consequences occur.

The monitoring infrastructure for agentic AI is substantially more demanding than for other AI types, and governance must ensure that this infrastructure is in place before agentic systems are deployed. Deploying agentic AI without adequate real-time monitoring is deploying with the assumption that the agent will always operate within intended scope — an assumption that agentic AI governance cannot afford to make.

The cascade failure risk

Agentic AI systems that interact with other systems — accessing databases, calling APIs, modifying records, initiating transactions — create cascade failure risks: situations where an AI error or an out-of-scope action triggers cascading consequences across multiple systems before any single component recognizes a problem.

Consider an AI agent tasked with updating vendor records that, due to a data quality problem in its input, applies incorrect updates across a database — and those updates are then used by other systems before the error is detected. Or an AI agent tasked with scheduling that creates cascading booking conflicts because its optimization logic failed to account for a constraint not represented in its training. Or an AI agent interacting with financial systems that initiates a sequence of transactions that each individually appear valid but that together constitute an unauthorized pattern.

Cascade failure governance requires: sandboxing principles — designing agentic systems so that their actions are contained within defined system boundaries that limit the scope of potential cascade; transaction review thresholds — requiring human review before actions that would affect more than a defined number of records, transactions, or external parties; rollback capabilities — ensuring that the systems the agent interacts with support rollback of agent-initiated changes, and that those rollback capabilities are tested before deployment; and incident detection that spans multiple systems rather than monitoring each system in isolation.

The human oversight design challenge for agentic systems

Designing meaningful human oversight for agentic AI is genuinely difficult, because the efficiency value of agentic systems derives precisely from their ability to operate autonomously without requiring human review of each action. If every action requires human authorization, the agent is not autonomous — it is a more complex interface for human action. If no actions require human review, governance is absent. The governance design challenge is to find the appropriate points of human oversight that preserve meaningful control without eliminating operational value.

Effective human oversight design for agentic AI typically involves a combination of: goal authorization — humans define and authorize the goals the agent pursues, with clear scope and constraints; plan review — for complex multi-step tasks, humans review the agent's plan before execution begins, with opportunity to modify goals, add constraints, or decline authorization; action-level review for high-consequence actions — a defined set of high-consequence or irreversible actions that require human authorization even within an authorized goal; results assessment — humans review what the agent accomplished and how, with opportunity to assess whether the execution was within intended scope and consistent with institutional values; and anomaly escalation — the agent is designed to pause and request human guidance when it encounters situations outside its programmed scope rather than making its best autonomous judgment.

This oversight architecture is not appropriate for every agentic deployment — the right balance depends on the task complexity, the consequence level of available actions, the reversibility of actions, and the institution's risk tolerance. Governance must define the oversight architecture specifically for each agentic deployment, not apply a generic template, because the governance-relevant characteristics of agentic deployments vary enormously.

When categories overlap: compound governance challenges

The three categories discussed in this chapter — generative AI, automated decision systems, and agentic AI — are not mutually exclusive. Many institutional AI deployments combine characteristics of multiple categories, and those combinations often create governance challenges that exceed the sum of the individual category challenges.

Generative automated decision systems

Systems that use generative AI capabilities to make automated decisions combine the open-ended output risk of generative AI with the high-stakes, high-volume character of automated decision systems. A benefits eligibility system that uses a language model to interpret applicant narratives and determine eligibility combines hallucination risk with due process implications. A hiring system that uses generative AI to evaluate candidate materials and produce screening decisions combines content appropriateness risk with anti-discrimination obligations. A clinical system that uses generative AI to produce clinical risk assessments combines reliability risk with patient safety implications.

The governance of these combinations requires addressing the full scope of both category-specific governance requirements: the verification and explainability requirements of generative AI, plus the due process, threshold calibration, and cumulative impact requirements of automated decision systems. The compound governance requirements are more demanding than either category alone, and governance processes must be explicitly designed to address both dimensions.

Agentic generative systems

Agentic systems that use generative AI capabilities — agents that compose communications, generate reports, create content, or interact with people through natural language — combine the autonomous action risks of agentic AI with the content reliability and appropriateness risks of generative AI. A customer service agent that autonomously handles service requests through generated responses combines prompt injection risk with the authorization and scope problems of autonomous action. A research agent that autonomously accesses information and produces synthesized reports combines hallucination risk with cascade failure risk if the reports are used as inputs to other systems.

The governance of these combinations requires specific attention to the intersection of content governance and action governance: ensuring that the agent's generated content is subject to appropriate review requirements, that the agent's action scope is defined specifically in relation to its generative capabilities, and that monitoring addresses both the quality of generated content and the scope of autonomous actions.

Fully autonomous decision and action systems

The most governance-demanding category — representing the intersection of all three categories — is systems that autonomously gather information, make decisions about specific individuals, and take actions based on those decisions, all without individual human review. These systems are currently relatively rare in institutional settings, but they are developing rapidly. A loan processing system that autonomously reviews applications, determines eligibility, sets terms, and initiates loan agreements represents this category. A benefits management system that autonomously reviews eligibility, determines benefit levels, adjusts benefits in response to changing circumstances, and communicates those adjustments to recipients represents this category.

The governance of fully autonomous systems requires the full compound of requirements from all three categories, and raises a more fundamental governance question: should fully autonomous systems with high-consequence decision authority be deployed in institutional settings at all, absent robust governance infrastructure that may not yet be available? This question is not rhetorical — for some categories of high-consequence decisions, the answer may be that current AI capabilities, current explainability techniques, and current governance frameworks are not yet adequate to support full autonomous operation without meaningful human review in the loop.

Building governance capacity for these categories

The governance of generative AI, automated decision systems, and agentic AI requires institutional capacity that the standard governance framework may not yet have developed. Several capacity investments are particularly important.

Technical expertise for generative AI governance requires understanding of how language models work, what hallucination risk looks like in specific deployment contexts, what prompt injection vulnerabilities exist in specific system configurations, and how to evaluate the content governance measures that vendors claim to have implemented. This expertise may need to be obtained through training existing governance staff, hiring staff with specific technical backgrounds, or engaging external advisors.

Legal expertise for automated decision system governance requires understanding of the legal frameworks that apply to automated decision-making in the institution's specific sector and jurisdiction — not only general data protection law but sector-specific requirements, anti-discrimination frameworks applicable to automated decision-making, and the emerging AI-specific regulatory requirements that are developing in most major jurisdictions.

Operational expertise for agentic AI governance requires understanding of the systems the agent will interact with, the action sequences it will execute, the external parties it will engage with, and the potential failure modes in each. This operational expertise typically resides in the functions that own the systems the agent will operate within, and governance must engage those functions specifically in agentic AI governance design.

A note on rapidly evolving capabilities

These three categories of AI are among the most rapidly evolving in current AI development. Generative AI capabilities are expanding in capability, modality, and deployment accessibility faster than any previous AI category. Automated decision systems are being applied to increasingly consequential domains. Agentic AI is advancing from research prototype to commercial product at significant speed.

This pace of development creates a specific governance challenge: the governance frameworks described in this chapter address these categories as they exist now. As capabilities evolve, governance frameworks will need to evolve with them. An institution whose AI governance for generative AI was designed around 2023-era capabilities may find that 2026-era capabilities present governance challenges that 2023-era frameworks do not adequately address. The same applies to automated decision systems as they are deployed in increasingly sensitive domains, and to agentic AI as it develops more sophisticated capabilities for autonomous action.

The governance response to rapidly evolving AI capabilities requires: regular review of governance frameworks for these categories, specifically assessing whether current frameworks remain adequate given current capabilities; active monitoring of AI development in these categories, through industry publications, regulatory guidance, academic research, and peer institution practice; and willingness to invest in governance improvements proactively rather than reactively — building governance capacity in anticipation of capability growth rather than scrambling to catch up when new capabilities are already deployed.

The institutions that will govern generative, automated, and agentic AI most effectively are not those that develop perfect frameworks today and apply them unchanged as capabilities grow. They are those that build governance cultures and governance functions capable of continuous adaptation — of recognizing when governance frameworks need to evolve and of having the institutional capacity and commitment to evolve them.

Chapter 21: Legal and Regulatory Basics

The legal landscape that governance must navigate

AI governance does not exist in a legal vacuum. Every institutional AI deployment occurs within a web of legal and regulatory requirements that shape what is permitted, what is required, and what creates liability. These requirements are not static — they are evolving faster than almost any other area of law, driven by rapid AI development, high-profile AI failures, and legislative attention across every major jurisdiction. An institution whose AI governance framework was legally adequate two years ago may have significant compliance gaps today, and significant additional gaps are likely to develop before any governance document written now can be updated.

This chapter provides a practical legal and regulatory orientation for institutional AI governance. It is not a substitute for legal counsel — governance decisions with legal dimensions require legal advice specific to the institution's jurisdiction, sector, regulatory environment, and specific circumstances. It is a foundation: the legal and regulatory literacy that governance leaders, governance team members, and institutional decision-makers need to understand what the legal landscape requires, what questions they must bring to legal counsel, and how to build legal compliance into governance architecture rather than treating it as an afterthought.

The chapter is organized around the major legal frameworks and regulatory domains that affect institutional AI governance, followed by guidance on how to monitor an evolving legal landscape and build legal considerations into the governance system.

The foundational legal principle: technology does not change obligations

Before addressing specific legal frameworks, one foundational principle deserves emphasis: existing legal obligations do not disappear or diminish when institutions use AI to perform functions those obligations govern. Anti-discrimination law that prohibits discriminatory employment decisions applies to employment decisions made with AI assistance. Healthcare privacy law that governs the handling of patient information applies to AI systems that process patient information. Consumer protection law that prohibits deceptive practices applies to AI systems that engage in consumer-facing communication. Professional licensing requirements that govern clinical practice apply to clinical AI that assists with clinical decisions.

This principle has several important implications. First, it means that governance must identify the existing legal obligations relevant to each AI use case and ensure that AI-assisted processes honor those obligations — not only the AI-specific legal requirements that are developing but the established legal frameworks within which AI operates. Second, it means that legal defenses that AI was merely a tool — that the institution bears no responsibility for discriminatory AI outcomes because the discrimination was algorithmic rather than intentional — have been consistently rejected by courts and regulators. Third, it means that legal compliance for AI governance requires understanding both the existing legal framework that governs the underlying activity and the emerging AI-specific requirements that add to that framework.

This principle is not merely theoretical. Healthcare institutions have faced HIPAA enforcement for AI vendor relationships that exposed patient data. Financial institutions have faced fair lending enforcement for algorithmic credit decisions that produced discriminatory outcomes. Employers have faced employment discrimination claims for AI hiring tools with disparate impact. The legal system is actively applying existing frameworks to AI failures, and the governance response must address that existing framework alongside emerging AI-specific regulation.

Data protection and privacy law

The global data protection landscape

Data protection and privacy law — governing how personal information is collected, used, retained, and protected — is the legal framework most universally relevant to institutional AI governance. AI systems process personal information as a fundamental feature of their operation, and that processing occurs within a legal framework that imposes substantial obligations regardless of institution type or AI use case.

The global data protection landscape is characterized by significant variation across jurisdictions combined with a gradual movement toward more comprehensive regulation. Understanding the frameworks applicable in the institution's jurisdictions of operation is a legal compliance prerequisite, not an optional governance enhancement.

The European Union: GDPR and the AI Act

The General Data Protection Regulation — the GDPR, in force since 2018 — is the most comprehensive and most influential data protection framework currently in effect. Its influence extends beyond the European Union: any institution that processes personal data of people in the EU is subject to GDPR regardless of where the institution is located, which means that many institutions outside Europe must comply with GDPR requirements for at least some of their data processing.

GDPR requirements most relevant to AI governance include several that have been addressed in earlier chapters but warrant legal framing here.

The lawful basis requirement — the obligation to process personal data only on a recognized legal basis — applies to all AI processing of personal data. For each AI system that processes personal data, the institution must identify a valid legal basis: consent, contractual necessity, legal obligation, vital interests, public task, or legitimate interests (subject to balancing). The choice of legal basis has practical consequences: consent-based processing requires specific consent mechanisms and creates rights to withdraw; legitimate interests-based processing requires a documented balancing test; each basis has specific conditions and limitations.

The purpose limitation principle — the prohibition on processing personal data for purposes incompatible with the purpose for which it was collected — directly constrains the use of operational data for AI training, the use of data collected for one service in AI systems for different services, and many other AI data uses that involve repurposing previously collected data.

Article 22 — the provision specifically addressing automated decision-making — creates specific rights for individuals when automated processing produces decisions that significantly affect them. These rights include the right not to be subject to solely automated decisions with significant effects (with exceptions for contract performance, legal authorization, and explicit consent), the right to human review, the right to explanation, and the right to contest. Article 22 compliance is required for any AI system that makes automated decisions with significant effects on individuals, and its requirements shape the human oversight and explainability governance described in Chapters 13 and 20.

The EU AI Act — entering into force progressively from 2024 — adds AI-specific regulatory requirements on top of GDPR's data protection framework. The AI Act establishes a risk-based classification system that categorizes AI systems by risk level and imposes corresponding requirements.

Prohibited AI practices under the AI Act include: AI systems that manipulate persons through subliminal techniques; AI that exploits vulnerabilities of specific groups; AI-based social scoring by public authorities; most uses of real-time remote biometric identification in public spaces; AI systems that assess the risk of persons committing offenses; AI that infers emotions in workplaces and education institutions in most circumstances; and biometric categorization systems based on sensitive attributes.

High-risk AI systems — defined by both the sector of deployment and the type of use — face the most significant compliance requirements. High-risk systems include AI used in critical infrastructure, educational and vocational training, employment and worker management, access to essential private and public services, law enforcement, migration and border control, administration of justice, and democratic processes. High-risk AI requirements include conformity assessment before market placement, technical documentation, logging requirements, transparency and provision of information to users, human oversight design, and registration in an EU database.

General-purpose AI models — large language models and other foundation models that can be used for many tasks — face their own regulatory requirements under the AI Act, with additional requirements for models deemed to pose systemic risk.

GDPR and AI Act compliance together represent a substantial governance compliance requirement for institutions operating in or serving people in the EU. Governance frameworks for these institutions must be specifically designed to address both frameworks.

United States: a sectoral patchwork

The United States does not have a comprehensive federal AI law or a comprehensive federal data protection law equivalent to GDPR. Instead, AI governance in the US operates within a complex patchwork of federal sectoral laws, state laws, and regulatory guidance from multiple agencies.

Federal sectoral frameworks relevant to AI governance include several that are particularly important for specific institution types.

The Health Insurance Portability and Accountability Act — HIPAA — governs the handling of protected health information by covered entities (healthcare providers, health plans, healthcare clearinghouses) and their business associates. AI vendors that process PHI on behalf of covered entities are business associates subject to HIPAA requirements, and covered entities must execute Business Associate Agreements that impose HIPAA obligations on those vendors. HIPAA compliance for AI systems requires specific assessment of what PHI the AI processes, under what authorization, with what security protections, and under what contractual terms with vendors.

The Family Educational Rights and Privacy Act — FERPA — governs educational records at institutions receiving federal education funding, restricting disclosure of student records and creating student and parent rights. AI systems used in educational contexts that access or process student educational records must comply with FERPA requirements, including restrictions on third-party disclosure that affect what data can be provided to AI vendors.

The Equal Credit Opportunity Act and the Fair Housing Act — ECOA and FHA — prohibit discrimination in credit and housing decisions on the basis of protected characteristics. These frameworks apply to AI systems used in credit scoring, loan processing, insurance pricing, housing eligibility, and related decisions, requiring that AI-assisted decisions meet fair lending and fair housing standards regardless of whether discrimination is intentional. The Consumer Financial Protection Bureau and Department of Housing and Urban Development have issued guidance specifically addressing AI in credit and housing decisions.

Title VII of the Civil Rights Act and related employment discrimination laws prohibit employment discrimination on the basis of protected characteristics, applying to AI systems used in hiring, promotion, performance evaluation, and other employment decisions. The Equal Employment Opportunity Commission has issued guidance on AI and employment discrimination, and multiple enforcement actions have targeted algorithmic hiring tools with disparate impact.

The Children's Online Privacy Protection Act — COPPA — governs the collection of personal information from children under 13, with specific requirements for consent, data minimization, and security that apply to AI systems used in contexts that serve children.

State-level frameworks add significant complexity to US AI governance. California's Consumer Privacy Act and its amendments through the California Privacy Rights Act — CCPA and CPRA — create comprehensive data protection requirements for businesses operating in or serving residents of California, including requirements for automated decision-making disclosure and opt-out rights that are among the most significant AI-specific state requirements in the US. Illinois' Biometric Information Privacy Act — BIPA — creates specific requirements for collection and use of biometric data, including facial recognition, with a private right of action that has generated significant litigation. Several other states have enacted or are developing comprehensive privacy laws with AI-relevant provisions.

AI-specific state legislation is developing rapidly. Multiple states have enacted laws addressing AI in employment decisions — requiring disclosure of AI use in hiring, prohibiting certain AI-based practices, or creating rights to explanation. Several states have enacted or are considering requirements for healthcare AI, including disclosure and oversight requirements. A growing number of states have addressed AI-generated content, deepfakes, and AI in political advertising. The state legislative landscape is changing continuously and requires ongoing monitoring.

Federal regulatory guidance — from agencies including the FTC, EEOC, CFPB, HHS, and others — is increasingly addressing AI-specific issues within existing regulatory frameworks. This guidance does not have the force of law that statutes and regulations carry, but it provides authoritative interpretation of how existing frameworks apply to AI and often precedes formal rulemaking. Institutions should monitor agency guidance relevant to their sectors as an important source of compliance intelligence.

Canada

Canada's federal privacy law — the Personal Information Protection and Electronic Documents Act, PIPEDA, and the provincial laws that are substantially similar to it — governs commercial handling of personal information and applies to AI systems that process personal information. PIPEDA's accountability principle, purpose limitation requirements, and individual rights create compliance obligations for AI deployments similar in structure to GDPR, though with different specific requirements.

Canada is in the process of developing more comprehensive AI-specific legislation. Bill C-27, the Digital Charter Implementation Act, includes the Artificial Intelligence and Data Act — AIDA — which would establish requirements for high-impact AI systems including impact assessments, risk management, monitoring, and transparency. The status of this legislation and its final requirements should be verified as it progresses through the legislative process.

Other jurisdictions

China has enacted comprehensive AI regulation, including the Interim Measures for the Management of Generative Artificial Intelligence Services and regulations governing algorithmic recommendations and deep synthesis technologies. These regulations apply to AI services provided in China and create specific requirements for generative AI operators, algorithmic recommendation systems, and deep synthesis applications.

The United Kingdom has taken a sector-based regulatory approach to AI, with existing sector regulators applying their frameworks to AI within their domains, supplemented by cross-cutting principles developed by the AI Safety Institute and relevant guidance bodies. UK data protection — governed by the UK GDPR and the Data Protection Act 2018, which retained GDPR requirements following Brexit — imposes obligations similar to EU GDPR.

India, Brazil, Japan, Singapore, Australia, and other major jurisdictions are at various stages of developing AI-specific regulatory frameworks, with each building on their existing data protection and sector regulatory foundations. Institutions operating internationally must track the regulatory development in each relevant jurisdiction.

Anti-discrimination and civil rights law

Anti-discrimination law is the second foundational legal framework for AI governance, applying whenever AI systems make or influence decisions that affect people's access to employment, housing, credit, education, healthcare, public accommodations, or other protected domains.

Employment discrimination

Employment discrimination law — Title VII and related federal statutes in the US, the Equality Act in the UK, the Employment Equality Directive in the EU, and equivalent national laws across jurisdictions — prohibits discrimination in employment decisions on the basis of protected characteristics. These frameworks apply to AI-assisted employment decisions through both disparate treatment theory (intentional discrimination, which AI may replicate from biased training data) and disparate impact theory (practices that are facially neutral but produce disproportionately adverse outcomes for protected groups).

Disparate impact theory is particularly significant for AI hiring tools: an algorithmic screening system that produces differential selection rates across racial, gender, or age groups must be justified by job-related necessity and lack of less discriminatory alternative. The EEOC's Uniform Guidelines on Employee Selection Procedures — which predate AI but apply to algorithmic selection — establish specific statistical thresholds (the four-fifths rule) for identifying adverse impact that requires justification.

Practical compliance requirements for AI employment systems include: adverse impact analysis before deployment and on an ongoing monitoring basis; documentation of the job-relatedness of any selection criteria the AI uses; assessment of whether less discriminatory alternatives exist; and disclosure to applicants that AI was used and how it affected their consideration.

Fair lending and fair housing

The Equal Credit Opportunity Act, Fair Housing Act, and related frameworks prohibit discrimination in credit and housing decisions. These frameworks apply to AI credit scoring, automated underwriting, AI-assisted loan processing, and AI-assisted housing and rental decisions.

Regulatory enforcement of fair lending and fair housing law has specifically addressed algorithmic decision-making. Enforcement actions and supervisory guidance from the CFPB, OCC, Federal Reserve, and FDIC have established that lenders using AI must be able to explain credit decisions, must monitor for disparate impact, and must not use factors that are proxies for protected characteristics. The adverse action notice requirement — the obligation to provide applicants denied credit with the specific reasons for the denial — applies to AI-assisted denials and requires explainability capabilities that many AI systems do not natively provide.

Healthcare and disability discrimination

Section 504 of the Rehabilitation Act and the Americans with Disabilities Act — in the US — and equivalent frameworks in other jurisdictions prohibit discrimination against people with disabilities in healthcare, education, employment, and access to programs receiving federal funding. AI systems used in healthcare that perform differently across disability groups, that make eligibility assessments that disadvantage people with disabilities, or that are deployed in ways that create accessibility barriers may implicate these frameworks.

The specific healthcare AI concern that has attracted the most regulatory attention is AI systems that perform differently across racial and ethnic groups in clinical contexts. Section 1557 of the Affordable Care Act prohibits discrimination in healthcare programs and activities, and the HHS Office of Civil Rights has issued guidance specifically addressing AI and health equity. Healthcare institutions using clinical AI must address differential performance across demographic groups as a civil rights compliance matter, not only a fairness ethics matter.

Healthcare-specific legal frameworks

Healthcare institutions face AI governance legal requirements that are more extensive and more specific than those facing most other institution types, reflecting both the sensitivity of health information and the life-and-death stakes of clinical decisions.

HIPAA in depth

HIPAA's Security Rule, Privacy Rule, and Breach Notification Rule together create a comprehensive compliance framework for protected health information. For AI governance, the most significant HIPAA requirements include: the requirement for Business Associate Agreements with AI vendors that process PHI; the minimum necessary standard, requiring that AI systems process only the PHI needed for their specific purpose; the security safeguards required for PHI in AI system environments; and the breach notification requirements that apply when PHI is exposed through AI system incidents.

HIPAA compliance for AI specifically requires attention to: whether PHI is being transmitted to AI vendor systems and whether BAAs are executed; whether de-identification of PHI for AI training meets

HIPAA's specific de-identification standards; whether AI system logging and access controls meet Security Rule requirements; and whether the institution's training on appropriate AI use of PHI is adequate for workforce compliance.

FDA regulation of AI medical devices

The Food and Drug Administration regulates software that meets the definition of a medical device, including AI/ML-based software used in clinical decision-making. The FDA's Digital Health Center of Excellence and the Center for Devices and Radiological Health have developed regulatory frameworks specifically addressing AI/ML-Based Software as a Medical Device — SaMD.

Clinical AI systems that meet the FDA's device definition — software intended to diagnose, cure, treat, prevent, or mitigate disease or conditions, or that is intended to affect the structure or function of the body — require FDA clearance or approval before deployment in US clinical settings. Healthcare institutions deploying clinical AI must assess whether FDA regulation applies, and must not deploy AI medical devices that have not received appropriate FDA authorization.

The FDA's approach to AI medical devices is evolving. The concept of predetermined change control plans — pre-approved frameworks for how AI systems can be updated without requiring new regulatory submissions for each change — is under development and will affect how healthcare institutions govern AI system updates.

Clinical standards and professional licensing

Beyond statutory regulatory requirements, clinical AI governance must address the professional standards and licensing requirements that govern clinical practice. Physicians, nurses, and other licensed clinicians bear professional responsibility for clinical decisions, and that responsibility does not transfer to AI systems. Clinical AI that influences clinical decisions does not reduce clinicians' professional obligations; it adds an obligation to use AI responsibly within the framework of professional standards.

Medical malpractice liability for AI-assisted clinical decisions is an evolving area of law. Courts and legal commentators are working through questions of liability allocation among institutions, clinicians, and AI vendors when AI-assisted clinical decisions contribute to patient harm. The governance implication for healthcare institutions is that documentation of AI use in clinical decision-making, governance of clinical AI oversight, and clear human oversight in clinical AI workflows are both ethical requirements and potential legal protections.

Education-specific legal frameworks

Educational institutions face specific legal requirements that affect AI governance in their context.

FERPA — addressed above — restricts disclosure of educational records and creates student and parent rights that apply to AI systems processing student data. The FERPA "school official" exception — which allows disclosure to vendors providing services to the school under specific conditions — has been applied to AI vendors, but requires that the vendor be subject to the institution's FERPA obligations through contractual terms and that the vendor use the data only for the specified educational purpose.

COPPA — also addressed above — applies when educational institutions use AI systems with children under 13, requiring specific parental consent mechanisms and data minimization requirements.

The Individuals with Disabilities Education Act — IDEA — and Section 504 create specific requirements for educational institutions regarding students with disabilities that apply to AI systems used in educational assessment, placement, and accommodation decisions. AI systems that affect educational decisions for students with disabilities must be consistent with the institution's obligations to provide appropriate accommodations and to make placement decisions through processes that honor IDEA's procedural requirements.

State education privacy laws in many US states add requirements beyond FERPA and COPPA. Several states have enacted specific student data privacy laws that create requirements for vendor contracts, student data use limitations, and disclosure requirements that affect AI governance in educational contexts.

Consumer protection law

Consumer protection law — governing deceptive and unfair practices in consumer-facing contexts — applies to institutional AI in several important ways.

The Federal Trade Commission's authority over unfair or deceptive practices — Section 5 of the FTC Act — has been applied to AI-related deception, including deceptive AI performance claims by vendors, undisclosed AI use in consumer-facing contexts, and deceptive AI-generated content. The FTC has issued extensive guidance on AI and has brought enforcement actions addressing AI-related deception and unfair practices. Institutions using AI in consumer-facing contexts must ensure that their AI practices are not deceptive or unfair under FTC standards.

State consumer protection laws — including California's Unfair Competition Law and similar statutes in other states — provide additional consumer protection requirements that may apply to institutional AI use in consumer-facing contexts.

Emerging requirements for disclosure of AI-generated content — particularly AI-generated political advertising and AI-generated content in commercial contexts — are developing in multiple jurisdictions and represent a growing consumer protection compliance dimension for institutions that use generative AI in consumer communication.

Sector-specific regulatory frameworks

Beyond the cross-cutting legal frameworks described above, numerous sector-specific regulatory requirements affect AI governance in specific institutional contexts.

Financial services regulation — from the SEC, FINRA, banking regulators, and insurance regulators — addresses AI in investment advice, trading, credit, insurance underwriting, fraud detection, and customer service. AI governance in financial services must address model risk management requirements, explainability requirements for automated decisions, fair lending obligations, and the rapidly developing regulatory guidance on AI in financial services from multiple regulatory bodies.

Social services and benefits administration at the state and federal level face legal requirements from the statutes authorizing the programs administered — Medicaid, SNAP, housing assistance, child welfare — that constrain how automated decision systems can be used in eligibility determination, benefit calculation, and service delivery. Due process requirements under the Constitution's Fifth and Fourteenth Amendments apply to government automated decision-making affecting legally protected interests.

Government AI use faces additional constitutional and administrative law constraints. Due process requirements, equal protection requirements, and administrative law requirements for reasoned decision-making apply to government AI use in ways that do not apply to private institutions. The algorithmic accountability of government AI — the requirement that government decision-making be explainable and contestable — has been the subject of significant litigation and legislative attention.

Emerging AI-specific regulatory frameworks

Beyond the application of existing legal frameworks to AI, a growing body of AI-specific regulation is developing across jurisdictions. The EU AI Act — addressed above — is the most comprehensive enacted framework, but it is far from alone.

The United States has no comprehensive federal AI law as of this writing, but federal AI regulatory activity is substantial: executive orders on AI have directed regulatory agencies to address AI in their domains; sector regulators have issued AI-specific guidance and proposed rulemaking; and Congress has considered multiple AI-focused bills. The regulatory landscape is developing rapidly, and institutions should monitor federal AI regulatory activity as a governance compliance matter.

AI-specific state legislation in the United States is proliferating. Colorado, Connecticut, Illinois, Maryland, New York, Texas, and other states have enacted or are developing AI-specific requirements in areas including employment, healthcare, consumer services, automated decision-making, biometrics, and AI-generated content. The diversity and pace of state AI legislation creates significant compliance complexity for institutions operating across multiple states.

International AI governance frameworks are developing in parallel with domestic regulation. The OECD AI Principles, the G7 Hiroshima AI Process, the Council of Europe AI Convention, and bilateral and multilateral AI governance agreements are shaping the international legal environment within which institutional AI governance operates.

Building legal compliance into governance architecture

Understanding the legal landscape is necessary but not sufficient. Effective AI governance must translate legal requirements into the governance architecture — the policies, processes, monitoring systems, and documentation — that ensures ongoing compliance.

Legal review as a governance process component

Legal review should be built into governance processes at defined points rather than applied reactively when problems arise. The intake and risk screening process (Chapter 10) should include legal assessment as a standard component for medium- and high-risk use cases: identifying what legal frameworks apply, what requirements those frameworks impose, and whether the proposed use case and its governance arrangements are legally adequate.

Vendor contract review (Chapter 11) should include legal review of AI-specific provisions: data handling terms, liability allocation, audit rights, breach notification, and exit provisions — assessed against the specific legal requirements that apply to the institution's use of the vendor's AI system.

The AI policy (Chapter 8) should reflect current legal requirements and should be reviewed at least annually for legal currency. Policy provisions that were legally adequate when written may become inadequate as new requirements are enacted or existing requirements are newly applied to AI contexts.

Regulatory monitoring as a governance function

The regulatory landscape for AI is changing fast enough that institutions cannot rely on periodic legal reviews to maintain currency. Governance frameworks should include ongoing regulatory monitoring: systematic tracking of legislative and regulatory developments relevant to the institution's AI use.

Regulatory monitoring responsibilities should be assigned explicitly — typically to legal counsel, supported by a governance team member with specific responsibility for tracking AI regulatory developments. The outputs of regulatory monitoring should feed into governance team review: significant regulatory developments should trigger governance team discussion of compliance implications and may trigger policy updates, process changes, or reassessment of specific AI deployments.

External resources for regulatory monitoring include: law firm AI practice group newsletters, regulatory agency notification services, industry association AI governance resources, and specialized AI policy tracking services. No single source provides comprehensive coverage across all jurisdictions and sectors; effective monitoring typically requires several sources.

Documentation as legal protection

The documentation practices built into AI governance — intake records, testing documentation, monitoring reports, incident records, vendor assessment files — serve legal protection functions as well as governance functions. When an institution faces a regulatory inquiry, a litigation matter, or a compliance audit, the documentation of its AI governance demonstrates the due diligence that is both legally relevant and institutionally protective.

Documentation should be maintained with the understanding that it may be reviewed in adversarial legal or regulatory proceedings. This means that documentation should be accurate rather than aspirational — documenting what governance actually does, not what the governance framework aspires to do. It means that governance gaps should be documented and addressed rather than papered over with optimistic characterizations. And it means that incident documentation should reflect honest assessment of what occurred rather than defensive framing that minimizes institutional culpability — because documentation created in real time, before litigation, is far more credible than documentation that appears to have been shaped by legal strategy.

Working effectively with legal counsel

Governance teams that include legal counsel and that have relationships with external counsel for specialist matters are better positioned for AI governance legal compliance than those that treat legal counsel as a last resort. Several practices improve the effectiveness of governance-legal collaboration.

Briefing legal counsel on AI governance fundamentals — the risk categories, the governance processes, the vendor relationship dynamics, the monitoring framework — ensures that legal review is substantive rather than merely formal. Legal counsel who understand how AI systems work and what institutional AI governance requires provide more useful advice than those applying legal frameworks to a technical domain they do not understand.

Bringing legal counsel into governance processes proactively — at the intake stage, at vendor assessment, at policy review — is more effective and less expensive than engaging counsel after problems have materialized. Legal review at the intake stage can prevent legal problems from being built into deployments; legal review after incident is damage limitation.

Building a relationship with counsel who have specific AI law expertise — rather than relying exclusively on general counsel — is increasingly important as AI law develops as a specific practice area. AI law expertise is developing rapidly in the legal profession; institutions with significant AI portfolios benefit from access to counsel who track AI law developments as a primary professional focus.

Communicating regulatory developments between legal and governance functions in both directions — governance alerting legal to institutional AI developments that may have legal implications, legal alerting governance to regulatory developments that may require governance response — creates the continuous compliance awareness that the pace of AI regulatory development requires.

The legal future: preparing for continued change

The legal landscape for AI governance will continue to change substantially. Several trends in that change are predictable enough to inform governance planning.

Comprehensive federal AI legislation in the United States is increasingly likely, though its specific form and timeline are uncertain. Governance frameworks should be designed with the expectation that federal requirements will develop and should be adapted accordingly — which means avoiding governance designs that would require complete reconstruction to accommodate federal requirements.

International regulatory convergence — and divergence — will continue. The EU AI Act is likely to influence AI regulation in other jurisdictions, as GDPR has influenced global data protection law. But AI regulatory frameworks will not converge completely; significant differences across jurisdictions will persist, creating ongoing compliance complexity for internationally operating institutions.

AI-specific sector requirements will proliferate. Every major regulatory domain — healthcare, finance, education, employment, housing, criminal justice, government benefits — is likely to develop AI-specific requirements that add to the general AI regulatory framework. Sector specialists will need to track AI regulatory development in their specific domains as a governance function.

Private litigation will develop alongside regulatory enforcement. Class action litigation, individual claims, and public interest litigation addressing AI governance failures are all developing and will create legal precedents that further shape what governance is legally required. Legal counsel should monitor litigation developments as a compliance intelligence source alongside regulatory monitoring.

The institutions that navigate this continuing legal evolution most effectively will be those with governance frameworks designed for adaptability — with regular legal review cycles, regulatory monitoring functions, and governance processes that can accommodate legal requirement changes without complete reconstruction. Legal compliance and governance quality are not the same thing, but they reinforce each other: institutions that govern AI well are typically in better legal compliance, and institutions that maintain legal compliance are typically governing AI more responsibly than those that do not.

Chapter 22: Audits, Metrics, and Accountability

The question governance must answer

Every governance system faces a fundamental accountability challenge: how does the institution know whether its governance is actually working? Not whether governance documents exist, not whether governance processes are formally in place, not whether the governance team meets regularly — but whether governance is achieving what it is supposed to achieve. Whether AI systems are performing fairly, safely, and reliably. Whether oversight is genuine rather than nominal. Whether the people the institution serves are protected from the harms governance was designed to prevent. Whether the institution's stated commitments to responsible AI use are honored in practice rather than merely declared in policy.

This question cannot be answered by governance processes examining themselves. An intake process that produces approvals, a monitoring function that generates reports, and an oversight system that achieves high procedural compliance rates — all of these may be operating exactly as designed while failing at their purpose. The intake process may be approving use cases it should decline because its criteria are inadequate. The monitoring function may be generating reports that no one adequately reviews. The oversight system may be producing the documentation of human review without the substance of human judgment. Governance that assesses only whether its processes are running misses whether those processes are working.

Audit is the governance function that closes this gap. It is the systematic, periodic assessment of whether governance is achieving its purposes — examining not only whether processes are followed but whether they are effective, not only whether metrics are collected but whether they are adequate, not only whether responsibilities are assigned but whether they are fulfilled. Metrics are what audit measures. Accountability is what audit enables.

This chapter describes what institutional AI governance auditing requires: how to design audit programs, what to measure, how to interpret what measurements reveal, how to distinguish governance that is working from governance that appears to be working, and how to build the accountability structures that convert audit findings into governance improvement rather than merely documentation of governance adequacy.

What audit is and is not

Before describing how to audit AI governance, it is important to be clear about what auditing means in this context — and what it does not mean.

An AI governance audit is a structured, systematic assessment of whether the institution's AI governance is achieving its purposes. It examines governance processes, governance outcomes, and the relationship between them. It is conducted by people with independence from the governance functions being assessed, applying defined criteria and methodologies, and producing findings and recommendations that are acted on rather than filed.

An audit is not a monitoring report. Monitoring — described in Chapter 16 — is continuous and operational, tracking AI system performance as it occurs. Audit is periodic and evaluative, stepping back from the continuous data stream to assess whether the overall governance picture is adequate. Monitoring provides the data that audit draws on and assesses; audit assesses whether monitoring itself is functioning adequately.

An audit is not a compliance checklist. Compliance documentation — confirming that required processes have occurred — is one component of what audit examines, but it is not the purpose of audit. An audit that confirms process completion without assessing whether processes are achieving their governance purposes is compliance documentation masquerading as audit. The test of AI governance is not whether the intake form was completed but whether the intake review identified and addressed the governance-relevant risks of the proposed use case. Not whether monitoring reports were produced but whether they detected what they were designed to detect. Not whether training was delivered but whether it changed understanding and behavior.

An audit is not an investigation. Investigation — described in Chapter 19 — is triggered by specific incidents or concerns and focuses on understanding what happened and why. Audit is proactive and systematic, assessing governance quality across the full scope of the institution's AI activities rather than examining a specific event.

An audit is also not a rubber stamp. The governance team that commissions an audit and treats unfavorable findings as problems to be managed rather than information to be acted on has not audited its governance; it has created documentation of a review process. Genuine audit requires genuine accountability: findings that reveal governance failures must produce governance improvements, and the institution must be able to demonstrate that they did.

The audit program: structure and scope

An institutional AI governance audit program is the organized set of audit activities — what will be audited, how frequently, by whom, using what methods, to what standards, with what accountability for findings — that constitutes the institution's systematic self-assessment of AI governance quality.

Defining the audit scope

The audit program must cover the full scope of institutional AI governance, not only the dimensions that are easiest to assess or most likely to produce favorable findings. A comprehensive scope includes: AI policy and its implementation; the intake and risk screening process; vendor assessment and contract management; pre-deployment testing; human oversight design and effectiveness; monitoring and ongoing review; incident response; staff training and AI literacy; communication with affected parties; and the governance team's own functioning.

For each of these dimensions, the audit program should define what aspects will be assessed and at what level of depth. Not every dimension requires equally intensive audit attention. Risk-based prioritization — investing more intensive audit in the dimensions most consequential for governance outcomes — is appropriate and necessary given limited audit resources. The dimensions that most directly protect the people the institution serves from harm — oversight effectiveness, bias monitoring, incident response — warrant more intensive audit than dimensions whose governance failures are less consequential.

The audit scope should also include a cross-cutting question that is harder to audit but more fundamental than any process-specific assessment: is the institution's governance culture — its actual commitment to responsible AI use as evidenced by behavior rather than stated values — supportive of effective governance? A governance system whose processes are formally adequate but whose culture undermines them — where workarounds are tolerated, where governance requirements are treated as obstacles rather than obligations, where leadership does not visibly comply with the requirements it has established — is a governance system that is failing at the level that no process improvement can fix.

Audit frequency

Different components of the AI governance program warrant different audit frequencies, based on their risk relevance, the pace at which conditions change, and the resources available for audit activity.

The most fundamental audit activity is the annual governance review — a comprehensive assessment of whether the institution's AI governance program is operating effectively across its full scope. Annual review provides the systematic governance health assessment that governance leaders and institutional leadership need to understand the overall quality of the institution's AI governance and to make investment and improvement decisions.

For specific high-risk AI systems — clinical AI, AI used in benefit determinations, AI used in employment decisions — more frequent targeted audits are appropriate. Quarterly or semi-annual audits focused on specific high-risk systems allow earlier detection of performance problems, governance compliance failures, and emerging concerns than annual cycles would permit.

For components where conditions change rapidly — vendor relationships where contracts are expiring, regulatory environments where new requirements are developing, AI systems where model updates occur frequently — triggered audits that assess governance adequacy when specific changes occur are appropriate supplements to calendar-based audit cycles.

Independence

The effectiveness of audit depends fundamentally on the independence of the audit function from the functions being assessed. Self-assessment — the intake process assessing whether it is effective, the monitoring function assessing whether monitoring is adequate, the governance team assessing whether governance team functioning is effective — is useful input into audit but is not a substitute for independent assessment.

The appropriate degree of audit independence depends on the significance of what is being assessed and the institutional resources available to support independent audit. Several models are available.

Internal audit functions — professional audit staff who are organizationally separate from the governance functions they audit and report to leadership rather than to the governance team — provide meaningful independence for most governance assessment purposes. Where institutions have internal audit capacity, AI governance audit should be incorporated into the internal audit program.

External audit — assessment conducted by third-party auditors who are independent of the institution entirely — provides the highest degree of independence and is appropriate for high-stakes governance assessments, for assessments where internal independence is questioned, and for audits that will be shared with external parties including regulators, accreditors, or the public. For high-risk AI applications with significant regulatory implications, external audit may be legally required or practically necessary for regulatory credibility.

Peer review — assessment by governance professionals from comparable institutions who exchange assessments — provides meaningful external perspective at lower cost than formal external audit. Peer review works well for governance process assessment where professional judgment matters more than technical precision.

For smaller institutions with limited internal audit capacity, creative approaches to independence may be necessary. A retired professional with relevant expertise engaged as a periodic reviewer, a board committee with appropriate expertise conducting governance reviews, or a consortium arrangement with peer institutions are all mechanisms that provide more independence than pure self-assessment while being more accessible than full external audit.

What to measure: the metrics architecture

Governance audit is only as good as what it measures. The metrics architecture for AI governance audit must capture what governance is trying to achieve — not only whether governance processes are being followed but whether they are working.

The following describes the primary measurement categories for each major governance dimension.

Measuring intake and risk screening effectiveness

The intake process is supposed to ensure that AI use cases with significant governance concerns are identified before deployment and either declined, conditioned, or modified to address those concerns. Metrics for intake effectiveness should assess whether it is actually doing this.

Intake completeness — the proportion of AI use cases going live in the institution that went through the intake process — is the threshold measure. An intake process that is formally well-designed but that is being bypassed for a significant proportion of actual AI deployments is not providing governance coverage. Completeness is assessed by comparing the AI inventory to the intake records: every system in the inventory should have a corresponding intake record. Systems that do not represent governance gaps.

Risk identification accuracy — whether intake reviews correctly identified the risk levels of the use cases they assessed — is a more demanding measure. Post-deployment comparison of the risk levels assigned at intake with what monitoring subsequently revealed about actual risk patterns provides evidence of whether intake risk assessment is accurate. Systematic patterns in which intake consistently underestimates risk for specific categories of use case indicate intake assessment methodology problems.

Decision quality — whether approval decisions were appropriately calibrated to risk findings — assesses whether the governance team made the right decisions given what intake found. Review of a sample of intake decisions, with attention to whether conditions attached to approvals were appropriate to the risks identified, provides audit evidence about decision quality. This assessment requires judgment, not only metrics, and should involve reviewers with sufficient expertise to assess whether governance decisions were reasonable.

Condition compliance — whether conditions attached to conditional approvals were actually implemented — tests whether governance approval conditions had practical effect. For a sample of conditionally approved use cases, audit should verify that the specified conditions were met before deployment, that compliance was confirmed rather than assumed, and that conditions are being maintained in ongoing operation.

Measuring vendor governance effectiveness

The vendor governance system is supposed to ensure that AI vendor relationships protect institutional and stakeholder interests. Metrics for vendor governance effectiveness assess whether it is doing this.

Due diligence completeness — whether vendor assessments were conducted to the required depth for each risk level — assesses whether the vendor assessment process was applied systematically. Audit review of vendor assessment documentation for a sample of vendor relationships, comparing documented due diligence to the requirements established in governance policy, provides evidence of completeness.

Contract adequacy — whether vendor contracts include the provisions that governance policy requires — assesses whether the institution has the contractual protections it needs. Systematic review of AI vendor contract provisions against the governance requirements described in Chapter 11 reveals gaps in the institution's contractual protection.

Vendor compliance monitoring — whether the institution is actively monitoring vendor compliance with contractual obligations — assesses whether the institution is exercising its governance rights in the vendor relationship. Evidence of compliance monitoring includes: documentation of periodic performance reviews, exercise of audit rights, review of vendor change notifications, and escalation records when vendor performance concerns arose.

Vendor notification compliance — whether vendors are meeting their notification obligations — assesses a specific contractual requirement that is frequently inadequately monitored. If the institution has experienced AI system changes without receiving the notification its contracts require, that represents both a vendor compliance failure and an institutional monitoring failure.

Measuring oversight effectiveness

Human oversight is supposed to ensure that AI errors are caught and corrected before causing harm, and that human judgment is genuinely exercised in AI-assisted decisions. Measuring whether oversight is actually achieving this is one of the most important and most challenging governance audit tasks.

Override rates — the proportion of AI recommendations that human reviewers modify or reject — are the primary behavioral indicator of oversight quality. The appropriate override rate varies by use case, AI system accuracy, and operational context, so audit assessment requires comparison against expected ranges rather than universal benchmarks. Rates that are systematically near zero, particularly in contexts where the AI system cannot be perfect, suggest automation bias or nominal oversight. Audit should examine override rates across operational functions, time periods, and demographic groups (to detect whether certain populations' cases receive more or less genuine oversight).

Escalation rates — the proportion of AI outputs that are elevated for additional review — provide complementary insight into oversight culture. In any AI deployment with genuine oversight, some cases will present uncertainties or concerns that warrant escalation. Consistently near-zero escalation rates across extended periods suggest either that escalation culture is not functioning or that the escalation threshold is set impractically high.

Documentation adequacy — whether required documentation of AI-assisted decisions is being maintained — assesses a specific oversight requirement that is both legally important and governance-relevant. Sample review of AI-assisted decision records, assessing whether documentation reflects the oversight that was supposed to have occurred, provides evidence of documentation compliance.

Override decision quality — for a sample of cases where reviewers deviated from AI recommendations, whether the deviation represented genuine exercise of professional judgment — is a more demanding audit assessment. This assessment requires domain expert involvement and produces qualitative evidence about whether overrides reflect genuine independent assessment rather than arbitrary deviation.

Simulated scenario testing — presenting reviewers with AI outputs that contain known errors or problems and assessing whether they are detected — provides direct evidence of oversight effectiveness that behavioral metrics alone cannot. For high-risk AI systems, periodic simulation testing by audit or governance team members provides evidence that oversight is capable of catching the kinds of failures the AI system might produce.

Measuring fairness monitoring adequacy

The fairness monitoring system is supposed to detect differential AI performance across demographic groups in time to address it before significant harm accumulates. Metrics for fairness monitoring adequacy assess whether it is doing this.

Monitoring coverage — whether the institution has adequate demographic data to monitor fairness for the populations its AI systems serve — is the foundational measurement. Audit should assess whether demographic data collection is adequate for meaningful fairness monitoring, what groups can and cannot be monitored with statistical confidence given available sample sizes, and what gaps in monitoring coverage represent governance risks.

Detection sensitivity — whether the fairness monitoring system would detect meaningful performance differentials given available data — is a statistical assessment of monitoring adequacy. Audit should include assessment of the statistical power of fairness monitoring: given the sample sizes available, what magnitude of performance differential could be detected at what confidence level? If the answer is that only very large differentials would be statistically detectable, governance must acknowledge this limitation and address it through either more aggressive data collection or more conservative oversight requirements.

Monitoring currency — whether fairness monitoring is being conducted at the required frequency and whether reports are being reviewed and acted on — assesses operational compliance with monitoring requirements. Audit review of monitoring records, report distribution, and governance team review documentation provides evidence of operational currency.

Response adequacy — when monitoring has identified fairness concerns, whether the governance response was appropriate — assesses whether the monitoring feedback loop is functioning. For incidents where monitoring produced fairness-related signals, audit should assess whether those signals received appropriate governance attention, whether investigation occurred, and whether responses were proportionate to what was found.

Measuring incident response effectiveness

The incident response system is supposed to detect, investigate, remediate, and learn from AI incidents. Metrics for incident response effectiveness assess whether it is doing this.

Reporting completeness — whether the incidents that occurred during the audit period were reported through the incident response system — is assessed by comparing incident reports to other evidence of AI problems: monitoring data, complaints, external sources, staff interviews. A significant gap between the evidence of AI problems and the number of formal incident reports suggests reporting culture problems.

Response timeliness — whether incidents received responses within the timeframes that governance policy requires — assesses procedural compliance with incident response requirements. Audit review of incident records provides evidence of whether response timeliness standards were met.

Investigation quality — whether incident investigations produced findings that adequately explain what occurred and identify contributing factors — requires qualitative assessment of investigation documentation. Investigations that conclude only that a technical error occurred without identifying governance contributing factors, investigations that do not assess systemic implications, or investigations that lack domain expert involvement should be flagged as inadequate.

Remediation completion — whether remediation commitments made in response to incidents were actually implemented — assesses whether the accountability of the incident response system has practical effect. For all incidents during the audit period, audit should verify that remediation commitments were completed rather than merely documented.

Learning integration — whether lessons from incidents were incorporated into governance improvements — assesses the highest-value function of incident response. Evidence of learning integration includes: policy updates reflecting incident findings, training updates addressing issues identified in incidents, monitoring improvements addressing detection gaps revealed by incidents.

Measuring training effectiveness

AI literacy training is supposed to produce the understanding and behavior change that governance requires. Metrics for training effectiveness assess whether it is achieving this.

Completion rates — the proportion of required training completed by relevant staff — are the threshold measure. They are necessary but entirely insufficient: high completion rates with no behavior change indicate training that produces completion records rather than learning.

Knowledge assessment results — scores on knowledge checks and scenario assessments that test application of governance understanding

— provide evidence of whether training is producing the understanding it is supposed to produce. Systematic patterns of poor performance on specific topics indicate training content or design problems.

Behavior change indicators — changes in governance-relevant behavior following training delivery — are the most governance-relevant training effectiveness measures. Analysis of override rates, escalation rates, and documentation compliance before and after training delivery provides evidence of whether training is producing the behavior changes it is designed to produce. Where behavior metrics do not improve following training, the training is not achieving its governance purpose regardless of what completion records show.

Application survey evidence — periodic surveys asking staff how they are applying AI governance learning in their work — provides qualitative evidence about training effectiveness and identifies gaps between training content and operational reality.

The governance scorecard: integrating metrics into a coherent picture

Individual metrics tell individual stories. Governance accountability requires an integrated picture — a way of synthesizing diverse metrics into an overall assessment of governance health that leadership and governance teams can understand and act on.

A governance scorecard provides this integration: a structured summary of governance performance across key dimensions that presents an honest overall picture of where governance is strong, where it has gaps, and where it is failing. The scorecard should be designed before it is populated — defining what dimensions will be assessed, what evidence will be used, and what performance levels will be characterized as strong, adequate, or inadequate — so that assessment is not shaped by what the evidence happens to show.

Scorecard dimensions and performance levels

A practical AI governance scorecard for most institutions covers six to eight dimensions — enough to represent the full scope of governance without becoming unwieldy. The following dimensions form a foundational scorecard that institutions should adapt to their specific governance architecture.

Policy and framework completeness — whether the institution has an adequate, current, and implemented AI governance framework — assesses the foundational governance infrastructure. Performance levels range from no governance framework (unacceptable) through a framework that exists in documents but is not implemented (inadequate) to a framework that is current, understood by relevant staff, and honored in practice (adequate).

Intake process functioning — whether new AI use cases are systematically reviewed before deployment — assesses the primary prevention function of governance. Performance levels range from no systematic intake (unacceptable) through intake that is formally required but frequently bypassed (inadequate) to intake that captures all significant AI deployments and produces risk-appropriate review quality (adequate).

Vendor governance quality — whether AI vendor relationships are assessed, contracted, and managed to governance standards — assesses the protection of institutional interests in external AI relationships. Performance levels assess the completeness of due diligence, the adequacy of contract provisions, and the quality of ongoing relationship management.

Oversight effectiveness — whether human oversight of AI systems is genuine rather than nominal — assesses the primary harm prevention mechanism in operational AI use. Performance levels assess whether override rates are within expected ranges, whether escalation culture is healthy, whether documentation is adequate, and whether simulation testing reveals oversight capability.

Fairness monitoring adequacy — whether the institution has the monitoring infrastructure to detect differential AI performance across demographic groups — assesses a governance dimension whose inadequacy may not be visible until harm has occurred at scale.

Performance levels assess monitoring coverage, detection sensitivity, and response quality.

Incident response readiness — whether the institution can detect, investigate, remediate, and learn from AI incidents — assesses governance resilience when prevention fails. Performance levels assess reporting completeness, response timeliness, investigation quality, and learning integration.

Training effectiveness — whether staff have the AI literacy governance requires — assesses the human capacity that makes all other governance dimensions operational. Performance levels assess completion rates alongside the behavior change evidence that completion rates alone cannot provide.

Governance culture — whether the institution's actual behavior reflects genuine commitment to responsible AI use — assesses the foundation on which all process governance rests. This dimension resists quantification but is assessed through qualitative evidence: whether governance requirements are visibly supported by leadership, whether workarounds are tolerated, whether staff feel safe raising governance concerns.

Rating and trend assessment

Scorecard dimensions should be rated on a consistent scale that allows meaningful comparison across dimensions and over time. A four-level scale works well for most institutional AI governance scorecards: exemplary (governance in this dimension exceeds requirements and is a model for others), adequate (governance meets requirements and is functioning as designed), developing (governance has the right framework but has significant implementation gaps), and inadequate (governance in this dimension is not meeting its requirements and requires immediate attention).

Equally important as the rating itself is the trend: is governance in each dimension improving, stable, or deteriorating? A governance dimension rated adequate and improving warrants less concern than one rated adequate but deteriorating. Governance trends require longitudinal data — comparing current assessments to prior periods — which is why consistent audit methodology over time is more valuable than episodically rigorous audit.

Accountability: what happens with audit findings

Audit findings that produce no accountability are audit findings that have no governance effect. The accountability structures that convert audit findings into governance improvement are as important as the audit itself.

Reporting lines and obligations

Audit findings should be reported to audiences with both the authority and the obligation to act on them. The appropriate reporting structure depends on what the audit found and who has the authority to address it.

Audit findings about specific governance process failures — intake reviews that are inadequate, monitoring configurations that miss important signals, oversight designs that produce nominal review — should be reported to the governance team, which has authority and responsibility for governance process quality. The governance team's accountability for these findings is to address them: developing specific improvements, assigning responsibility for implementation, and tracking completion.

Audit findings about governance program-level failures — systematic patterns of inadequate governance across multiple dimensions, governance culture problems that undermine process-level governance, resource inadequacy that prevents governance from functioning effectively — should be reported to senior leadership, which has the authority to make the institutional investments and cultural changes that program-level failures require.

Audit findings about specific AI systems with significant governance failures — bias patterns that monitoring has not adequately addressed, oversight inadequacy in high-risk contexts, vendor relationships with significant contractual governance gaps — should be reported to the governance team with a defined timeline for remediation, with escalation to senior leadership if remediation is not accomplished within that timeline.

For institutions with audit committees of the board, significant AI governance audit findings should reach that committee. Board-level accountability for AI governance quality is appropriate for institutions with significant AI portfolios and is increasingly expected by regulators and accreditors.

Remediation tracking

Audit findings produce recommendations. Recommendations produce commitments. Commitments must be tracked to completion. The accountability architecture for audit findings must include a systematic mechanism for tracking whether commitments made in response to audit recommendations are actually implemented.

Remediation tracking should assign each audit recommendation to a specific responsible party, establish a specific implementation timeline, define what evidence will demonstrate completion, and schedule verification that completion has occurred. Governance teams that accept audit recommendations but have no systematic mechanism for tracking implementation have substituted the process of accepting recommendations for the substance of acting on them.

Incomplete remediation — audit recommendations that were accepted but not implemented — should itself trigger governance attention. When audit findings from one cycle remain unaddressed when the next cycle occurs, the pattern reveals a governance culture that treats audit as compliance performance rather than accountability. Governance leadership must treat incomplete remediation as a serious failure, not as a normal feature of busy institutional life.

External accountability

Internal audit and accountability mechanisms are necessary but not sufficient. External accountability — the institution's accountability to parties outside its governance system — provides a check on the adequacy of internal governance that internal accountability alone cannot provide.

Regulatory accountability — the institution's obligation to meet legal requirements and to demonstrate that obligation to regulatory bodies — is the most direct external accountability mechanism. Regulatory examinations, compliance reviews, and enforcement actions assess governance from outside the institution and impose consequences for inadequacy that internal accountability cannot replicate. Institutions whose internal governance audit is rigorous and honest will typically be better positioned in regulatory accountability contexts than those whose internal audit is more comfortable than accurate.

Public accountability — accountability to the communities the institution serves, through transparency about AI governance quality — is developing as a significant dimension of external accountability, particularly for institutions with public missions. AI governance reports, voluntary disclosures of AI use and governance practices, and community engagement about AI governance all represent forms of public accountability that go beyond regulatory minimum requirements and that signal genuine governance commitment.

Accreditation and certification accountability — external assessments by bodies that set professional or quality standards — increasingly includes AI governance dimensions. Healthcare accreditors, educational accreditors, and financial services auditors are all developing AI governance assessment components. Governance programs that meet robust internal standards are well-positioned for these external assessments; governance programs that are more form than substance are exposed by them.

The governance gap analysis: measuring what should be versus what is

A specific audit activity that deserves explicit attention is the governance gap analysis — a systematic comparison of what the institution's AI governance framework requires with what is actually occurring. Gap analysis is what distinguishes audit that measures governance process completion from audit that measures governance effectiveness.

Gap analysis for AI governance should examine each major governance commitment — policy provisions, process requirements, oversight designs, monitoring specifications — and assess whether actual institutional practice meets the commitment. The methodology involves: documenting what the governance framework requires; gathering evidence about what actually occurs; comparing the two; and characterizing the gap.

The most common governance gaps in institutional AI governance programs include:

Intake bypass — the gap between the policy requirement that all AI use cases go through intake review and the actual proportion of AI systems that have intake records. This gap is typically discovered through the AI inventory exercise described in Chapter 9, which reveals systems in operation that have no corresponding intake records.

Oversight nominalization — the gap between the oversight design that governance approval established and the oversight that is actually occurring. This gap is most visible in override rates that are systematically near zero, but also appears in documentation that is formally complete but substantively empty — records that confirm review occurred without evidence of what the review found.

Monitoring non-review — the gap between monitoring reports that are produced and monitoring data that is genuinely reviewed and acted on. This gap is common and difficult to detect without direct audit inquiry: monitoring infrastructure may generate comprehensive reports that are technically distributed to governance team members who do not substantively engage with them.

Remediation non-completion — the gap between governance commitments made in response to incidents, audit findings, or monitoring concerns, and the actual implementation of those commitments. This gap is systematically undercounted in governance programs that do not systematically track commitment completion.

Training non-transfer — the gap between training completion records and the behavior change training is designed to produce. This gap requires behavior evidence rather than completion records to detect, which is why training effectiveness audit must examine behavior metrics rather than relying on attendance data.

Gap analysis findings should be treated as governance improvement priorities rather than as governance embarrassments. Every governance program has gaps; the governance programs that improve are those that find their gaps honestly and address them systematically. The governance programs that do not improve are those that avoid finding their gaps by avoiding honest measurement.

Accountability for governance leaders

A dimension of governance accountability that is often overlooked is accountability for the governance function itself — for the governance team, governance leaders, and the senior leadership that established and resources the governance program. Governance that is accountable only to others and not to itself is governance that cannot improve.

The governance team should establish regular self-assessment — distinct from external audit — that asks honestly whether the team is fulfilling its governance responsibilities. Self-assessment questions should include: Are intake reviews substantive or perfunctory? Are vendor assessments thorough or checkbox exercises? Are monitoring reviews engaged or passive? Are incident responses rigorous or reputation-protective? Is the governance team's own culture one of genuine commitment to responsible AI use or procedural compliance?

Senior leadership accountability for AI governance requires that leadership regularly assess whether the governance program is adequately resourced, whether governance requirements are consistently enforced including for powerful operational functions, whether governance findings are honestly communicated and acted on, and whether the institution's AI practices are consistent with its stated values.

Board accountability requires that the board receive honest AI governance reporting — not a sanitized version that presents governance as more effective than it is — and that the board asks the questions that genuine oversight requires: What are the most significant AI governance risks the institution faces? What incidents have occurred? What monitoring has revealed? What are the most significant governance gaps? What is the trend in governance quality?

The accountability standard that governance should hold itself to is the same standard it holds AI use to: not perfection, but genuine commitment to improvement, honest acknowledgment of limitations, proportionate response to failures, and demonstrable progress over time.

Building a governance improvement cycle

The ultimate purpose of audit, metrics, and accountability is not to document current governance quality but to improve it. Governance that produces thorough audit findings, comprehensive metrics, and clear accountability assignments but whose governance quality does not improve over time has built accountability infrastructure without building improvement culture.

The governance improvement cycle — the structured process through which audit findings generate governance change — should be explicit and systematic. Annual governance reviews produce findings. Findings produce recommendations. Recommendations produce commitments. Commitments are tracked to completion. Completed improvements are assessed in the subsequent audit cycle for their effectiveness. This cycle is what converts the accountability mechanisms described in this chapter from instruments of documentation into instruments of change.

Governance improvement requires not only responding to specific audit findings but developing the meta-level learning described at the end of Chapter 16: examining patterns across findings over time, identifying systemic conditions that generate recurring problems, and addressing those conditions rather than only their individual manifestations. An institution whose audit consistently finds oversight quality problems in high-volume operational contexts should address the structural conditions — staffing levels, workflow designs, performance management systems — that create those conditions, not only establish requirements that the conditions make practically difficult to meet.

The most governance-capable institutions are not those that have perfect governance at any point in time. They are those that have built genuine improvement capacity — the honest assessment, accountable leadership, and systematic follow-through that make governance better year over year rather than maintaining a stable level of adequacy.

A final word on the honesty requirement

Everything in this chapter depends on honesty — specifically on the institutional willingness to measure what governance actually achieves rather than what governance hopes it achieves, to report findings accurately rather than favorably, and to treat uncomfortable findings as information to act on rather than problems to manage.

This honesty requirement is harder than it sounds. Governance programs are built and staffed by people who are invested in their quality. Audit findings that reveal significant governance gaps reflect on those people's work. Reporting those findings honestly to leadership and boards requires courage and institutional culture that supports truth-telling over comfort.

But the alternative — governance programs that measure selectively, report favorably, and act primarily to maintain the appearance of effectiveness — are governance programs that have substituted performance for function. They produce the documentation of governance while failing the people governance is supposed to protect. The patients who receive biased clinical AI recommendations. The applicants who are screened out by discriminatory hiring AI. The clients who are denied services by AI systems whose errors were not caught.

Honest governance measurement is not a bureaucratic nicety. It is the mechanism through which governance programs know whether the people they are responsible for protecting are actually protected. That knowledge — however uncomfortable it sometimes is — is the foundation of governance that serves its purpose.

Chapter 23: Sunset, Rollback, and Replacement

The decision that governance rarely prepares for

Every AI governance framework described in this book addresses the beginning and middle of the AI system lifecycle with considerable care: how to evaluate systems before adoption, how to test them before deployment, how to oversee and monitor them in operation. The end of the lifecycle receives far less attention, in governance frameworks and in institutional practice alike. Systems are adopted deliberately; they are rarely retired deliberately. They continue in use because inertia, sunk costs, vendor relationships, embedded workflows, and staff habits all create resistance to change — not because continuing use remains the right governance decision.

This asymmetry is a governance failure. The decision to stop using an AI system is as governance-relevant as the decision to start using it. A system whose performance has degraded below acceptable thresholds should be retired. A system found to have caused systematic harm should be suspended. A system whose vendor relationship has become ungovernable, whose governance conditions cannot be maintained, or whose technology has been superseded by substantially better alternatives with better governance profiles — all of these warrant retirement decisions that governance should make deliberately rather than postpone indefinitely.

The governance language for this set of decisions is sunset, rollback, and replacement. Sunset refers to the planned, gradual phase-out of an AI system that has reached the end of its useful or appropriate institutional life. Rollback refers to rapid suspension or reversal of a deployment — either a recent deployment that has not performed as expected or an established system that has failed in ways requiring immediate operational cessation. Replacement refers to the transition from one AI system to another, which should be governed as carefully as the original deployment. These three processes are distinct in their triggers, their urgency, and their operational requirements — but they share a common governance foundation: the recognition that stopping AI use is a governance decision that requires the same deliberateness and accountability as starting it.

This chapter describes when each process is appropriate, how to conduct it responsibly, what governance the process itself requires, and how to manage the human and operational dimensions that make end-of-lifecycle decisions among the most practically difficult governance acts an institution undertakes.

Why AI systems should be retired: the trigger framework

Governance needs a framework for identifying when AI systems should be considered for sunset or rollback — when the case for continued operation no longer outweighs the case for cessation. The following categories of trigger represent the primary conditions that should prompt governance review of whether a system should continue.

Performance deterioration below acceptable thresholds

AI systems can deteriorate in performance over time through the drift mechanisms described in Chapter 16. A system whose accuracy, fairness, or reliability has declined to the point where it no longer meets the governance thresholds established at deployment — or that shows a trajectory of decline that will reach unacceptable levels without intervention — is a candidate for retirement if that deterioration cannot be remediated.

The governance question when performance deterioration is identified is sequenced: can the deterioration be addressed? The first response to identified performance decline should always be remediation: working with the vendor to identify whether a model update, a training data refresh, or a deployment condition adjustment can restore acceptable performance. Retirement is appropriate when remediation is not available, not achievable within acceptable timeframes, or has been attempted and failed.

Performance deterioration triggers should be defined in governance documentation before they occur. The system's original governance approval established minimum performance thresholds; those thresholds define the boundary below which performance triggers sunset consideration. Governance that responds to performance deterioration only when deterioration becomes severe has allowed harm to accumulate during the period of inadequate performance that earlier response would have prevented.

Identified harm to affected people

When monitoring, incident response, or audit reveals that an AI system has caused or is causing harm — through biased outputs, safety failures, privacy violations, or other failure modes — the governance response must address not only the specific incident but the question of whether the system should continue operating at all.

The governance calculus for harm-triggered retirement weighs the severity and scope of identified harm against the operational value of the system and the availability of alternatives. Severe harm to identifiable individuals, systematic harm to specific populations, or harm that the institution cannot adequately remediate through oversight or system adjustments all weigh heavily toward retirement. The operational inconvenience of retiring an embedded system — however significant — cannot be allowed to override the governance obligation to protect the people the institution serves from ongoing harm.

Harm-triggered retirement should be considered on an expedited governance timeline. When harm is occurring and continuing, the standard governance review timeline is not appropriate; accelerated decision-making with appropriate senior leadership involvement is required. Governance frameworks should define expedited decision processes for harm-triggered retirement that can reach a decision within days rather than weeks.

Irremediable governance failure

Some AI systems cannot be adequately governed within the institution's governance framework because the conditions that governance requires cannot be maintained for those systems. A vendor that is unresponsive to governance concerns, that refuses audit access, that makes undisclosed system changes, and that will not renegotiate inadequate contract provisions is a vendor with whom adequate governance is not possible. A system whose complexity or opacity prevents meaningful explainability, whose bias testing cannot be conducted for technical reasons, or whose oversight requirements cannot be met within operational constraints represents an irremediable governance gap.

When governance failure is irremediable — when the conditions that adequate governance requires cannot be achieved and cannot be reasonably expected to be achieved — continued operation is not adequately governed operation; it is operation without governance. The governance response to irremediable governance failure is retirement. The institution that continues operating AI systems it cannot adequately govern has not found a pragmatic accommodation with operational reality; it has abandoned its governance obligations.

This is a difficult conclusion in practice, because systems with irremediable governance failures often have genuine operational value. The AI system that cannot be adequately assessed for bias may also be the system whose efficiency gains have become embedded in operational workflows. The vendor that refuses meaningful audit access may also provide capabilities the institution relies on. The governance discipline required is to hold the line: operational dependency on a system that cannot be governed does not justify continuing ungoverned operation indefinitely. It justifies urgently prioritizing alternative governance arrangements — including system replacement — as a governance response.

Regulatory or legal developments that make continued use non-compliant

Changes in the legal and regulatory environment — new legislation, regulatory guidance, enforcement actions against the institution or peer institutions for similar AI use, court decisions establishing new legal standards — may make continued operation of an existing AI system legally non-compliant or legally risky in ways that require retirement.

When regulatory developments require governance response, the first question is whether the system can be modified to become compliant — through deployment changes, oversight augmentation, or vendor-negotiated system modifications. If compliance can be achieved through modification, modification is preferable to retirement. When compliance cannot be achieved through modification — because the fundamental nature of the system's operation is inconsistent with new requirements — retirement is required.

Governance should monitor regulatory developments (as described in Chapter 21) specifically to identify when existing deployed systems may be affected, providing lead time for compliant retirement planning rather than requiring emergency cessation when non-compliance is discovered.

Strategic obsolescence

AI systems become obsolete — not because they fail in ways that cause harm but because substantially better alternatives have become available whose performance, governance characteristics, or operational fit are significantly superior. The availability of alternatives that would better serve the institution's mission and better protect the people it serves is a governance consideration for existing deployments, not only for new adoption decisions.

Strategic obsolescence retirement is the least urgent trigger category and the one most frequently indefinitely postponed. Operational disruption, transition costs, vendor relationship obligations, and staff change resistance all create momentum against retiring systems that are performing adequately even when better alternatives exist. The governance case for strategic obsolescence retirement is not urgency but responsibility: institutions that can serve the people they serve better, at acceptable transition cost, have a governance obligation to pursue that improvement rather than deferring indefinitely to operational inertia.

The governance framework for strategic obsolescence should include periodic portfolio review — examining whether each significant AI system in the inventory remains the best available option for its purpose — as a standard governance function rather than an exceptional one. Systems that have been in operation for multiple years without reassessment of whether better alternatives exist may be candidates for strategic obsolescence review.

Distinguishing sunset from rollback: urgency and process

Sunset and rollback both result in an AI system ceasing operation, but they differ significantly in urgency, process, and governance requirements.

Rollback: emergency cessation

Rollback is the rapid suspension or reversal of an AI deployment in response to a condition that requires immediate operational cessation. It is the governance equivalent of an emergency stop — appropriate when continuing operation creates unacceptable ongoing risk that cannot wait for planned phase-out.

The triggers that warrant rollback rather than planned sunset include: active ongoing harm that will continue and accumulate with each additional day of operation; a security incident that creates immediate data exposure or system compromise; discovery of a severe performance failure that makes continued AI-assisted decisions potentially dangerous; regulatory action that requires immediate cessation; or vendor notification of a critical system failure that makes the system unreliable for its intended purpose.

Rollback is a rapid decision requiring immediate operational action. The governance process for rollback should be defined in advance — specifically, who has authority to direct rollback without waiting for full governance team review, what the operational procedure for immediate system cessation is, and what notification and documentation must accompany rollback. For high-risk AI systems in particular, these pre-defined rollback authorities and procedures are essential; improvising rollback process in an emergency produces delay that allows harm to continue accumulating.

Rollback does not mean permanent retirement, though it may lead there. A rolled-back system may be reinstated after the condition that triggered rollback is addressed, if investigation determines that reinstatement is appropriate. Rollback is an operational pause that creates space for governance assessment; that assessment determines whether the pause becomes permanent.

Sunset: planned phase-out

Sunset is the planned, deliberate phase-out of an AI system that has been determined appropriate for retirement but that does not require emergency cessation. It is the governance-managed end of a system's operational life, conducted in a way that minimizes operational disruption, protects the people the system has served, preserves institutional records and knowledge, and honors governance obligations associated with the system's operation.

Planned sunset allows for deliberate transition planning — time to prepare staff, identify alternative arrangements, address vendor contract obligations, manage data retention and deletion, and communicate with affected parties. The planning horizon for sunset should be proportionate to the system's operational significance: systems that are deeply embedded in critical workflows may require months of planned transition; systems with limited operational integration may be retired quickly.

The governance of sunset should be as deliberate as the governance of original deployment. A formal sunset decision — documented in governance records, communicated to relevant stakeholders, with a defined transition plan and timeline — is the appropriate governance act for system retirement. Systems that gradually cease to be used without a formal governance decision are not governed into retirement; they drift into disuse in ways that create institutional ambiguity about their status, complicate data governance, and may leave vendor obligations unaddressed.

The sunset process: governance in detail

The following describes the governance process for planned sunset. Rollback processes, where urgency compresses this timeline, should follow the same steps in accelerated form, with post-rollback review completing any steps that emergency cessation prevented.

Step one: sunset trigger identification and governance team notification

The sunset process begins when a trigger condition is identified through monitoring, audit, regulatory notification, or other sources, and that condition is assessed as warranting sunset consideration rather than remediation. This assessment may be made by the AI governance coordinator, by a monitoring reviewer, by the governance team during periodic review, or by any institutional actor who identifies a sunset-relevant condition.

The governance team should be formally notified when sunset consideration is triggered, with documentation of what the trigger condition is, what evidence supports it, and what initial assessment has been conducted. This notification creates a formal governance record that the sunset process has begun and assigns governance team accountability for completing it.

Step two: retirement assessment

The governance team should conduct a structured retirement assessment: a systematic evaluation of whether retirement is appropriate and, if so, what the retirement approach should be.

The assessment should address: the nature and severity of the trigger condition; whether remediation alternatives exist that would address the condition without retirement; the operational significance of the system and the disruption that retirement would cause; the availability of alternative arrangements for the functions the system performs; the timeline urgency — whether emergency rollback is needed or planned sunset is appropriate; the data governance implications of retirement; the vendor contract implications; and the communication obligations associated with retirement.

The retirement assessment should produce a documented recommendation to the governance team, which makes the formal retirement decision. For high-risk systems or systems with significant operational importance, this decision should involve senior leadership consultation. For systems with regulatory implications, legal counsel should be involved.

Step three: transition planning

Once the retirement decision is made, transition planning begins. A well-designed transition plan addresses every dimension of the change that retirement creates.

Operational continuity — how the functions the AI system performed will be handled during and after the transition. For some uses, the pre-AI workflow can simply be restored: staff return to the processes they used before the AI system was adopted. For uses where the pre-AI workflow no longer exists — where staff no longer have the skills or capacity to perform the function without AI assistance — transition planning must either develop those capabilities, identify alternative AI tools, or restructure the operational function. The institution should never allow itself to be in the position where it cannot safely retire an AI system because it has lost the capacity to function without it.

Staff preparation — communicating the retirement decision to staff who use the system, explaining what will change, providing any training needed for alternative workflows, and addressing the concerns and questions that change management creates. Staff who have worked with an AI system for an extended period may have significant questions about whether the retirement reflects problems with their use, what the institution's confidence in AI governance is, and what the implications for other AI systems they use are. Honest, transparent communication that addresses these questions directly is more effective than minimally informative announcements.

Data governance — addressing the data that the AI system has created, processed, or retained during its operation. Retirement creates specific data governance obligations: determining what data must be retained for audit, accountability, or legal hold purposes; what data should be deleted because its retention is no longer justified by the operational purpose it served; how to ensure vendor deletion of institutional data; and how to address the disposition of AI-generated records that have become part of institutional files.

Vendor obligations — managing the end of the vendor relationship in accordance with contractual terms. Contract exit provisions should specify notice periods, transition support obligations, data return and deletion requirements, and financial terms for early termination. The governance function should coordinate with procurement and legal to ensure that vendor relationship termination is conducted in compliance with contractual obligations and with appropriate protection of institutional interests.

Affected party communication — notifying people who have been affected by the AI system about its retirement, where those people have a reasonable interest in knowing. Patients who received AI-assisted care recommendations, clients whose service delivery was AI-assisted, applicants whose applications were AI-processed — depending on the nature of the system and the nature of the retirement trigger, these parties may have interests in knowing that the system is being retired and what that means for the institution's handling of their cases.

Governance documentation — creating the formal governance record of the retirement: the trigger that prompted it, the assessment that led to the retirement decision, the transition plan and its execution, the data governance actions taken, the vendor relationship termination, and the lessons identified for future governance improvement.

Step four: phased operational transition

For planned sunset of significant systems, a phased transition — mirroring the staged deployment approach described in Chapter 15 — is generally preferable to abrupt cessation. The phased approach allows operational learning about what the transition requires, identifies and addresses transition problems before they affect the full operational scope, and provides time to refine alternative arrangements before full reliance on them.

The transition phases should be defined in the transition plan, with evaluation criteria at each stage: what must be demonstrated before the transition advances, what conditions would require pausing or accelerating the transition, and what governance monitoring will be conducted during the transition.

For some retirement triggers — harm that is ongoing, regulatory requirements with specific timelines, security incidents that require immediate cessation — phased transition is not available. These situations require the rapid rollback process rather than planned sunset, with transition planning occurring after cessation rather than before.

Step five: final decommissioning

When operational transition is complete — when the AI system is no longer in use for any institutional purpose — formal decommissioning closes the governance lifecycle.

Decommissioning actions include: confirmation that the system has been fully removed from institutional workflows and is no longer being accessed by any staff; completion of data governance actions including vendor certification of data deletion; final vendor relationship termination; archiving of governance records related to the system; and formal governance team documentation that decommissioning is complete.

The AI inventory entry for the decommissioned system should be updated to reflect retirement status, the retirement date, the reason for retirement, and the archive location of governance records. Retired systems should be retained in the inventory — not deleted — because the institutional record of what AI systems were used, for what purposes, and how they were governed is a governance accountability resource that must be preserved.

Step six: post-retirement review

The post-retirement review is the governance reflection that extracts learning from the retirement process and incorporates it into governance improvement. It should address: what the retirement trigger reveals about governance adequacy — whether the condition that triggered retirement should have been detected earlier, whether governance processes were effective in managing the retirement, and whether lessons from this retirement should change how other systems are governed or how future systems are adopted.

For retirements triggered by performance deterioration, the post-retirement review should assess whether monitoring was adequate to detect the deterioration when it occurred and whether the detection-to-response timeline was appropriate. For retirements triggered by identified harm, the review should assess whether governance failed to prevent the harm, at what governance stage the failure occurred, and what systemic changes are needed. For retirements triggered by irremediable governance failure, the review should assess how the governance condition developed and whether earlier governance attention could have prevented it or enabled earlier detection.

Post-retirement review findings should feed into the governance improvement cycle described in Chapter 22, contributing to the institutional learning that makes governance better over time.

Rollback: the emergency process

When rollback is required — rapid suspension in response to urgent governance conditions — the governance process must be compressed without being abandoned. The following describes how rollback governance differs from planned sunset governance.

Pre-authorized rollback authority

Rollback decisions cannot wait for full governance team deliberation when ongoing harm requires immediate cessation. Pre-authorization of rollback authority — designating specific individuals who can direct immediate system suspension without convening a governance team meeting — is a governance design requirement for all high-risk AI systems.

The pre-authorized rollback authority should be: clearly designated in governance documentation before deployment, known to IT and operational staff who would implement rollback, accessible on short notice including outside normal business hours, and accountable to governance team review within a defined timeframe following the exercise of rollback authority.

Rollback authority pre-authorization does not eliminate governance accountability; it provides for governance-appropriate rapid response followed by governance team review. The person who exercises rollback authority should document the decision, the evidence that triggered it, and the expected timeline for governance team review. The governance team should review rollback decisions promptly — within one to two business days — confirming that the trigger warranted rollback and determining the appropriate path forward.

Immediate operational actions

When rollback is directed, immediate operational actions include: directing IT to suspend the AI system's operation; notifying operational leaders whose workflows depend on the system so that they can activate fallback procedures; confirming that fallback procedures are operational; and documenting the rollback action in governance records.

These actions should follow a documented procedure that has been prepared and tested before they are needed. As Chapter 15 emphasized, fallback procedures must be defined before deployment precisely because they may be needed rapidly in situations like rollback. Institutions that have not prepared fallback procedures and documented rollback procedures will face operational chaos during rollback in addition to the governance challenge that triggered it.

Communication during rollback

Rollback creates immediate communication needs. Staff who depended on the system need to know it is suspended and what they should do instead. If the system affected the people the institution serves — patients, clients, students — those parties may need immediate notification depending on the nature of the failure. Regulatory notification may be required if the rollback involves a reportable incident.

Communication during rollback must be managed under time pressure and with incomplete information — investigation is still underway when initial communication needs to occur. The principle established in Chapter 18 and Chapter 19 applies: honest acknowledgment of what is known, honest acknowledgment of what is not yet known, and commitment to further communication as investigation proceeds. Defensive or minimizing communication during rollback compounds governance failures rather than addressing them.

Rollback investigation

Following rollback, investigation of the condition that triggered it should proceed as described in Chapter 19's incident response framework. The investigation must determine: what the system did that triggered rollback, what governance contributed to the condition, who was affected and how, and what remediation is required.

The investigation's findings determine the path forward: whether the system can be reinstated with modifications and conditions, whether it should remain suspended pending vendor remediation, or whether rollback should become permanent retirement. This determination should be made explicitly through the governance team rather than allowing rollback to default to permanent retirement without a governance decision, or allowing pressure for operational restoration to drive reinstatement without adequate governance assessment.

Replacement: transitioning to something better

Replacement — transitioning from one AI system to a different one — is not simply the simultaneous retirement of one system and adoption of another. It is a governance process with specific challenges that arise from the interaction between the legacy system being retired and the new system being adopted.

Why replacement is not just retirement plus adoption

If replacement were simply conducted as a sequential retirement and adoption, each governed separately by the processes described in this chapter and in Chapter 15, the governance challenges of replacement would be relatively straightforward. The specific challenges of replacement governance arise from three dimensions that sequential treatment misses.

Continuity requirements — many AI system retirements are driven by the adoption of a replacement, and operational continuity requires that the replacement be operational before the legacy system is retired. This creates a period of concurrent operation during which governance must address both systems simultaneously. Governance of this overlap period

— ensuring that the legacy system is genuinely retired rather than continuing in informal use, that staff transition fully to the replacement rather than maintaining dual practices, and that data governance addresses both systems' records appropriately — is a specific replacement governance requirement.

Legacy bias and data contamination — the replacement system may be trained on, tested against, or configured using data that was generated by the legacy system. If the legacy system had governance problems — bias patterns, performance inadequacies, incorrect classifications — the data it generated carries those problems. Training a replacement system on legacy system outputs risks replicating the legacy system's governance failures in a technically different form. Replacement governance must specifically assess the legacy data contamination risk for proposed replacement systems.

Institutional memory and baseline disruption — when a replacement system is adopted, the monitoring baselines established for the legacy system are no longer relevant, and new baselines must be established for the replacement. The institutional knowledge accumulated about the legacy system's performance characteristics, failure modes, and governance requirements does not transfer automatically to the replacement system. Replacement governance must ensure that pre-deployment assessment and testing of the replacement system is genuinely fresh — not compromised by assumptions that the replacement will behave similarly to the legacy system it replaces.

The replacement governance process

Replacement governance should proceed in three overlapping phases.

Replacement selection and assessment — conducted before legacy system retirement — follows the full governance process described for new AI adoption: intake and risk screening, vendor assessment, testing, oversight design, and deployment planning. The specific replacement governance additions are: assessment of legacy data contamination risk for the proposed replacement; assessment of whether the replacement addresses the governance problems that motivated the replacement (a replacement adopted because the legacy system had bias problems must be specifically assessed for whether it addresses those problems, not merely assessed on general governance dimensions); and evaluation of vendor relationship continuity (if the replacement is from the same vendor as the legacy system, assess whether the vendor relationship problems that may have contributed to retirement are addressed in the new relationship).

Parallel operation and transition — the period during which both legacy and replacement systems are operating, with progressive migration of users and use cases from legacy to replacement. Governance during parallel operation must: maintain monitoring for both systems; ensure that the legacy system is genuinely being phased out rather than informally maintained as a fallback; track whether transition is proceeding at the planned pace and quality; and assess whether early replacement system performance is consistent with pre-deployment testing results.

Legacy retirement and replacement stabilization — the completion of the replacement process, when the legacy system is formally retired and governance shifts fully to the replacement system. The legacy retirement follows the decommissioning process described above. Replacement stabilization follows the deployment monitoring process described in Chapter 15 and transitions to standard operational monitoring as described in Chapter 16.

Managing staff through replacement

Replacement creates specific staff management challenges that governance must address. Staff who have learned to work with a legacy AI system, who have developed professional routines around its outputs and limitations, and who may have developed confidence or distrust toward it based on extended operational experience must now develop equivalent experience with a replacement system they may not yet understand.

Change management for replacement should: acknowledge and respect the knowledge staff have developed about the legacy system, framing the replacement as building on rather than discarding that knowledge; provide specific training on how the replacement system differs from the legacy system, particularly in behavior characteristics that affect oversight; create opportunities for staff to develop confidence in the replacement system before legacy system retirement removes the option of relying on the familiar system; and establish clear escalation channels for staff who observe replacement system behavior that differs from legacy system behavior in unexpected ways.

The replacement transition period is when automatic bias (described in Chapter 13) takes an interesting form: staff familiar with the legacy system may unconsciously evaluate the replacement system's outputs against their mental model of the legacy system rather than against the appropriate performance standard for the use case. This comparative bias can cut either direction — staff may be inappropriately skeptical of replacement system outputs that differ from legacy patterns, or inappropriately accepting of replacement system outputs that resemble familiar legacy patterns even when those patterns were governance problems that the replacement was supposed to address.

Governance should specifically address this transitional bias in replacement training: helping staff understand that the appropriate reference for evaluating replacement system outputs is the governance standard for the use case, not the behavior of the legacy system, and that differences between replacement and legacy system outputs are not themselves evidence of replacement system error.

Governance obligations that survive retirement

Retirement does not end all governance obligations associated with an AI system. Several governance responsibilities persist after a system is retired, sometimes for significant periods.

Record retention

Records associated with the AI system's operation — governance approvals, testing documentation, monitoring reports, incident records, vendor assessments, deployment documentation — must be retained for periods that reflect their accountability and legal relevance. Governance records may be needed in subsequent regulatory inquiries, litigation, audit, or accountability processes. The retention periods for different record categories should be defined in data governance policy, and retirement should not result in records being deleted before their retention period expires.

Records of AI system decisions — the outputs the system produced and the human decisions made in relation to those outputs — may need to be retained as part of the institutional records of decisions affecting the people the institution serves. If those records fall within the institution's general records retention framework — as clinical records, employment records, or educational records, for example — they are governed by that framework regardless of the AI system's operational status.

Remediation obligations

When a system is retired because of identified harm — bias, safety failures, privacy violations — the retirement does not end the institution's remediation obligations to people who were harmed by the system during its operation. Ongoing remediation commitments — reviewing decisions made during the affected period, notifying affected individuals, providing recourse — continue after retirement until the remediation plan has been completed.

Governance should ensure that retirement planning specifically addresses remediation continuity: that the people responsible for ongoing remediation are identified and accountable, that remediation timelines are established and tracked, and that the governance team receives regular updates on remediation progress until completion.

Data deletion obligations

The retirement of an AI system creates specific data deletion obligations: institutional data that was provided to the vendor and that the vendor retains must be deleted in accordance with the contract's data return and deletion provisions. Vendor certification of deletion must be obtained and documented. Institutional data held in systems directly associated with the retired AI must be addressed according to applicable retention and deletion requirements.

Data deletion obligations associated with retirement may be legally required — particularly for personal data subject to data protection law rights to erasure — and are also governance obligations that protect the people whose data was processed. The institution that retires an AI system but leaves its institutional data in vendor systems without addressing deletion has not completed the governance obligations of retirement.

Continuing accountability for past use

The institution remains accountable for the AI system's decisions during its operational period even after retirement. Regulatory inquiries, litigation, complaints from affected individuals, and audit assessments may all require the institution to account for what the system did and why, how governance functioned during its operation, and what the institution knew and when about any governance failures.

Post-retirement accountability is why governance records must be retained, why the governance record-keeping described throughout this book must be genuine rather than performative, and why honest governance — governance that acknowledges problems as they are identified rather than concealing them — is protective rather than merely ethical. The institution with honest governance records is better positioned for post-retirement accountability than the institution whose records were designed for favorable appearance rather than accurate documentation.

The institutional posture toward AI system endings

The way an institution handles the end of AI systems' lifecycles reveals its actual governance values more clearly than the way it handles their beginnings. Adoption decisions are visible, deliberate, and supported by the organizational attention that new initiatives receive. Retirement decisions are typically low-visibility, resistant to organizational attention, and opposed by the inertia of established practice.

Institutions that govern AI well develop the institutional posture — the leadership commitment, the governance discipline, and the organizational culture — to make retirement decisions as deliberately as adoption decisions. They establish clear criteria for when retirement is warranted. They fund and staff transition planning. They communicate honestly with staff and affected parties. They complete their remediation obligations. They retain their records. They learn from what retirement reveals about governance gaps.

This posture does not come naturally. It requires explicit cultivation — governance frameworks that include sunset and replacement processes as prominently as intake and deployment processes, leadership that is willing to make difficult retirement decisions when governance requires them, and governance cultures that treat retirement as governance maturity rather than governance failure.

AI systems end. Governance that is not prepared for endings is governance that is only half-built. The institution that can adopt AI responsibly, govern it through its operational life, and retire it with integrity when retirement is warranted has built governance that honors the full scope of its obligations to the people it serves.

Sunset, rollback, and replacement in the governance lifecycle

The processes described in this chapter do not stand alone; they complete the governance lifecycle that has been the subject of this book from its beginning. Intake and screening (Chapter 10) evaluate whether systems should be adopted. Testing (Chapter 14) validates whether they are ready to deploy. Deployment (Chapter 15) makes them operational under governance conditions. Monitoring (Chapter 16) sustains governance through the operational life. Audit (Chapter 22) assesses whether governance has functioned. And sunset, rollback, and replacement (this chapter) close the cycle, retiring systems that should no longer operate and transitioning to what comes next.

The lifecycle is a circle, not a line. What institutions learn from retiring AI systems — about governance gaps, about what monitoring should have detected earlier, about what the replacement needs to address — feeds back into how they adopt and govern future systems. This circular learning is what makes governance a practice that improves over time rather than a framework that is established once and applied unchanged.

Governance that takes the ending of AI systems as seriously as their beginning is governance that treats AI use as the ongoing institutional responsibility it is — not a series of adoption decisions with consequences that end when something new replaces what came before, but a continuing commitment to the people the institution serves, maintained through every phase of every AI system's life.

Part V: Tools and Templates

Chapter 24: A Starter AI Policy

How to use this policy

The policy that follows is a model — a complete, usable starting point that institutions can adapt rather than draft from scratch. It is written in policy language, with the active obligations, specific requirements, and defined accountability that Chapter 8 described as the characteristics of effective policy. It is not a template with blanks to fill in; it is a substantive document that reflects the governance principles, processes, and requirements described throughout this book.

No institution should adopt this policy without adaptation. Every institution's legal environment, operational context, risk profile, and governance capacity differs. Provisions appropriate for a large hospital may be disproportionate for a small nonprofit. Requirements adequate for an institution with limited AI use may be insufficient for one with an extensive AI portfolio. Legal requirements that apply in one jurisdiction may not apply in another, and legal requirements that do not yet apply may apply by the time this document is reviewed.

The adaptation process should involve: legal counsel reviewing the policy for compliance with applicable law and consistency with existing institutional policies; governance team members adapting scope, thresholds, and process requirements to institutional capacity and risk profile; operational leaders assessing whether requirements are practically achievable in operational contexts; and where possible, consultation with staff and affected community representatives about whether the policy reflects values and protections they recognize as meaningful.

Several provisions in this policy are marked [ADAPT] to indicate points where institutional-specific information, thresholds, or choices are required. These are minimum adaptation points; other provisions may also require adaptation based on institutional context.

The policy is organized into ten sections that follow the structure described in Chapter 8: purpose and scope, definitions, principles, acceptable and prohibited uses, roles and responsibilities, review and approval process, data governance requirements, human oversight requirements, incident reporting and response, and training and compliance.

ARTIFICIAL INTELLIGENCE GOVERNANCE POLICY

[INSTITUTION NAME] Policy Number: [ADAPT] **Effective Date:** [ADAPT] **Review Date:** [ADAPT — typically one year from effective date] **Policy Owner:** [ADAPT — typically the governance team or designated governance lead] **Approved By:** [ADAPT — senior leadership]

Section 1: Purpose and Scope

1.1 Purpose

This policy establishes requirements for how [Institution Name] uses, evaluates, oversees, and manages artificial intelligence systems. It exists to ensure that AI use at [Institution Name] serves our mission, protects the people we serve, upholds our legal obligations, and reflects our institutional values of [ADAPT — fairness, transparency, safety, and accountability, or institution-specific values].

AI systems can provide genuine value — improving efficiency, extending reach, and supporting better outcomes for the people we serve. They also present risks: they can produce biased or inaccurate outputs, create privacy risks, generate safety concerns, and fail in ways that harm individuals and communities. This policy governs AI use to capture its benefits while managing its risks responsibly.

1.2 Scope

This policy applies to:

Who: All staff, contractors, volunteers, and any other individuals acting on behalf of [Institution Name], regardless of employment status, seniority, or the specific role in which they use AI.

What activities: All use of AI systems for institutional purposes, including use on institutional systems, use on personal devices for work purposes, and use of AI systems provided by or through third-party vendors.

What systems: All AI systems as defined in Section 2 of this policy, including standalone AI tools, AI features embedded in existing software, AI capabilities in vendor-provided systems, and AI used by third-party service providers on the institution's behalf.

What does not require specific compliance under this policy: Basic automation, rules-based systems, and conventional software that does not use machine learning or similar techniques to generate outputs, make predictions, or produce recommendations.

This policy applies in addition to, and does not replace, [Institution Name]'s existing data privacy policy, acceptable use of technology policy, and other applicable institutional policies. Where this policy and other institutional policies address the same subject, the more protective or more specific requirement applies. Legal counsel should be consulted when policies appear to conflict.

1.3 Geographic and regulatory scope

This policy is designed to meet the requirements of [ADAPT — list applicable jurisdictions, such as: applicable US federal law, [State] law, and the data protection frameworks applicable to individuals whose information we process]. Where applicable law imposes requirements more stringent than this policy, those legal requirements govern.

Section 2: Definitions

For purposes of this policy, the following terms have the meanings specified:

Artificial Intelligence (AI) System: A system that uses machine learning, neural networks, large language models, or similar computational techniques to generate outputs, produce predictions, provide recommendations, classify inputs, or take actions that affect institutional operations, decisions, or the people [Institution Name] serves. This definition encompasses: standalone AI tools and applications; AI features embedded in broader software platforms; AI capabilities in vendor-provided enterprise systems; custom or internally developed AI systems; and AI used by third-party service providers on [Institution Name]'s behalf.

Approved AI System: An AI system that has completed [Institution Name]'s review and approval process and is authorized for use within its specified scope, conditions, and oversight arrangements.

AI Governance Team: The cross-functional group established under this policy with authority and responsibility for AI governance at [Institution Name], as described in Section 5.

AI Governance Coordinator: The designated staff member responsible for administering AI governance processes, maintaining the AI inventory, and serving as the primary operational contact for AI governance matters.

AI Output: Any result produced by an AI system in response to inputs, including text, images, scores, classifications, recommendations, decisions, or actions.

Personal Information: Information that identifies or can reasonably be used to identify a specific individual, including but not limited to: names, contact information, identification numbers, health information, financial information, educational records, employment information, and any other information that applicable law treats as personal or protected.

Sensitive Information: Personal information in categories that receive heightened protection under this policy and applicable law, including: health and medical information; financial information; information about minors; biometric data; information about legally protected characteristics including race, ethnicity, gender, sexual orientation, disability status, religion, and national origin; immigration status; and any other categories designated as sensitive by applicable law or by the AI Governance Team.

High-Risk AI Use: AI use that involves any of the following: making or significantly influencing decisions that affect individuals' access to services, employment, healthcare, education, housing, or financial products; processing sensitive information; operating with limited human oversight of individual outputs; interacting directly with vulnerable populations; or use in contexts identified by the AI Governance Team as high-risk.

AI Incident: Any event involving an AI system that has caused, may have caused, or creates meaningful risk of causing: harm to people; legal or regulatory exposure for [Institution Name]; significant operational failure; or material breach of institutional governance commitments.

Vendor: Any external party that provides, develops, operates, or maintains an AI system used at [Institution Name].

Section 3: Principles

3.1 Governing principles

[Institution Name]'s use of AI is governed by the following principles. These principles apply to all AI use decisions and should guide staff judgment when specific policy provisions do not address a particular situation.

Fairness: AI systems used at [Institution Name] must not produce unjustified differential outcomes across demographic groups. We are committed to identifying, monitoring, and addressing bias in AI systems, and to ensuring that AI use does not replicate or amplify historical patterns of discrimination.

Transparency: We are honest about our AI use with the people it affects. Staff who use AI in ways that influence decisions about specific people must be prepared to acknowledge that AI was used and to explain its role. We provide meaningful disclosure of AI use to the people we serve.

Safety: AI systems must not cause foreseeable harm to the people we serve. Safety requirements are calibrated to the stakes of each AI use, with heightened requirements for systems operating in contexts where errors could cause physical, psychological, or material harm.

Privacy: AI systems must handle personal information in ways that respect the reasonable expectations of the people it concerns, comply with applicable law, and serve the purposes for which information was collected. We do not use AI to process personal information in ways people would not anticipate or consent to.

Accountability: Specific people are responsible for the AI systems [Institution Name] uses. Responsibility is clearly assigned, documented, and exercised. When AI systems cause problems, the institution acknowledges what occurred, remediates harm to affected individuals, and makes governance improvements.

Security: AI systems and the information they process are protected against unauthorized access, manipulation, and misuse. AI security risks are assessed alongside other cybersecurity risks.

Human Dignity: AI use at [Institution Name] treats the people it affects as individuals with inherent worth. AI systems do not substitute for the human relationship and judgment that our work requires. People affected by AI-assisted decisions have access to human review.

3.2 Applying the principles

When specific policy provisions do not address a situation, staff should apply these principles to determine what responsible AI use requires. When principles appear to conflict, staff should seek guidance from their supervisor or the AI Governance Coordinator rather than resolving the conflict independently.

Section 4: Acceptable and Prohibited Uses

4.1 Permitted uses without prior governance review

The following categories of AI use are permitted without completing the formal review and approval process, provided they comply with all other provisions of this policy:

- Use of AI writing assistance tools to draft communications, documents, or other content that is reviewed and substantially revised by a staff member before use, and that does not involve personal information about the people we serve
- Use of AI tools for personal productivity tasks that do not involve institutional data or institutional decision-making
- Use of AI translation tools for internal communications not involving sensitive information
- Use of AI scheduling or calendar tools for internal scheduling purposes
- Use of AI tools to assist with research on general topics where outputs are verified against authoritative sources before use

Even for these permitted uses, staff must comply with data governance requirements in Section 7 and must not enter personal or sensitive information into AI systems that are not covered by appropriate data processing agreements.

4.2 Uses requiring review and approval

The following categories of AI use require completion of the review and approval process described in Section 6 before implementation:

- Any AI system used in a process that produces outputs influencing decisions about specific individuals, including decisions about service eligibility, clinical care, employment, educational assessment, or benefits
- Any AI system that processes personal information about the people we serve

- Any AI system deployed for direct interaction with the people we serve, including chatbots, virtual assistants, and automated response systems
- Any AI system used to automate decisions that were previously made by human staff
- Any AI system integrated into institutional workflows in ways that affect how staff perform their core functions
- Any AI tool that is new to the institution, regardless of whether similar tools have been previously approved
- Use of an approved AI system in a context, for a population, or with data types not covered by the original approval

4.3 Absolutely prohibited uses

The following uses of AI are prohibited regardless of any approval, operational need, or vendor capability claim. These prohibitions may be revised only by a policy amendment approved by senior leadership.

Prohibited decision-making:

- Using AI as the sole basis for final, unreviewable decisions that significantly affect individuals' access to services, employment, healthcare, education, or benefits, without human review and authority
- Using AI to make determinations about individuals that would be unlawful if made by human decision-makers on the same basis

Prohibited data practices:

- Entering personal information about the people we serve into AI systems that are not covered by appropriate data processing agreements, regardless of whether the information appears to be de-identified
- Using sensitive information — as defined in Section 2 — in AI systems not specifically approved for that purpose
- Using AI to process children's data in ways not authorized by applicable law

- Providing institutional data to AI vendors for model training purposes without specific governance review and approval

Prohibited representations:

- Representing AI-generated content as human-created work in contexts where the distinction is material — including academic submissions, professional certifications, regulatory filings, and legal proceedings — without disclosure
- Deploying AI systems that deny being AI when sincerely asked whether they are AI or human
- Using AI to generate content that fraudulently impersonates real individuals

Prohibited surveillance and manipulation:

- Using AI systems designed to manipulate individuals through techniques that bypass their conscious judgment
- Using AI for unauthorized surveillance of staff, clients, patients, or students
- Using AI to infer sensitive personal characteristics — including health conditions, sexual orientation, political beliefs, or religious views — for purposes not authorized under this policy

Prohibited adoption:

- Implementing any AI system for institutional use without completing the required review and approval process
- Continuing to use an AI system whose approval has been withdrawn or that has been suspended by the AI Governance Team

4.4 Conditional uses

Many AI uses are appropriate under specific conditions that this policy or governance approvals specify. Staff who are uncertain whether a specific use is permitted, prohibited, or conditional should consult the AI Governance Coordinator before proceeding.

Section 5: Roles and Responsibilities

5.1 Senior leadership

[ADAPT — CEO/Executive Director/President] is responsible for:

- Approving this policy and ensuring it reflects [Institution Name]'s values and commitments
- Allocating resources adequate for the governance program this policy requires
- Modeling compliance with AI governance requirements
- Receiving and acting on AI governance reports from the AI Governance Team
- Making decisions on AI governance matters that exceed the AI Governance Team's authority
- Communicating institutional AI governance commitments to external stakeholders

5.2 Board of directors [ADAPT — if applicable]

The board is responsible for:

- Receiving regular reports on institutional AI governance, including significant AI-related risks, incidents, and governance program performance
- Asking questions that hold leadership accountable for AI governance quality
- Ensuring that AI governance receives appropriate board-level oversight as part of institutional risk management

5.3 AI Governance Team

The AI Governance Team is responsible for:

- Governing institutional AI use in accordance with this policy

- Reviewing and deciding on AI use case proposals submitted through the intake process
- Establishing and updating AI governance standards, processes, and tools
- Monitoring and reviewing AI system performance across the institution
- Investigating AI incidents and directing governance response
- Reporting to senior leadership on AI governance program performance
- Updating this policy as needed and recommending policy amendments to senior leadership

The AI Governance Team is composed of: [ADAPT — list roles: senior leadership representative, legal/compliance representative, IT/security representative, operations representative, data governance representative, and any other roles appropriate to institutional context]. Terms of reference for the AI Governance Team are maintained separately from this policy.

The AI Governance Team meets [ADAPT — monthly / quarterly] as a standing body, with additional meetings called when governance matters require. A quorum of [ADAPT — specify quorum, e.g., four of six members] is required for governance decisions.

5.4 AI Governance Coordinator

The AI Governance Coordinator [ADAPT — specify role title or name] is responsible for:

- Maintaining the AI inventory
- Administering the intake and review process, including receiving submissions, conducting preliminary triage, and coordinating governance team review
- Maintaining AI governance documentation
- Serving as the first point of contact for staff with AI governance questions or concerns
- Monitoring AI governance compliance and escalating concerns to the governance team
- Coordinating AI literacy training activities

- Producing governance reports as required

5.5 Legal and compliance

The legal and compliance function is responsible for:

- Advising on the legal and regulatory requirements applicable to institutional AI use
- Reviewing AI vendor contracts for legal adequacy
- Assessing AI use cases for legal risk
- Monitoring regulatory developments affecting institutional AI governance
- Supporting incident response when AI incidents have legal implications

5.6 Information technology and information security

IT and information security is responsible for:

- Assessing the technical feasibility and security implications of proposed AI systems
- Implementing and maintaining technical controls for AI system access and security
- Monitoring AI systems for technical performance and security anomalies
- Managing technical integration of AI systems with institutional infrastructure
- Assessing vendor technical security practices
- Supporting the governance team with technical information needed for governance decisions

5.7 Procurement

Procurement is responsible for:

- Incorporating AI governance requirements into vendor assessment and contract negotiation

- Ensuring that AI vendor contracts include provisions required by this policy and applicable law
- Managing vendor relationships in a manner consistent with AI governance requirements
- Coordinating with legal, IT, and the governance team in AI vendor assessment and contracting

5.8 Department and operational leaders

Leaders of departments and operational functions that use or are considering using AI are responsible for:

- Submitting AI use cases through the intake process before implementation
- Ensuring that staff in their functions complete required AI literacy training
- Creating oversight environments that support genuine rather than nominal human review of AI outputs
- Receiving and acting on escalations from staff regarding AI concerns
- Monitoring AI governance compliance within their functions
- Reporting AI incidents and concerns to the AI Governance Coordinator

5.9 All staff

All staff who use AI systems in their work are responsible for:

- Using AI systems only in ways that comply with this policy and with governance approvals applicable to their specific use
- Completing required AI literacy training
- Exercising genuine independent professional judgment in reviewing AI outputs, rather than deferring to AI recommendations without assessment
- Reporting AI concerns, unusual AI behavior, and potential AI incidents to their supervisor and to the AI Governance Coordinator
- Maintaining required documentation of AI-assisted work

- Not entering personal or sensitive information into AI systems not authorized for that purpose

5.10 Vendors

AI vendors are expected to:

- Provide accurate documentation of AI system performance, including performance across demographic groups
- Honor data handling commitments made in their contracts with [Institution Name]
- Notify [Institution Name] of material changes to AI systems within the timeframe their contracts require
- Cooperate with audit and assessment activities as provided in their contracts
- Respond substantively and promptly to governance concerns raised by [Institution Name]

Section 6: Review and Approval Process

6.1 Requirement for review

No AI system may be implemented for institutional use without completing the review and approval process described in this section, except as specifically provided in Section 4.1. This requirement applies regardless of the procurement method, the cost of the system, the vendor relationship, or the seniority of the person proposing the use.

Staff who are uncertain whether a proposed use requires formal review should contact the AI Governance Coordinator. When in doubt, review is required.

6.2 How to submit for review

AI use case proposals must be submitted using the AI Intake Form [ADAPT — specify where form is located and how to submit]. The form requires information about the proposed AI system, its vendor, its intended use, the data it will process, the people it will affect, and the oversight arrangements proposed for it.

Submissions should be as complete as possible. The AI Governance Coordinator will conduct a completeness check and will return incomplete submissions with specific requests for additional information.

6.3 Review timeline

The AI Governance Team will complete reviews within the following timelines, measured from receipt of a complete submission:

- **Low-risk proposals:** [ADAPT — e.g., 7 business days]
- **Medium-risk proposals:** [ADAPT — e.g., 15 business days]
- **High-risk proposals:** [ADAPT — e.g., 25 business days]

Expedited review may be available in time-sensitive circumstances. Requests for expedited review must explain the operational need and will be assessed by the AI Governance Coordinator. Expedited review does not reduce the substantive rigor of review; it compresses the administrative timeline.

6.4 Possible outcomes

The AI Governance Team may respond to a proposal with one of the following outcomes:

Approved: The use case is approved within its specified scope, with any conditions specified in the approval. The AI Governance Coordinator will create an inventory entry and communicate the approval and any conditions to the submitter.

Conditionally approved: The use case is approved subject to specific conditions that must be met before or during operation. Conditions will be specified in writing. The submitter must confirm to the AI Governance Coordinator that all conditions have been met before the system goes live.

Declined with guidance: The use case is not approved in its current form. The AI Governance Team will provide specific reasons for declining and, where possible, guidance on what changes would make the use case approvable. Declined proposals may be resubmitted after addressing the reasons for decline.

Deferred: The review cannot be completed because specific information is needed. The AI Governance Team will specify what information is required and a deadline for providing it.

6.5 Changes to approved use cases

If a previously approved AI system is proposed for use in a new operational context, with new data types, for a new population, or with materially different oversight arrangements, a new submission is required. Changes that do not affect the substantive scope or risk profile of an approved use case should be communicated to the AI Governance Coordinator, who will determine whether a new submission is needed.

6.6 Vendor-initiated changes

Vendors who make material changes to AI systems — including changes to AI model capabilities, training data, data handling practices, or output characteristics — must notify [Institution Name] as required by their contracts. Upon receiving notification of a material vendor change, the AI Governance Coordinator will assess whether the change requires governance review and will notify the governance team when it does.

Staff who become aware of changes to AI systems they use should notify the AI Governance Coordinator promptly.

Section 7: Data Governance Requirements

7.1 General data governance obligations

All AI use at [Institution Name] must comply with applicable data protection law, [Institution Name]'s data privacy policy, and the requirements of this section. Where data protection obligations and AI governance requirements interact, both sets of obligations apply.

Staff who are uncertain about data governance requirements applicable to a specific AI use should consult the AI Governance Coordinator or legal counsel before proceeding.

7.2 Restrictions on information entered into AI systems

Staff must not enter the following categories of information into AI systems that have not been specifically approved for that purpose:

- Personal information about clients, patients, students, customers, or other individuals the institution serves
- Employee personal information, including performance data, health information, or other employment-related personal data
- Sensitive information as defined in Section 2
- Confidential institutional information, including financial projections, legal strategy, personnel matters, and other information the institution has obligations to protect
- Information subject to legal privilege
- Information the institution is contractually obligated to protect

Even for AI systems that have been approved for use with certain types of information, staff must apply the minimum necessary standard: providing only the information the AI system needs for its specific intended purpose, not all available information.

7.3 Vendor data handling requirements

[Institution Name] will not enter into relationships with AI vendors whose data handling practices do not meet the following minimum requirements:

- The vendor's data processing activities are governed by a written agreement that addresses data handling, security, and the institution's rights
- The vendor does not use [Institution Name]'s data to train AI models without [Institution Name]'s specific prior consent

- The vendor maintains security practices appropriate to the sensitivity of the information it processes
- The vendor will return or delete institutional data upon request or contract termination
- The vendor will notify [Institution Name] of security incidents affecting institutional data within [ADAPT — e.g., 72 hours] of discovery

Contracts with AI vendors must include provisions addressing these requirements. Procurement and legal counsel are responsible for ensuring that vendor contracts meet these standards before execution.

7.4 Use of institutional data for AI training

[Institution Name]'s operational data — including information about the people we serve, our programs, and our operations — may not be used to train AI models, whether by [Institution Name] itself or by vendors, without specific governance review and approval. Any proposal to use institutional data for AI training must be submitted through the intake process as a proposed AI use case.

7.5 Data retention and deletion

AI-generated outputs that become part of institutional records — including clinical records, personnel files, educational records, and case management records — are subject to the retention requirements applicable to those records regardless of their AI-generated character.

AI-generated outputs that are not incorporated into institutional records should not be retained beyond the period needed for their immediate operational purpose unless retention is required for audit, legal hold, or other specified purposes.

7.6 Individual rights

When individuals whose information is processed by AI systems exercise applicable data rights — including rights of access, correction, deletion, explanation, and objection to automated processing — [Institution Name] will respond in accordance with applicable law. Staff who receive requests from individuals seeking to exercise data rights in connection with AI processing should direct those requests to [ADAPT — legal/compliance or designated contact].

Section 8: Human Oversight Requirements

8.1 The requirement for meaningful oversight

AI systems used at [Institution Name] must be subject to meaningful human oversight. Oversight is meaningful when the human reviewer exercises genuine independent judgment — not merely acknowledging that a review occurred, but actually assessing whether the AI output is correct, appropriate, and consistent with the circumstances of the specific situation.

Oversight that consists of approving AI outputs without substantive review is not adequate oversight. Staff are expected to apply their professional judgment to AI outputs, not to defer to AI recommendations without assessment.

8.2 Oversight requirements by risk level

The following oversight requirements apply based on the risk level of the AI use case, as determined through the intake and approval process:

High-risk AI uses:

- Human review by a qualified staff member is required before any AI output influences a decision affecting a specific individual
- Reviewers must form and document their independent assessment before reviewing the AI output, except in operational contexts where this is infeasible, in which case equivalent structural independence must be demonstrated in the oversight design

- Override of AI recommendations is a normal and expected professional judgment, not an exception requiring special justification
- Decisions made with AI assistance must be documented, including what the AI recommended, what the human decided, and the basis for any deviation from the AI recommendation
- Oversight quality — including override rates — will be monitored as specified in governance approvals

Medium-risk AI uses:

- Human review is required before AI outputs are acted on or communicated externally
- Documentation of AI use is required at the level specified in governance approvals
- Override of AI recommendations is unrestricted and requires no special documentation beyond standard decision records

Low-risk AI uses:

- Human review before acting on AI outputs is expected as good practice but is not formally required for every individual output
- Staff retain full authority to disregard, modify, or reject AI outputs based on their professional judgment

8.3 Categories of decisions requiring human authority

The following categories of decision must be made by a human with appropriate authority and accountability, regardless of AI system capabilities or recommendations:

- Decisions to deny or terminate an individual's access to a service or benefit the institution provides
- Decisions to take adverse action against an employee
- Clinical decisions of the types specified by [ADAPT — clinical leadership or applicable professional standards]
- Decisions subject to due process requirements under applicable law

- Any other decision designated as requiring human authority by the AI Governance Team

AI systems may assist with these decisions — providing analysis, information, or recommendations — but the final decision must be made by an authorized human decision-maker.

8.4 Escalation of oversight concerns

Staff who encounter AI outputs that seem incorrect, unusual, or inconsistent with their professional judgment must escalate those concerns through the following pathway:

1. Document the concern, including what the AI system produced, why it seems problematic, and what information the staff member has that conflicts with the AI output
2. Do not act on the AI output without additional human review if the concern relates to a consequential decision
3. Report the concern to their supervisor and to the AI Governance Coordinator using [ADAPT — specify the reporting mechanism, e.g., the AI concern reporting form at link/location]

Staff will not face adverse consequences for reporting good-faith concerns about AI outputs, regardless of whether subsequent investigation confirms that the concern was warranted.

8.5 Disclosure to affected individuals

Individuals affected by AI-assisted decisions have a right to know that AI was used. [Institution Name] will provide meaningful disclosure of AI use to the people it serves in the following circumstances:

- When AI systems contribute to decisions about their care, services, benefits, or eligibility
- When AI systems are used in direct interaction with them, including automated responses and AI-powered support systems
- When required by applicable law

Disclosure should be: in plain language accessible to the intended audience; specific about what AI does in the relevant context; honest about AI's limitations and the human oversight in place; and accompanied by information about how to request human review.

Section 9: Incident Reporting and Response

9.1 Reporting obligation

All staff must report AI incidents — as defined in Section 2 — promptly upon becoming aware of them. Prompt means as soon as practicable and no later than [ADAPT — e.g., 24 hours] after the incident is identified, except for potential safety incidents which must be reported immediately.

Reports must be made to the AI Governance Coordinator using [ADAPT — specify the reporting mechanism, e.g., the AI incident report form at link/location, or by contacting the governance coordinator directly at contact information].

Staff should report potential incidents even when uncertain whether the event meets the definition of an AI incident. The AI Governance Coordinator will assess whether the event requires formal incident response. The cost of over-reporting is low; the cost of under-reporting is high.

9.2 Non-retaliation

[Institution Name] will not retaliate against any staff member who reports a good-faith AI incident or concern. This protection applies regardless of whether subsequent investigation confirms that an incident occurred, whether the incident was caused by the reporting staff member's use of the system, or whether the incident was previously unknown to institutional leadership.

Staff who believe they have experienced retaliation for reporting an AI concern should report that retaliation to [ADAPT — HR, the ombudsperson, or other appropriate institutional contact].

9.3 Incident response

Upon receiving an incident report, the AI Governance Coordinator will:

1. Acknowledge receipt within [ADAPT — e.g., 4 business hours]
2. Conduct an initial assessment of the incident's apparent nature and severity
3. Classify the incident as requiring immediate governance team escalation, standard investigation, or operational resolution
4. Initiate the appropriate response process

For incidents classified as requiring immediate escalation — those involving potential significant harm, potential safety failure, significant data breach, or conditions requiring immediate system suspension — the AI Governance Coordinator will convene emergency governance team consultation within [ADAPT — e.g., 4 hours of classification].

The AI Governance Team will oversee investigation, remediation, and communication for all significant incidents. Incident response will include: investigation to understand what occurred and why; immediate protective measures where ongoing harm requires them; notification to affected individuals as required by this policy, applicable law, and ethical obligation; governance system remediation to address contributing factors; and post-incident review to integrate learning into governance improvement.

9.4 Rollback authority

The following individuals have authority to direct immediate suspension of an AI system without waiting for AI Governance Team deliberation, when they determine that ongoing operation presents unacceptable immediate risk:

- [ADAPT — e.g., the CEO/Executive Director]
- [ADAPT — e.g., the Chief Medical Officer, if applicable]
- [ADAPT — e.g., The AI Governance Team Chair]

Exercises of rollback authority must be documented and reported to the full AI Governance Team within [ADAPT — e.g., 24 hours].

Section 10: Training and Compliance

10.1 Required training

The following AI literacy training requirements apply. Staff must complete required training within the specified timeframe and must maintain training currency as required.

All staff who use AI systems in their work:

- Foundational AI literacy training: must be completed within [ADAPT — e.g., 60 days] of this policy's effective date for current staff, and within [ADAPT — e.g., 30 days] of the start of employment for new staff
- Annual refresher training: must be completed annually within [ADAPT — e.g., 60 days] of each training cycle

Staff designated as direct users of approved AI systems:

- Role-specific training for each AI system they use: must be completed before the staff member uses the system in institutional work
- Training must include: what the specific AI system does and its known limitations, the governance requirements applicable to the specific use, what oversight is required, and how to identify and report concerns

Supervisors and department leaders:

- Management AI literacy training covering oversight culture, governance compliance monitoring, and AI concern escalation: must be completed within [ADAPT — e.g., 90 days] of this policy's effective date and annually thereafter

AI Governance Team members:

- Governance-level AI literacy covering the full governance framework, legal requirements, vendor assessment, and audit: to be completed as specified by the AI Governance Team and updated annually

Completion records will be maintained by [ADAPT — HR or the AI Governance Coordinator]. Department leaders are responsible for ensuring that staff in their functions complete required training within specified timeframes.

10.2 Policy compliance

Compliance with this policy is a condition of employment and of any contractor or vendor relationship with [Institution Name]. Violations of this policy will be addressed through [Institution Name]'s standard personnel processes, taking into account the nature and severity of the violation, whether the violation was intentional, the harm caused or risked, and any mitigating circumstances.

Policy violations will not be treated identically regardless of severity. Minor unintentional violations — such as inadvertent use of an unapproved tool for a low-risk purpose — may be addressed through additional training and guidance. Serious violations — such as deliberate circumvention of the review process for high-risk AI use, unauthorized processing of sensitive information, or failure to escalate a known AI incident — may result in disciplinary action up to and including termination.

10.3 Questions and guidance

Staff with questions about this policy, about whether a specific AI use is permitted, or about their obligations under this policy should contact the AI Governance Coordinator at [ADAPT — contact information]. The AI Governance Coordinator will respond to routine inquiries within [ADAPT — e.g., 3 business days] and will escalate complex questions to legal counsel or the governance team as needed.

10.4 Policy review and updates

This policy will be reviewed annually by the AI Governance Team, with revisions recommended to [ADAPT — senior leadership / the board] as needed. Off-cycle review will be conducted when significant changes in institutional AI use, applicable law, or AI governance practice warrant it.

Staff will be notified of material changes to this policy with sufficient explanation of what changed and why. Changes that create new obligations for staff will be communicated with reasonable notice before the new obligations take effect, except where urgent circumstances require immediate implementation.

The current version of this policy is maintained at [ADAPT — specify location, e.g., the institutional intranet, the policy management system]. Archived versions are maintained by the AI Governance Coordinator.

Appendix A: Quick reference — prohibited and permitted uses

[ADAPT — Institutions should develop a one-page quick reference guide that summarizes the key permitted and prohibited use categories from Section 4 in plain language accessible to all staff. This appendix placeholder indicates where that reference should appear.]

Appendix B: Governance contacts

Role	Name	Contact
AI Governance Coordinator	[ADAPT]	[ADAPT]
Governance Team Chair	[ADAPT]	[ADAPT]
Legal/Compliance Contact	[ADAPT]	[ADAPT]
IT Security Contact	[ADAPT]	[ADAPT]
After-hours incident reporting	[ADAPT]	[ADAPT]

Appendix C: Key governance documents and resources

The following documents implement and support this policy:

- AI Inventory: [ADAPT — location]
- AI Intake Form: [ADAPT — location, also Chapter 25 of this governance handbook]
- Vendor Due Diligence Questionnaire: [ADAPT — location, also Chapter 26]
- Testing and Review Checklist: [ADAPT — location, also Chapter 27]
- Incident Report Template: [ADAPT — location, also Chapter 28]
- Monitoring Dashboard Template: [ADAPT — location, also Chapter 29]
- AI Governance Team Terms of Reference: [ADAPT — location]
- AI Literacy Training: [ADAPT — location]

Policy certification

By approving this policy, [Institution Name] commits to implementing, maintaining, and enforcing its requirements in a manner consistent with our institutional values and our obligations to the people we serve.

Approved by: ______________________________

Title: ______________________________

Date: ______________________________

Next review date: ______________________________

Notes on adaptation

The most important adaptations this policy requires are those that connect its requirements to institutional reality — making them specific to the institution's actual AI use, specific to applicable law, and specific to the governance capacity the institution actually has or can build.

Several provisions deserve particular attention in adaptation.

The definitions section should be reviewed by legal counsel to ensure that the definition of AI captures what the institution needs to govern while being workable in the institution's specific context. A definition that is technically precise but practically unworkable will be circumvented.

The review timeline in Section 6 should be calibrated to what the institution's governance function can actually achieve. Timelines that cannot be met in practice will be treated as aspirational, which will undermine the requirement for review before implementation. It is better to commit to longer but achievable timelines than to establish shorter timelines that the governance function regularly misses.

The oversight requirements in Section 8 should be calibrated to the actual risk levels and operational contexts of the institution's AI use. An institution that does not use high-risk AI in consequential decision contexts does not need the full apparatus of Section 8.2's high-risk requirements; an institution whose AI use is primarily in such contexts should strengthen those requirements beyond what this model provides.

The training timeline in Section 10 should reflect what the institution has actually built or can realistically build in training capacity. Committing to training that has not been developed, delivered by trainers who have not been identified, is committing to an obligation the institution will not meet.

This policy is a beginning, not an end. The institution that adopts it thoughtfully, implements it genuinely, and improves it continuously will have built something that serves both governance and mission. The institution that adopts it as a compliance artifact and files it will have produced a document — which is a very different thing.

Chapter 25: AI Intake Form

How to use this form

The AI intake form is the primary instrument through which institutional AI governance begins its work on any proposed new AI use. It is the document that translates a staff member's or department's interest in using an AI system into a structured governance submission — providing the governance team with the information it needs to assess whether the proposed use is appropriate, what risks it presents, what conditions should govern it, and what oversight it requires.

This chapter provides a complete intake form that institutions can adapt. It is organized as a form with guidance: each section includes the questions to be answered and explanatory notes for submitters explaining why each question matters and what level of detail is expected. These guidance notes can be retained in the version distributed to staff, removed if they make the form unwieldy for high-volume use, or converted into a separate guidance document that submitters consult alongside a cleaner form.

The form is designed to be completed by the person or team proposing the AI use — not by the governance function conducting the review. A form completed by governance staff based on a brief oral summary does not provide the accountability and specificity that intake governance requires. The submitter is the person with operational knowledge of the proposed use; their documentation of what they are proposing and why is both a governance information source and an accountability act.

The form is designed to be proportionate in length and complexity to what governance review actually requires. It will take most submitters between thirty minutes and two hours to complete thoughtfully, depending on the complexity of the proposed use and how much of the relevant information the submitter already has in hand. For high-risk proposals, additional information may be requested during review; this form represents the minimum required for complete submission.

Institutions should adapt this form to their specific context, terminology, and governance requirements. The [ADAPT] markers indicate fields where institutional-specific information is needed. Other provisions may also require adaptation based on institutional context, regulatory requirements, and governance architecture.

AI USE CASE INTAKE AND REVIEW FORM

[INSTITUTION NAME] — AI GOVERNANCE PROGRAM

This form must be completed for all proposed AI uses that require review under [Institution Name]'s AI Governance Policy. If you are uncertain whether your proposed use requires review, contact the AI Governance Coordinator at [ADAPT — contact information] before proceeding.

Submitting this form initiates the review process. You will receive an acknowledgment within [ADAPT — e.g., 2 business days] of submission. Do not proceed with the proposed AI use until you have received a governance decision.

Submit completed form to: [ADAPT — specify submission channel: email address, form portal, or other mechanism]

Questions about this form: [ADAPT — AI Governance Coordinator contact]

Part A: Submission Information

This section identifies the submitter and the nature of the submission.

A1. Submission date

____

A2. Submitter information

Field	Response
Submitter name	
Job title	
Department / function	
Email address	
Phone number	
Supervisor's name	

A3. Operational owner

If the person who will be responsible for this AI system's ongoing governance is different from the submitter, provide their information here. The operational owner is the person accountable for compliance with governance conditions, monitoring obligations, and escalation responsibilities if this use case is approved.

Field	Response
Operational owner name (if different from submitter)	
Job title	
Department / function	
Email address	

A4. Submission type

Check all that apply:

☐ New AI system — not previously used at [Institution Name] ☐ New use of an existing approved AI system — expanding scope, population, or data types beyond original approval ☐ AI feature newly added by vendor to existing software we already use ☐ Renewal of a previously approved use case — for governance reassessment ☐ Custom or internally developed AI system ☐ AI system used by a third-party service provider on our behalf ☐ Other — describe:

____

Guidance: Select the type that best describes what you are proposing. If you are proposing to use a tool that has been approved for one purpose in a new context, select "New use of an existing approved AI system" and describe both the prior approval and the new proposed use.

A5. Proposed implementation timeline

Field	Response
Target implementation date	
Is there a hard deadline? If yes, what is it and why?	
Are there consequences to a delay? If yes, describe	

Guidance: Provide your realistic implementation timeline. If there is a contract deadline, a funder requirement, or another constraint that creates urgency, explain it here. The governance team may be able to prioritize urgent reviews if time constraints are genuine. However, artificial urgency — claiming time pressure to accelerate review — is not appropriate and will be recognized. Governance review quality will not be compromised for convenience.

Part B: AI System Description

This section describes what the AI system is and what it does. Be specific. Vague descriptions produce inadequate reviews and delayed decisions.

B1. System identification

Field	Response
AI system name	
Vendor name	
Vendor website	
Product version or model (if known)	
Is this system already in use elsewhere at [Institution Name]? If yes, where?	

B2. What does this AI system do?

Describe in plain language what this AI system does — how it works, what it produces, and what problem it is designed to solve. Write this description for a reader who is not familiar with the system and does not have technical expertise.

____
____

____
____

____
____

Guidance: A good description explains the system type (what kind of AI it is — classification, generative, predictive, etc.), what inputs it receives, what outputs it produces, and what it is designed to accomplish. Example: "This system uses machine learning to review submitted grant applications and produce a score from 1-100 predicting likelihood of program success, based on factors including applicant history, project description, and budget. Staff would use this score as one input in the application review process."

B3. Proposed specific use

Describe specifically how you propose to use this AI system at [Institution Name]. This should be more specific than the vendor's description of the system's general capabilities — describe what this system will do in your specific operational context.

____

____

Guidance: Describe the specific workflow: what triggers use of the AI, what information staff will provide to it, what outputs it produces, how those outputs will be used, and what happens next. Example: "After initial intake, case workers will enter client identifying information, program eligibility criteria responses, and case notes into the system. The system will produce an eligibility recommendation and flag factors it identified as relevant. Case workers will review the recommendation and make a final eligibility determination."

B4. Operational scale

Field	Response
How many staff will use this system?	
Which specific staff roles will use it?	
How frequently will it be used (daily / weekly / monthly / other)?	
Approximate number of transactions or outputs per month	
Will use be concentrated in a specific time period (e.g., seasonal, during specific program cycles)?	

B5. AI system type

Check all that apply to this AI system:

☐ Classification system — categorizes inputs into defined categories ☐ Prediction system — estimates probabilities or future events ☐ Recommendation system — suggests options, content, or actions ☐ Generative AI / large language model — generates text, images, or other content ☐ Decision support — assists human decision-making with analysis or recommendations ☐ Automated decision system — makes decisions with limited individual human review ☐ Agentic system — takes sequences of actions to accomplish goals with limited human involvement in individual steps ☐ Chatbot or conversational AI — interacts with users through natural language ☐ Image or document analysis — processes visual or document content ☐ Other — describe: ______________________________

B6. What alternatives were considered?

Describe what alternatives to this AI system you considered, including non-AI alternatives. Why is this AI system the proposed approach rather than an alternative?

____

____

Guidance: Governance review considers whether AI is the appropriate approach for this use case. Describing what alternatives you considered and why you chose AI helps the governance team understand whether this is a use case where AI adds genuine value. If you did not consider alternatives, explain why.

Part C: People Affected

This section identifies who will be affected by this AI system — who it will process information about, who will interact with it, and who will be affected by its outputs.

C1. Who is directly affected by this AI system?

Describe the people whose information the AI system will process, to whom the AI system will produce outputs, or about whom the AI system will make recommendations or decisions.

____

____

Examples: clients applying for services; patients receiving care; students enrolled in programs; job applicants; current employees; members of the public contacting our service line.

C2. Population characteristics

Question	Response
Approximate number of people who will be affected per month or year	
Does the affected population include minors (people under 18)?	☐ Yes ☐ No ☐ Unknown
Does the affected population include people who may be in crisis or acute distress?	☐ Yes ☐ No ☐ Possible
Does the affected population include people with disabilities?	☐ Yes ☐ No ☐ Unknown
Does the affected population include people from specific racial or ethnic communities? If yes, describe	
Is the affected population economically vulnerable?	☐ Yes ☐ No ☐ Partially
Are there language barriers in the affected population?	☐ Yes ☐ No ☐ Some
Are there other vulnerability characteristics relevant to this population? Describe	

Guidance: The governance team uses population information to assess whether heightened protections are needed. Honest characterization of your population is essential. If you are uncertain about population characteristics, indicate that uncertainty rather than leaving fields blank.

C3. Consequences for affected people

What could happen to a person as a result of this AI system's outputs? Describe both the intended consequences (benefits) and the potential adverse consequences if the system makes an error.

Intended benefits to affected people	
Potential adverse consequences if the system produces an incorrect or biased output	
How reversible are potential adverse consequences?	☐ Easily reversed ☐ Reversible with effort ☐ Difficult to reverse ☐ Irreversible

---

C4. Will affected people be informed that AI is being used?

Question	Response
Will the people directly affected by this AI system be informed that AI is being used?	☐ Yes ☐ No ☐ Partially
If yes, how and when will they be informed?	
If no or partially, explain why complete disclosure is not proposed	
Will affected people be told how to request human review of AI-assisted decisions?	☐ Yes ☐ No ☐ Not applicable

Guidance: [Institution Name]'s AI governance policy requires meaningful disclosure to affected parties in most circumstances. If you are proposing not to disclose AI use to the affected population, explain your reasoning. The governance team will assess whether non-disclosure is appropriate.

Part D: Data

This section describes what information the AI system will process. Complete this section carefully — it is the basis for data governance and privacy risk assessment.

D1. What information will be provided as inputs to the AI system?

List all categories of information that will be entered into or processed by the AI system. Be specific — do not simply list "client information" but describe what specific types of information about clients.

Information category	Does this include personal information about individuals?	Does this include sensitive information?	Approximate volume
	☐ Yes ☐ No	☐ Yes ☐ No	
	☐ Yes ☐ No	☐ Yes ☐ No	
	☐ Yes ☐ No	☐ Yes ☐ No	
	☐ Yes ☐ No	☐ Yes ☐ No	
	☐ Yes ☐ No	☐ Yes ☐ No	

Add rows as needed.

D2. Sensitive information categories

Check all sensitive information categories that will be processed by this AI system:

☐ Health and medical information ☐ Mental health information ☐ Financial information (beyond basic contact/billing) ☐ Information about minors ☐ Biometric data (facial images, fingerprints, voice prints, etc.) ☐ Racial or ethnic origin ☐ Political opinions ☐ Religious or philosophical beliefs ☐ Sexual orientation or gender identity ☐ Immigration status ☐ Criminal history ☐ Disability status or history ☐ Social services or benefits information ☐ Educational records ☐ Employment or performance records ☐ None of the above

For each sensitive category checked, describe specifically what information and in what context:

____
____

D3. Data sources

Question	Response
Where will the data entered into this system come from? (describe sources)	
Is the data being repurposed from an original collection for a different purpose?	☐ Yes ☐ No
If yes, what was the original purpose and what is the new purpose?	
Is there a legal basis for using this data for the proposed AI purpose?	☐ Yes ☐ No ☐ To be confirmed by legal
If yes, what is that legal basis?	

D4. Vendor data practices

Question	Response
Does the vendor retain inputs submitted to the system?	☐ Yes ☐ No ☐ Unknown
Does the vendor use inputs for model training or improvement?	☐ Yes ☐ No ☐ Unknown
Where does the vendor store institutional data (country/jurisdiction)?	
Is there a data processing agreement with this vendor?	☐ Yes ☐ No ☐ In negotiation
For healthcare contexts: Is there a HIPAA Business Associate Agreement?	☐ Yes ☐ No ☐ Not applicable
Has legal or procurement reviewed the vendor's data terms?	☐ Yes ☐ No ☐ Not yet

Guidance: "Unknown" answers will require follow-up before review can be completed. If you do not have information about the vendor's data practices, contact the vendor before submitting or note that you are following up and provide an expected date for that information.

D5. Data security

Question	Response
Has IT security assessed this system's security practices?	☐ Yes ☐ No ☐ In progress
If yes, what were the findings?	
Does the vendor have relevant security certifications? (e.g., SOC 2, ISO 27001) If yes, specify	
What access controls will limit which staff can use the system?	

Part E: Workflow and Oversight

This section describes how the AI system fits into your workflows and what human oversight will be in place. This section is critical for the governance team's assessment of whether oversight is adequate.

E1. Workflow description

Describe step by step how this AI system will function within your operational workflow. Include what happens before the AI is used, what inputs are provided, what the AI produces, and what happens with those outputs.

____
____

____
____

Guidance: Walk through the workflow concretely. Who does what in what order? Where does the AI appear in the process? What does a staff member see? What do they do with the AI's output? What is the next step? If this is a complex workflow, a diagram or numbered step list is helpful.

E2. Human oversight design

Question	Response
Will a human review AI outputs before they influence decisions about specific individuals?	☐ Always ☐ Usually ☐ Sometimes ☐ Rarely ☐ Never
If not always, describe the circumstances where AI outputs will not receive individual human review	

Question	Response
Who specifically is responsible for reviewing AI outputs? (describe role, not name)	
What qualifications or training will reviewers have?	
What information will reviewers have access to when reviewing AI outputs?	
Can reviewers override or modify AI recommendations?	☐ Yes, unrestricted ☐ Yes, with documentation ☐ Yes, with supervisor approval ☐ No
Approximately how many AI outputs will each reviewer assess per hour / day?	
Will reviewers document their review and any deviation from AI recommendations?	☐ Yes ☐ No ☐ Partially
How will the AI output be presented to reviewers — will they see it before or after forming their own assessment?	

Guidance: Be honest about oversight. If the workflow is designed so that AI outputs are acted on without systematic individual human review — because volume is too high, because the workflow doesn't include a review step, or because outputs are incorporated into records automatically — describe that accurately. The governance team needs to know what oversight will actually occur, not what might ideally occur.

E3. Decision authority

Question	Response
Will this AI system make final decisions about individuals, or will humans retain final decision authority?	☐ AI makes final decisions ☐ AI recommends, human decides ☐ AI

Question	Response
	assists, human decides independently
For decisions where AI recommends and human decides: describe what the human decision looks like in practice	
Are there circumstances where AI outputs will be acted on without human review?	☐ Yes ☐ No
If yes, describe those circumstances and explain why human review is not feasible	

E4. Exception handling

Question	Response
What will happen when the AI system produces an output that seems incorrect, unusual, or low-confidence?	
Is there a mechanism for staff to escalate AI concerns?	☐ Yes ☐ No
If yes, describe the escalation pathway	
What will happen if the AI system is unavailable? Is there a fallback process?	
Describe the fallback process	

Part F: Vendor Information and Assessment

This section gathers information about the vendor and the vendor's AI governance practices. Complete this section based on information you have from the vendor. If you have not yet had conversations with the vendor about governance, conduct those conversations before submitting.

F1. Vendor details

Field	Response
Vendor company name	
Vendor headquarters location	
Vendor primary contact name and title	
Vendor contact email and phone	
How long has this vendor been providing this product?	
Is this vendor currently used by [Institution Name] for other purposes?	☐ Yes ☐ No

---

F2. AI system performance documentation

Question	Response
Has the vendor provided documentation of AI system performance?	☐ Yes ☐ No
If yes, attach documentation or describe what was provided	
Has the vendor provided data on system performance across demographic groups?	☐ Yes ☐ No ☐ Requested, not yet received
If yes, summarize the findings	
What accuracy rate or performance standard does the vendor claim for this system?	
What evaluation data was this performance claim based on?	
Has this system been independently evaluated or audited?	☐ Yes ☐ No ☐ Unknown
If yes, by whom and what were the findings?	

F3. Vendor governance practices

Question	Response
Does the vendor have a published responsible AI / AI ethics policy?	☐ Yes ☐ No ☐ Unknown
If yes, provide a link or attach	
Does the vendor provide ongoing performance monitoring and reporting to customers?	☐ Yes ☐ No
Does the vendor notify customers of material changes to the AI system?	☐ Yes ☐ No ☐ Contract language to be reviewed
Will the vendor provide audit access to the institution?	☐ Yes ☐ No ☐ To be negotiated
Has the vendor responded substantively to governance questions?	☐ Yes — describe ☐ No — describe ☐ Not yet asked

---

F4. Contract status and terms

Question	Response
Is there a proposed or executed contract with this vendor?	☐ Yes, executed ☐ Yes, proposed ☐ No, to be negotiated
Has legal counsel reviewed the contract?	☐ Yes ☐ No ☐ In progress
Does the contract include: data handling provisions?	☐ Yes ☐ No ☐ Unknown
Does the contract include: audit rights?	☐ Yes ☐ No ☐ Unknown
Does the contract include: breach notification obligations?	☐ Yes ☐ No ☐ Unknown
Does the contract include: data return / deletion upon termination?	☐ Yes ☐ No ☐ Unknown
Does the contract include: performance standards?	☐ Yes ☐ No ☐ Unknown

Question	Response
Does the contract include: exit provisions and transition support?	☐ Yes ☐ No ☐ Unknown
Contract term length	
Contract value (if known)	

Part G: Risk Self-Assessment

This section asks you to assess the risks associated with your proposed AI use. Your honest assessment helps the governance team calibrate its review and identify areas requiring deeper scrutiny. You will not be penalized for identifying risks — identifying them is the responsible and expected approach.

G1. Overall risk assessment

Based on your understanding of this AI system and its proposed use, how would you assess its overall risk level?

☐ Low — limited consequences for errors, robust human oversight, no sensitive data, not affecting vulnerable populations ☐ Medium — some consequence for errors, meaningful human oversight, limited personal data, limited vulnerability concerns ☐ High — significant consequences for errors, limited human oversight, sensitive data involved, or vulnerable populations affected

Explain the basis for your assessment:

____

G2. Risk category assessment

For each risk category, indicate your assessment of the risk level for this specific proposed use and briefly explain your reasoning.

Bias and discrimination risk

Risk level: ☐ Low ☐ Medium ☐ High ☐ Unknown

Could this AI system produce outputs that disadvantage specific demographic groups? Explain:

____

____

Privacy risk

Risk level: ☐ Low ☐ Medium ☐ High ☐ Unknown

What are the privacy risks of this AI system processing the data described in Part D? Explain:

____

____

Safety risk

Risk level: ☐ Low ☐ Medium ☐ High ☐ Unknown

Could errors or failures in this AI system contribute to physical, psychological, or material harm to anyone? Explain:

____

____

Hallucination and unreliability risk *(for generative AI systems)*

Risk level: ☐ Low ☐ Medium ☐ High ☐ Not applicable

What are the risks of incorrect or fabricated AI outputs? How will those be detected and managed? Explain:

____

____

Overreliance risk

Risk level: ☐ Low ☐ Medium ☐ High ☐ Unknown

Is there a risk that staff will defer to AI outputs without exercising genuine independent judgment? What will prevent this? Explain:

____

____

Legal and regulatory risk

Risk level: ☐ Low ☐ Medium ☐ High ☐ Unknown

Are there legal or regulatory requirements that specifically govern this type of AI use? Have those requirements been assessed? Explain:

____

____

G3. Known limitations

What are the known limitations of this AI system as described by the vendor or as identified through your research?

____

Guidance: Every AI system has limitations. If the vendor has not described any, that itself is a concern worth noting here. Common limitations include: performance variability for certain input types, performance differences across demographic groups, tendency to produce confident but incorrect outputs for certain question types, language or dialect limitations, reliance on training data that may not reflect current conditions.

G4. Concerns and open questions

Are there aspects of this AI system, its vendor, or its proposed use that concern you or that you believe warrant careful governance scrutiny? Are there questions you were unable to answer in this form?

____

Guidance: This question provides space for honest reflection. If there are things about this proposal that you think the governance team should know or carefully assess — uncertainties, concerns, vendor responsiveness issues, staff readiness questions, operational complications — describe them here. Surfacing concerns at intake is not a mark against your proposal; it demonstrates governance awareness and allows the team to address concerns proactively.

Part H: Implementation and Monitoring Plans

This section describes your plans for implementing and monitoring this AI system if it is approved. These plans will be assessed as part of governance review and will form the basis of monitoring requirements in any approval.

H1. Implementation plan

Question	Response
Have staff who will use this system been identified?	☐ Yes ☐ No ☐ Partially
What training will staff receive before using the system?	
Who will provide that training and when?	
How will compliance with oversight requirements be ensured?	
What documentation of AI use will be maintained?	
How will the institution verify that conditions attached to approval (if any) are met?	

H2. Monitoring plan

Question	Response
How will you monitor this AI system's performance after deployment?	
Who will be responsible for monitoring?	
How frequently will monitoring occur?	
What performance indicators will you track?	
Will you monitor for differential performance across demographic groups?	☐ Yes ☐ No — explain

Question	Response
How will staff concerns about AI performance be collected and acted on?	
How will monitoring findings be reported to the AI Governance Team?	

H3. Incident response readiness

Question	Response
Do relevant staff know how to report an AI incident under [Institution Name]'s policy?	☐ Yes ☐ No ☐ Will be covered in training
Is there a designated escalation contact for this AI system if a problem arises?	☐ Yes — name: ________ ☐ No
What will happen operationally if this AI system needs to be suspended?	

Part I: Supporting Materials

Attach all relevant supporting materials. Check each item that is included with this submission.

☐ Vendor product documentation or data sheet ☐ Vendor performance documentation, including accuracy and reliability metrics ☐ Vendor bias and fairness testing documentation (demographic performance data) ☐ Vendor privacy / data handling documentation or privacy policy ☐ Proposed or executed vendor contract ☐ Data processing agreement or equivalent ☐ HIPAA Business Associate Agreement (if applicable) ☐ Vendor security certifications or assessments ☐ IT security assessment (if completed) ☐ Legal counsel review notes or memo (if completed) ☐ Workflow diagram or process description ☐ Sample AI outputs or interface screenshots (optional but helpful) ☐ Other — describe: ____
_

Guidance: Submissions without vendor performance documentation, data handling documentation, and a proposed or executed contract cannot be reviewed as complete. If these documents are not yet available, indicate when they will be available and whether you would like to hold the submission pending their receipt or have the team begin review with acknowledgment that these items are outstanding.

Part J: Submitter Certification

By signing below, you certify the following.

I certify that:

1. The information provided in this form is accurate and complete to the best of my knowledge, and I have made reasonable efforts to obtain information I did not have at the time of submission.
2. I understand that [Institution Name]'s AI Governance Policy requires governance approval before this AI system can be implemented, and I will not proceed with implementation until I have received written governance approval.
3. I understand that if this use case is approved, I am responsible for ensuring that the system is used in compliance with all conditions of approval and all requirements of [Institution Name]'s AI Governance Policy.
4. I will notify the AI Governance Coordinator promptly if: circumstances materially change from what is described in this form; I become aware of AI system performance that raises governance concerns; a vendor changes the AI system in ways that may be material to governance; or I identify information relevant to governance that was not available when this form was submitted.
5. I am submitting this form in good faith as an honest representation of the proposed AI use and its risks. I understand that providing materially inaccurate information, or proceeding with AI use without authorization, may result in disciplinary action.

Submitter name (print):

____

Submitter signature:

____

Date: ____

Supervisor name (print):

____

Supervisor signature:

____

Date: ____

For Governance Team Use Only

The following section is completed by the AI Governance Coordinator and governance team during review. Do not complete.

Submission received: ____________ **Received by:** ____________

Completeness check: ☐ Complete — proceed to triage ☐ Incomplete — returned to submitter on ____________ for: ______________________

Preliminary risk classification: ☐ Low risk — fast track ☐ Medium risk — standard review ☐ High risk — intensive review ☐ Requires additional information before classification

Risk classification rationale:

____

Governance team reviewers assigned:

- Primary reviewer: ____
- Legal review: ____
- IT/security review: ____
- Domain expert (if needed): ____

Review decision date: ___________

Decision: ☐ Approved ☐ Conditionally approved ☐ Declined ☐ Deferred

Conditions / reasons / guidance:

____

____

Monitoring requirements:

____

____

Inventory entry created: ☐ Yes ☐ No **Entry ID:** ___________

Decision communicated to submitter on: ___________ **By:** ___________

Condition confirmation received: ___________ (for conditional approvals)

Governance team members who reviewed:

Name Role Date reviewed Signature

Notes on adapting this form

The form above is comprehensive — covering the full range of information that governance review requires for complex, high-risk proposals. Institutions should consider whether a tiered form structure is appropriate for their use: a shorter initial screening form that collects the information needed to determine risk level, followed by additional sections required only for medium- and high-risk proposals. This tiered approach reduces the burden on submitters of low-risk proposals while ensuring that high-risk proposals receive the full information collection that comprehensive review requires.

The guidance notes throughout the form are an important design feature. Submitters who understand why a question is being asked produce better answers than those who encounter questions without context. Institutions should retain the guidance notes in staff-facing versions of the form, or provide them in a companion guidance document, rather than presenting the form as a bare questionnaire.

The for-governance-team-use section should be completed consistently and stored with the submission. This section creates the governance record that supports accountability and audit. Governance teams that do not systematically complete this section lose the institutional memory that the governance record is supposed to preserve.

Finally, the submitter certification is not merely a formality. It creates explicit accountability for the accuracy of the submission and for compliance with conditions of approval. Institutions should ensure that submitters understand they are making a meaningful commitment when they sign, and that governance will follow up on that commitment through condition verification and monitoring.

Chapter 26: Vendor Due Diligence Questionnaire

How to use this questionnaire

The vendor due diligence questionnaire is the instrument through which institutions systematically assess AI vendors before entering or renewing a vendor relationship. It translates the vendor assessment requirements described in Chapter 11 into a structured set of questions that procurement teams, compliance staff, legal counsel, and governance team members can use to gather the information that responsible AI procurement requires.

This questionnaire serves two distinct functions. First, it is an information-gathering instrument — a structured way to collect from vendors the documentation and answers that governance review requires. Second, it is a governance instrument — the act of asking these questions, and assessing how vendors respond to them, reveals information about vendors' AI governance practices and their willingness to engage with governance requirements that is itself governance-relevant. Vendors who respond substantively, who provide requested documentation, and who engage constructively with difficult questions are demonstrating governance partnership. Vendors who are evasive, who provide generic assurances in place of specific answers, or who treat governance questions as obstacles are demonstrating something different.

The questionnaire is organized into eight sections covering AI system performance and validation, data governance and privacy practices, security, transparency and explainability, vendor governance practices, contractual terms, ongoing relationship management, and references and track record. Not every section will be equally relevant for every vendor assessment — institutions should apply sections selectively based on the nature of the proposed AI system and the risk level of the proposed use case.

This questionnaire is designed to be sent to vendors as a formal information request, with a defined response deadline. Vendors should be informed that their responses will be reviewed by the institution's procurement, legal, and governance functions, that supporting documentation should be provided where indicated, and that the institution reserves the right to ask follow-up questions before making a procurement decision.

The [ADAPT] markers indicate fields where institution-specific information is needed. Institutions should customize the questionnaire header, instruction language, and any provisions that reflect institution-specific requirements before sending to vendors.

AI VENDOR DUE DILIGENCE QUESTIONNAIRE

[INSTITUTION NAME] — AI GOVERNANCE PROGRAM

Questionnaire Reference Number: [ADAPT — assign for tracking] **Date Issued:** ___________ **Response Deadline:** ___________ **Issued By:** [ADAPT — procurement contact name and contact information] **Purpose:** Pre-procurement assessment for [ADAPT — describe proposed AI system and use case]

Instructions for Vendors

[Institution Name] is conducting due diligence on your AI system and your organization's AI governance practices in connection with a proposed procurement. This questionnaire is a formal information request that forms part of our procurement and governance review process.

Please respond to all questions that apply to your AI system and organization. Where a question does not apply, indicate "Not applicable" and briefly explain why. Where you do not have information to respond to a question, indicate that directly rather than leaving it blank or providing a general answer — we will follow up as needed.

Please provide supporting documentation where indicated. Documentation should be current — generally dated within the past twelve months unless historical documentation is specifically requested.

Your responses will be reviewed by [Institution Name]'s procurement, legal, and governance functions. We may request follow-up information or meetings to discuss specific responses. We will treat your responses as confidential within our procurement and governance functions, subject to our legal obligations including potential disclosure obligations in litigation or regulatory proceedings.

Incomplete or vague responses will delay review and may result in the procurement being declined or deferred. We understand that some information may be proprietary; where you cannot provide specific information for proprietary reasons, explain what you can share and what you cannot and why.

Please return completed questionnaire and supporting documentation to: [ADAPT — specify submission address/portal/email]

Questions about this questionnaire: [ADAPT — procurement contact]

Section 1: AI System Performance and Validation

This section assesses how well your AI system performs and how that performance has been documented and validated. We are looking for specific, documented evidence of performance — not general capability claims.

1.1 System overview

Field	Response
Product name	

Field	Response
Current version or model	
Date of most recent significant update	
Brief description of what the system does	
Primary use cases for which the system is designed	
Use cases for which the system is NOT designed and should NOT be used	

1.2 Performance metrics

Provide documented performance metrics for your AI system. For each metric, specify: the metric itself, the value achieved, the evaluation dataset used, the date of evaluation, and who conducted the evaluation.

Performance metric	Value	Evaluation dataset	Evaluation date	Evaluated by

Supporting documentation required: Please attach your most recent performance evaluation report or technical documentation containing performance metrics.

1.3 Evaluation methodology

Question	Response
Describe the methodology used to evaluate system performance	
Was evaluation data independent from training data? How was independence verified?	
What was the composition of the evaluation dataset (source, time period, demographics represented)?	
Does evaluation performance reflect performance in real-world deployment? If not, explain differences	

Question	Response
Are performance claims auditable by customers? If yes, describe how	

1.4 Performance in contexts similar to the proposed use

Question	Response
Has this system been used in contexts similar to the proposed use at [Institution Name]?	☐ Yes ☐ No
If yes, describe those contexts and provide available performance data	
Has the system been evaluated on data similar in characteristics to what [Institution Name] would use?	☐ Yes ☐ No ☐ Not yet
If yes, provide that evaluation data. If no, are you willing to conduct evaluation on representative sample data?	
What performance variability can [Institution Name] expect across different input types or populations?	

1.5 Bias and fairness testing

Question	Response
Has this AI system been tested for differential performance across demographic groups?	☐ Yes ☐ No
If yes, which demographic groups were assessed?	
What methodology was used to assess differential performance?	
What were the findings for each demographic group tested? Provide specific metrics, not summary characterizations	
Were any demographic groups found to have meaningfully different performance? If yes, describe the differentials and what was done in response	

Question	Response
Is demographic performance data available for the specific use case [Institution Name] is proposing?	
How frequently is bias testing conducted and when was the most recent assessment?	

Supporting documentation required: Please attach bias and fairness testing documentation, including the specific metrics for each demographic group tested.

If your system has not been tested for demographic performance differentials, explain why and describe what testing you plan to conduct and when.

1.6 Known limitations and failure modes

Question	Response
What are the known limitations of this AI system?	
What types of inputs or use cases is the system less reliable for?	
What failure modes have been identified through testing or deployment?	
Are there input types or populations for which the system performs significantly worse?	
What does the system do when it encounters inputs it was not designed to handle?	
What error types are most common and what are their typical consequences?	

1.7 Confidence and calibration

Question	Response
Does the system provide confidence scores or probability estimates with its outputs?	☐ Yes ☐ No
If yes, are these scores calibrated — i.e., do they accurately reflect actual reliability rates?	
Provide calibration documentation or describe calibration methodology	
Is there evidence that users over-rely on system outputs? If yes, how is this addressed?	

Section 2: Data Governance and Privacy Practices

This section assesses how your organization handles the data that customers provide to and through your AI system. These questions are critical for our compliance with applicable data protection law.

2.1 Data collection and processing

Question	Response
What categories of data does this AI system collect from users?	
What categories of data does the system collect passively (usage patterns, metadata, inferences)?	
For each data category collected: what is it used for?	
Where is customer data stored (country/jurisdiction)?	
Is customer data processed or stored by any third parties (subprocessors)?	☐ Yes ☐ No
If yes, list all subprocessors that may process customer data, their locations, and their functions	

Supporting documentation required: Please attach your data processing documentation or privacy policy specific to this product.

2.2 Training data use

Question	Response
Is customer data used to train, fine-tune, or otherwise improve your AI models?	☐ Yes ☐ No ☐ Depends on configuration
If yes, describe what data is used and how	
Can customers opt out of having their data used for training?	☐ Yes ☐ No ☐ Opt-out is default
If opt-out is available, describe the mechanism and its effectiveness	
If customer data is used for training, how is it protected from exposure to other customers?	
Has customer data ever been accidentally incorporated into model outputs accessible to other customers?	☐ Yes ☐ No ☐ Unknown
If yes, describe what occurred and how it was addressed	

2.3 Data retention and deletion

Question	Response
How long do you retain customer data (inputs, outputs, logs)?	
What triggers deletion of customer data?	
Upon contract termination, what happens to customer data?	
What is your timeline for data deletion upon customer request or contract termination?	
Do you provide certification of deletion?	☐ Yes ☐ No
Are there any categories of customer data that cannot be fully deleted? If yes, describe	

Question	Response
How do you handle data deletion requests where data has been used in model training?	

2.4 Sensitive data handling

Question	Response
Does your system have specific capabilities or safeguards for handling health information?	☐ Yes ☐ No ☐ Not applicable
Are you able to execute HIPAA Business Associate Agreements?	☐ Yes ☐ No ☐ Depends on configuration
Does your system have specific capabilities or safeguards for data about minors?	☐ Yes ☐ No
Does your system have specific capabilities or safeguards for other sensitive data categories (financial, biometric, legally protected characteristics)?	
Describe any technical controls that prevent staff from accessing customer personal data	

2.5 Data processing agreements

Question	Response
Do you execute data processing agreements with customers?	☐ Yes ☐ No
Is your standard DPA available for review? Please attach or provide a link	
Are DPA terms negotiable?	☐ Yes ☐ No ☐ Limited
Do your DPA terms extend equivalent obligations to subprocessors?	☐ Yes ☐ No

Question	Response
Do you maintain records of data processing activities as required under applicable data protection law?	☐ Yes ☐ No

2.6 Data subject rights

Question	Response
Can you support data subject rights requests (access, correction, deletion, portability) for data processed by your system?	☐ Yes ☐ No ☐ Partially
Describe your process for responding to data subject rights requests received through your customers	
Can you identify and provide data about a specific individual upon request?	☐ Yes ☐ No
What is your response time commitment for data subject rights requests?	

Section 3: Security

This section assesses your organization's security practices for protecting customer data and the integrity of your AI system.

3.1 Security certifications and standards

Question	Response
What security certifications does your organization hold?	
SOC 2 Type II report: available? Current? Please provide or describe scope	
ISO 27001 certification: current?	☐ Yes ☐ No

Question	Response
Other relevant certifications (e.g., FedRAMP, HITRUST, PCI-DSS): specify	
Date of most recent security assessment by a qualified third party	

Supporting documentation required: Please provide your most recent SOC 2 Type II report or equivalent security assessment documentation.

3.2 Data security practices

Question	Response
How is customer data encrypted in transit?	
How is customer data encrypted at rest?	
What access controls limit which of your staff can access customer data?	
Is customer data access logged? Are logs reviewed?	
Is customer data logically separated from other customers' data?	
Describe your network security architecture at a high level	
What controls prevent unauthorized external access to customer data?	

3.3 AI-specific security

Question	Response
Has your AI system been tested for adversarial vulnerabilities (adversarial inputs that cause incorrect outputs)?	☐ Yes ☐ No
If yes, what vulnerabilities were found and how were they addressed?	

Question	Response
Has your system been tested for prompt injection vulnerabilities?	☐ Yes ☐ No ☐ Not applicable
If yes, describe findings and mitigations	
Has your system been tested for model inversion or membership inference vulnerabilities (ability to extract training data)?	☐ Yes ☐ No
What measures protect against data poisoning of your AI models?	
Describe any AI-specific security testing your organization conducts	

3.4 Security incident history

Question	Response
Have you experienced any security incidents affecting customer data in the past three years?	☐ Yes ☐ No
If yes, describe each incident including: nature of incident, data affected, date, how discovered, how resolved, and customer notification	
Have you experienced any security incidents specifically affecting your AI systems (model compromise, adversarial attacks, unauthorized access to AI infrastructure) in the past three years?	☐ Yes ☐ No
If yes, describe each incident	

3.5 Breach notification

Question	Response
What is your breach notification policy?	
What is your committed timeline for notifying customers of a security incident?	

Question	Response
What information do you provide in breach notifications?	
Have you ever failed to notify a customer of a security incident within applicable legal timeframes?	☐ Yes ☐ No
If yes, describe the circumstances	
Will you commit to breach notification within 72 hours of discovery in your contract with us?	☐ Yes ☐ No ☐ Open to negotiation

3.6 Vulnerability management

Question	Response
How frequently do you conduct security vulnerability assessments?	
What is your process for addressing identified vulnerabilities?	
What is your typical timeline from vulnerability identification to remediation for critical vulnerabilities?	
Do you have a responsible disclosure / bug bounty program?	☐ Yes ☐ No

Section 4: Transparency and Explainability

This section assesses whether your AI system can explain its outputs sufficiently for institutional governance and for meeting obligations to people affected by AI-assisted decisions.

4.1 Explainability capabilities

Question	Response
Can your AI system explain the basis for individual outputs — i.e., what factors influenced a specific recommendation or decision?	☐ Yes ☐ No ☐ Partially
If yes, describe the explanation format and what it conveys	
Are explanations understandable by non-technical users?	☐ Yes ☐ No ☐ With translation
Are explanations technically accurate — do they reflect what the model actually computed?	
What are the limitations of the explanations your system provides?	
For automated decision systems: can you produce explanations adequate to meet adverse action notice requirements?	☐ Yes ☐ No ☐ Not applicable

---

4.2 System documentation

Question	Response
Do you provide documentation describing how your AI system works?	☐ Yes ☐ No
Please provide or attach product technical documentation	
Does your documentation describe: training data characteristics?	☐ Yes ☐ No
Does your documentation describe: known limitations and failure modes?	☐ Yes ☐ No
Does your documentation describe: intended use cases and use cases to avoid?	☐ Yes ☐ No
Does your documentation describe: performance across demographic groups?	☐ Yes ☐ No
How frequently is documentation updated?	

4.3 System changes and updates

Question	Response
How do you notify customers of material changes to your AI system?	
What counts as a "material change" that triggers customer notification?	
What advance notice do you provide before deploying material changes?	
Do customers have any control over when updates are applied to their instance?	☐ Yes ☐ No
Can customers maintain a previous version of the system if an update creates governance concerns?	☐ Yes ☐ No
Do you provide release notes or change logs? If yes, please provide an example	
Have material changes to your system ever significantly altered its performance characteristics? If yes, describe	

4.4 Audit and inspection rights

Question	Response
Will you grant customers the right to audit system performance using their own data and methods?	☐ Yes ☐ No ☐ Open to negotiation
Describe what an audit process would look like — what access is provided, what methodology customers can use, what the vendor provides in support	
Will you participate in customer-commissioned third-party audits?	☐ Yes ☐ No ☐ Open to negotiation
Are there limitations on audit scope that you require? If yes, describe	
Have you undergone third-party audits of your AI system? If yes, can you share those audit reports (or summaries)?	

Section 5: Vendor AI Governance Practices

This section assesses how your organization governs the AI systems it develops and provides. We are assessing whether you have the governance practices that would make you a responsible partner in our AI governance program.

5.1 Responsible AI framework

Question	Response
Does your organization have a published responsible AI or AI ethics framework?	☐ Yes ☐ No
If yes, please provide a link or attach	
Who in your organization is responsible for AI governance? (title, not name)	
Does your organization have a dedicated AI safety, ethics, or governance team?	☐ Yes ☐ No
How are AI governance principles operationalized in your development and deployment practices? Provide specific examples, not general statements	

5.2 AI development practices

Question	Response
Describe your process for assessing bias and fairness before releasing a new AI system or significant update	
Describe your process for safety testing before release	
Do you conduct red-team testing or adversarial testing as part of your development process?	☐ Yes ☐ No
If yes, describe the process	
Do you have a process for customers to report AI performance concerns?	☐ Yes ☐ No

Question	Response
If yes, describe the process and typical response timeframes	
Describe how you respond when customers identify bias or performance problems in deployed systems	

5.3 Incident history — AI performance

Question	Response
Have there been significant AI performance failures in this system in the past three years?	☐ Yes ☐ No
If yes, describe each failure, its scope, how it was discovered, and how it was addressed	
Have bias or discrimination concerns been identified in this system by customers, researchers, or regulators?	☐ Yes ☐ No
If yes, describe the concerns and your response	
Has this system been the subject of regulatory investigation, enforcement action, or litigation?	☐ Yes ☐ No
If yes, describe the circumstances and outcome	

5.4 Regulatory compliance

Question	Response
What AI-specific regulatory frameworks does your organization comply with?	
How do you monitor for AI regulatory developments in the jurisdictions where your customers operate?	
If new AI regulations require changes to your system, what is your process for making those changes and notifying customers?	
Have you conducted an EU AI Act conformity assessment for this system?	☐ Yes ☐ No ☐ In progress ☐ Not applicable

Question	Response
If yes, what risk classification was assigned and what were the findings?	
What is your approach to compliance with Article 22 of GDPR (automated decision-making)?	

5.5 Customer support for governance

Question	Response
Do you provide specific support for customers' AI governance programs?	☐ Yes ☐ No
If yes, describe what governance support you offer	
Is there a designated contact for governance-related inquiries from customers?	☐ Yes ☐ No
What is the typical response time for governance-related inquiries?	
Do you provide performance reporting to customers on an ongoing basis?	☐ Yes ☐ No
If yes, describe what reporting is provided, in what format, and at what frequency	
Do you provide customers with monitoring data or tools to monitor AI system performance?	☐ Yes ☐ No

---

Section 6: Contractual Terms and Commitments

This section identifies your position on key contractual terms relevant to AI governance. We are not asking you to execute these terms here — we are gathering information about your contractual flexibility to inform our negotiations.

6.1 Performance standards

Question	Response
Will you commit to specific performance standards in a contract?	☐ Yes ☐ No ☐ Open to negotiation
If yes, what performance standards are you willing to commit to?	
What are the contractual consequences if performance falls below committed standards?	
Will you commit to specific performance standards for demographic groups (e.g., no performance differential exceeding a defined threshold)?	☐ Yes ☐ No ☐ Open to negotiation

---

6.2 Data handling contractual commitments

Question	Response
Will you contractually commit to not using customer data for model training without explicit customer consent?	☐ Yes ☐ No ☐ Open to negotiation
Will you contractually commit to data deletion within a specified timeframe upon contract termination?	☐ Yes ☐ No ☐ Open to negotiation
Will you provide written certification of data deletion?	☐ Yes ☐ No
Will you contractually limit subprocessor access to customer data to those disclosed in the agreement?	☐ Yes ☐ No ☐ Open to negotiation
Will you notify customers before adding new subprocessors who will have access to their data?	☐ Yes ☐ No ☐ Open to negotiation

---

6.3 Audit and transparency commitments

Question	Response
Will you contractually commit to audit rights — allowing customer-initiated performance assessment?	☐ Yes ☐ No ☐ Open to negotiation
If yes, describe the audit rights you are willing to commit to	
Will you contractually commit to providing advance notice of material system changes?	☐ Yes ☐ No ☐ Open to negotiation
If yes, what notice period?	
Will you contractually commit to breach notification within 72 hours of discovery?	☐ Yes ☐ No ☐ Open to negotiation

6.4 Liability and indemnification

Question	Response
What limitations on liability does your standard contract include?	
Are you willing to accept liability for harm resulting from inaccurate performance representations?	☐ Yes ☐ No ☐ Open to negotiation
Are you willing to provide indemnification for claims arising from AI system bias or discrimination?	☐ Yes ☐ No ☐ Open to negotiation
What warranty, if any, do you provide regarding AI system performance?	

6.5 Exit provisions

Question	Response
What are the terms for early termination of your contracts?	
Do you charge early termination fees? If yes, describe	
Are auto-renewal provisions in your standard contracts? If yes, describe notice requirements	

Question	Response
What transition support do you provide when a customer ends the relationship?	
Do you export customer data in portable formats upon request? What formats?	
What is your timeline for providing customer data export upon termination request?	

6.6 Governing law and dispute resolution

Question	Response
What governing law does your standard contract specify?	
What dispute resolution process does your standard contract specify?	
Are you open to negotiating governing law and dispute resolution provisions?	☐ Yes ☐ No ☐ Limited

---

Section 7: Ongoing Relationship Management

This section assesses what the ongoing vendor relationship will look like from a governance perspective.

7.1 Customer support and engagement

Question	Response
What customer support do you provide? Describe tiers and response time commitments	
Is there a dedicated account manager for customers of our expected contract size?	☐ Yes ☐ No

Question	Response
How are governance-related inquiries handled — through the same support channel as technical issues?	
What is the escalation path if a customer's governance concern is not resolved at the account level?	
Are executive or governance-level contacts accessible to customers for significant concerns?	☐ Yes ☐ No

7.2 Ongoing performance monitoring

Question	Response
Do you proactively monitor deployed systems for performance degradation or fairness issues?	☐ Yes ☐ No
If yes, describe your monitoring approach and what you monitor for	
How do you notify customers if monitoring reveals performance concerns with their deployment?	
Do you share aggregate performance data from deployed instances with customers?	☐ Yes ☐ No
Have you ever proactively notified customers of performance concerns before they were raised by the customer?	☐ Yes ☐ No
If yes, describe an example	

7.3 System improvement and roadmap

Question	Response
How frequently do you update your AI system?	
Do customers have input into the product roadmap?	☐ Yes ☐ No
How do you incorporate customer feedback about AI system limitations or failures?	

Question	Response
Are there known limitations of the current system that you are working to address? If yes, describe and provide expected timeline	
What is your approach to providing backward compatibility when significant system changes occur?	

7.4 Reference customers

Question	Response
Can you provide references from customers using this system in contexts similar to our proposed use?	☐ Yes ☐ No
Please provide contact information for three reference customers:	
Reference 1: Organization, contact name and title, contact information, how long they have used this system	
Reference 2: Organization, contact name and title, contact information, how long they have used this system	
Reference 3: Organization, contact name and title, contact information, how long they have used this system	
Are there customers who have stopped using this system? If yes, can you explain why (without identifying the customers if they prefer confidentiality)?	

Section 8: Organization and Financial Stability

This section assesses whether your organization has the stability, capacity, and commitment to be a reliable long-term governance partner.

8.1 Organization overview

Question	Response
Organization type (public company, private company, nonprofit, subsidiary, etc.)	
Year founded	
Headquarters location	
Number of employees	
Number of customers for this specific AI product	
Approximate annual revenue (or revenue range)	
Is the organization profitable or on a funded runway?	

8.2 Financial stability

Question	Response
Have there been significant changes in organizational leadership, ownership, or financial condition in the past two years?	☐ Yes ☐ No
If yes, describe	
Are there pending legal proceedings, regulatory investigations, or other matters that could materially affect your ability to continue serving customers?	☐ Yes ☐ No
If yes, describe to the extent you are able	
Is the organization actively seeking acquisition or considering a business model change that would affect this product?	☐ Yes ☐ No ☐ Cannot disclose

8.3 AI-specific organizational capacity

Question	Response
How many employees work specifically on this AI product?	
Does your organization have dedicated AI safety or governance staff? If yes, approximately how many?	
What is your organization's AI research and development investment (as a percentage of revenue or in absolute terms)?	

Question	Response
Is this AI product a core product for your organization, or a secondary offering?	
What is your long-term commitment to maintaining and improving this product?	

Section 9: Attestations

The following attestations should be made by an authorized representative of your organization with knowledge of the matters attested to.

Please attest to each of the following by checking the box and having an authorized representative sign below:

☐ The information provided in this questionnaire is accurate and complete to the best of our knowledge as of the date of this response.

☐ We will notify [Institution Name] promptly if, following submission of this questionnaire, we become aware of information that would materially change any of our responses.

☐ We will notify [Institution Name] of material changes to our AI system in accordance with the notification practices described in Section 4.3 of this questionnaire.

☐ We have not omitted material information about security incidents, performance failures, bias findings, regulatory actions, or litigation affecting our AI system.

☐ We understand that [Institution Name] will rely on the accuracy of our responses in making its procurement decision, and that material inaccuracies may result in termination of any contract entered into in reliance on these responses.

Completed by:

Field	Response
Name	
Title	
Email	
Phone	
Organization	
Date	
Signature	

Supporting Documentation Checklist

Please confirm which supporting documents you are providing with this questionnaire response:

Performance documentation: ☐ Performance evaluation report with specific metrics ☐ Bias and fairness testing documentation with demographic group data ☐ Third-party audit reports (or summaries) ☐ Technical documentation describing system architecture and training approach

Data and privacy documentation: ☐ Privacy policy for this product ☐ Data processing documentation ☐ Standard data processing agreement (DPA) ☐ Subprocessor list ☐ HIPAA Business Associate Agreement (if applicable)

Security documentation: ☐ SOC 2 Type II report (or equivalent) ☐ Security certifications ☐ Penetration testing summary (current year)

Governance documentation: ☐ Responsible AI / AI ethics framework ☐ EU AI Act conformity assessment (if applicable) ☐ Product documentation including limitations and appropriate use cases

Contractual documentation: ☐ Standard master services agreement or equivalent ☐ Standard order form or equivalent

Other documentation provided:

____

____

For Internal Use: Vendor Assessment Scoring and Notes

The following section is for [Institution Name] procurement, compliance, and governance team internal use. Do not return to vendor.

Assessment conducted by:

Reviewer Function Date

Section-by-section assessment summary:

For each section, record: overall assessment (Satisfactory / Concerns / Significant Concerns / Unsatisfactory), key findings, and questions requiring follow-up.

Section	Assessment	Key findings	Follow-up required
1. Performance and Validation			
2. Data Governance and Privacy			
3. Security			
4. Transparency and Explainability			
5. Vendor Governance Practices			

Section	Assessment	Key findings	Follow-up required
6. Contractual Terms			
7. Ongoing Relationship			
8. Organization and Stability			

Red flags identified:

Red flag	Section reference	Severity	Proposed response

Documentation gaps — required documentation not provided:

____
____

Follow-up questions for vendor:

____
____

Contract negotiation priorities based on assessment:

____
____

Overall vendor assessment:

☐ Recommended to proceed — vendor meets governance requirements
☐ Proceed with conditions — describe conditions:

___ ☐ Proceed with caution — significant concerns identified, describe:

___ ☐ Do not recommend — describe disqualifying concerns:

___

Assessment approved by: ______________________________
Date: ___________

Notes on interpreting vendor responses

The quality of a vendor's responses to this questionnaire is itself governance information. The following patterns in vendor responses warrant specific attention during assessment.

Responses that substitute generality for specificity — claims such as "we are committed to responsible AI" or "our system is designed with fairness in mind" without specific metrics, processes, or documentation to support those claims — indicate that the vendor either does not have specific information to provide or is not willing to provide it. Either situation is a governance concern. Push for specificity: when a vendor says their system has been tested for bias, ask for the specific metrics, the specific demographic groups tested, and the specific evaluation methodology.

Consistent "unknown" responses regarding what the system does with customer data, how data is retained, and whether data is used for training are not acceptable for any AI system that processes personal information. Vendors who do not know what their products do with customer data do not have adequate data governance practices, and institutions should not entrust them with sensitive information.

Reluctance to commit contractually to positions stated verbally is a significant red flag. Vendors who assert during sales conversations that they do not use customer data for training, that they will provide audit access, that they will notify customers of material changes — but who will not put those commitments in a contract — are not making commitments; they are making representations that have no legal force. Governance requires contractual commitments, not verbal assurances.

Incident history gaps — vendors who report no security incidents, no performance failures, no bias findings, and no customer complaints over multiple years of operating a widely deployed AI system — are either genuinely exceptional or are not monitoring adequately or disclosing honestly. Ask follow-up questions that make honest disclosure of past issues easy: frame questions as seeking to understand how the vendor responded to challenges rather than whether challenges occurred.

Evasiveness about training data for AI models is increasingly a governance concern. Vendors who cannot describe the characteristics of their training data — its composition, its time period, its known limitations — cannot adequately assess or represent the fairness and performance characteristics of their systems. This evasiveness may reflect proprietary concerns, but it may also reflect inadequate documentation practices that themselves indicate governance gaps.

Chapter 27: Testing and Review Checklist

How to use this checklist

The testing and review checklist is the governance instrument that confirms an AI system is ready for deployment. It translates the pre-deployment testing requirements described in Chapter 14 and the oversight design requirements described in Chapter 13 into a structured sequence of verifications that must be completed — and documented — before any AI system goes live in institutional operations.

This checklist is not a box-ticking exercise. Each item represents a genuine governance verification: a check that something has been done, done adequately, and documented in a form that supports accountability. Items that cannot be checked because the work has not been done are not items to be skipped — they are deployment blockers. An AI system that proceeds to deployment with unchecked items on this checklist has not completed pre-deployment governance. It has proceeded without governance, with a record that makes that non-governance visible.

The checklist is organized into ten sections that follow the sequence of pre-deployment governance work: system understanding, data governance, performance testing, bias and fairness testing, robustness and reliability testing, safety testing, security testing, oversight and workflow verification, operational readiness, and final governance authorization. Each section includes items with space for documentation of completion, responsible party, date, and notes. A final section records the deployment decision and its authorization.

The checklist is designed to be completed by the team responsible for pre-deployment review — typically a combination of the AI governance coordinator, the operational function proposing the deployment, IT and information security, legal counsel, and where relevant clinical or domain experts. Different sections of the checklist may be completed by different functions, with the governance coordinator responsible for ensuring that all sections are completed and that the completed checklist is reviewed by the governance team before deployment authorization is granted.

Risk-level adaptation: This checklist is comprehensive — it covers all dimensions of pre-deployment review for medium- and high-risk AI systems. For low-risk systems, institutions may use an abbreviated version that focuses on the highest-priority items in each section. The items marked [HIGH RISK] are specifically required for high-risk deployments and may be omitted for low-risk systems with documented governance team justification. Items not marked are required for all deployments regardless of risk level.

Institutions should adapt this checklist to their specific context, regulatory requirements, and governance architecture. [ADAPT] markers indicate fields requiring institution-specific information.

AI PRE-DEPLOYMENT TESTING AND REVIEW CHECKLIST

[INSTITUTION NAME] — AI GOVERNANCE PROGRAM

Checklist Header

Field	Response
AI system name	
Vendor	
Version / model being deployed	
Intake submission reference number	
Proposed deployment scope	
Proposed go-live date	
Risk level (from intake assessment)	☐ Low ☐ Medium ☐ High
Checklist completion lead	
Checklist start date	

How to complete this checklist

For each item:

Status: Mark one of: ✓ Complete | ✗ Not complete — deployment blocked | N/A — with justification | Deferred — with governance team approval

Responsible party: The role or name of the person who completed or verified this item.

Date: Date the item was completed or verified.

Evidence / notes: Brief description of what was done, what was found, and where supporting documentation is located. "Evidence" does not mean a generic reference to work having occurred — it means a specific pointer to documentation that a reviewer could examine to verify the work.

Items marked ✗ Not complete are deployment blockers and must be resolved before the deployment authorization section is completed. Items cannot be deferred without explicit governance team approval, which must be documented.

Section 1: System Understanding and Baseline Documentation

Before testing can be meaningful, the governance team must understand what system is being tested, what it is supposed to do, what its documented capabilities and limitations are, and what the institution's governance requirements for it are. This section verifies that foundational understanding is in place.

1.1 The AI system's function, inputs, outputs, and intended use case are documented and consistent with the approved intake submission.

Status Responsible party Date Evidence / notes

1.2 The vendor's product documentation has been reviewed, including: system description, intended use cases, use cases the system is NOT designed for, known limitations, and applicable performance documentation.

Status Responsible party Date Evidence / notes

Document location: ________________________________

1.3 The governance requirements that apply to this deployment have been identified and documented: what testing standards must be met, what oversight arrangements are required, what monitoring must be in place, and what conditions the intake approval specified.

Status Responsible party Date Evidence / notes

Conditions from intake approval:

____

1.4 Minimum acceptable performance thresholds for this deployment have been defined and documented in advance of testing. These thresholds reflect the governance requirements for this use case — not merely whatever performance the system happens to achieve.

Status Responsible party Date Evidence / notes

Defined thresholds: ________________________________

Note: Thresholds must be set before testing results are known. Post-hoc threshold setting — defining "acceptable" as whatever the system achieved — is not governance-adequate.

1.5 The people and populations that will be affected by this AI system have been identified, including any vulnerable groups, and their characteristics have been documented to inform testing design.

Status Responsible party Date Evidence / notes

1.6 [HIGH RISK] A test plan has been developed, reviewed, and approved by the governance team before testing began. The test plan specifies: what will be tested, what datasets will be used, who will conduct each testing component, what success criteria apply, and how findings will be documented.

Status Responsible party Date Evidence / notes

Test plan document location:

____

Section 2: Data Governance Verification

AI systems are only as reliable as the data they process. This section verifies that data governance requirements are in place before deployment and that testing used representative, appropriate data.

2.1 The categories of data this system will process in deployment have been documented and verified against the intake submission. No data categories beyond those reviewed at intake will be processed without additional governance review.

Status Responsible party Date Evidence / notes

2.2 A data processing agreement with the vendor is executed, current, and has been reviewed by legal counsel for adequacy. The DPA addresses: data use limitations, training data use restrictions, retention and deletion, subprocessors, and breach notification.

Status Responsible party Date Evidence / notes

DPA execution date: _______ Legal review date: _______ DPA document location: ___________

2.3 For healthcare deployments: A HIPAA Business Associate Agreement is executed with the vendor and has been reviewed by legal counsel.

☐ Applicable ☐ Not applicable — reason: ___________________________

Status Responsible party Date Evidence / notes

2.4 The legal basis for processing personal information in this AI system has been identified, documented, and confirmed as adequate by legal counsel.

☐ Applicable — legal basis: ____________________ ☐ No personal information processed

Status Responsible party Date Evidence / notes

2.5 Staff have been briefed on data governance requirements for this system: what information may and may not be entered, minimum necessary principles, and consequences of inappropriate data entry.

Status Responsible party Date Evidence / notes

2.6 The test dataset used for pre-deployment testing has been validated as: representative of the deployment population, independent from training data (no data leakage), and adequate in size to support meaningful performance assessment.

Status Responsible party Date Evidence / notes

Dataset characteristics:

____

Independence verification method:

____

2.7 The vendor's practices regarding use of institutional data for model training have been reviewed and documented. If the vendor uses or may use institutional data for training, the institution has made an explicit, governance-reviewed decision about whether this is acceptable.

Status Responsible party Date Evidence / notes

Vendor training data use practice:

____

Institution's decision: ☐ Acceptable ☐ Opted out ☐ Contractually prohibited ☐ Not applicable

---

2.8 [HIGH RISK] For systems processing sensitive information: additional legal review has confirmed compliance with applicable law (HIPAA, FERPA, COPPA, state privacy laws, sector-specific regulations) and any required additional safeguards are in place.

☐ Applicable — specify relevant frameworks: ______________________ ☐ Not applicable

Status Responsible party Date Evidence / notes

Section 3: Accuracy and Performance Testing

This section verifies that the AI system meets the minimum performance thresholds defined for this deployment.

3.1 Accuracy testing has been conducted on a test dataset representative of the deployment context. Testing was not conducted on training data or data known to the model.

Status Responsible party Date Evidence / notes

Testing conducted by: ________________________________

3.2 Performance metrics have been calculated and documented for all metrics identified in the test plan. Results are compared against pre-defined minimum thresholds.

Performance metric Result Threshold ☐ Met / ✗ Not met

Testing documentation location: ____

3.3 Performance results have been compared against: vendor performance claims (verifying that institutional testing is consistent with vendor representations), pre-AI baseline (verifying that AI provides meaningful improvement), and human performance baseline where applicable.

Comparison	Finding	Consistent with governance requirements?
vs. vendor claims		☐ Yes ☐ No — describe discrepancy
vs. pre-AI baseline		☐ Yes ☐ No ☐ N/A
vs. human baseline		☐ Yes ☐ No ☐ N/A

3.4 Confidence calibration has been assessed: expressed confidence scores accurately reflect actual reliability rates, and overconfidence patterns have been identified and documented.

☐ Applicable — system provides confidence scores ☐ Not applicable — system does not provide confidence scores

Status Responsible party Date Evidence / notes

Calibration finding: ____

3.5 Output consistency has been tested: equivalent inputs produce consistent outputs, and sensitivity to superficial input variations is within acceptable bounds.

Status Responsible party Date Evidence / notes

Consistency findings:

____

3.6 [HIGH RISK] For generative AI systems: hallucination rate assessment has been conducted for the specific output types and use cases this system will be used for. Findings have informed verification requirements and oversight design.

☐ Applicable — system is generative AI ☐ Not applicable

Status Responsible party Date Evidence / notes

Hallucination assessment findings:

____

Verification requirements established:

____

3.7 For systems that did not meet minimum performance thresholds on any metric: the governance team has reviewed the finding, assessed whether deployment is appropriate with enhanced oversight or other conditions, and documented its decision.

☐ All thresholds met — this item not applicable ☐ One or more thresholds not met — governance team decision required

Status Responsible party Date Evidence / notes

Governance team decision and rationale: ____

Section 4: Bias and Fairness Testing

This section verifies that the AI system has been assessed for differential performance across demographic groups and that the findings are within acceptable bounds or are addressed through governance measures.

4.1 The demographic groups to be assessed in bias testing have been defined in advance, based on: the groups most relevant to anti-discrimination requirements, the groups that could be most affected by differential performance, and the groups for which adequate test data is available.

Status Responsible party Date Evidence / notes

Groups assessed: ____

Groups not assessed and reason (sample size, data availability): ____________________________

4.2 Acceptable differential performance thresholds have been defined in advance of testing, with legal counsel input where anti-discrimination law is relevant.

Status Responsible party Date Evidence / notes

Acceptable differential threshold:

____

Legal counsel reviewed threshold: ☐ Yes ☐ No ☐ Not applicable

4.3 Bias and fairness testing has been conducted for all groups identified in item 4.1. Results include statistical significance assessment alongside magnitude of differentials.

Demographic group	Performance metric	Group result	Overall result	Differential	Statistically significant?	Within threshold?

Testing documentation location:

____

4.4 Vendor-provided bias testing documentation has been reviewed and compared against institutional testing results. Any significant discrepancies have been investigated and documented.

Status Responsible party Date Evidence / notes

Vendor documentation reviewed: ☐ Yes ☐ No — reason:

____

Discrepancies identified: ☐ None ☐ Yes — describe:

____

4.5 For demographic groups where testing revealed differentials exceeding defined thresholds: the governance team has reviewed findings, assessed implications, and documented its decision on how to proceed, including any additional oversight or monitoring requirements.

☐ No differentials exceeded thresholds — this item not applicable ☐ One or more differentials exceeded thresholds — governance team decision required

Status Responsible party Date Evidence / notes

Governance team decision and rationale:

____

4.6 For groups where sample sizes were insufficient for statistically meaningful bias testing: the governance team has acknowledged this limitation, documented it, and established compensating governance measures (more conservative oversight, specific monitoring for these groups, or other measures).

☐ All groups had adequate sample sizes — this item not applicable ☐ Some groups had inadequate sample sizes

Status Responsible party Date Evidence / notes

Groups with inadequate sample sizes and compensating measures:

____

4.7 [HIGH RISK] Intersectional bias testing — assessing performance across combinations of demographic characteristics — has been conducted where sample sizes permit, and findings have been reviewed.

☐ Applicable ☐ Not applicable — reason: ______________________________

Status Responsible party Date Evidence / notes

4.8 Monitoring for differential performance across demographic groups has been designed into the ongoing monitoring plan, with defined metrics, measurement frequency, and alert thresholds.

Status Responsible party Date Evidence / notes

Fairness monitoring plan location: ____

Section 5: Robustness and Reliability Testing

This section verifies that the AI system performs reliably under the range of conditions it will encounter in deployment, not only under optimal testing conditions.

5.1 Input variation testing has been conducted: the system has been tested with equivalent inputs expressed in different forms (rephrasing, different formats, minor variations) to assess output consistency. Findings have been documented.

Status Responsible party Date Evidence / notes

Consistency findings: ____

5.2 Edge case testing has been conducted: the system has been tested with inputs at the margins of its intended scope, unusual case types, and cases that combine features in uncommon ways. Findings and any performance limitations at the margins have been documented.

Status Responsible party Date Evidence / notes

Edge case findings: ____

5.3 Degraded input testing has been conducted: the system has been tested with inputs of the quality levels that may be encountered in real operational conditions — incomplete data, formatting variations, documentation inconsistencies — and findings documented.

Status Responsible party Date Evidence / notes

Findings with degraded inputs:

____

5.4 Temporal robustness has been assessed: the system has been tested on data from different time periods where available, and any performance variation over time has been documented and assessed for governance implications.

☐ Applicable — temporal data available ☐ Not applicable — reason:

____

Status Responsible party Date Evidence / notes

5.5 Distributional shift has been assessed: differences between the vendor's training/evaluation data distribution and the institution's deployment population have been identified, and their potential impact on performance has been assessed.

Status Responsible party Date Evidence / notes

Identified distributional differences:

____

Assessed impact on performance:

____

5.6 Performance drift monitoring has been designed: baseline performance metrics have been established and a monitoring plan is in place to detect performance degradation after deployment.

Status Responsible party Date Evidence / notes

Baseline performance established: ☐ Yes ☐ Will be established during staged deployment

Drift monitoring plan location:

____

Section 6: Safety Testing

This section verifies that the AI system has been assessed for potential harms in the specific deployment context and that safety safeguards are adequate.

6.1 Safety definition has been completed: the specific harms that could result from AI system failure in this deployment context have been documented, including physical, psychological, material, and dignitary harms, and the populations most vulnerable to those harms.

Status Responsible party Date Evidence / notes

Safety definition document location:

____

6.2 Failure mode testing has been conducted: the system has been specifically tested for the failure modes identified in the safety definition, with particular attention to the inputs and situations most likely to produce harmful outputs.

Status Responsible party Date Evidence / notes

Failure mode testing findings:

____

6.3 Minimum safety performance thresholds specific to this deployment context have been defined and tested against. Thresholds reflect the stakes of the use case, not generic performance standards.

Status Responsible party Date Evidence / notes

Safety thresholds defined:

____

Thresholds met: ☐ Yes ☐ No — governance decision required

6.4 [HIGH RISK] For systems deployed in direct interaction with people in vulnerable circumstances (clinical contexts, crisis support, child-serving contexts, mental health contexts): adversarial safety testing has been conducted, simulating the specific high-risk interaction types that could occur in the deployment context.

☐ Applicable ☐ Not applicable — reason:

____

Status Responsible party Date Evidence / notes

Adversarial safety testing findings:

____

6.5 [HIGH RISK] Human oversight-safety interaction testing has been conducted: human reviewers have been presented with AI outputs containing known safety-relevant errors to assess whether the oversight design reliably catches those errors. Automation bias mitigation has been tested.

☐ Applicable ☐ Not applicable — reason:

____

Status Responsible party Date Evidence / notes

Oversight-safety interaction findings:

____

6.6 Domain expert review has been conducted: qualified subject matter experts (clinical staff, social work professionals, educators, or other relevant experts) have reviewed AI outputs for professional appropriateness, not only technical accuracy.

☐ Required for this use case ☐ Not required — reason:

____

Status Responsible party Date Evidence / notes

Domain experts involved:

____

Domain expert findings:

____

6.7 For generative AI systems deployed in contexts where content appropriateness matters: content appropriateness testing has been conducted using realistic test inputs, including attempts to elicit inappropriate, harmful, or off-scope content.

☐ Applicable ☐ Not applicable

Status Responsible party Date Evidence / notes

Content testing findings:

____

Section 7: Security Testing

This section verifies that the AI system's security has been assessed and that deployment will not create unacceptable security risks.

7.1 IT information security assessment of this AI system has been completed. The assessment covered: vendor security practices, data transmission security, access controls, AI-specific security risks, and integration security.

Status Responsible party Date Evidence / notes

IT security assessment findings:

____

Assessment report location:

____

7.2 Access controls have been configured: only authorized staff with appropriate roles can access the AI system, and access is enforced technically rather than relying solely on policy compliance.

Status Responsible party Date Evidence / notes

Access control configuration:

____

7.3 For systems that process external content (documents, emails, web content): prompt injection vulnerability has been assessed and mitigations are in place.

☐ Applicable — system processes external content ☐ Not applicable

Status Responsible party Date Evidence / notes

Prompt injection assessment findings:

____

7.4 [HIGH RISK] For systems processing sensitive personal information: specific security testing has been conducted for data extraction and model inversion vulnerabilities.

☐ Applicable ☐ Not applicable

Status Responsible party Date Evidence / notes

Security testing findings:

____

7.5 Security vulnerabilities identified during assessment have been: disclosed to the vendor where applicable, remediated or mitigated, and residual risks documented and accepted by the appropriate governance authority.

☐ No significant security vulnerabilities identified ☐ Vulnerabilities identified — describe remediation

Status Responsible party Date Evidence / notes

Vulnerabilities and remediation status:

____

7.6 Vendor security review has been completed, including: review of vendor security certifications, review of vendor security incident history, and verification that vendor security practices meet institutional requirements.

Status Responsible party Date Evidence / notes

Vendor security assessment summary:

____

Section 8: Oversight and Workflow Verification

This section verifies that the human oversight design is adequate and that the workflow in which the AI system will operate has been tested and is ready.

8.1 The oversight design for this deployment has been documented: who reviews AI outputs, what information they have access to, what their review process is, what documentation is required, and what the escalation pathway is.

Status Responsible party Date Evidence / notes

Oversight design document location:

____

8.2 The oversight design has been assessed for adequacy: reviewers have access to the information they need, the presentation of AI outputs does not anchor reviewers before independent assessment, override authority is unrestricted and not procedurally burdensome, and volume requirements are consistent with genuine review.

Question	Assessment
Do reviewers see underlying information or only AI outputs?	
Is AI output presented before or after reviewer forms independent view?	

Question	Assessment
Are there procedural barriers to overriding AI recommendations?	
How many AI outputs will reviewers assess per hour? Is this consistent with genuine review?	
Is there a meaningful escalation pathway for uncertain cases?	

Status Responsible party Date Evidence / notes

8.3 The workflow integration has been tested in a realistic simulation or pilot: staff have used the system in conditions approximating real deployment, workflow gaps have been identified, and the integration has been refined based on that testing.

Status Responsible party Date Evidence / notes

Workflow testing findings and adjustments:

____

8.4 [HIGH RISK] Simulated oversight testing has been conducted: staff have been presented with AI outputs containing known errors to assess whether the oversight design reliably catches those errors under realistic conditions.

☐ Applicable ☐ Not applicable — reason:

____

Status Responsible party Date Evidence / notes

Oversight simulation findings:

____

8.5 Automation bias risk has been specifically addressed in the oversight design and will be addressed in staff training: staff understand what automation bias is, how it affects their role, and what practices reduce its impact.

Status Responsible party Date Evidence / notes

8.6 The documentation requirements for AI-assisted work have been defined and are operationally feasible: required documentation of AI use, AI outputs, and human review decisions can be maintained without impractical burden under realistic operational conditions.

Status Responsible party Date Evidence / notes

Documentation requirements:

____

8.7 For systems used in direct interaction with affected people: disclosure mechanisms have been tested and are in place. People interacting with or affected by the system will receive meaningful notification that AI is being used and how to request human review.

☐ Applicable ☐ Not applicable

Status Responsible party Date Evidence / notes

Disclosure mechanism and content:

____

Section 9: Operational Readiness

This section verifies that all operational preparations required for responsible deployment are complete.

9.1 Required staff training has been completed by all staff who will use this AI system before deployment. Training completion has been verified and documented — not only scheduled or planned, but confirmed.

Status Responsible party Date Evidence / notes

Training completed by: ___________ of ___________ required staff

Verification method:

____

9.2 Supervisors and operational leaders whose teams will use this system have received appropriate briefing on: what the system does, what governance requirements apply, how to monitor oversight quality, and how to receive and act on staff escalations.

Status Responsible party Date Evidence / notes

9.3 The escalation pathway for AI concerns is operational: staff know how to report concerns, the designated escalation recipient knows they are the designated recipient, and the escalation mechanism (form, channel) is accessible.

Status Responsible party Date Evidence / notes

Escalation pathway tested: ☐ Yes ☐ No — must be tested before deployment

Escalation pathway: ___________________________________

9.4 Fallback procedures are documented and operational: there is a defined, tested process for handling the work this AI system supports when the system is unavailable. Staff know the fallback procedures.

Status Responsible party Date Evidence / notes

Fallback procedure document location:

____

Fallback tested: ☐ Yes ☐ No — must be tested before deployment

---

9.5 Incident response readiness has been verified: the AI incident report template is accessible to staff, the AI governance coordinator knows that this system is being deployed, and incident response procedures for this specific system type are understood by relevant parties.

Status Responsible party Date Evidence / notes

9.6 Technical integration has been verified by IT: the AI system is correctly integrated with institutional systems, data flows are functioning as designed, access controls are in place and working, and the system is receiving inputs of the type and quality that testing used.

Status Responsible party Date Evidence / notes

IT integration sign-off: ___________________________ **Date:** ___________

9.7 Monitoring infrastructure is operational from day one: performance metrics collection is configured, reporting mechanisms are functioning, alert thresholds are set, and the persons responsible for reviewing monitoring data know they are responsible and know what to review.

Status Responsible party Date Evidence / notes

Monitoring dashboard / reporting location: ____

Monitoring review responsibility: ____

9.8 Rollback authority and procedure for this system are defined: the person with authority to direct immediate system suspension is identified, knows they hold that authority, and the operational procedure for suspension is documented.

Status Responsible party Date Evidence / notes

Rollback authority holder: ____

Rollback procedure: ____

9.9 Staged deployment plan has been defined: the deployment will begin at limited scope with intensive monitoring before expanding. Stages, expansion criteria, and evaluation timeline are documented.

☐ Staged deployment plan in place ☐ Full deployment without staging — governance team has specifically authorized:

____

Status	Responsible party	Date	Evidence / notes

Staged deployment plan location:

____

9.10 The AI inventory has been updated to reflect this pending deployment, with all fields completed and linked to the intake submission and this checklist.

Status	Responsible party	Date	Evidence / notes

Inventory entry ID: ____

9.11 All conditions attached to the intake approval have been confirmed as met. The operational owner has certified that each condition has been fulfilled.

☐ No conditions were attached to approval ☐ Conditions were attached — all confirmed as met

Condition	Confirmed met?	Confirmed by	Date
	☐ Yes ☐ No		
	☐ Yes ☐ No		

Condition Confirmed met? Confirmed by Date

☐ Yes ☐ No

Status Responsible party Date Evidence / notes

Section 10: Legal and Regulatory Verification

This section verifies that legal and regulatory requirements have been assessed and addressed.

10.1 Legal counsel has reviewed this deployment and confirmed it is consistent with applicable law, including: data protection law, anti-discrimination law, sector-specific regulatory requirements, and any AI-specific legal requirements in applicable jurisdictions.

Status Responsible party Date Evidence / notes

Legal review memo / confirmation location:

____

Legal counsel name and date of review:

____

10.2 Applicable regulatory disclosure requirements have been identified and will be met. If this deployment requires regulatory notification, registration, or prior approval, those obligations have been addressed.

Status Responsible party Date Evidence / notes

Regulatory requirements identified:

____

Requirements addressed:

____

10.3 For systems making or significantly influencing decisions affecting individuals: due process requirements (right to explanation, right to contest, access to human review) have been assessed and appropriate mechanisms are in place.

☐ Applicable ☐ Not applicable — reason:

____

Status Responsible party Date Evidence / notes

Due process mechanisms in place:

____

10.4 [HIGH RISK] For systems subject to EU AI Act requirements: conformity assessment has been completed or is not required, and applicable transparency and documentation obligations are addressed.

☐ Applicable ☐ Not applicable — reason:

____

Status Responsible party Date Evidence / notes

Section 11: Open Items and Exception Log

Document any items that are incomplete, deferred, or subject to exception. All items in this log must be reviewed by the governance team before deployment authorization.

Item number	Description of issue	Proposed resolution	Governance team decision	Date

---

Section 12: Deployment Authorization

This section is completed by the governance team after reviewing the completed checklist and all supporting documentation. Deployment may not begin until this section is completed.

Checklist review summary:

Total items applicable to this deployment: ___________

Items confirmed complete: ___________

Items not applicable with documented justification: ___________

Items in exception log: ___________

Items blocking deployment (not resolved): ___________

Governance team assessment:

The governance team has reviewed the completed checklist, supporting documentation, and testing findings. Based on this review:

☐ **Deployment authorized** — all required items are complete, testing results meet defined thresholds, operational readiness is confirmed, and the governance team authorizes deployment to proceed under the conditions specified.

☐ **Deployment authorized with additional conditions** — the governance team authorizes deployment subject to the following additional conditions:

____
____

____
____

☐ **Deployment deferred** — the following items must be resolved before deployment authorization will be granted:

____
____

☐ **Deployment declined** — testing findings or governance review have identified concerns that preclude deployment at this time. See attached governance team decision memo.

Special deployment conditions, monitoring requirements, and review schedule:

____
____

____
____

Scheduled first-stage review date: ____________ **Scheduled full deployment review date:** ____________

Governance team sign-off:

Governance team member Role Signature Date

Final authorization:

Authorized by: ____________________________________

Title: ____________________________________

Date: ____________________________________

Authorized go-live date:
____

Authorized scope: ____________________________________

Checklist archived by: _______________________ **Location:**
____

Notes on checklist administration

The completed checklist — including all supporting documentation referenced in evidence fields — should be stored as the governance record for this deployment. It should be linked to the corresponding intake submission and inventory entry and retained for at least the operational life of the AI system plus [ADAPT — specify retention period consistent with institutional records retention policy].

Checklist items that reference specific document locations should link to documents that actually exist and can be retrieved. A reference to "testing documentation — on file" that does not specify where the documentation is located, and where subsequent retrieval proves the documentation does not exist or is not what the reference implied, represents a governance record failure that is worse than acknowledged incompleteness.

The governance team should treat this checklist as a live accountability document during the pre-deployment period — reviewing its status at governance team meetings, tracking completion progress against the target deployment date, and escalating items that are at risk of not being completed before deployment. Rushing checklist completion in the days immediately before deployment, in ways that compromise the quality of testing or verification, defeats the purpose of the checklist. If the deployment timeline does not allow adequate time for genuine completion of required checklist items, the deployment timeline should move — not the checklist requirements.

Chapter 28: Incident Report Template

How to use this template

The incident report template is the documentation instrument through which AI-related failures, concerns, near-misses, and misuse events are formally recorded, investigated, and acted on. It is the mechanism that converts a staff member's observation — something felt wrong with this AI output, something unexpected happened, someone may have been harmed — into a governance record that can be reviewed, investigated, escalated, and learned from.

The template serves multiple distinct functions simultaneously. It is a detection instrument: structured documentation forces the person reporting to articulate what they observed with enough specificity that others can assess its significance. It is an investigation guide: the questions it asks shape the scope and methodology of subsequent investigation. It is an accountability record: a completed incident report creates a documented chain of accountability from initial observation through investigation findings to remediation actions. It is an institutional learning resource: the archive of incident reports, reviewed in aggregate, reveals patterns that individual incidents do not.

This chapter provides two related components. The first is the staff-facing incident reporting form — the form that any staff member completes when they identify a potential AI incident. This form is designed to be accessible to non-technical staff, requiring no specialized knowledge to complete, and short enough that the barrier to reporting is low. The second is the governance investigation record — the more detailed documentation that the governance team and AI governance coordinator complete during and after investigation. Together, these two components constitute the full incident record.

Both components should be understood as living documents. The initial report captures what is known at the moment of observation. The governance record accumulates information as investigation proceeds, is updated as findings develop, and is finalized when investigation and remediation are complete. A well-maintained incident record tells the full story of what happened, how governance responded, and what the institution learned — in a form that supports both internal accountability and external scrutiny.

The [ADAPT] markers indicate fields requiring institution-specific information. Institutions should also adapt the escalation pathways, response timelines, and severity classifications to reflect their specific governance architecture and risk profile.

PART ONE: STAFF INCIDENT REPORT FORM

AI Incident Report

[INSTITUTION NAME] — AI GOVERNANCE PROGRAM

This form should be completed by any staff member who observes, suspects, or receives a report of an AI-related incident. You do not need to be certain that an incident has occurred to submit this form. If something about an AI system seems wrong, harmful, or inconsistent with how it should work, report it. The AI Governance Coordinator will assess whether formal investigation is needed.

You will not face negative consequences for submitting this report in good faith, regardless of whether investigation confirms that an incident occurred.

How to submit: [ADAPT — specify submission method: online form link, email address, physical form location]

Urgent incidents — potential harm occurring now: Contact [ADAPT — AI Governance Coordinator name and direct contact, plus after-hours contact if applicable] immediately by phone. Do not wait to complete this form.

Questions about whether to report: Contact [ADAPT — AI Governance Coordinator] at [ADAPT — contact information]. When in doubt, report.

Section A: Reporter Information

Field	Response
Your name	
Your job title	
Your department	
Your email address	
Your phone number	
Date you are submitting this report	
Your supervisor's name	

Do you wish to remain anonymous? ☐ No — I am willing to be contacted about this report ☐ Yes — please do not share my name outside the investigation team

Note: Anonymous reports will still be investigated but may be more difficult to follow up. If you have concerns about reporting, please speak with the AI Governance Coordinator before deciding to report anonymously.

Section B: Basic Incident Information

B1. When did the incident occur or when did you first observe the concern?

Date: ___________ Time (approximate): ___________

B2. When did you first become aware of this incident or concern?

☐ I observed it directly ☐ A colleague told me about it on: ___________ ☐ A person we serve raised it on: ___________ ☐ I noticed it in reviewing records or outputs ☐ Other:

____

B3. Which AI system is involved?

AI system name: ____

Vendor (if known): ____

Department or function using the system:

____

How the system was being used when the incident occurred:

____

B4. Incident type — check all that apply:

☐ The AI system produced output that appears to be incorrect, inaccurate, or misleading ☐ The AI system produced output that appears to be biased or discriminatory toward specific individuals or groups ☐ The AI system produced output that caused or may have caused harm to a person ☐ The AI system was used in a way that violated policy or its approved scope ☐ The AI system accessed, exposed, or processed data it should not have ☐ The AI system produced content that is inappropriate, offensive, or contrary to institutional values ☐ The AI system behaved in an unexpected or unexplained way ☐ A staff member's use of AI created a problem (misuse, over-reliance, failure to exercise required oversight) ☐ A vendor did something concerning (undisclosed system change, data practice concern, inadequate notification) ☐ An affected person (patient / client / student / applicant / employee) raised a concern about AI use ☐ A near-miss — no harm occurred but something happened that could have caused harm ☐ Other — describe:

____

Section C: What Happened

C1. Describe what you observed or were told about this incident. Please be as specific as possible.

Describe: what the AI system did or did not do; what inputs were involved; what outputs were produced; what happened as a result; and any other relevant circumstances.

____

____

____

____

____

____

____

____

Guidance: Write what you know, not what you think caused it or what should have happened. "The AI recommended treatment X for a patient who had a documented contraindication in their record, and the treating clinician initially accepted the recommendation before catching the error during a second review" is a specific description. "The AI made a mistake" is not.

C2. Is there documentation of what the AI system produced?

☐ Yes — describe what documentation exists and where:

____

☐ No — explain why documentation is not available:

____

☐ Uncertain — describe: _____________________________________

Note: If documentation exists — screenshots, system logs, printed outputs, records — preserve it now if you can do so easily and appropriately. Do not alter or delete records. Contact the AI Governance Coordinator if you are uncertain whether or how to preserve records.

C3. Was any person harmed or potentially harmed by this incident?

☐ Yes, harm appears to have occurred — describe: ____

☐ Possible harm — uncertain — describe: ____

☐ Near-miss — no harm occurred but could have — describe: ____

☐ No harm — concern is about system behavior or policy compliance, not harm to a specific person

If a person was or may have been harmed:

How many people are affected or potentially affected: ____________

Who are the affected people (describe role or relationship to institution — do not provide identifying information in this form): ____

Nature of harm or potential harm: ____

C4. Is the incident ongoing — is the AI system still operating in the way that produced this concern?

☐ Yes — the AI system is still operating and may be producing the same type of problematic output

☐ No — the problem appears to have been a one-time occurrence or the situation has changed

☐ Unknown

If yes, or if you are uncertain, please contact the AI Governance Coordinator directly in addition to submitting this form. Ongoing harm requires faster response than this form alone can initiate.

C5. Have any immediate actions been taken in response to this incident?

☐ No — no actions taken yet

☐ Yes — describe what actions were taken, by whom, and when:

____

____

Section D: Context

D1. How long has this AI system been in use in this context?

____

_

D2. Has this or a similar problem with this AI system occurred before, to your knowledge?

☐ Yes — describe what you know about previous occurrences:

____
____

☐ No, not to my knowledge

☐ Uncertain

D3. Is there anything else you think the AI Governance Coordinator or governance team should know about this incident?

____
____

____
____

Section E: Reporter Certification

By submitting this form, I certify that:

- The information I have provided is accurate and complete to the best of my knowledge
- I am submitting this report in good faith based on genuine concern about AI system behavior or governance
- I understand that the information I provide may be shared with the AI Governance Coordinator, governance team members, legal counsel, and other institutional parties involved in investigating and responding to this incident
- I understand that if I have identified myself, I may be contacted for follow-up

Submitter signature (if submitting paper form):

____

Date: ___________

For electronic submissions, submission of the form constitutes certification.

Immediate next steps for reporters

After submitting this form:

If you believe harm is occurring now or may continue: Call [ADAPT — AI Governance Coordinator direct line and after-hours number] immediately.

You will receive: An acknowledgment of your report within [ADAPT — e.g., 4 business hours / 1 business day]. The acknowledgment will confirm receipt and provide a reference number. It will not necessarily describe what investigation has been initiated — some aspects of investigation must remain confidential.

If you are a supervisor: In addition to submitting this form, ensure that the immediate operational situation is managed — that staff understand what to do, that any ongoing AI use that may be creating the problem is handled appropriately, and that records relevant to the incident are preserved.

If you have questions: Contact [ADAPT — AI Governance Coordinator] at any time.

PART TWO: GOVERNANCE INVESTIGATION RECORD

AI Incident Governance Record

For AI Governance Coordinator and Governance Team Use

This record is initiated when an incident report is received and is maintained through investigation completion, remediation, and post-incident review. It is a confidential governance document. Access is restricted to: the AI Governance Coordinator, governance team members, legal counsel, and other parties specifically authorized by the governance team for purposes of investigation and response.

Administrative Information

Field	Response
Incident reference number	[ADAPT — assign sequential number: INC-YYYY-NNN]
Date report received	
Date governance record opened	
Record maintained by	
Intake form reference number (if incident relates to a reviewed use case)	
AI inventory entry reference	

Phase 1: Initial Assessment and Classification

To be completed by the AI Governance Coordinator within [ADAPT — e.g., 4 business hours for potential harm incidents; 1 business day for other reports] of receipt.

IA-1. Report completeness and reliability assessment

Question	Assessment
Is the report sufficiently specific to initiate assessment?	☐ Yes ☐ No — follow-up needed
Is there any reason to question the good faith of the report?	☐ No concern ☐ Some uncertainty — describe
What additional information is needed before initial classification?	
Follow-up contact made with reporter?	☐ Yes — date/time: _____ ☐ Not needed ☐ Pending

---

IA-2. Initial incident classification

Incident type — primary classification:

☐ Harm incident — AI system has caused or may have caused harm to identifiable people ☐ Governance failure incident — AI governance requirements were not followed ☐ Near-miss incident — harm was avoided but conditions were present that could cause harm ☐ Misuse incident — AI system was used deliberately in ways inconsistent with policy ☐ Performance concern — AI system behavior raises questions not rising to incident level ☐ Vendor concern — vendor behavior raises governance concerns

Severity classification:

☐ **Critical** — Potential significant harm to identifiable people; ongoing harm that may be continuing; potential major legal or regulatory exposure; potential systemic failure affecting many people; requires immediate governance team notification and possible system suspension

☐ **High** — Harm has occurred or is likely; significant governance failure; regulatory implications; affects vulnerable population; requires governance team notification within 24 hours and prioritized investigation

☐ **Medium** — Possible harm; moderate governance failure; concerning pattern identified; no immediate ongoing risk; requires governance team notification at next regular meeting and investigation within defined timeline

☐ **Low** — Near-miss with no harm; minor governance gap; single occurrence with low recurrence risk; can be addressed operationally with documentation; governance team notification in periodic reporting

Classification rationale:

____
____

IA-3. Immediate action assessment

Question	Decision
Does this incident require immediate system suspension?	☐ Yes — initiate rollback ☐ No ☐ Under assessment
Does this incident require immediate notification of affected people?	☐ Yes ☐ No ☐ Under assessment
Does this incident require immediate legal counsel notification?	☐ Yes ☐ No
Does this incident require immediate regulatory notification?	☐ Yes ☐ No ☐ Under assessment with legal
Does this incident require immediate senior leadership notification?	☐ Yes ☐ No

Immediate actions taken:

Action Taken by Date/time

IA-4. Escalation pathway

Escalation level	Notified?	Date/time	By whom
AI Governance Coordinator (initiating this record)	✓		
Relevant operational leader	☐ Yes ☐ No		
Legal counsel	☐ Yes ☐ No		
Governance team — standard notification	☐ Yes ☐ No		
Governance team — emergency meeting convened	☐ Yes ☐ No		
Senior leadership	☐ Yes ☐ No		
Board / board committee	☐ Yes ☐ No		
Vendor	☐ Yes ☐ No		
External regulator	☐ Yes ☐ No		

Phase 2: Investigation

To be completed during investigation. Investigation timeline and depth are determined by severity classification. Critical and High severity incidents should be substantially investigated within [ADAPT — e.g., 5 business days]. Medium severity within [ADAPT — e.g., 15 business days]. Low severity within [ADAPT — e.g., 30 business days].

INV-1. Investigation team

Role	Name	Function	Involvement scope
Lead investigator			
Legal counsel			
IT/security			
Domain expert			
Operations representative			
Other			

Independence assessment: Is the investigation team sufficiently independent from the functions whose practices are under investigation?

☐ Yes — no significant independence concern ☐ Partial — describe: ____ ☐ Independence concern — describe and explain how addressed: ______________________

INV-2. Investigation scope

Describe what the investigation will examine: what questions it will address, what evidence it will review, and what time period it will cover.

____

____

Is there reason to believe the problem may be broader than the reported incident — potentially affecting more people or occurring over a longer period than the initial report indicates?

☐ No — investigation will focus on reported incident ☐ Yes or possibly — investigation will include broader scope assessment. Describe:

____

____

INV-3. Evidence collected

Document all evidence reviewed during investigation. Each entry should identify the evidence type, source, date obtained, and where it is stored.

Evidence type	Source	Date obtained	Location
AI system logs			
AI outputs (screenshots, printouts, records)			
Incident-related institutional records			
Staff interviews			
Technical system assessment			
Vendor communications			
Vendor documentation			
Monitoring data			
Other			

INV-4. Technical findings

Describe what the AI system actually did, based on evidence. What inputs were processed? What outputs were produced? How do those outputs compare to what the system should have produced? Is there a technical explanation for the behavior?

____

____

____

____

Technical cause determination:

☐ Technical cause identified — describe:

____

☐ Technical cause not identified — system behavior is unexplained at this point

☐ Technical cause determination requires vendor input — vendor has been / will be contacted

---

INV-5. Harm assessment

Describe the harm that occurred or may have occurred, based on evidence gathered in investigation. Be specific about: who was affected, what harm they experienced, the severity and duration of harm, and whether harm is reversible.

People directly affected:

Category	Number	Nature of harm	Severity	Reversibility

Narrative harm assessment:

____

____

Were specific identifiable individuals harmed?

☐ Yes — [Do not record identifying information in this general record. Maintain a separate restricted-access document identifying affected individuals for remediation and notification purposes.]

☐ No — harm was systemic or potential, not identified for specific individuals

☐ Unknown at this stage of investigation

INV-6. Governance failure analysis

Identify where in the governance lifecycle this incident's contributing factors arose. For each governance stage, assess whether failures at that stage contributed to the incident.

Governance stage	Did failure here contribute?	Describe the failure
Intake and risk screening — was this risk identified and assessed?	☐ Yes ☐ No ☐ Partial	
Vendor assessment — were vendor practices adequately assessed?	☐ Yes ☐ No ☐ Partial	
Pre-deployment testing — was this failure mode tested for?	☐ Yes ☐ No ☐ Partial	
Oversight design — was oversight adequate to catch this type of failure?	☐ Yes ☐ No ☐ Partial	
Training — did staff have the knowledge to prevent or detect this?	☐ Yes ☐ No ☐ Partial	
Monitoring — should monitoring have detected this earlier?	☐ Yes ☐ No ☐ Partial	
Escalation — was escalation appropriate when concern arose?	☐ Yes ☐ No ☐ Partial ☐ N/A	
Vendor performance — did vendor system performance contribute?	☐ Yes ☐ No ☐ Partial	
Vendor notifications — did vendor fail to notify of relevant changes?	☐ Yes ☐ No ☐ Partial	
Policy — was policy adequate, or did it have gaps this incident exposed?	☐ Yes ☐ No ☐ Partial	

Summary of primary governance contributing factors:

____
____

INV-7. Scope assessment — broader than initial report?

Based on investigation, does the incident appear to be broader than the initial report indicated?

Question	Finding
Is this an isolated occurrence or part of a pattern?	
Over what time period may the problem have been occurring?	
How many people may have been affected beyond those in the initial report?	
Are there other AI systems or use cases where the same contributing factors may be present?	

INV-8. Vendor assessment

If a vendor's AI system, practices, or contractual compliance is relevant to this incident:

Question	Finding
What role did vendor AI system performance play in this incident?	
Did the vendor fulfill its notification obligations prior to this incident?	
How has the vendor responded to this incident notification?	
Are there contractual obligations the vendor may have breached?	
What vendor remediation has been requested?	

Question	Finding
What is the vendor's response to remediation requests?	

INV-9. Legal and regulatory assessment

Question	Assessment
Does this incident create legal exposure for [Institution Name]? Describe	
Does this incident trigger regulatory notification obligations?	
Which regulators, if any, must be notified? By when?	
What are the applicable notification requirements?	
Has legal counsel been engaged and what are their recommendations?	
Are there litigation preservation obligations?	
What documentation must be preserved?	

INV-10. Investigation findings summary

Provide a plain-language summary of what the investigation found: what happened, why it happened, who was affected, what governance failed, and what needs to be fixed.

What happened:

____

____

Why it happened (root cause analysis):

____

____

Who was affected and how:

____

____

What governance failed:

____

____

What needs to change:

____

____

INV-11. Governance team review of findings

The governance team has reviewed investigation findings and determined the following:

☐ Investigation findings accepted as presented ☐ Investigation findings accepted with modifications — describe: _________________________
☐ Further investigation required — describe:
____

Governance team review date: ___________ **Meeting reference:** ___________

Governance team member Role Date reviewed

Phase 3: Remediation

Document all remediation actions — for affected individuals, for AI system performance, and for governance processes.

REM-1. Remediation for affected individuals

For each category of affected person, describe what remediation is being provided.

Affected population	Remediation action	Responsible party	Timeline Status

Direct outreach to affected individuals:

☐ Direct outreach required and planned — describe plan:

____

____

☐ Direct outreach not required — reason:

____

____

Outreach completed: ☐ Yes — date: ___________ ☐ In progress ☐ Not yet initiated

---

REM-2. AI system remediation

Remediation action	Responsible party	Target completion	Status
System suspension / rollback			☐ Not needed ☐ Completed ☐ In progress

Remediation action	Responsible party	Target completion	Status
Vendor notification and remediation request			
System modification or reconfiguration			
Additional testing / validation			
Override of problematic decisions / outputs			
Other system-level action			

System current status:

☐ System remains in operation with enhanced oversight ☐ System suspended pending remediation ☐ System suspended — retirement being considered ☐ System restored after remediation ☐ System retired as result of this incident

---

REM-3. Governance system remediation

For each governance failure identified in INV-6, describe the specific remediation action that will address it.

Governance failure identified	Remediation action	Responsible party	Target completion	Status

---

REM-4. Personnel actions

If this incident involved staff behavior that requires a personnel response — inadequate oversight, deliberate policy violation, failure to escalate — document that a personnel response is being addressed through appropriate channels. Do not document personnel action details in this governance record.

☐ Personnel matter identified and referred to appropriate institutional process — date referred: ___________ ☐ No personnel action required ☐ Under assessment

---

REM-5. Remediation tracking

Commitment	Responsible party	Target date	Completion date	Verified by

Remediation completion assessment:

☐ All remediation commitments complete — date: ___________ ☐ Remediation ongoing — expected completion: ___________ ☐ Remediation delayed — reason and revised timeline: ________________________

Phase 4: Communication Log

Document all communications related to this incident. This log creates the communication record that supports accountability and regulatory compliance.

COM-1. Internal communications

Date	Communication	Audience	Method	By whom
	Acknowledgment to reporter	Reporter		
	Governance team notification	Governance team		
	Senior leadership notification	Leadership		
	Operational staff notification	Affected staff		
	Board notification	Board		
	Other			

COM-2. External communications

Date	Communication	Recipient	Content summary	By whom	Legal review?
	Affected individual notification				☐ Yes ☐ No
	Vendor notification				☐ Yes ☐ No
	Regulatory notification				☐ Yes ☐ No
	Media / public statement				☐ Yes ☐ No
	Other				☐ Yes ☐ No

COM-3. Regulatory notification status

☐ No regulatory notification required ☐ Notification required — status:

Regulator	Notification deadline	Notification sent	Confirmation received

---

Phase 5: Post-Incident Review

To be completed after initial remediation is underway, typically [ADAPT — e.g., 4-8 weeks] after the incident.

PIR-1. Post-incident review conducted

Date of post-incident review: ___________

Participants:

Name	Role

PIR-2. Governance system assessment

Question	Assessment
Was the incident detected as quickly as governance systems should have detected it? If not, why not?	
Was the initial classification accurate?	
Was the investigation appropriately scoped and resourced?	
Was the response timely and adequate?	
Was communication to affected parties appropriate?	
Were remediation commitments made and kept?	
Were there aspects of incident response that worked well and should be repeated?	
Were there aspects of incident response that should be improved?	

PIR-3. Learning that generalizes

Beyond this specific incident, what does it reveal about governance adequacy across the institution's AI portfolio?

Learning	Implication for other AI systems or governance processes	Action required

---

PIR-4. Governance improvement commitments from this incident

Improvement	Responsible party	Target completion

These commitments should be tracked in the governance improvement cycle described in Chapter 22.

PIR-5. Pattern analysis

Is this incident part of a pattern identified in prior incident reports or monitoring data?

☐ Yes — describe pattern and implications: ______________________________________

☐ No — appears to be a standalone incident

☐ Uncertain — warrants monitoring for recurrence

Phase 6: Record Closure

To be completed when investigation, remediation, and post-incident review are all complete.

RCL-1. Closure criteria assessment

Criterion	Met?
Investigation is complete and findings are documented	☐ Yes ☐ No
All remediation commitments are complete or have defined completion plans	☐ Yes ☐ No
Regulatory notification obligations have been addressed	☐ Yes ☐ No
Direct outreach to affected individuals is complete (where required)	☐ Yes ☐ No
Post-incident review has been conducted	☐ Yes ☐ No
Governance improvement commitments have been assigned and tracked	☐ Yes ☐ No
Governance team has reviewed and approved record closure	☐ Yes ☐ No

---

RCL-2. Incident summary for governance reporting

Provide a brief summary suitable for inclusion in governance team reports and, where appropriate, in public governance reporting. This summary should be honest about what occurred and what was done in response.

____
____

____
____

RCL-3. Record closed

Record closed by: ________________________________

Date: __________

Governance team approval of closure:

Member Role Date

Record archived at: _________________________________

Retention period: [ADAPT — specify, e.g., 7 years from closure date, or as required by applicable law]

Notes on maintaining this record

The incident record is only as valuable as the honesty and completeness of its documentation. Several principles should guide how this record is maintained.

Document what happened, not what the institution wishes had happened. Incident records that minimize findings, use passive constructions that obscure accountability, or characterize governance failures as isolated technical issues are governance documents that have been shaped by reputation management rather than accountability. When regulators, courts, or auditors review incident records, documents that appear to have been crafted for favorable appearance rather than accurate documentation undermine institutional credibility far more than honest records of imperfect governance.

Maintain the record in real time, not retrospectively. Documentation that is completed in the days and weeks following an incident, as it develops, is more credible and more useful than documentation assembled after the fact. Investigation findings should be recorded when they are made. Remediation actions should be recorded when they are taken. Communications should be logged when they occur. Retrospective reconstruction of incident timelines is both less accurate and less credible than contemporaneous documentation.

Distinguish what is known from what is suspected. Investigation findings should clearly distinguish between established facts — what evidence shows — and inferences or assessments — what the evidence suggests. Using appropriately hedged language ("evidence indicates," "investigation suggests," "the balance of evidence supports") where certainty is not established is more honest and more defensible than asserting conclusions that the evidence does not fully support.

Preserve all relevant evidence. The evidence log in INV-3 should be comprehensive and should link to preserved evidence that can actually be retrieved. Evidence that is described in an incident record but cannot be produced when requested provides no governance value and creates credibility problems. When evidence cannot be preserved — when logs have already been overwritten, when records have been discarded in normal retention cycles, when vendor-side evidence is not accessible — that absence should be documented rather than ignored.

Protect confidentiality appropriately. The governance record contains sensitive information about affected individuals, personnel matters, and legal assessments that must be handled with appropriate confidentiality. The record itself should not contain identifying information about affected individuals — that information should be maintained in a separate restricted-access document linked to but not part of the general governance record. Legal counsel communications and assessments should be maintained separately under applicable privilege protections, linked to the record but not incorporated into it.

Chapter 29: Glossary and Further Reading

How to use this chapter

This chapter serves two purposes. The glossary provides definitions of the key terms used throughout this book — a reference for readers who encounter unfamiliar language or who want precise definitions of terms used in governance contexts. The further reading section identifies resources for readers who want to go deeper on specific topics than a governance handbook can address.

The glossary is not exhaustive — AI terminology is expanding faster than any static document can track, and technical terminology not essential to governance practice has been omitted. The definitions here prioritize governance relevance over technical precision. Where a concept has both a technical definition used by AI researchers and a practical meaning relevant to institutional governance, this glossary defines the latter.

The further reading section is organized by topic rather than by chapter, allowing readers to pursue specific areas of interest. It identifies types of resources rather than specific titles where possible, because specific publications date quickly in a field changing as rapidly as AI governance. Where specific resources are named, readers should verify that current editions or versions are available and that the content remains accurate given subsequent developments.

Part One: Glossary

Accountability The mechanism by which people and institutions are answerable for decisions and outcomes, including those produced with AI assistance. In governance contexts, accountability requires that specific responsibilities are clearly assigned, that failures produce consequences, and that affected parties have meaningful recourse. Accountability is distinct from blame — its primary function is ensuring that problems are identified, acknowledged, and addressed, not that punishment is assigned.

Adversarial input An input deliberately designed to cause an AI system to produce incorrect, harmful, or unintended outputs. Adversarial inputs exploit the statistical nature of AI systems by crafting examples that are misleading to the system while appearing normal to humans. In governance contexts, adversarial input vulnerability is a security risk that must be assessed before deployment and monitored during operation.

Agentic AI An AI system that takes sequences of actions to accomplish goals with a degree of autonomy — browsing the web, executing tasks, interacting with other systems, sending communications — without requiring human authorization for each individual action. Agentic AI presents governance challenges distinct from AI that produces outputs for human review, because the AI's actions may have real-world consequences before human oversight is possible. See Chapter 20.

AI inventory A systematic record of every AI system an institution uses, plans to use, or has recently retired, containing information sufficient to support governance oversight of each system. The AI inventory is the empirical foundation of AI governance — the document that allows the governance team to know, at any time, what it is responsible for overseeing. See Chapter 9.

AI lifecycle The full arc of an AI system's relationship with an institution — from initial evaluation and adoption through deployment and operation to modification and eventual retirement. Governance applies across the entire lifecycle, not only at the adoption or deployment stages.

AI literacy The understanding of AI systems — how they work, what their characteristics are, what their limitations are, and what responsible use requires — that allows institutional staff to use AI tools effectively and exercise their governance responsibilities. AI literacy is not technical expertise; it is the functional knowledge that different roles need to do their jobs responsibly in AI-augmented environments. See Chapter 17.

Algorithm A defined set of steps or rules for solving a problem or making a decision. In common usage, "algorithm" often refers specifically to the computational processes underlying AI systems. In governance contexts, the term is sometimes used to describe AI-assisted decision systems, particularly those used in consequential determinations about individuals.

Algorithmic bias See *Bias*.

Algorithmic impact assessment A structured evaluation of the potential effects of an AI system on affected individuals and communities before deployment. Algorithmic impact assessments typically examine accuracy, fairness, transparency, and legal compliance. Several jurisdictions require algorithmic impact assessments for specific categories of AI use.

Artificial intelligence (AI) A broad term referring to computational systems designed to perform tasks that would previously have required human intelligence — pattern recognition, prediction, language understanding and generation, decision-making, and similar capabilities. In governance contexts, the relevant category is systems that use machine learning or similar techniques to generate outputs, make predictions, provide recommendations, or take actions affecting people or institutional operations.

Audit (AI governance) A structured, systematic assessment of whether AI governance is achieving its purposes — examining governance processes, governance outcomes, and the relationship between them. Governance audit is distinct from monitoring (which is continuous and operational) and from investigation (which is triggered by specific incidents). See Chapter 22.

Automated decision system An AI system that makes or significantly determines decisions affecting specific individuals with limited or no individual human review of each decision. Automated decision systems are subject to specific governance requirements around due process, explainability, and the rights of affected individuals. See Chapter 20.

Automation bias The tendency of humans to favor automated recommendations over their own independent judgment, at rates that exceed what the accuracy of those recommendations would warrant. Automation bias is a well-documented cognitive phenomenon that is the primary mechanism through which nominal human oversight replaces genuine oversight. Understanding and counteracting automation bias is a core AI literacy requirement and a fundamental oversight design consideration. See Chapters 3 and 13.

Baseline In monitoring contexts, the documented performance characteristics of an AI system established during early deployment, against which subsequent performance is compared to detect drift or degradation. In testing contexts, a comparison standard — such as the performance of human decision-makers or a simple rules-based system — against which AI system performance is evaluated.

Bias (in AI systems) Systematic patterns in AI outputs that disadvantage or unfairly affect identifiable groups of people. Bias in AI systems typically arises from training data that reflects historical patterns of discrimination, from feature selection that uses proxies for protected characteristics, or from feedback loops that amplify initial disparities. Bias is not limited to deliberate discriminatory design — systems designed without discriminatory intent can produce biased outcomes through the mechanisms described above. See Chapter 3.

Calibration The correspondence between an AI system's expressed confidence scores and its actual accuracy rates. A well-calibrated system that expresses 90% confidence is correct approximately 90% of the time. Poorly calibrated systems — typically overconfident ones — express high confidence in outputs that are less reliable than the scores suggest, which can misdirect human oversight away from outputs that most need scrutiny.

Chatbot A conversational AI system designed to respond to questions and requests from users through natural language. Chatbots that are deployed to interact with the people an institution serves require specific governance because they place AI in direct contact with potentially vulnerable people, often with limited per-interaction human oversight. See Chapter 20.

Classification model An AI system trained to assign inputs to categories — spam or not spam, fraudulent or legitimate, high-risk or low-risk. Classification models are among the most widely deployed AI systems in institutional settings and are particularly associated with bias risk, because the categories themselves may reflect historical patterns and the criteria used to assign them may have differential effects across demographic groups.

Conditional approval A governance outcome in which an AI use case is approved subject to specific requirements that must be met before or during operation. Conditions might include enhanced oversight arrangements, mandatory monitoring, specific training requirements, or vendor contract modifications. See Chapter 10.

Conformity assessment Under the EU AI Act, the process by which high-risk AI systems are assessed for compliance with applicable requirements before being placed on the market or put into service. Conformity assessments may be conducted by the provider itself or by a notified third-party body, depending on the system category.

Contextual integrity A framework for evaluating information flows: information flows appropriately when it matches the norms of the context in which it was originally shared. Medical information shared with a healthcare provider for treatment purposes flows appropriately to other treating clinicians but not to employers. Contextual integrity provides a useful heuristic for assessing whether AI uses of personal information honor reasonable privacy expectations.

Data governance The policies, processes, and practices that manage how an institution collects, uses, stores, shares, retains, and deletes data. Data governance for AI encompasses all standard data governance requirements plus AI-specific dimensions: training data quality and bias, operational data privacy, inference and derived data, vendor data practices, and the use of institutional data for AI training. See Chapter 12.

Data minimization The principle that personal information should be collected and retained only to the extent necessary for the specific purpose it serves. Data minimization applies to AI systems as an obligation to limit what information the system collects and processes to what the use case genuinely requires.

Data poisoning A security attack in which an adversary introduces corrupted or misleading data into an AI system's training data, causing the system to learn incorrect patterns or to behave in ways that serve the adversary's goals. Data poisoning is an AI-specific security risk that requires specific governance attention.

Deepfake AI-generated synthetic media — typically video or audio — that realistically depicts people saying or doing things they did not actually say or do. Deepfakes are a governance concern in institutional contexts involving AI-generated content, authentication, and the risk of AI-generated disinformation.

Deployment The stage at which an AI system begins operating in an institution's actual workflows, producing outputs that affect real people and real decisions. Deployment is distinguished from testing by the presence of real operational conditions. Safe deployment requires staged rollout, operational preparation, and monitoring from the first day. See Chapter 15.

Differential performance Variation in AI system accuracy, reliability, or error rates across demographic groups. Differential performance is the primary empirical measure of AI bias: a system that performs significantly better for some groups than others may be producing discriminatory outcomes regardless of whether any discriminatory intent was present in its design.

Disparate impact In anti-discrimination law, a practice or policy that is facially neutral but produces disproportionately adverse outcomes for members of protected groups. Disparate impact theory applies to AI systems used in employment, housing, credit, and other protected domains, making differential performance a legal compliance matter, not only an ethical one.

Drift Gradual degradation of AI system performance or governance compliance over time. Model drift occurs when the statistical relationship between inputs and appropriate outputs changes as conditions evolve. Population drift occurs when the characteristics of the population the system serves change. Behavioral drift occurs when staff use patterns evolve in ways that undermine oversight design. Monitoring for drift is a core ongoing governance function. See Chapter 16.

Due diligence The structured assessment of an AI vendor's systems, practices, and contractual terms before entering a vendor relationship. Due diligence for AI vendors goes substantially beyond standard technology vendor assessment to include performance documentation, demographic testing, data governance practices, security assessment, and governance practice evaluation. See Chapter 11 and Chapter 26.

Due process The legal and ethical requirement that decisions significantly affecting individuals be made through fair procedures that include appropriate notice, explanation, opportunity to be heard, and access to review. Due process requirements apply to AI-assisted decisions and require that AI systems used in consequential determinations can provide explanations, honor appeal rights, and accommodate human review.

EU AI Act The European Union's comprehensive regulation of artificial intelligence, which classifies AI systems by risk level and imposes corresponding requirements. The EU AI Act prohibits certain AI practices outright, imposes substantial requirements on high-risk AI systems including healthcare, employment, and benefits administration AI, and establishes requirements for general-purpose AI models. The Act entered into force progressively from 2024 and applies to AI used in or serving people in the EU regardless of where the provider is located. See Chapter 21.

Explainability The capacity of an AI system to provide a meaningful account of why it produced a particular output — what factors influenced the recommendation, what patterns in its training support the conclusion. Explainability is required for AI systems used in consequential decisions, both as a due process obligation (affected people deserve to understand decisions affecting them) and as an oversight enabler (reviewers cannot meaningfully assess outputs they cannot understand). Explainability in practice is limited — explanations may be simplified, post-hoc, or technically approximate — and governance should assess the adequacy and accuracy of available explanations.

FERPA (Family Educational Rights and Privacy Act) A US federal law that governs educational records at institutions receiving federal education funding. FERPA restricts disclosure of student educational records and creates student and parent rights that apply to AI systems processing student data. See Chapter 21.

Foundational model (Foundation model) A large AI model trained on broad data that can be adapted to a wide range of tasks. Large language models such as GPT and Claude are foundational models; so are large image models and multimodal models. Foundational models are increasingly the technical basis for institutional AI applications, accessed through APIs or built into commercial products. Their governance implications include opacity about training data, variability in output reliability across use cases, and rapidly evolving capabilities.

GDPR (General Data Protection Regulation) The European Union's comprehensive data protection regulation, which governs the processing of personal data of people in the EU regardless of where the processor is located. GDPR is among the most significant legal frameworks for AI governance globally, imposing requirements for lawful basis, purpose limitation, data minimization, and individual rights, and including specific provisions governing automated decision-making in Article 22. See Chapter 21.

Generative AI AI systems that produce new content — text, images, audio, code, or other media — in response to inputs. Generative AI includes large language models used for writing, summarization, and conversation, as well as image and audio generation systems. Generative AI presents governance challenges including hallucination, output appropriateness, intellectual property, and prompt injection. See Chapters 3 and 20.

Governance (AI governance) The system an institution uses to make and oversee consequential decisions about AI — including what tools to use, how to use them, under what conditions, and what to do when things go wrong. Governance is a system, not a document or a committee; it requires functioning processes, clear accountability, active oversight, and genuine institutional commitment. See Chapter 2.

Governance team The cross-functional group responsible for institutional AI governance, with authority to approve, decline, or condition AI use cases, establish governance standards, monitor AI system performance, and direct governance responses when problems arise. See Chapter 6.

Hallucination The production by a generative AI system of outputs that are fluent, confident, and factually incorrect. Hallucination is a structural feature of how language models generate text — they produce statistically plausible continuations of inputs without a reliable internal mechanism for verifying factual accuracy. Governance for hallucination requires verification requirements, oversight design, and training that builds appropriate skepticism. See Chapters 3 and 20.

High-risk AI A category of AI use characterized by significant potential consequences for affected individuals, limited reversibility of errors, genuine individuation requirements, or accountability obligations that require human authority. High-risk AI use cases require the most intensive governance, including comprehensive pre-deployment testing, robust human oversight, intensive monitoring, and specific legal compliance assessment. Different governance frameworks, including the EU AI Act, define high-risk AI with varying specificity.

Human dignity The governance principle that AI systems should treat the people they affect as individuals with inherent worth — not reducing them to data points, optimization targets, or problems to be processed efficiently. Human dignity provides the normative grounding for governance requirements around transparency, explanation, human oversight, and the preservation of genuine human relationship in institutional contexts. See Chapter 7.

Human oversight The active involvement of human judgment in reviewing, evaluating, and intervening in AI-assisted processes. Human oversight is meaningful when reviewers have the information, capability, authority, and time to exercise genuine independent judgment — as opposed to nominal oversight, where humans are present in the process but are not actually exercising independent assessment. See Chapter 13.

HIPAA (Health Insurance Portability and Accountability Act) A US federal law that governs the handling of protected health information by covered entities and their business associates. AI vendors that process PHI on behalf of healthcare institutions are business associates subject to HIPAA requirements and must execute Business Associate Agreements. See Chapter 21.

Incident (AI incident) Any event involving an AI system that has caused, may have caused, or creates meaningful risk of causing harm to people, legal or regulatory exposure for the institution, significant operational failure, or material breach of institutional governance commitments. Incidents include harm incidents, governance failure incidents, near-miss incidents, and misuse incidents. See Chapter 19.

Incident response The structured process through which institutions detect, escalate, investigate, remediate, communicate about, and learn from AI incidents. Incident response capability requires pre-defined processes, designated responsible parties, and readiness infrastructure that must be established before incidents occur. See Chapter 19.

Intake process The governance process through which proposed new AI use cases are submitted to the governance team, assessed, and decided before adoption. The intake process is the primary prevention function of AI governance — the point at which governance has the greatest leverage to shape AI use. See Chapter 10.

Large language model (LLM) A type of AI system trained on vast quantities of text to generate, summarize, translate, classify, and respond to text. Large language models are the technology underlying AI chatbots, writing assistants, document summarization tools, and many other widely deployed AI products. Their governance implications include hallucination risk, opacity about training data, sensitivity to prompt design, and rapidly evolving capabilities.

Legal basis Under data protection law, the recognized grounds that justify processing personal data. For AI systems, identifying the appropriate legal basis for each type of data processing is a compliance prerequisite. Common legal bases include consent, contractual necessity, legal obligation, vital interests, public task, and legitimate interests, each with specific conditions and limitations.

Lock-in (vendor lock-in) The condition in which an institution becomes dependent on a specific AI vendor's systems in ways that make switching costly, disruptive, or practically impossible. Vendor lock-in reduces institutional governance leverage, constrains accountability options, and limits the institution's ability to respond to vendor performance failures. See Chapter 3.

Machine learning A category of AI approaches in which systems learn patterns from data rather than being explicitly programmed with rules. Machine learning systems adjust their parameters through training processes to improve performance on defined tasks. Most contemporary AI systems used in institutional settings — whether called machine learning, deep learning, neural networks, or AI — use machine learning approaches.

Membership inference A security attack in which an adversary queries an AI model to determine whether specific individuals' data was included in the model's training set. Membership inference attacks can expose sensitive information about individuals even when training data is not directly accessible. See Chapter 14.

Model In AI contexts, a mathematical structure that has been trained on data to recognize patterns and produce outputs in response to inputs. A model is distinct from the AI system that incorporates it — the system includes the model plus interfaces, infrastructure, integrations, and the operational context in which it is used.

Model inversion A security attack in which an adversary reconstructs training data by querying an AI model. Model inversion attacks can recover sensitive personal information about individuals who appeared in training data. See Chapter 14.

Monitoring The continuous process of tracking AI system performance, oversight quality, fairness metrics, and harm signals after deployment to detect problems while they can still be addressed before causing significant harm. Monitoring is distinguished from audit (which is periodic and evaluative) and from incident response (which is triggered by specific events). See Chapter 16.

Near-miss An incident in which harm was avoided or was minimal, but where the AI system's behavior, a staff member's response, or an operational circumstance reveals conditions that could produce harm if not addressed. Near-miss reporting is a valuable governance intelligence source that should be actively cultivated rather than dismissed because "nothing actually happened." See Chapter 19.

Nominal oversight The appearance of human oversight without its substance — when a human is present in the workflow but is not actually exercising independent judgment. Nominal oversight is the governance failure that automation bias produces: reviewers who are formally compliant with oversight requirements but who are effectively deferring to AI recommendations without substantive assessment. See Chapter 13.

Operational data Data that flows through an AI system in operation — the inputs users provide, the outputs the system produces, and the logs generated by system activity. Operational data governance addresses how this data is handled, retained, protected, and managed, distinct from training data governance.

Overreliance The behavioral pattern produced by automation bias: systematically deferring to AI recommendations without adequate independent evaluation. Overreliance manifests as declining to seek information that would allow independent verification, failing to probe unusual AI outputs, and accepting AI-generated summaries without reviewing underlying sources. See Chapter 3.

Policy (AI policy) The written expression of governance decisions — the document that records what an institution has decided about AI use, who is responsible for what, what processes must be followed, and what happens when things go wrong. Policy creates governance only when paired with institutional structures that give it effect. See Chapters 2 and 8.

Prediction model An AI system that estimates the likelihood of future events — a patient's probability of readmission, a student's probability of course completion, a borrower's probability of default. Prediction models raise governance concerns similar to classification models: what outcome is being predicted, what data is used, how accurate predictions are across demographic groups, and what actions are taken based on predicted probabilities.

Principle (AI governance principle) A value commitment that guides AI governance decisions — fairness, transparency, safety, privacy, accountability, security, and human dignity. Principles provide the normative foundation for governance requirements and serve as interpretive guides when specific provisions do not address a situation. See Chapter 7.

Privacy The governance principle that AI systems handle personal information in ways that respect the reasonable expectations of the people it concerns, comply with applicable law, and serve the purposes for which information was collected. Privacy governance for AI addresses both explicit data handling and AI-specific privacy risks including inference, training data use, and distributed data flows. See Chapters 3 and 7.

Prompt An input provided to a language model to direct its behavior — a question, instruction, or piece of context that shapes the model's response. Prompt design significantly affects AI output quality, and prompt governance addresses both how system-level prompts shape AI behavior and what users are permitted to provide as inputs. See Chapter 4.

Prompt injection A security attack in which instructions embedded in content an AI processes override the system's intended behavior. Prompt injection attacks are particularly relevant for AI systems that process external content — documents, emails, web pages — that may contain adversarially crafted instructions. See Chapters 14 and 20.

Protected characteristics Characteristics on the basis of which discrimination is legally prohibited — typically including race, ethnicity, sex and gender, age, disability, religion, national origin, and sexual orientation, with specific characteristics varying by jurisdiction and legal framework. AI systems used in contexts governed by anti-discrimination law must be assessed for differential performance along protected characteristics.

Recommendation model An AI system that predicts which outputs — content, products, people, options — a user or system is likely to prefer or benefit from. Recommendation models raise governance concerns including feedback loops, demographic differential performance, and the encoding of historical preferences as future recommendations.

Risk screening The component of the intake process that assesses what risk level a proposed AI use case presents and what governance requirements apply. Risk screening uses defined criteria to classify use cases as low, medium, or high risk, calibrating the depth of governance review to the significance of the risk. See Chapter 10.

Rollback Rapid suspension or reversal of an AI deployment in response to a condition that requires immediate operational cessation — active harm, security incident, severe performance failure, or regulatory requirement. Rollback authority and procedures should be defined before deployment and should not require full governance team deliberation to exercise. See Chapter 23.

Safety The governance principle that AI systems do not cause foreseeable physical, psychological, or material harm to the people they affect, and that appropriate safeguards prevent, detect, and respond to harm when it occurs. Safety requirements are context-dependent and should be calibrated to the harm potential of the specific use case. See Chapters 3 and 7.

Security The governance principle that AI systems and the data they process are protected against unauthorized access, manipulation, misuse, and failure. AI security encompasses both standard cybersecurity measures and AI-specific security risks including adversarial inputs, prompt injection, data poisoning, and model extraction. See Chapters 3 and 7.

Sensitive information Categories of personal information that receive heightened governance and legal protection because of the particular harms that their mishandling can cause. Typically includes health information, financial information, information about minors, biometric data, and information about legally protected characteristics. AI systems that process sensitive information require more intensive governance than those that do not.

Staged rollout A deployment approach in which an AI system is introduced at limited scope with intensive monitoring, expanding to full deployment only as evidence accumulates that performance is adequate. Staged rollout is the primary structural governance measure for limiting the harm of deployment problems discovered after deployment begins. See Chapter 15.

Sunset The planned, deliberate phase-out of an AI system that has reached the end of its useful or appropriate institutional life — because of performance deterioration, identified harm, irremediable governance failure, regulatory non-compliance, or strategic obsolescence. Sunset should be governed as deliberately as initial deployment. See Chapter 23.

Training data The collection of examples on which an AI model is trained. Training data is among the most consequential determinants of model behavior — what the model learns to do, how accurately it does it, for whom it works well, and what biases it encodes are substantially determined by training data composition and quality. See Chapter 4.

Transparency The governance principle that institutions are open about what AI they use, how it works, what it can and cannot do, and what role it plays in decisions that affect people's lives. Transparency applies at multiple levels: internal transparency (governance teams having information needed for governance decisions), external transparency (affected people having information about AI use that affects them), and systemic transparency (practices being accountable to oversight). See Chapters 3 and 7.

Use case A specific application of AI within an institution — using AI to screen job applications, generate patient summaries, draft communications, flag suspicious transactions, and so forth. AI governance operates at the level of use cases, not only at the level of AI in the abstract. The same AI tool may present very different governance requirements in different use cases.

Vendor An external party that provides, develops, operates, or maintains an AI system used by an institution. Most institutional AI use involves vendor relationships, which creates specific governance requirements: vendor assessment, contract protections, ongoing relationship management, and governance of the accountability gaps that vendor relationships create. See Chapters 11 and 26.

Part Two: Further Reading

This section identifies types of resources and specific works for readers who want to go deeper on particular topics. Given the pace of change in AI governance, readers should verify that recommended resources reflect current understanding and should supplement with more recent materials as needed.

Foundational AI governance frameworks

Several organizations have published AI governance frameworks that provide useful reference points for institutional governance program design. These include:

Government and intergovernmental frameworks: The OECD AI Principles provide a widely referenced international framework for responsible AI. The US National Institute of Standards and Technology AI Risk Management Framework (NIST AI RMF) provides a detailed, practical framework for AI risk management. The EU AI Act and its accompanying guidance documents from the European AI Office provide the most comprehensive legally binding AI governance framework currently in force. These primary documents are available from the relevant agencies and should be consulted directly rather than through summaries.

Sector-specific guidance: Healthcare AI governance has been addressed by the FDA, NHS AI Lab, WHO, and numerous professional medical associations. Education AI governance has been addressed by UNESCO, the US Department of Education, and various national education ministries. Financial services AI governance has been addressed by banking and financial regulators in most major jurisdictions. Readers should identify the sector-specific guidance most relevant to their institutional context.

Academic and research frameworks: Several research institutions have published AI governance frameworks that inform both policy and practice. The Ada Lovelace Institute, AI Now Institute, Partnership on AI, and the Alan Turing Institute have each published governance-relevant research. Academic journals including the ACM FAccT conference proceedings, Ethics and Information Technology, and AI and Society publish governance-relevant research.

AI bias and fairness

Understanding bias requires both technical and sociotechnical perspectives. Technical resources address how bias enters models, how it is measured, and what technical mitigations exist. Sociotechnical resources address the social and institutional contexts that shape what bias means and how it should be addressed.

Key concepts to explore: Differential performance measurement, fairness metrics and their trade-offs (demographic parity, equalized odds, predictive parity), the impossibility theorems showing that multiple fairness criteria cannot simultaneously be satisfied, proxy discrimination, feedback loops, and the relationship between algorithmic fairness and structural inequality.

Recommended starting points: Solon Barocas, Moritz Hardt, and Arvind Narayanan's online textbook *Fairness and Machine Learning* (available at fairmlbook.org) provides a rigorous technical treatment of fairness concepts. Kate Crawford's *Atlas of AI* provides a critical sociotechnical perspective on AI's structural dimensions. Safiya Umoja Noble's *Algorithms of Oppression* examines bias in information systems. The ACM FAccT conference proceedings provide current research on fairness, accountability, and transparency in AI systems.

Privacy and data protection

Legal frameworks: Readers needing depth on GDPR should consult the regulation itself, the Article 29 Working Party and European Data Protection Board guidance, and practitioner-oriented legal commentaries. For US privacy law, the IAPP (International Association of Privacy Professionals) publishes regularly updated resources on the evolving state landscape. Sector-specific guidance from HHS on HIPAA, from the FTC on consumer data privacy, and from the FTC and DOE on FERPA provides authoritative interpretations.

AI-specific privacy: The intersection of AI and privacy is addressed in academic work on differential privacy, membership inference, model inversion, and data minimization for machine learning. The NIST Privacy Framework and its AI-specific supplements provide a practitioner-oriented approach.

Anti-discrimination law and AI

Governance teams need working knowledge of how anti-discrimination law applies to AI in their specific sectors and jurisdictions. Key legal frameworks to understand include:

Employment: EEOC guidance on AI and employment discrimination, the Uniform Guidelines on Employee Selection Procedures, and recent enforcement actions involving algorithmic hiring tools provide practical guidance. Legal scholarship on disparate impact theory and its application to algorithmic decision-making provides theoretical grounding.

Housing and credit: CFPB guidance on algorithmic underwriting, adverse action notice requirements for AI-assisted credit decisions, and FHA and ECOA enforcement in algorithmic contexts are essential for institutions operating in these domains.

Healthcare: Section 1557 ACA guidance, OCR guidance on AI and health equity, and emerging literature on algorithmic discrimination in clinical AI inform healthcare governance.

Readers in specific sectors should engage legal counsel with specific expertise in the intersection of anti-discrimination law and AI for their context rather than relying on general resources.

AI safety and human oversight

Automation bias: Scholarly literature on automation bias spans cognitive psychology, human factors engineering, and aviation and healthcare safety research. Work by Raja Parasuraman and colleagues established foundational understanding of automation bias. More recent work by Bran Knowles and others has addressed automation bias specifically in AI contexts.

Human-AI interaction: Research on how AI system design affects human oversight quality is an active area. Work by Berkeley Dietvorst on algorithm aversion and algorithm appreciation, by Eric Strickland and others on clinical AI and clinician behavior, and by various researchers on AI-assisted hiring and decision-making provides empirical grounding for oversight design.

AI safety (technical): For readers interested in the technical dimensions of AI safety — beyond the institutional governance focus of this book — resources from the Machine Intelligence Research Institute, Anthropic's alignment research, and academic AI safety literature address AI safety at a technical level.

Generative AI governance

Generative AI governance is a rapidly evolving topic. Resources current as of any publication date may be substantially outdated given the pace of development.

Starting points: Policy papers from AI safety research organizations, guidance from data protection authorities on generative AI (including the Italian DPA's early investigation of ChatGPT, which established precedents others have followed), and sector-specific guidance from healthcare and education regulators address the governance of generative AI in institutional contexts.

Hallucination: Research literature on language model factuality, calibration, and confabulation — published in AI research venues including NeurIPS, ICML, and ACL — provides technical grounding for understanding hallucination risk.

Prompt injection: Security research on prompt injection attacks is published in cybersecurity venues. Practitioners should follow AI security researchers' current work as this threat landscape evolves rapidly.

AI law and regulation

EU AI Act: The official text of the EU AI Act is available from the European Union's legislative database. The European AI Office has published guidance on implementation. Law firm analyses from major practices provide accessible interpretations of compliance implications.

US regulatory landscape: The NIST AI RMF and associated resources provide a voluntary framework that increasingly informs regulatory expectations. Congressional Research Service reports on AI regulation provide accessible policy overviews. Agency-specific guidance from the FTC, EEOC, CFPB, FDA, and other regulators addresses AI in their respective domains.

International: The Council of Europe's Framework Convention on AI represents the first binding international AI treaty. The OECD AI Policy Observatory tracks AI policy developments globally and is a useful resource for monitoring international regulatory developments.

AI governance in specific sectors

Healthcare: The FDA's Digital Health Center of Excellence publishes guidance on software as a medical device. The NHS AI Lab and NHS AI and Digital Regulations Service publish practical governance resources for healthcare AI. Academic literature in journals including *npj Digital Medicine*, *The Lancet Digital Health*, and *JAMA* provides research on clinical AI performance and governance.

Education: UNESCO's guidance on AI in education, the US Department of Education's AI reports, and the EdTech sector's emerging governance frameworks address educational AI governance. Research on student data privacy and AI in education is published in educational technology journals.

Social services and government: Academic literature on algorithmic decision-making in child welfare, benefits administration, and criminal justice provides extensive evidence about governance challenges. Work by Virginia Eubanks (*Automating Inequality*) and Cathy O'Neil

(*Weapons of Math Destruction*) provides accessible critical perspectives on algorithmic systems in public sector contexts.

Financial services: The Financial Stability Board, Bank for International Settlements, and major financial regulators have published extensively on AI in financial services. The NIST AI RMF has been adapted for financial services contexts.

Practical AI governance implementation

Organizational resources: Organizations including the Partnership on AI, CSET (Center for Security and Emerging Technology), and various think tanks publish practical guidance on AI governance implementation. Professional associations in healthcare, law, and other sectors are developing sector-specific governance guidance.

Case studies: Documented AI governance failures — in hiring, healthcare, benefits administration, criminal justice, and other domains — provide essential learning about what governance failures look like and how they could have been prevented. Academic case study literature, investigative journalism, and regulatory enforcement records provide access to this learning.

Practitioner communities: AI governance practitioners are developing shared resources through communities including the AI governance community on LinkedIn, GovAI, and various professional associations. Academic conferences including the ACM FAccT conference and the IEEE AI Ethics conference bring together researchers and practitioners.

Staying current

The most important resource for AI governance practitioners is a system for staying current — because the regulatory environment, the technical landscape, and the accumulated evidence about AI governance challenges are all changing rapidly.

Effective staying-current systems typically include: monitoring regulatory bodies relevant to the institution's sector and jurisdiction for guidance and enforcement updates; following two or three reliable sources for AI policy and governance news; participating in professional networks where AI governance practitioners share emerging challenges and solutions; and scheduling time — at minimum quarterly — to actively seek out what is new and relevant.

No governance framework, including this one, can remain adequate without updating. The institution's AI governance program needs a mechanism for incorporating new information: a policy review cycle, a regulatory monitoring function, and governance team discussions that engage with current developments rather than applying static frameworks to a changing world.

A final note on navigating a rapidly evolving field

Readers of this book will encounter AI governance challenges that it does not specifically address — because new AI capabilities, new use cases, new regulatory requirements, and new evidence about AI impacts will continue to develop. The appropriate response to those gaps is not to conclude that governance does not apply to novel situations, but to apply the principles and reasoning described throughout this book to situations the book did not anticipate.

The principles — fairness, transparency, safety, privacy, accountability, security, and human dignity — do not become irrelevant when AI capabilities evolve. The governance logic — assess before deploying, oversee in operation, monitor for problems, respond when things go wrong, learn from experience — does not become obsolete when new AI types emerge. The commitment to governing AI on behalf of the people institutions serve, rather than adopting AI for its own sake, is not superseded by technological change.

Good governance in a rapidly evolving field is not about having all the answers in advance. It is about having the principles, the processes, and the institutional commitment to ask the right questions — and to act responsibly on what those questions reveal.